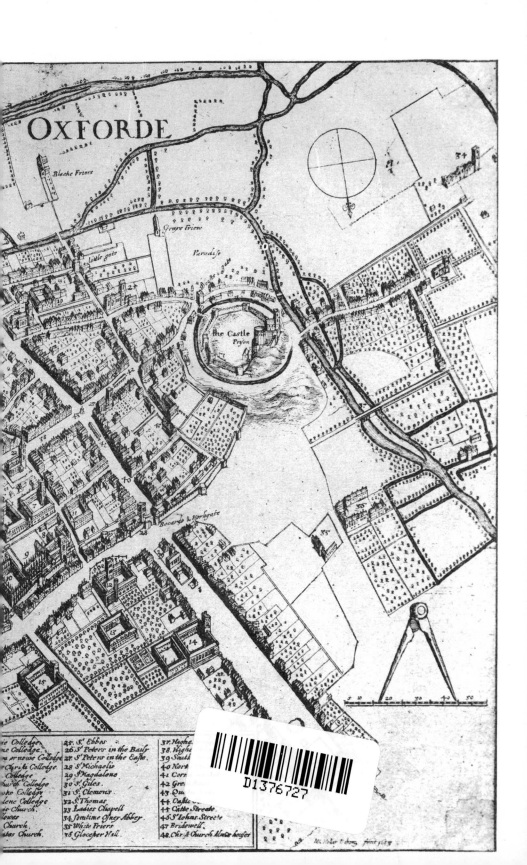

OXFORDE

Blacke Friers

Graye Friers

Paradise

litle gate

the Castle
Pryon

Bocardo & Northgate

D1376727

W. Hole Librar. fecit 1605

JOHN AUBREY

By the same author

ANATOLE FRANCE
THE IMAGE OF FRANCE

JOHN AUBREY

A LIFE

David Tylden-Wright

HarperCollins*Publishers*

DA
93
A8
.T95
1991
1

Front cover painting of John Aubrey from original painting (now lost) by Sir Peter Lely. Reproduced by kind permission of John Rylands University Library, Manchester.

Back cover illustration of original manuscript in John Aubrey's handwriting (MS.Aubrey.3 Fol.163;recto), reproduced courtesy of the Bodleian Library, Oxford.

Front endpaper: Hollar's map of Oxford, 1643, the year after Aubrey went up.

Back endpaper: Aubrey's map of south-west England, from the *Monumenta Britannica* (MS. Top. Gen. c 24. fol 250–1) reproduced by courtesy of the Bodleian Library, Oxford.

HarperCollins *Publishers*,
77–85 Fulham Palace Road,
Hammersmith, London W6 8JB.

Copyright © David Tylden-Wright 1991

Published by HarperCollins *Publishers* 1991

9 8 7 6 5 4 3 2 1

David Tylden-Wright has asserted his moral right
to be identified as the author of this work.

A catalogue record for this book
is available from the British Library

Typeset in Linotron Ehrhardt at The Spartan Press, Lymington, Hampshire
Printed and bound in Great Britain by
Hartnolls Limited, Bodmin, Cornwall

25246799

To our son, Roy,
without whose help this book
might never have been started,
and to our daughter, Sue,
without whom it would certainly
never have been finished.

Contents

List of Illustrations

Preface

To elaborate on the first of my two dedications. When I decided I wanted to write a book on Aubrey, the difficulty was to combine the study of the mass of material in the Bodleian with an active farming life. The occasional trip to Oxford only served to show the extent of the task, and the time needed to fulfil it. So the idea went to join several others in the deep freeze. It only partially came out of it when my eldest son Roy, having taken his degree, was uncertain what he wanted to do. It occurred to me that it would serve both our purposes if I financed Roy to stay on for a further year at Oxford during which he transcribed what he could of the manuscripts, and during which he would have time to make up his own mind about his future. Roy seemed happy with this, and from his year in Duke Humfrey's Library produced four large notebooks in which he had transcribed much of the 'Lives', a good part of *Monumenta Britannica*, and the *Idea of Education*, as well as several of Aubrey's minor, but informative and interesting, manuscripts such as *Faber Fortunae*, *Collectio Geniturarum*, his *Miscellanies* and a number of 'loose papers'. He did not touch on Aubrey's Wiltshire work or his Letters. All of this gave me much to ponder, and provided an invaluable stepping stone without which I might never have crossed my Rubicon.

But, of course, in itself Roy's work was not enough to back a book. One can not transcribe everything Aubrey wrote even in a year, and different readers look for different things. In the end I had to go through everything myself. But to do this I had to wait until I was of an age when I could reasonably ease myself out of farming, not altogether, but enough to give me the time to write 'Aubrey' and do other things I had long wanted to. So, some three years ago, I sold one of the two farms we had until then been running together, and have since been spending on average a day a week in the Bodleian. This involves a round trip of over three hundred miles from where we now live and farm on the Devon-Somerset border – which is tedious – but I have enjoyed much of the work itself. There can be no more beautiful library in which to work than Duke Humfrey's and reading manuscripts is in itself exciting. One always has the feeling that one is going to find something new, which, in the way of detail, one often does. Also, Aubrey is so personal a writer that he is rarely dull. I wish one could say the same of all of his correspondents.

I am most grateful to the Keeper of Western Manuscripts, Mrs Mary Clapinson, for giving me the Library's formal permission to quote from the manuscripts, without which this book would hardly have been possible, for Aubrey is quoted on more pages than not. The desk staff in the Library have been as helpful as it was possible to be and in the final search for illustrations guided even my forays into other departments. Comically the longest search of all – for the edition of Dugdale's *Monasticon Anglicanum* containing the reproduction of the drawing of Osney Abbey which Aubrey commissioned as an undergraduate – ended with one of the venerable volumes that are on permanent display in Duke Humfrey's, in the alcove where I was actually working. I would also like to thank the staff of the Museum at Devizes and in particular Mrs Colman, the Librarian. The Museum is the home of the Wiltshire Archaeological and Natural History Society, which I warmly recommend as a very worthwhile body to which to belong. I have also been helped, as often in the past, by the staff of the London Library, and also by Alan Clark, himself an expert on Avebury and co-author of the recently published *Avebury Reconsidered*, and the staff of the Reading Room of the Royal Society. I would also like to thank Richard Ollard for much scholarly comment and constructive criticism from which I and the book have greatly benefited. I am also most grateful to the librarian at Worcester College, Mrs Lesley LeClaire, for showing me Aubrey's books.

On a more purely personal note, I greatly enjoyed and valued over many years the friendship of Justin MacCarthy, who lived in the house that stands (almost) on the site of that in which Aubrey was born, and his wife Ann, who still lives there. I often used to stay there when we ourselves had left the district. Finding oneself looking out over much the same 'glorious prospect' as the one Aubrey knew – 'the best between Marshfield and Burford' – has played no small part in the writing of the book. I would also like to add to the love that my wife knows she always has my thanks for her patience over the long period of pondering and her encouragement during the shorter period of writing.

Finally to my second dedication, a particularly well-earned one. Our youngest daughter, Sue, who happily for us, farms next door, has word-processed a volume of manuscript that amounts in all to about three or four times the length of the book, while coping with her own work, and producing our first grandchild. Even more miraculously, she has developed a remarkable and rare skill in reading my writing so that she can now do so with no more difficulty than I do myself. For whatever it is worth I feel this book is in part hers and Roy's, as well as mine.

Introduction

When, more years ago now than I care to count, we decided to leave London, and – we hoped – divide our time between writing books, farming and bringing up our family, we ended up, after a long search, in a small farm with a large house in north Wiltshire. Purely by chance, our farm bordered that on which Aubrey was born and which he later inherited from his maternal grandfather. He was to live there for twelve years, until, to his 'greate griefe' he had to yield to the pressure of the massive debt that had been accumulating ever since the death of his father, seven years before that of his grandfather, and sell it. This ended a family possession, as both tenants and owners, of over two hundred and fifty years. When we took over our farm, the previous owner handed us his field map on which we noted that the three fields on our northern boundary were collectively called 'the Vernall'. It was in 'Vern-knoll, my Lord Lucas's' that Aubrey 'bored clay as blue as Ultra-marine', which he thought 'might make Porcelayne'. The lane which connected these three fields was clearly part of an old lane which had led through to Easton Piers, Aubrey's home. As the crow flew, our house, which was there in his day, was no more than a mile and a half from his. Even at a distance of three centuries it is difficult not to be curious about one's neighbours. One of the purposes of this book is to show how interesting a neighbour and a person Aubrey proved to be.

But the lane which led to Aubrey led to very much more. Aubrey was lucky in the age in which he lived. He himself would have denied it – and did, often declaring that many of his misfortunes were due to the fact that, astrologic-ally, he was born in 'an ill-howre'. But in fact the timing was perfect for anyone as observant and curious and interested in life as he was. When he went up to Oxford in 1642, it was on the eve of the Civil War, and so already full of unacademic activity. When he returned a year later, it had the King and the court in it and was the headquarters of the Royalist war effort. There can have been few more fascinating, if fraught, moments in Oxford's long and distinguished history. When he came back to finish his studies after the war and three long years in the country which he found extremely tedious, with few books and even fewer friends around him, he was to find himself caught up in an exciting mood and movement of intellectual experiment and discovery. He was in the company of many who were to prove the most eminent of his generation. Over the next few years Petty, Wren, Hooke, Boyle and many other subsequently famous figures were to become his friends. He was to join a club at Oxford which was to prove the nucleus of the Royal Society, of which he was to be an original member. Because he was interested in people rather than politics, he was to be present at Whitehall when Cromwell held court there, as he was in the early years of the Restoration at the court of Charles II, whom he was to introduce to the greatness of Avebury, which by chance he had rediscovered on a hunting trip. Even when he had lost his money and his estates, and his social life was centred on coffee-houses and the meetings of the Royal Society rather than the court and its surrounding *salons*, he always remained a member of the intelligentsia and a friend of the famous. In the last years of his life one finds Evelyn annotating the manuscript of his *Natural History of Wiltshire* and Dryden helping him to find a printer for the only work he succeeded in getting published in his lifetime, his *Miscellanies*.

Yet behind this appearance of a life of extreme sociability lay a background of constant work, of great integrity, often innovative, always interesting. In the main, Aubrey's motive was to record as much as he could of what he valued in the world around him before it disappeared, or was destroyed, as so much had been in the course of the Civil War and the Puritan purge which followed. He was conscious, too, of the hurt that had been caused to scholarship by the Dissolution of the Monasteries, from the evidence which still lay around him, even though it had occurred a century earlier. In an effort to counter a recurrence of such a situation he wrote his *North Wiltshire Collections*, concerned with his particular corner of the county; then his *Natural History*, which covered the whole of it; and at the same time his *Monumenta Britannica*, which ranged, although very haphazardly, across Britain. All these are, in their different ways, pioneering works, often fumbling and feeling for their way forward, and incomplete. Yet they were an amazing achievement all the same. Perhaps even more remarkable was the act of faith which lay behind them, for he was always writing for posterity not for his contemporary world, being correctly conscious that it would be difficult to get his work published. When the constricting circumstances of his later life had forced him to look for other material, and so produced the creative outburst in which he wrote his 'Lives', he had achieved a remarkably complete picture of the people and places of his time.

Aubrey was a very likeable character. One can be certain of this simply from the mass of friends that he always had, once he had escaped from the confines of a surprisingly secluded childhood. His appeal still comes across in his work. Over the many years I have been pondering and writing this book,

I have always found him a pleasant, interesting, often entertaining companion. It has also given me much personal pleasure to write about the corner of north Wiltshire – in which lie both Easton Piers, where Aubrey lived, and Allington, where we did – of which in the ten years we were there we became just as fond as Aubrey did in his time.

```
                                              WILLIAM AUBREY
                                              'the little doctor'
                                              b. 1529  d. 1595


SIR EDWARD AUBREY          SIR THOMAS AUBREY              6 daugh
    of Brecon                 m. Mary Mansell
                           d. of Anthony Mansell
  6 sons, of whom          of Llantrithyd, Glam.
the elder had 7 sons
                             SIR JOHN AUBREY
                               of Llantrithyd
                                  1st Bart.
                             b. 1606  d. 1679


                             SIR JOHN AUBREY
                               of Llantrithyd
                                  d. 1708
                           m. 1. Margaret Lonsdale
                             d. of Lord Lonsdale
                                2. Mary Lewis
                             d. of Wiliam Lewis
                             of Boarstall, Bucks


                                MARY AUBREY
                          m. Sir William Montagu
                      Lord Chief Baron of the Exchequer
```

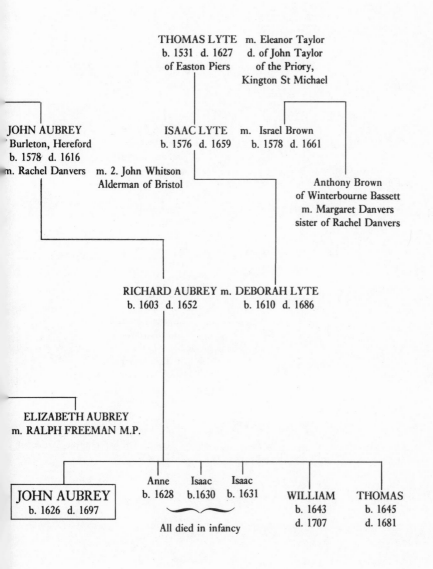

THOMAS LYTE   m. Eleanor Taylor
b. 1531 d. 1627   d. of John Taylor
of Easton Piers   of the Priory,
Kington St Michael

JOHN AUBREY   ISAAC LYTE   m. Israel Brown
Burleton, Hereford   b. 1576 d. 1659   b. 1578 d. 1661
b. 1578 d. 1616
m. Rachel Danvers   m. 2. John Whitson
Alderman of Bristol
                                                   Anthony Brown
                                                   of Winterbourne Bassett
                                                   m. Margaret Danvers
                                                   sister of Rachel Danvers

RICHARD AUBREY m. DEBORAH LYTE
b. 1603 d. 1652   b. 1610 d. 1686

ELIZABETH AUBREY
m. RALPH FREEMAN M.P.

JOHN AUBREY   Anne   Isaac   Isaac
b. 1626 d. 1697   b. 1628   b.1630   b. 1631   WILLIAM   THOMAS
                                                          b. 1643   b. 1645
                     All died in infancy   d. 1707   d. 1681

Easton Piers
and Kington St Michael

If you take the Chippenham turning off the M4 – at Junction 17 – and then at a distance of about half a mile, roughly at the point on the Chippenham to Malmesbury Road where a turnpike used to stand, turn right, you will shortly come to the village of Kington St Michael – a long straggling village that always gives the impression of being on the way to somewhere else. As, indeed, it is, being on the way to Grittleton, Hullavington, Leigh Delamere, Stanton St Quintin, Castle Combe, Yatton Keynell, all places that Aubrey included in the survey of north Wiltshire which he started in 1660 but had not completed when he died in 1697. It is also on the way to Easton Piercy, as it is now called – Easton Piers in Aubrey's time – a small hamlet, technically a tything, half a mile or so to the north-west, now part of the parish of Kington St Michael, but with an individuality of its own. This perhaps stems from the fact that during the thirteenth to sixteenth centuries it was a parish in its own right, with a chapel, a manor and its own lord and master, who in 1250 was a Sir Piers, who took his second name from his property, becoming Sir Piers de Easton. Subsequently he gave both his names back to the hamlet, although time has twiddled them around – hence Easton Piers or Piercy.

Nowadays, as you drive through Kington St Michael, you are very conscious that it has properly and, on the whole, pleasantly, moved with the times. On either side you pass a motley of buildings thrown up by the tides of the centuries. On the right, two sixteenth- or seventeenth-century farm houses – of grey stone, with just a hint of honey to mellow their colour, mullioned windows, stone-tiled roofs mottled with lichen; on the left their Edwardian counterparts, of red brick with grey slate roofs – clear evidence that the passage of years does not necessarily lead to improvement; a row of almshouses built by a contemporary cousin of Aubrey's, Alderman Lyte; a Georgian pub – or rather a pub in a Georgian building – facing its alcoholic rival, the local club, a modern building which, in our day, had a tin roof.

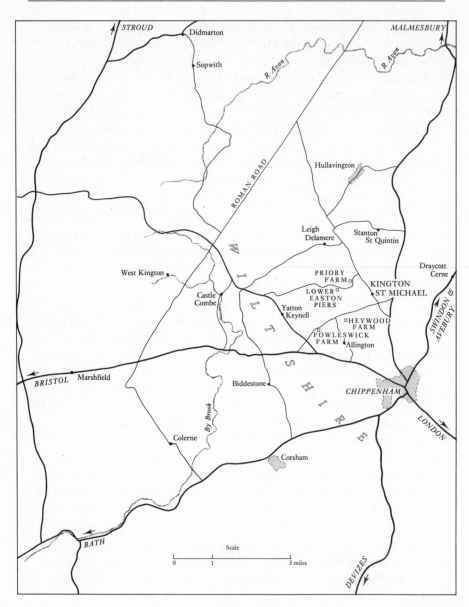

Easton Piers and its neighbourhood

Between buildings the spaces, which even when we first knew the village we remember as fields coming up to the edge of the road, are now filled by housing estates, but they are well designed, discreetly placed, and blend in well with the older buildings. Overall, Kington St Michael gives the impression of a characterful village that has kept its links with the past but yet faces up confidently and cleverly to its role in the present, which is increasingly that of a dormitory for Chippenham, only two miles distant.

But if at the far end of the village, you turn down the small side-road – still little more than a lane, and a dangerous one at that, with high hedges, steep slopes, blind corners, which leads at a distance of about a couple of miles to the neighbouring village of Yatton Keynell – it is quite a different matter. For here time seems almost to have stood still. Easton Piercy is still composed of the same four farms – no more and no less – that Easton Piers had in Aubrey's day. Some farm cottages have come and gone, some boundaries have altered, but the division of land is still roughly the same as it was three centuries ago. Of the four main houses, three are still recognizable as those that were there in his time. Sadly, the only one that has been completely demolished is the house, built by Aubrey's maternal great-grandfather Thomas Lyte, in which Aubrey was born and which he later inherited. But the house which stands in its stead – or almost in its stead, it is slightly lower down the slope – was built of its stone, and although smaller, it is very much of the same character as the house one sees on Aubrey's sketches. Seasoned now by two centuries of existence and Wiltshire weather – it bears the date 1785 – it seems of an age with the others, and one has constantly to remind oneself that this, in fact, is not the house in which Aubrey was born. On the edge of the tything, separated from it only by the brook which forms the boundary, stand the buildings and fields of what is now known as Priory Farm, but which for the four centuries preceding the Dissolution was St Mary's Priory, supposedly founded by the Empress Matilda, mother of Henry II. It is not technically in the tything, but in all geographical, social and other ways it is quite clearly a part. If you add it to Easton Piercy's four farms then you have a country entity that has remained remarkably unchanged over four centuries.

The Priory and the four farms of Easton Piercy are all strung along the road to Yatton Keynell which, once it has crossed the brook, rises rapidly to a ridge which widens out as it approaches its end. It is a remarkable ridge, unexpected and unobtrusive, from bottom to top rising only a few hundred feet, yet it dominates the neighbourhood. From its north side, one looks across miles of not flat but low countryside towards Stroud and Gloucester; from its southern slopes one can see the distant downs above Beckhampton. Canon J. E. Jackson, the excellent Victorian editor of Aubrey's *Wiltshire Collections* and a distinguished antiquarian in his own right – also for a long time vicar of Leigh Delamere, the neighbouring village to the north, where two and a half centuries earlier Aubrey had gone to school – describes it as 'a well wooded grassy ridge . . . yielding healthy dry pasture . . . as high ground as any in the neighbourhood; . . . traversed through its full length by a very narrow winding lane crossed by gates, and overshadowed by steep banks and old picturesque trees'.[1] Sadly, many of the trees, after the onslaught of Dutch Elm disease, have gone, but the lane is no less narrow, or winding than ever it was, and at least two of the gates remained even in our Wiltshire time, although to the considerable relief of anyone using the road, these too have now been taken away.

The original manor stood, and in part still stands, a field's length to the north of the road which crowns the ridge. Of this, Aubrey tells us his Lyte ancestors had held the lease for 'time out of mind'. In a more precise mood, he writes that they were there for 249 years. He thought it 'not improbable that the Lytes of Easton might have originally come from Evilton [Yeovilton] but 2 miles from Lytes Cary in Somerset [the family home, now a National Trust property] and may have taken their first lease from the family', who succeeded Piers of Easton as owners at the beginning of the fourteenth century, 'and might relate to them as Stewards'.[2] It was not improbable that they were also related in a more normal way – for surely only the strength of some family tie would have brought up two families from the considerable distance that south Somerset then was. The de Yeoviltons and their descendants held the estate, and the Lytes their lease, for the following two centuries, with the exception of a brief period following the accession of Richard III when the then Lord Daubeney, a descendant through marriage of the de Yeovilton family, backed the wrong side and so forfeited his estates. However, Easton was soon returned to him – only for him to sell it in 1507 to a Thomas Essex, whom Aubrey relates to a 'William Essex, Lord Treasurer and Knight of the Privy Council'. His much later descendant in Aubrey's time, 'Sir Thos. Essex Kt. and Baronet', was 'Governour of Bristowe for the Parliam[ent] under the E[arl] of Essex. A Batchelor'. In 1564, William Essex sold Easton to Sir Richard Sackville. Ten years later it was from his son, Thomas Sackville, the poet and statesman – who was to become the Earl of Dorset, but who at that time had risen only one rung up the aristocratic ladder to the barony of Buckhurst – that the Lytes, at very long last, were able to buy the estate of which they had been tenants for nearly two and a half centuries. Aubrey dates the sale 'A.D.1574. Thomas Lord Buckhurst sold Easton Pierse to John and Thomas Light. The deed of purchase beareth date November the sixth, in the sixteenth yeare of the reigne of Queen Elizabeth.' But, annoyingly, he leaves in the place of what would have been the most interesting detail, the price, one of his famous, or infamous, never filled-in blanks – 'The price was . . . poundes.'[3]

Even as tenants, there can be no doubt that the Lytes had prospered at Easton Piers. Aubrey wrote that his great-great-grandfather, Richard Lyte, received £800 a year from his various leases which included the whole of Easton Piers – except for the smallest farm of the four, Cromwells, taking its name from its fourteenth-century owner, a Ralph de Cromhales – and that of a large farm at Didmarton and Sopworth, two neighbouring hamlets some twenty miles to the north-west. But Aubrey's figures are always suspect, and when one makes the massive multiplication needed to cover four centuries of inflation, one realizes that it becomes too large a figure to be credible, however well the Lytes had farmed, or sublet their farms, and husbanded their revenue and resources. Particularly since we know that when, only a few weeks after the two brothers had at last bought the manor and its lands, the elder brother John sold off what was clearly his share – the manor house itself and most of the land to the north of the road – for 'three hundred fower gross five pounds lawfull money';[3] in other words for less than half the amount Richard Lyte was supposed to receive annually as income.

The manor and its surrounding land were sold on 1 January 1575 to John Snell and his son Thomas, who already owned the manor of Kington St Michael, at the other end of the village from Easton Piers, and most of the surrounding land. At the time of the Dissolution, John Snell's grandfather, Richard, had been steward at Kington St Michael for the Abbey of Glastonbury, which then owned the manor and its land, and in fact most of Kington St Michael. His father Nicholas was its purchaser from the Crown some eight years later, in 1543, for £803. According to Jackson, the name Snell is 'an old Wiltshire word signifying "sharp"'. Local rumour had it that at that time, the Snells lived up to their name, withholding the last years of rent due to the Abbey, and using the money to buy the property. Aubrey, to some extent, endorses the rumour: 'The Manourhouse at Kington was the Lord Abbots. It was bought by . . . Snell, the Abbot's Reeve, who payed halfe the money to the King: the arrears he kept in his hands foreseeing the Fall of the Abbeyes.'[4]

Once they had changed from stewards to squires, the Snells quickly flourished. Nicholas himself was three times a Member of Parliament, knighted and in 1565 Sheriff of Wilts. His grandson, Sir Thomas, went into the navy and was, Aubrey tells us when in the course of his survey of Kington St Michael church for his *North Wiltshire Collections* he came to the place in the chancel where Sir Thomas was buried in 1612, 'a good Astrologer; understood Navigation; was a Captain in the Island voyage'.[4] More important, perhaps, as a buttress to the family fortunes than his seafaring skill was his marriage to the daughter of an important local land owner, Sir Robert Long of Draycot. But this seems to have been the zenith of the family fortunes. The only son, Charles, who inherited, seems to have been a man of a very different calibre from the old sea-captain. He was a friend of Sir Walter Raleigh, whose companions Aubrey tells us 'were boisterous blades, but generally those that had wit, except otherwise upon designe to gett them engaged for him; as for instance Sir Charles Snell of Kington St Michael . . . my good neighbour, an honest young gentleman, but kept a perpetual sott. Sir W. engaged him to build a ship (The Angel Gabriel) for the designe for Guiana, . . . which ship upon Sir Walter's attainder was forfeitted'.[5] This cost Snell several properties which included the manor and lands at Easton Piers which John Snell had bought from John Lyte forty-eight years before. Sir Charles was the last of the male Snell line at Kington, dying a bachelor in 1651, but the property in and around the village was held by the descendants of his three surviving sisters, who split the estate between them, until well into the twentieth century, our own house and farm at Allington at the south-west corner of the parish being part of it.

Sir Charles Snell sold Easton Piers Manor in 1623, to a Bristol merchant, John Langton, whose family held it for the rest of the seventeenth century. Shortly after he had bought it, Langton pulled down and rebuilt a great part of the old house. This, of course, is the house that Aubrey would have known, rather than that in which his ancestors lived, for he was born three years after the sale, and its reconstruction would have taken place during the years of his childhood. Part of the house still stands, but it is surprising that it does, for clearly a century ago it was on the point of total collapse. Jackson talks of its 'perilous state of dilapidation' at that time. In his day, the hall of the old house was still standing, and shows the considerable style in which Aubrey's ancestors must have lived, even while they were still tenants:

> The older part which they [the Langtons] did not take down is still left, and forms a north wing . . . The windows . . . being of ecclesiast-ical style with cinquefoil heads, and its angles being flanked by bold buttresses with a substantial moulding running all round, about a yard from the ground, the wing looks not unlike a chapel; but it was the original hall. The room is paved with freestone, in lozenge. It was once wainscotted with carved oak panels: and a few relics of better days, such as stags' antlers, etc., still linger on the walls, as if to declare that it was not always filled with piles of sacks, cider-presses, and other farm house gear as it is now.[6]

A few years later this part had fallen down and it seemed that all else was about to. Kilvert the diarist, then a curate at Clyro, but back on a visit to his father, vicar of near-by Langley Burrell, describes a walk that he made to it on 24 August 1871, with Edward Awdry, the vicar of Kington:

We put the carriage up at the Vicarage and Edward Awdry walked up with us to Easton Pierse, by the old paths which I used to travel and which seemed so familiar to me. From the meadows above Lower Easton we caught the first glimpse of the grey gables. The old manor house has fallen into sad ruin since I used to come here to see old Mrs Buckland seven years ago. The great hall and the grand staircase both gone. All the back of the house tottering and the tall carved chimney stack trembling to its fall. From the huge oak beam which runs across and supports the vast ruined kitchen chimney, we stripped off large pieces of the bark which had never been removed and which looked as fresh as when the beam was placed there, perhaps hundreds of years ago. The house seemed empty and deserted. Heaps of stone and rubbish lay round the yards. The orchards were tangled and overgrown, the garden run wild with weeds, rank and neglected. Pink stonecrop and some straggling Virginia Stock ran over the heaps of waste and rubbish stone. There was not a sound or sign of life or living thing about the ruinous deserted place. Nothing but silence and desolation. A shepherd lives in a part of the house which still stands but as the staircase has fallen he is obliged to go out of doors and across a rude scaffolding stage before he can reach his bedroom.[7]

But, amazingly, the front part of the house is still there, bearing on two of its chimneys the Langton initials, and if one walks up to it from Lower Easton, the points of its three gables rise up out of the ground in front of you, like dragons' teeth, just as they would have for Aubrey when he walked up from his house to visit his neighbours, or for that matter for Kilvert when he walked up with Edward Awdry.

At the time of the Lyte purchase in 1574, Aubrey's great-grandfather Thomas Lyte, unlike his elder brother John, had chosen to keep his share of the proceeds in land rather than money and had retained most of the Easton Piers land south of the Kington St Michael to Yatton Keynell road. On it he built himself a new house. As Aubrey tells us: 'When my greatgrandfather Thomas Lyte sold the mannor-Howse with the lands near it in 1575, he built another howse on the brow of the Hill above the Brook facing the south-east . . . It was built the same yeare my Grandfather was born. In the parlour chimney is TL 1576.'[8]

It may have been the proximity of the Priory on the other side of both the brook and the road, but still near enough in winter, when the leaves were down, for the two buildings to look straight across at each other, that influenced the choice of the site. For the wife of Thomas Lyte, Aubrey's great-grandfather and the builder of the house, was the daughter of Isaac

Tayler, who then lived at the Priory and whose brother had bought it in 1556 from Sir Richard Long to whom it had been granted after the Dissolution. Aubrey made several drawings of the Priory in his time. One can see from them that although a chapel has disappeared at one end, a porch at the other, and a storey of bedrooms has been inserted in the top strata of the great Hall, the main body of buildings remains remarkably the same as it was in his time. In all probability, it had been much the same when the Priory provided a home not only for the nuns but also for 'widows and grave single women'. These brought, of course, their endowments with them. Here 'young maids', the daughters of parents who could afford to pay for their tuition, were taught 'needlework, the art of confectionary, surgery (anciently no apothocaries or surgeons: the gentlewomen did cure their poor neighbours: their hands are now too fine); physic, writing drawing, etc'.[9] Or so Aubrey tells us, although he was born nearly a hundred years after the Dissolution, and had it only on hearsay from 'old Jacques who lived where Charles Hadnam did'. It was probably also from 'old Jacques' that Aubrey learnt that at that time around the cross which 'stood at the [fork] going to the Priory was a little market frydayes – for fish, eggs, butter . . . perhaps chiefly for the Nunnes.' In Aubrey's time there was 'on Michaelmas day . . . a Fayre famous for ale and stubble-geese'.[10]

Aubrey, in fact, tells us much less about his great-grandfather's, his grandfather's and what was finally to become his own house, than he does about the 'grave single women' and the 'young maids' of the Priory. But a drawing which he made of it from the slope on the other side of the brook shows a typical substantial Elizabethan manor house with two wings, one of which one assumes, because of the size of the chimney stack and because it has only two levels of windows, to have been the hall. The other we know to have had on its first floor the main bedroom of the house, since on his sketch Aubrey marked its windows with a cross and wrote in red ink an explanatory legend in the bottom left-hand corner – 'My Grandfather Lyte's chamber wherein I drew my first breath'.[11]

But even if the obvious route to his grandfather's house, where Aubrey was born, was along the road from Kington St Michael, the approach which I prefer follows the flow of the stream which runs northwards out of the fields that were ours, into those that were his. At the top of the Vernall the length of lane, in our time separated from our barley fields by a hedge that flared with spindle in the autumn, had led, in the days of Aubrey's forebears, from Allington – where we lived – to a cross at Easton Piers, and then on to Leigh Delamere, the neighbouring village on the other side. In those days, as well as its cross, Easton Piers had its own chapel, which was destroyed shortly before Aubrey's time, but which he refers to in his *North Wiltshire Collections* as being 'but small', to which Jackson, added in a footnote 'and so its perquisites. A.D. 1446 Allowance to the Clerk for stipend, 4d'. But, according to Aubrey, it had 'a turret for two tintinnabulums', a phrase which has the ring of the bells themselves in it; a burial ground, from which for some time, according to Jackson, after the destruction of the chapel, bones were often turned up by the plough; and a pound for straying cattle. Aubrey remembered the font from the chapel being used in his day as a cattle trough at Cromwells. By his time, part of the Allington lane close to Easton Piers had already been overgrown, so that although he mentions it, he adds also, surprisingly, 'but of that now no signe left'.[12] Yet the end that ran through our fields only finally disappeared when, after our time, the spindle hedge was grubbed out and the lane ploughed up to make a few extra yards of barley.

If, from Vernall, you followed downstream but northwards for about half a mile, through sloping grass fields whose appearance can have changed little since Aubrey's day, past a rowan tree that flames like fire in the autumn, you find yourself looking up at the farmhouse which replaced Aubrey's house – standing as his did 'in the eye of the sun', the ridges that shored up the slope in his day still serving their purpose. Below stand a range of stone-built farm buildings, most of them as old as the house itself, or possibly even older. On the banks of the brook below the house Aubrey found 'maiden-haire, harts tongue, phyllitis, brooke-lime etc., cowslip and primroses . . . In this ground calver-keys, hare parsley, wild vetch, maiden's honesty, polypodium . . . and many vulnerary plants by me forgot'.[13] He seems to have remembered plenty all the same.

At this point, if you cross the stream, and climb the bank opposite, you will find yourself on the spot from which Aubrey made his sketch of his grandfather's house, in which he marked the first floor bedroom on the right as you look at it, with the cross to indicate his birthplace. It was the main bedroom in the house and had, by Aubrey's description, massive beams and a fine fireplace. From his sketch one can see that between the two wings an arched doorway led into the main body of the house. In front of the house on both its southern and eastern sides, the ground shows as sharply terraced, which will not surprise anyone who knows the lie of the land and how steeply at that point it slopes to the brook. Around the house are a mass of bushy-topped trees – in Aubrey's talented but amateurish hand a tree is simply a tree and not distinguishable as oak, elm, ash or whatever it was. One knows, however, that on its southern aspect its view was clear – for this was the real feature of the house – as Aubrey tells us: 'The prospect from it is the best between Marshfield and Burford and though all along on that ridge between these two Towns are lovely prospects, yet none hath so many breakes and good ground objects.'

'Breakes and good ground objects'. By 'breakes', Aubrey presumably meant the slopes and contours of the ground, and the long vista of the view over them to which the distant Wiltshire Downs provided a perfect backcloth; and these are, of course, much the same as in his day. But so, surprisingly are most of the 'good ground objects'. If he was looking out from the site of the house today, he would miss the spire of Kington St Michael church, which shows in a sketch he made of the scene, but which fell down in 1705. Aubrey had forecast the fall some forty years before when describing the spire and steeple: 'I doe guess Michael, Abbot of Glastonbury . . . built the steeple, and I believe did sett the spire upon the old Tower which is too weake and cracks, and will shortly fall.'[14] He also made a careful full-page drawing of the spire, of which the purpose, one would think, was to point out the danger of its condition. Yet the dark mass of Hey Wood which can be seen in the same sketch, would still be there, although it has shrunk from the three hundred acres – 'chiefly of scrubbed and lopped oaks worth £142', as its size and value were assessed at the time of the Dissolution – to a fifty-acre Forestry Commission plantation. The character, and so the colour, of the trees would have changed, too, for now there are few oaks, 'scrubbed' or otherwise but mainly conifers. Nor would Aubrey – unless he looked to the left, where the housing estates of Kington St Michael are massing ominously on the skyline as if to make a cavalry charge down the slopes in front of them – see many more houses than were there in his day, although the cottages have shifted around a bit. Probably the only considerable change he would notice would be the division of land into fields, and the consequent increase of hedgerows. Before his time much of the land around Kington St Michael and Easton Piers was still common and although the process of enclosure was well under way by his day it was not until 1664, during the period of his ownership of Easton Piers, that the land, which shows in his sketch, was enclosed.

'Breakes' and 'good ground objects' are rarely recorded, nor is it possible to commit a glorious view to the confined care of an archive; but they are history none the less. Anyone in search of Aubrey, standing on or close to the site of his house, looking across to the distant downs, and seeing much the same of both as he did – knowing too how little the whole area in and around Easton Piers has changed – will feel very close to him.

'An eremeticall solitude'
1626–42

For the first twelve years of their married life Aubrey's parents lived with his Lyte grandparents, in the house with the glorious view on the brow of the hill, above the brook. The main reason for this was probably the extreme youth of Aubrey's mother, Deborah, who had married at fifteen and was only sixteen when he was born. Also, as an only child, the bond between her and her parents was probably particularly strong. But it is surprising all the same, for Richard Aubrey, her husband, who also was young when he married – only twenty-two – had extensive properties of his own, notably an estate at Burleton in Herefordshire, on which he was born, and which he inherited in 1616, on the early death of his father at the age of thirty-eight, when he himself was only a boy of twelve. He also owned another property, the Manor of Stretford, the other side of Hereford, near Bodenham, of roughly comparable size and value, if one can go by the price that Aubrey obtained when he was forced to sell both. But Richard Aubrey never lived in either house. Had he chosen to make either his home, Stretford might have been the better choice of the two, in spite of the family connections with Burleton, for it is in the heart of the rich red land district of Hereford, whereas at Burleton, by Aubrey's own account, the soil was 'compounded of sand and clay'. In fact, Richard Aubrey, throughout his married life, never lived in his own house in spite of these two obviously very suitable properties being available. When, for whatever reason, he and his wife decided it was time for a change, time to leave Easton Piers, he rented a farm on the Wilton Estate at Broadchalke (now written Broad Chalke). This refusal to stand on his own feet surely seems to point to a basic feeling of insecurity and a consequential need for support. At Easton Piers, he had that of his in-laws. At Broadchalke there were both Aubrey and Lyte connections with the Pembrokes, his landlords. Also the Penruddocks, from whom they were taking over the lease, had been family friends for generations. It was an understandable choice, yet how many men in the same position would have made it?

As in many cases, the cause of Richard Aubrey's sense of insecurity may simply have been a question of upbringing. His mother Rachel was a Danvers, a well-known Wiltshire family, with whom Aubrey had a double connection for his grandmother Israel Lyte's brother, Anthony Browne, had married Margaret, Rachel's sister. After the untimely death of her husband, Rachel Aubrey quickly remarried, becoming the fourth and last wife of a forceful expansive character, Alderman John Whitson, several times MP for Bristol, as well as its mayor. He was a self-made man who had begun his career as an apprentice to a Bristol merchant. Although Whitson was Aubrey's godfather as well as, of course, his step-grandfather, this did not deter Aubrey from recounting, in his 'Lives', a scandalous story about how he had got his start when he was an apprentice. 'He was a handsome young fellow; and his old Master being dead, his Mistress one day called him into the wine cellar and had him breach the best Butt in the cellar for her; and truly he breached his Mistresse who after married him.' Aubrey goes on to paint the picture of an active, energetic character – 'He had a very good healthy constitution and was an early riser; wrote all his letters and dispatched business betime in the morning. He had a good naturall witt, and gained by the Spanish trade a fair Estate. He lived nobly; kept a plentifull Table; was the most popular magistrate in the city . . . He kept his Hawkes.'[1] He was also the owner of the *Mayflower*.

It may not have been easy for Richard Aubrey, his stepson, being brought up under the aegis of so powerful a personality. One wonders whether the air of dissatisfaction that seems to hang over him throughout his life may not have stemmed from some early difficulty at this time, for which he compensated in later life by being over-strict with his sociable son and deliberately distancing himself from him, as Whitson possibly had from him. Anthony Powell aptly calls Richard Aubrey 'the victim of a long minority'. Certainly, Whitson seems to have abused his position of trust as his stepson's guardian – by, for example, cutting down timber on the Burleton estate, and not passing on the money for it. Aubrey would hardly have remembered Whitson, for he was only four when Whitson died, but he often used to stay with his grandmother, during what he called his 'youthhood'. This was in the manor house near Bristol that Whitson had left her, at Burnett, about two miles south of Keynsham, where the sight of all the city activity greatly intrigued Aubrey's ever-active curiosity and made him 'lament with my selfe that I lived not in a City, e.g. Bristowe, where I might have accesse to watchmakers, locksmiths etc.'

In general, Aubrey was extremely reticent in writing about either himself or his immediate family. Even the few pages of autobiography which he included in his 'Lives' were introduced apologetically – 'to be intersposed as a sheet of waste-paper only [in] the binding of a book.' With muddling modesty, he even at times writes about himself in the third person – or even as 'this person' – although this undue self-effacement rarely lasts longer than a few lines when, happily, his natural self-interest reasserts itself and he becomes the 'I' he should always have been. In these autobiographical fragments, Richard Aubrey, his father, shows as a shadowy figure whom it is difficult to bring into focus. The occasional references that Aubrey, in general a mild man and little given to harbouring resentment – particularly against his own family – makes to him, seem to show him in a disagreeable and discouraging light. When, for example, Aubrey describes how ' . . . at 8, I was a kind of Engineer, and fell then to drawing', he adds as an afterthought in the margin, 'crossed herein by father and schoolmaster'. Again, when describing a later stage in his education, he wrote 'my head was always working, never idle', he inserted above it 'my father discouraged me'. Later when at the start of the Civil War, Aubrey was summoned home from Oxford to Broadchalke where he found the country very dull after the stimulation of Oxford, he wrote 'conversed with none but servants and rustiques', and added in brackets 'to my great griefe, for in those days fathers were not acquainted with their children'. Richard Aubrey was probably, then, a difficult and distant parent, not entirely uncaring, otherwise he would not have 'sent for me home for feare' from Oxford when the Civil War was starting, but unsympathetic, unobservant of the sort of son he had – and obtuse. 'My father', wrote Aubrey, 'was not educated to learning but to Hawking.'[2]

In his ancestry there was nothing that should have made Richard Aubrey unsure of himself. In a worldly way, the Aubreys had more to offer than the Lytes, good sound country stock though they were. In origin they were a land-owning family of the Welsh Marches, who liked to trace their descent from a Sir Richard Aubrey who took part in the Norman invasion of Wales, and was rewarded by gift of land in Brecon. The great figure in the Aubrey pedigree was undoubtedly Aubrey's great-grandfather, William Aubrey. One would like to think that Aubrey's own spark of originality was struck from the same flint. William Aubrey was a brilliant lawyer, a Fellow of All Souls, who at the age of twenty-four became Regius Professor of Civil Law at Oxford. He served in the field and in France as Judge-Advocate with Elizabeth's armies during the campaign which culminated in the victory of St Quentin. He subsequently became a familiar figure at court, as well as Master in Chancery and Vicar-General to the Archbishop of Canterbury. Elizabeth liked him and called him her 'little doctor'. He was one of the Commissioners at the trial of Mary, Queen of Scots, but voted against the death penalty. In recognition of this James I, when he came to the throne, knighted his two eldest sons – the 'little doctor' himself having died in 1595 – and invited them to court, an invitation which they sensibly refused. For his friends, William Aubrey turned to men of learning like himself, although often in other and diverse fields. The figure of the sociable savant, which William Aubrey cut at Elizabeth's court, has an obvious similarity to the role which his great-grandson played in Restoration society. At the back of this liking for the company of intelligent, interesting people was an innate and insatiable curiosity about life, which Aubrey and the 'little doctor' clearly shared.

But in other ways they could hardly have been more different. William Aubrey was clearly as good at managing his private as his public affairs, whereas his great-grandson could hardly have been worse. The 'little doctor's' highly honourable career was undoubtedly very profitable also, so that he was able to buy the family seat at Abercynfrig from a cousin, as well as the Great House at Brecon which overlooks the Usk. He was reputed to be able to ride for nine miles without leaving his land. One could even today ride for nine miles over certain parts of Brecon without it being worth very much, but one cannot dispute that the income which he left of £2500 a year was, for those times, evidence of an immense fortune. Unfortunately, he seems to have left to his descendants his taste for litigation without his aptitude for succeeding in it. Much of the Aubrey fortune was squandered in the courts from which most of it originally came. Nor do any of his line, until one comes to Aubrey, seem to have inherited any part of his many-sided ability. Even Aubrey himself, when he looked into the lower branches of the family tree, admitted that William Aubrey 'engrossed all the witt of the family so that none descended from him can pretend to any'.

Aubrey made his great-grandfather the subject of one of the least brief of his 'Lives', and his pride in him shows throughout, not least by the comparative clarity of the manuscript, which, exceptionally, is little altered, well punctuated and hardly blemished by a blot. Aubrey balances his catalogue of William Aubrey's worldly successes with the picture of a family man who had married 'very young a Maiden and enjoyed to his death'. In the course of their enjoyment, and obviously a long and happy marriage, they produced three sons and six daughters, Aubrey's grandfather being the third of the sons. Physically Aubrey describes the 'little doctor', but obviously only from hearsay, as being of 'stature not taull, nor yet over low, not grosse in bodie and yet of good habit, somewhat inclining to fatnesse of visage – in his youth round, well favoured, well coloured and lively, and albeit in his latter yeares sicknesse had much impaired his strength and the freshnesse of his hew, yet there remained there still to the last in his countenance such comely and decent Gravity as that the change rather added to ... his former Dignitie.'[3]

Aubrey seems to have been devoted to his mother and greatly grieved at her death in 1686, when he himself was at the threshold of old age – there was, of course, only sixteen years difference of age between them – writing in a letter to Anthony Wood that since the news 'my heart has been a fountain of tears'.[4] She undoubtedly throughout the early part of his manhood had considerable influence on him. She twice stopped him setting off on the Grand Tour of France and Italy on which he had set his heart. It was, in fact, just the sort of experience that probably would have been invaluable for someone of his varied cultural and classical interests. Yet he gave way – 'my mother to my inexpressible grief and ruine, hindred my design'[5] – which surely shows the strength of her hold over him at this time.

But at the beginning, it may have been different. Following the birth of her first-born, Aubrey's mother had, in the course of the next five years, three children, all of whom died within a year of birth – Anne in 1628 and two Isaacs, one in 1630 and the second a year later. This wearying process of child-bearing and, more particularly, child-losing, cannot but have had an effect on both parents – and so on Aubrey himself. The understandable preoccupation of his parents with their own problems may well have been the reason why Aubrey seems to have had to turn for the affection and guidance that he, like every child, needed, to his grandparents, rather than to them. When his grandmother, Israel Lyte, died he made out an inscription for a monument he wished to raise to her memory. He never got around to having it erected but in his note on Kington church for his *North Wiltshire Collections* he recorded his intention. Even today, the message of his affection comes clearly through, as does the flavour of a charming and capable woman – 'In the north east aisle under our seate lies buried my deare grandmother Mrs Israel Lyte. If it shall please God to enable me I intend to sett up the following inscription in a decent white marble – "Here lies the body of Mrs Israel Lyte, daughter of Tho. Browne of Winterbourne Basset, Gent, the Relict of Isaac Lyte of Easton Pierse, Gent; ... a modest and sober matron; pious and charitable, an excellent menagere; delighting to be at home yet hospitable within her bounds to admiration. John Awbrey, her grandson, in duty to ye memory of her tendernesse, and diligence in his Education, hath placed this Monument"'.[6]

In his grandmother, Aubrey found affection; in his grandfather he found an influence that was probably as important as any in that early formative period of his life. His grandfather was, as Aubrey described him, a man of the 'old time'. He still wore a doublet and hose, and carried a dagger, in the Elizabethan style. He had been to court and provided his grandson with snippets of information about it. These still bring it alive to us as, no doubt, it did to Aubrey – such as that Sir Walter Raleigh's brother 'Sir Carew had a delicate, clear voice, and played singularly well on the Olpharion (which was the instrument in fashion in these days) to which he did sing'. Aubrey went on to add his own comments on a later generation of Raleighs – 'the grandchildren Walter and Tom (with whom I went to schoole at Blandford in Dorset 4 yeares) had also excellent tuneable voices, and played their parts well on the violl.: ingeniose, but all proud and quarrelsome.'[7] 'Ingeniose', one of Aubrey's favourite words, probably meant more to him than 'ingenious' does to us. 'Intelligent' would perhaps today fit the sense better, but it was intelligence of a particularly active, creative sort. 'A most ingeniose person' was Aubrey's highest commendation. Nobody, of course, fitted the description better than he himself.

'When a boy . . . was very curious', so Aubrey describes himself in one of his autobiographical fragments. 'I was always enquiring of my grandfather of the Oldtime, the Rood Loft, etc; ceremonies of the Priory, etc.' He comes back to it a page or so later – although this is one of the passages in which he writes of himself in the third person – 'When a boy he did ever love to converse with old men as Living Histories.' And yet again, in another fragment, he tells of his 'strong and early impulse to Antiquitie'.[8] Likewise, he opens his collection of diverse jotting on subjects of historical and archaeological interest which he called *Monumenta Britannica* by telling the Reader . . . 'I was inclined by my Genius from my childhood to the love of antiquities.'[9] Yet if this inclination and interest in the past was undoubtedly in him, would it ever have played so important a part in Aubrey's life had his grandfather not been on hand to encourage him, as his father never did?

A curious piece of flotsam from his grandfather's time has come to rest in Aubrey's correspondence in the Bodleian. Aubrey kept most of the letters that were sent to him during his adult life. These are now caringly arranged, and bound in two massive volumes. In most cases not only the text of the letters is preserved but also the full sheet of paper on part of which the address is written. The finished letter was folded several times, sealed (sometimes) and the address written on the exposed surface. This is often of considerable interest to the student of Aubrey – as it is often the only means of knowing where he was, and when. But with his own letters there is one sent to his grandfather, no doubt found at Easton Piers, and packed up, perhaps accidentally, with his own letters, when after the sale he had to move out. It is a letter of no consequence, simply a thank-you letter for hospitality of some sort or another, written in clear, characterful, spidery handwriting, yet it takes us a step further back into time than any of Aubrey's letters. It is addressed to

'Father Light' – presumably the writer was a younger man, and this was how he habitually called Aubrey's grandfather. It is dated 14 January 1635 – 'Father Light – T'is a vayne thinge to complement with him that regards it not. The Great Kindnesse that you and yours showed to me I do but intimate not requite; with what affection he knows that knows all things. . . .I am perpetually devoted. Hen. James.'[10] The message of affectionate gratitude comes through, and the attractive flavour of an older-fashioned, more formal style of writing.

The Aubrey side of his family, then, provided him with a useful network of family connections, with one particularly interesting and admirable ancestor in the 'little doctor'; while the Lytes provided a solid and reassuring base of country people, who had had the sense to stay more or less in one place not only for generations but for centuries, gradually improving themselves, their position and their possessions in the course of time. But so far as he, John Aubrey, is concerned, the story starts on that March day in 1626 when he was born in his grandfather's bedroom, the best in the house, in Lower Easton Piers Manor.

Aubrey describes his birth, at first in the third person: 'He was born at Easton-Pierse (a Hamlet in the parish of Kington St Michael) in the Hundred of Malmesbury in the Countie of Wilts.' He added in brackets 'his mother's inheritance'. Above this he jotted 'd. and h. of Mr. Isaac Lyte'. To the side of that he inserted 'longaevous, healthy kindred' – which the Lytes indeed were – Aubrey's great-grandfather living until he was ninety-six, and both his Lyte grandparents into their eighties. He goes on – 'March the 12 (St. Gregorie's day) about Sun-rising.' Above 'Sun-rising' he inserts 'A.D. 1626' – then continues 'being very weak and like to dye . . . he was christened before morning prayer.' At this point Aubrey's natural interest in himself overcame his effort at impersonality and he goes on in the first person: 'I gott not strength till I was 10 or 12 yeares old, but had sickness of vomiting' (here he writes in the margin 'the Bellyake and pains in the side') 'for 12 houres every fortnight for . . . yeares, then monthly, then quarterly, And at last once in half a yeare – about 12 it eased.'[11] My doctor wife suggests that this might well have been due to pyloric stenosis, a fault of the pylorus, the exit from the stomach, which occurs most often in first-born boys. Usually sufferers from this unpleasant and debilitating complaint grow out of it in much the same time sequence Aubrey describes. Yet, whether it was this, or some other gastric complaint, it surely must have meant that he was not a robust and healthy child, which could, as it generally does, have had its effect on his character.

Aubrey's formal education seems to have started when, at the late age of six, he was sent to learn to read and write to Thomas Brown, the clerk at

Kington St Michael. Obviously a quick learner, a year later – 'Ao 1633 I
entered into my Grammar and the Latin Schoole at Yatton Keynell in the
Church where the Curate taught'. Aubrey inserts above 'Mr. Hart'. Yatton
Keynell was a neighbouring parish, about a mile and a half along the lane on
to which his grandfather's house opened – in the opposite direction to
Kington St Michael. Evidently in the summer the curate and his charges
moved into the garden, for in his *Natural History* Aubrey refers to a
magnificent yew tree in the garden, under whose shade he used to do his
lessons. Whether in the church or the garden, Aubrey seems at that time to
have been more interested in the covers of his school books than the books
themselves. He may well have been right. They may well have been more
interesting, for 'the fashion then was to save the books by parchment, which
were old manuscripts, which I was too young to understand, but I was pleased
with the elegance of the writing and the coloured initial letter'. Even at this
early age it is easy to see the way Aubrey was going. But a habit of the
Rector's, whom Aubrey personally liked – 'Mr. Wm. Stump – a proper man
and good fellow . . . did grieve me then to see [for] when he brewed a barrell
of Special Ale, his use was to stop the bunghole with a sheet of manuscript: he
sayd nothing did it so well'.[12]

The following year, Aubrey changed school yet again, moving onto Leigh
Delamere, another neighbouring parish, but this time to the north of Kington
St Michael. Here for the first time he came under the influence of a good
scholar and a born teacher, Robert Latimer, who about thirty-five years
earlier had taught Thomas Hobbes, whose father was vicar of a Malmesbury
parish, Westport, on the Tetbury road. By Aubrey's account – he later wrote
a biography of Hobbes – Latimer at the time Hobbes came under his tuition
was himself 'a young man of about 19 newly come from the University . . . He
was a Batchelor and delighted in his scholar T.H's company. Here T.H. so
well profited in his learning that at fourteen years of age he went away a good
schoole-scholar to Magdalen Hall in Oxford.' At that time Latimer's school
was in his own house, which was in Westport, 'next door to the Smythe's
shop, opposite to the 3 Cuppes'[13] and so close to the Hobbes's family house
which was on the corner of the Horse Fair. But by the time Aubrey came to be
his pupil, Latimer had long been Rector of Leigh Delamere, and Aubrey was
taught in the church there.'

By a coincidence, which was indeed curious – for Aubrey, due to Latimer's
sudden and unexpected death, was his pupil only for some six months –
Thomas Hobbes came down during this time to Malmesbury to see family
and friends, foremost amongst whom, of course, was his old tutor. In the
course of his visit to Leigh Delamere he saw not only Latimer, but Aubrey.
What is even more curious is that on the following day Hobbes made a special

visit to Easton Piers to meet Aubrey's family. Aubrey tells us about it in his 'Life' of Hobbes – 'This summer', Aubrey jots on the opposite page, 'I remember 'twas in Venison season; July or August, Mr. T.H. came into his Native Country, to visitt his Friends and amongst others, he came then to see his old school-master Mr. Rob. Latimer at Leigh delamer where I was then at school at the church. I was then a little youth newly entered into my grammar . . ., here was the first place and time that ever I had the honour to see this worthy, learned man, who was then pleased to take notice of me, and the next day visited my relations. He was a proper man, briske, and in very good habit; his hayre was then quite black'.[14]

One wonders whether the real reason behind Hobbes's courtesy call and his obvious interest in Aubrey was that as a professional tutor – he had been at Chatsworth for twenty years as tutor and then secretary to the second Earl of Devonshire, and had thereafter taken several well-born sons through their lessons and on their travels (in this actual year he had been to France and Italy where he had met Galileo) – he was always on the look-out for future pupils. Aubrey was obviously intelligent; no doubt Latimer had given Hobbes a good account of him; and his family was clearly well-to-do. So – well worth a call. Hobbes would, of course, have been the ideal guide, companion and friend on the Grand Tour that Aubrey was to desire so ardently, and yet never achieve. It is a great pity that Hobbes's prescience – if it was such – was never rewarded.

Yet the first meeting between them was the start of what one can hardly, at that time, call friendship since the disparity of age between a boy of eight and a man of forty-six is obviously too great, but of a thread of connection between them that some twenty years later was to unravel into a rewarding relationship on both sides. As a man, Aubrey was to get to know Hobbes, when he returned from France to London in the earlier fifties. At that time, Aubrey, following the death of his father, was forgetting about law and following his own intellectual and social interests. As it happened, they lodged close to each other – Hobbes in Fetter Lane, Aubrey in Fleet Street – and had many friends in common. Later, at the time of the Restoration, Aubrey was to play a vital role in the rehabilitation of Hobbes. Hobbes, in return was to give Aubrey the satisfaction of knowing he was rubbing shoulders with greatness, of which he was always a good judge, and possibly influencing it as well. For, according to Aubrey, it was he who first suggested that Hobbes should write *De Legibus*. All of which seems a long way on from that first meeting in Leigh Delamere, but without the start there might have been nothing to follow.

Although, sadly, Aubrey was at Leigh Delamere for so short a time, he seems to have kept a vivid recollection of the six months during which he was taught by Latimer, and refers to it in three of his manuscripts – in the fragmentary autobiography inserted into his 'Lives'; in 'A Digression' which, for no obvious reason, Aubrey includes in his *Natural History*; and in his 'Life' of Hobbes. He was in one of his impersonal moods when he started these autobiographical notes: '1634 was entered in his Latin Grammar by Mr. R. Latimer Rector of Leigh Delamere.' Above 'Mr. R. Latimer', he put in a bracket 'Latimer Hobbes's Master' and also wrote in 'delicate little horse'. Above 'Leigh Delamere' he inserted 'a mile, fine walke'. Probably, whether he walked or rode to school depended on the weather. Latimer, he goes on 'had an easee way of teaching; and every time we asked leave to go forth, we had a Latin word from him, which at our return we were to tell him again: which in a little while amounted to a good number of wordes. 'Twas my unhappiness in half a year to loose this good Enformer, by his death.'[15] In his 'Digression', Aubrey tells us that at Latimer's school there was 'the like use of covering of books', using the old manuscripts dispersed at the Dissolution from the nearby abbeys, that there had been at Yatton Keynell. He goes on to expatiate on a misuse that obviously shocked him deeply: 'In my grandfather's days MSS. flew about like butterflies; all copie books, account books, etc were covered with manuscripts as we cover them now with blew paper or marbled paper. And the Glovers made great Harvest of them – and gloves were wrapt up no doubt in many good peices of antiquity. Before the late warres a world of good manuscripts perished hereabout; for within half a dozen miles of this place were the Abbey of Malmesbury, where it may only be presumed the Librarie was as well furnished with choice Copies as most Libraries of England; within the aforesaid compass Broadstock Abbey, Stanley Abbey, Farleigh Abbey, Bath Abbey 8 miles and Cyrencester abbey 12 miles.'[16] This was probably the first instance of man-made destruction that Aubrey came across. It made a deep impression on him that lasted throughout his life, becoming in fact something of an obsession, so that in later years when his older friends began to die off, he would often at news of their deaths rush off to salvage what he could of their manuscripts before 'woemen' used them to line their pie or pudding dishes. It may, too, have been a haunting remembrance of this early experience that in part at least lay behind the extraordinary care he took in his last years to see that his own manuscripts were in safe keeping.

Aubrey obviously had a particularly vivid remembrance of the pony, the 'delicate little horse' on which he used to ride to Latimer's school. In the margin of the note on Hobbes's visit in his Life of Hobbes, he also jots 'I had then a fine little horse and commonly rode.' Realizing, quite rightly, that this personal reminiscence is a bit out of place, he adds 'but this is impertinent'. Even so, he is determined to make his personal point quite clear and adds a further note, 'I was not a vulgar boy and carried not a satchell at my back.'[17] Aubrey remembered and wrote this in his middle age, when amidst the ruins of his material world, his social position was one of the few remaining props of his existence – and so probably more important to him than it had been in his youth. But even so, one can see that there was a barrier of social distinction round him as a child, which must have cut him off from contact with most of the village children, and which must have increased the loneliness of his life. Latimer's death was a tragedy for Aubrey. It meant the loss not only of a talented teacher, but of contact with other children, with the other pupils at the school. For the next four years he was taught by a succession of private tutors – 'dull ignorant teachers' in what he called 'Eremeticall Solitude' at Easton Piers, until some time around 1637 – he gives us no precise date – his parents moved to Broadchalke at the other end of Wiltshire. Shortly after the move – Aubrey says in 1638 – he was sent to boarding school at nearby Blandford.

Towards the end of his life, Aubrey wrote an *Idea of Education* that was intended to be the model for a series of schools for young gentlemen to be set up in stately homes throughout the country – the care of one of which, one imagines Aubrey hoped, might be a pleasant and lucrative occupation for his declining years and powers. Like most of his ideas it was never realized, yet he clearly spent a great deal of time and trouble over it. Although never finally finished, his *Idea* was sufficiently close to completion to be fit for circulation around various wealthy noblemen whom Aubrey hoped might back it. In it, Aubrey drew considerably on his own experience – mainly as a warning of errors to avoid – not only that of his years at school at Blandford, but also that of his earlier childhood education at Easton Piers. ' 'Twas a great disadvantage to me in my childhood to be bred-up in a kind of Parke, far from Neighbours and no child to converse withall . . . My father had one to teach me in the house, and I was pent-up in a Roome by myself melancholy . . . I am sensible of the inconvenience of my former private education to this very day.' Aubrey adds in brackets – 'besides it impaired my health', and inserts above 'melancholy, spleen'. He goes on – 'Sir Chr. Wren saith also the same of himselfe: wherefore he has sent his sonne to a great school – Eaton, not much caring what Latin he learnt, but to learn how to shift and live in the world.'[18]

Looking back on these last three or four years of his childhood at Easton Piers from the other end of his life, Aubrey seems to have found greater difficulty in bringing his own character into focus than he did those of his friends and other notable and noteworthy figures who provided his subject matter for his 'Lives'. Maybe the odd variation in the style of address he uses when writing about himself – 'this person', 'he', 'I' – reflects not only a normal embarrassment at looking at himself in the mirror, but a real difficulty in sizing up the, in more than one sense, curious child that he then was. Certainly, these autobiographical fragments are as disjointed, ill-decipherable and generally untidy as any part of his manuscripts, with many marginal additions, frequent insertions between the lines, constant corrections and crossings out. And yet, as one moves them around in one's mind, rather like the pieces of a jig-saw puzzle, they begin to form a picture: of a lonely child, of whom because 'at Easton' there were no children to mix or play with – 'the greatest delight [was] to be continually with the artificers that came there – e.g. joyners, carpenters, coupers, masons': of a child with a strong artistic impulse which he followed, in spite of his father's discouragement – 'I fell then to drawing, beginning first with plaine outlines, e.g. draughts of curtaines; then at nine to colours, copied pictures in the parlour . . if I had been good for anything, 'twould have been a Painter. I could fancy a thing so strongly and had so cleare an Idea of it'; of a scholarly child with an intense 'zeale to learning . . . though memory not tenacious . . . not very much care for Grammar . . . apprehension enough . . . an inventive and philosophical mind . . . but not adroit for verse'. Above all, as we have seen, he had this 'strong and early impulse to Antiquitie' about which he felt so strongly that he repeated in the margin 'strong impulse to' and then linked it with a curving line to 'Antiquitie'. Of his character in general, he sees himself as 'exceeding mild of spirit; mightily susceptible of Fascination'.[19] Looking back at his childhood, Aubrey clearly regretted and resented the lack of help, both in his formal and informal education, that he suffered after the death of Robert Latimer: 'bred ignorant at Eston', he writes bitterly at one point. At another he laments 'nobody to instruct me', and obviously feels so strongly about this that he repeats above 'being only my owne Instructor.' It would, in fact, have made all the difference to him to have had an imaginative, sympathetic and erudite teacher, such as Latimer, over these early formative years. Yet, in spite of the absence of help, in spite of, at times, actual discouragement, Aubrey seems in the end both to have made and found his own way. That he did so under such solitary conditions surely shows an independence of mind and force of spirit remarkable in a child of his age and which boded just as well for his creative and scholarly future as his 'susceptibility of Fascination' boded ill for his practical success.

*   *   *

When Aubrey was twelve his life changed dramatically. His parents moved out of Easton Piers. Whether this was the result of some tension between parents and grandparents one cannot know, but one would doubt it. There was, too, another relationship but of friendship rather than blood which may have played its part in the decision to move to Broadchalke. Aubrey tells us about it when describing the Armoury at Wilton, of which a large proportion of the contents had to be sold by Philip the fifth Earl, when he succeeded in

1650, because of the extravagant building of his father and because of the bad luck of a bad fire. 'The Armoury', writes Aubrey in his *Natural History* 'before the Civil Warres, I remember was . . . very full. The collection was not only great but the manner of obtaining it was much greater: which was by a victory at the battle of St Quintins, where William the first Earle of Pembroke was generall, Sir George Penruddock of Compton Chamberlaine, was Major Generall and William Aubrey L.L.D. my great grandfather was Judge Advocat'.[20] Relationships have a habit of repeating themselves. Was there a gravitational pull towards Broadchalke where an Aubrey was to take over a farm previously leased to a Penruddock, as a tenant of a Pembroke because their ancestors had served together in Elizabeth's victorious army? It is not beyond the bounds of, at least, conjecture.

Aubrey, by his own account, had known Wilton since he was eight, the same age at which, he wrote in his *Monumenta Britannica*, he first saw nearby Stonehenge and Salisbury Plain, which suggests that his parents spent some time considering their move before they actually made it. When it came Aubrey may not have minded too much, in spite of his undoubted affection for his grandparents and for Easton Piers itself. His childhood had been unduly solitary, particularly for someone, as his later life was to prove, of so sociable a temperament. The fact that from now on he ceased to have his sick attacks which had plagued his early years suggests that he was in a happier state of mind as well as of body. But what clearly he did at first mind very much was the fact that in the year following the move he was sent away to boarding school at Blandford. Aubrey's sheltered life at Easton Piers, insulated from outside shocks by the affection and attention primarily of his grandparents rather than his parents – also the fact that he was prevented from mixing with the other children of his age in the village by the cruel barrier of social distinctions – meant that he knew little of the ways of the world, and nothing of the ways of boys. He was an innocent, not at large, but at the mercy of his schoolfellows.

'At twelve years old', wrote Aubrey in his *Idea of Education*, 'I was putt to publick school at Blandford under Mr. W. Sutton M.D. I was like a Bird that was gott-out of his cage amongst the free citizens of the aire: 'twas the first time I knew the world and the wickedness of Boies. The boies mock't me, and abused me, that were stronger than myselfe.'[21] Aubrey was conscious that in some parts of his *Idea* he repeated himself and warned at the beginning: 'Here are somethings putt down in two places: I know it very well'. This was one of them. In a second very similar passage he wrote of being transplanted at twelve to the 'great schoole at Blandford, where there was as much Roguery as at Newgate . . . the towne-boies made a foole of me. Here I first knew what Theft was; Treachery, Envy. I began to munire [strengthten] . . .

myself with friendships . . . Children bred-up in Townes that [are] use[d] to buy things, and see people cheate and be cheated have their understandings opened as much at 16 as innocent Country people at 30.'²²

Aubrey was at a disadvantage at Blandford: not only because of his early upbringing, but because he was small. He also had a slight stutter which in later years he was to use as a convenient excuse for not going into the Church, but which at that moment must have provided an easy arm for his tormentors to twist. In such a situation one defends oneself as best one can. Aubrey's way of doing so was to reveal one of his greatest gifts. He made alliances with older and stronger boys, primarily to protect himself, but in doing so he showed a talent for friendship that was to prove one of the main strands and strengths of his life. These early friendships, press-ganged into service, were but the first of what was to prove an immense *confrérie* which gave Aubrey pleasure and amusement during his period of plenty, company and comfort, support and sustenance during his years of poverty, and in the end the material for some of his best work. Aubrey owed much to his friends, but his friendships were mainly of his creation. There was something stimulating in the company of this sociable, likeable character to which most people responded. Later on, as Aubrey himself realized, it was as a whetstone for other people's talents that he was to find one of the main purposes of his life.

Aubrey's power of making and keeping friends enabled him then to survive the hardships of school, as it did the misfortunes of his later life, but from his many references, both direct and indirect, to it, mainly in the *Idea* there can be no doubt that it was both a hard time and a hard school. Discipline was maintained by constant beating, and often carried to an extent and an excess far beyond that required for the orderly running of the school. It was not only for Aubrey that the memory of beatings at Blandford were still painful years afterwards. Aubrey had a school-fellow, later a distinguished soldier, who would wake in a sweat thirty years later, dreaming he was back there: 'This Tyranie at Blandford school was so great that yet upon any trouble Capt. Baynard dreams he is there at the hic, haec, hoc with fear and trembling, which was above XXX years hence. The like for XX yeares by dreams frequently happened to myselfe.'²³

Aubrey had a humane hatred of the ill-usage of children that was common at that time: 'It was a most ridiculous and imprudent way of breeding youth in K. James time or before. And at Bristowe much used yet, viz to damp poor lads spirits and so daunting them with whipping, cuffing and browbeating that often times a spirit thus broken never recovers itselfe again. This way made not only a strangenesse between Parent and children, but made the Child absolutely hate the parent . . . What a sad thing it is to see youths or girles come before strangers, hanging downe their heads, sneaking & voyed of spirit: whereas nature intended at this age their eies should dance with joy.'[24] Aubrey always wrote best when he felt strongly, and this is a good example of how vigorously, pleasantly and clearly he could express himself when his passions were roused. In his own case, Aubrey remembered that 'excessive whipping when I was a little childe did make a convulsive pain in my tender braine which doubtless did doe me a great deal of hurt'.[25] One can have nothing but sympathy and compassion for the suffering that he endured at Blandford, and which caused him to reiterate so constantly when formulating his own '*Idea of Education*' his hatred of the 'tyrannical beating and dispiriting of children'.

One can have some sympathy but not compassion for a different plaint that Aubrey has against his school, that of making him get up early. Clearly, by nature, Aubrey was not at his best in the morning. In his later years, late nights did not help this inclination, or disinclination. One knows that at this period he was not generally up until ten, which was the main reason why some of the 'Lives' were as brief as they were. To back his inherent dislike of early rising, Aubrey produced a theory for which he found support from his eminent friend Dr William Harvey, that it was unhealthy for children to be woken and made to get up before they had completed the process of perspiration which he believed took place in their sleep. He took this seriously to the point of including it in one of the 'Orders or Statutes' for the ideal school: 'Not to rise too early (especially in winter) because it checks the perspiration and so dulls them; and it shrinks their growth.' Of his own experience he wrote 'how contrary the course was at Blandford . . . for my part for want of perspiracon, I did nothing but gape an hower or two, the teares running down abundantly as if I had wept, which teares should have perspired.'[25] Schoolboys, no doubt, still continue to gape 'an hower or two' in the morning, and against early rising will always pour perpetual plaint, yet life is short, the day is short, particularly now, when the schoolboy has to digest so immense a curriculum. One feels that it cannot have been so different in Aubrey's day and that of the various accusations Aubrey levelled against his old school, this is the only one where he was making a fuss not quite about nothing, but about nothing very much. He believed that a boy's spirit could be so cowed by a harsh experience at this time that it never recovered and that such unfortunate boys were in consequence 'not fitt to live in the active world but for a monastique or collegiate life'. Yet despite the harsh experience which Aubrey himself underwent, there can be no doubt at all that he was not one of those to suffer permanently in this way.

His last years at Blandford, in fact, were clearly not nearly as bad as the early ones – in fact not bad at all. For 'here I recovered my health', as he would never have done if he had remained as miserable and maltreated as he was at the beginning 'and gott my Latin and Greeke'. The means by which he got his Latin and Greek show the continuing strength of his 'zeale of learning'. 'The Usher had by chance a Coupers Dict which I had never seen 'before. I was then in Terence. Perceiving his method I read all in the book where Ter[ence] was, and then Cicero, which was the meanes by which I gott my Latin – twas a wonderful helpe to my phansie.'[26] Looking back from his old age, and seeing the wide spread of learning over his life, Aubrey may have been tempted to elaborate a little on the early efforts from which it all flowed, and to show himself as the type of infant prodigy which he always so much admired. Yet, even allowing for this, he clearly possessed a powerful and persistent determination to learn that was entirely genuine. Nor was it only his scholarly inclination that he was now able to follow up at Blandford. Since 'he cared not for play . . . on play dayes he gave himselfe to Drawing and Painting'.

Aubrey heartily disliked his 'ill-natured' headmaster, from whom no doubt stemmed much of his school's severity, but he later referred to one of his senior masters as 'that worthy and gentle schoolmaster Mr. Gardener', and with some of the younger masters he made friendships that continued when he and they had left Blandford. From a Mr Stephens, only some five or six years older than himself, he 'reap't much information', and of another junior master, William Browne, he made a lifelong friend. It was possibly, and in fact probably, William Browne who built the bridge over which Aubrey crossed to the next, much happier and more fruitful stage of his education. Browne had been at Trinity College, Oxford, and it was to Trinity that Aubrey went up as an undergraduate at the beginning of the summer term of 1642.

Oxford in Peace and War
1642–3

In May 1642, Aubrey, then aged sixteen, was entered and took up residence as a gentleman-commoner at Trinity College, Oxford, the college of his friendly usher at Blandford, William Browne. In ordinary times, the Oxford that he came to would have been easily recognizable to anyone who knows the Oxford of today. The vast industrial complex that has grown up alongside, but has remained surprisingly separate from, university life, would not, of course, have been there. Fields, and so the country, still came up to the edge of the outlying colleges, of which Trinity was one. But the basic shape of the university was already complete. A glance at the map of Oxford of that time shows a number of bowling-greens that no longer exist, that Worcester was then called 'Glocester Hall', that Brasenose was known as 'Brasen Nose'; but all of the larger colleges – Christ Church, New College, Trinity, Magdalen – were recognizably the core of the colleges they are today.

War was, in fact, to break out in August. By the end of the year London had been abandoned by the Royalist army, in spite of its victory at Edgehill in October. Oxford was the obvious alternative as the Royalist capital, because of its central geographical position, and because of the convenient accommodation which its colleges provided. In consequence, from November 1642, it became the seat of the King and the court, the headquarters of the Royalist forces, and so at the heart of all the commotion, change and suffering that war of any sort involves.

Aubrey's first stay in Oxford was short. In August 'my father sent for me home for feare'.[1] For once Richard Aubrey showed a proper sense of responsibility, and even some sign of affection, for his son. Yet these few months, little longer than the length of a modern summer term, were vital to Aubrey. For the sip of scholarship they provided confirmed the taste for learning which lay at the core of his character. He also felt an immediate affinity with the place itself. 'In Febr. following (with much adoe)', he was to write in the autobiographical fragment he included in his 'Lives', 'I gott my

father to let me go to my beloved Oxford again.'² It was to remain 'my beloved
Oxford' for the rest of Aubrey's life.

Scholastically and socially the university of which Aubrey now became part
was a curious mixture. In some ways it had changed much since the time of its
inception, and in others very little. Its students no longer consisted mainly of
'poor and indigent' scholars, for seventy of whom New College, for example,
had been founded in 1379. At least half Aubrey's co-students were sons of
gentry. Another ten per cent were sons of clergy, which in most cases
amounted to the same thing. So that the poor scholars, for whose
advancement, both material and mental, most of the earlier colleges had been
created, were now already pushed well into the background, and of course,
into the worst rooms. This was inevitable since the fees varied according to
one's social status, a nobleman paying more than a gentleman-commoner, a
gentleman-commoner more than a scholar.

From the picture which Aubrey painted of Trinity under the remarkable
Dr Kettell, who had been President for nearly forty years when Aubrey
arrived there, it was clearly much more a school than a university college such
as we would understand it. This was partly because the students were on the
whole that much younger. Their ages varied considerably. Aubrey himself
was sixteen when he went up. Yet, unless there is some mistake about the date
of his birth, a co-student who was to become a life-long friend – 'one
J. Hoskyns' who in chapel would 'play the wag with the Doctor' by singing
'in a thin, shrill high treble' and 'making him straine his voice up to his'³ – can
only have been nine at the time, since he was born in 1634 and the Doctor
died in 1643. So it is hardly surprising that he could outstrip the Doctor up
the vocal scale.

But Trinity was also more like a school than a university college in that the
curriculum was more confined, and the teaching, because of the scarcity of
books, more personal. Instruction was still more by word of mouth than
through the written word. Lectures were often little more than lessons at
which long passages of textbooks were learnt by heart. Such were the notes
on logic written by Bishop Prideaux, Vice-Chancellor over the period of
Aubrey's first two sojourns in Oxford, which he was later to recommend on
the remembrance of his own experience: 'The logic notes of Trinity College,
Oxford are as good perhaps as any are (by Bishop Prideaux). They are short
and clear. We learned them by heart.'⁴ Students for the arts degrees were
taught to declaim and dispute, to develop an argument, to expound a thesis;
in other words, they were taught to think on their feet. Most of the various
examinations which marked the stages of the four-year course which led to
their degree were oral. It was a good mental training but more valuable to
those destined for the oratorical careers – for the Church, politics and law –

than for those with more meditative minds who thought better on paper, or for those who were naturally scholars and so more concerned with the search for knowledge than with developing their verbal dexterity.

Books, although no longer of such scarcity and value that they had to be chained to the desks, were still rare and expensive. Even those who had them were often not all that open-handed and open-hearted in lending them to those who had not. Many of the dons still looked upon books as tools of the trade and guarded them jealously. The 'currish Fellows', wrote Aubrey, still angry some forty years later, 'would not suffer their pupils to do it' [i.e. borrow or even read their books] 'like ill masters of trades that take good sums of money with their apprentices and never disclose to them the mystery of their trades'. Fortunately for Aubrey, one of his friends and co-students at Trinity was Ralph Bathurst, who, probably because his father was a Fellow – but clearly not at all 'currish' – had a well-stocked library which he encouraged Aubrey to use. In his *Idea of Education* Aubrey acknowledged the debt that he owed him. 'When I was a Gentleman Commoner at Trin. Coll. Oxon, 'twas my great happiness to have the friendship of the learned Mr. Ralph Bathurst (nowe Dean of Wells). He had an excellent Collection of well-chosen Bookes of all kinds of learning, and I still doe owe my thanks to him for his generous favour to let me turn them over and peruse them.'[5]

But the greatest debt that Aubrey contracted during his first two short sojourns at Oxford was to Dr Kettell. Dr Kettell was close to eighty when Aubrey came to Oxford. During his immensely long tenure of office he possibly did more than any other President before or since – with the possible exception of Bathurst, who also was to devote his life to his old college and to be President almost as long as Kettell – to further the fortunes of the college, organizing and extending its estates, rebuilding the hall, but above all moulding his students so that few who left Trinity during that period did not have his mark upon them. Just as Trinity at that time appears to us to have been more of a school than a college, so correspondingly Dr Kettell comes across more in the shape of a schoolmaster, if a headmaster, than that of a don nowadays. Aubrey shows Kettell as an imposing character with 'a very venerable presence' despite his age: 'He was a very tall, well growne man. His gowne and surplice and hood being on, he had a terrible gigantique aspect with his sharp grey eies.' Forty years on, Aubrey's picture still seems to carry something of the fright of the freshman.

Aubrey obviously admired Kettell's authoritative attitude and manner: 'He was an excellent Governor, one of his maxims of Governing was to keep down the Juvenilis impetus,' by which Aubrey presumably meant the hot blood of youth. Kettell did so by keeping a close eye and a tight grip on not only the studies but the personal life of the students. Anyone guilty of moral backsliding was liable to find himself castigated in college chapel. He was also particular about the appearance of his scholars and could not abide 'long haire', calling those who wore it 'hairy scalpes . . . When he observed the Scolars haire longer than ordinary . . . he would bring a paire of Cizers in his Muffe (which he commonly wore) and woe be to them that sate on the outside of the Table. I remember he cutt Mr. Radford's haire with the knife that chips the bread on the Buttery hatch.' Scolding his scholars, but one would think not in chapel, 'he used these names viz. Turds, Tararags (these were the worst sort, rude Rakills), Rascal-Jacks, Blindcinques, Scobberlotchers (these did no hurt but went idling about the Grove with their hands in their pockets).' One doubts whether Oxford still has its Tararags but one can be quite certain it still has its share of Scobberlotchers.

But there was a lot of common sense behind the Doctor's strictness. He saw to it that the college had the best beer in Oxford so that the students should be less tempted to go out to alehouses. There was kindness also. On his prowls around the college he would often slip small sums of money into the windows of penurious students, or alternatively arrange small unexacting jobs for them for which they would be overpaid. His students, and it is a clear sign of the affection in which they held him, were never so much in awe that they could not make fun of him. He slightly dragged one foot, Aubrey puts it vividly, 'like a rattlesnake', by which he gave warning of his approach: 'Will Egerton . . . a good witt and mimick . . . would goe so like him that sometimes he would make the whole Chapell rise up imagining he had been entring in.'

Like many autocratic heads of colleges or schools who want to run everything their own way, Kettell really got on much better with the students than his staff. According to Aubrey, 'there was a great Faction between Dr. Kettle and the Fellowes; and one time, at a Scrutiny, the doctor upbraiding them for their disrespect to him,' cried "Oh! You are brave Gentlemen and *learned* men, you dispise, and snort and fart at your poor President: I am an old blind-sucks; but who was it proposed you to be fellows from poor rackall-Jacks and Servitors; was it not your poor President? and yet none of your Friends were ever so gratefull to present me with so much as a wrought Night-cap".' The Doctor immediately and typically excused himself to one of the Fellows: 'I cry you mercy (Mr. Dr. Hobbs) indeed I remember, your Mother sent me once a gammon of Bacon'.[6] By small idiosyncratic detail such as this Aubrey brings the Doctor back to life.

Aubrey left Oxford for Broadchalke at his father's behest on 9 August, three days before the King raised his standard at Nottingham. So presumably he missed the flurry of military activity which followed the outbreak of war. As was to be expected, Oxford sympathies at that time were split along the traditional division of disagreement, the 'town' largely supporting Parliament, most of the 'gown' being ardently Royalist. For the moment, the 'gown' had the upper hand. Under the leadership of the energetic Warden of New College, Dr Pinke, bands of students, college servants, and so-called privileged men (those who by service or residence were entitled to enjoy the privileges of the university) were drilled in New College quad. Boulders were carried up into Magdalen Tower to be dropped on the heads of attackers crossing the bridge below. In default of other arms, bows and arrows were distributed. Most of these activities have the flavour of the academic rather than the military, but there can be no doubt of the enthusiasm which lay behind them, nor of the disruption they caused to normal studies. Clearly it was as well Aubrey saw something of the scholarly side of Oxford life before war broke out.

At this time in Oxford there was a schoolboy who was to play so important a part in the later part of Aubrey's life that it seems fair to mention him at this point even though their lifelines were not to link for more than twenty years. This was Anthony Wood, some six and a half years younger than Aubrey, and so a boy of ten at 'New College Schoole situated between west part of the chappell and east part of the cloyster', one would think in what is now the ante-chapel, when Aubrey first came up to Trinity as an undergraduate. Wood's grandfather had made a small fortune as lessee of the White Lion at Islington, and of the Axe Inn in Aldermanbury. His father had followed a similar trade in Oxford, becoming the owner of the Fleur de Luce in 1616. By this time Thomas Wood was already a man of property, having bought the lease of Postmaster's Hall, a house opposite Merton, in 1608. Here Anthony Wood was born in 1632, the fourth of six sons born of his father's second wife, and here he lived virtually all his life, save for two years during the siege of Oxford, when he was sent for safety to nearby Thame. In character, Wood seems to have been about as different from Aubrey as it was possible to be: mean where Aubrey was generous to the point of profligacy (when he had the money); anti-social, disagreeable in manner, unprepossessing in appearance, and, possibly because of this, a misogynist. In contrast, Aubrey was quickly likeable, extremely sociable with an immense capacity for making friends. Wood, seemingly, was much better at making enemies.

But the two qualities they shared which were to make their relationship on both sides probably the most important of their adult lives were an insatiable interest in scholarship, and an unshakeable belief in the worth of their work, even though their individual interests often varied. Wood devoted the greater part of his scholastic life to the history of Oxford and its antiquities, published under the title of *Historia et Antiquitates Univ. Oxon* and also compiled a biographical dictionary of past and present writers and bishops who had taken Oxford degrees, published under the title of *Athenae et Fasti Oxonienses*. Both are informative records but since Wood lacked Aubrey's skill with words and his human touch, they do not come to life in the way that Aubrey's work so often does. By a quirk of fate that Aubrey would have understood better, Wood is mainly remembered for a work he would have valued much less than his two main works, his *Life and Times*, based on his recollections of the early part of his life and the journal notes he made during the later part which covered his lifetime in Oxford. Much of this was written in retrospect, but like most self-centred people, Wood could vividly recall what he had seen, felt and thought many years in the past. Starting at the age of three his autobiography goes on until the year of his death, when he was sixty-two. It is a unique record of life in Oxford, mainly because of its unbroken continuity, seen through the eyes of an odd and on the whole unattractive character, who yet had his own integrity and courage.

As a pupil at New College School, Wood deeply disapproved of the disturbances caused in August 1642 by the training of undergraduates and privileged men which went on in the quadrangle under Dr Pinke, since it disrupted his co-pupils to the extent that 'some of them were so besotted with the training and activitie and gaitie there in that they could never be brought to their books again'.[7]

Aubrey was away for six months. During that time, Oxford underwent a violent fluctuation of fortune in the course of which it came face to face with the harsher reality of war. On 12 September 1642, it was occupied by a Parliamentary force commanded by Lord Saye and Sele, who immediately organized the demolition of such fortifications as the Royalists had erected – not one would imagine a very lengthy or difficult task. He also ordered a rigorous search of the colleges, not only for hidden plate, found in five colleges, but also for anything 'Popish' in the way of books, manuscripts, pictures, chapel decorations. Of the books and manuscripts thus condemned a great bonfire was made in front of the Star Inn, where Lord Saye was lodging. Their loss at a time when any book was a rare item, and in many a case irreplaceable, was tragic. Saye conducted some of the inspections himself, not sparing his own college, New College, of which he was a Fellow. It was, in fact, the first he visited, ransacking the plate and going through the papers of Dr Pinke, who by then was under arrest in the Tower of London, although he was soon released and allowed to return to Oxford. In Trinity, it was, according to Aubrey, only the presence of mind of Dr Kettell that saved two valued altar-pieces in the chapel from destruction: 'On the backside of the skreen had been two altars (of painting well enough for these times, and the colours were admirably fresh and lively). That on the right as you enter the Chapell was dedicated to St. Katherine, that on the left was of the taking our Saviour off from the crosse. My Lord Say saw that this was done of old time, and Dr. Kettle told his Lordship "Truly, my Lord, we regard them no more than a dirty Dish-clout". So they remained untoucht.'[8]

Within a few weeks the pendulum swung the other way. In the middle of October, in preparation for the battle that was to prove to be that of Edgehill, the Parliamentary force moved out, one of the troopers as he did so shooting the nose off a statue on the front of All Souls. At this time, Anthony Wood's eldest brother Thomas, then eighteen and a student at Christ Church, hearing of battle impending, 'left his gowne at the towns end, ran to Edgehill; did his majestie good service; returned on horseback well accountred; and afterwards was made an officer in the King's army'. However, Wood was not entirely happy with this, regretting his brother's transformation into 'a rude and boisterous soldier'.[9] When Edgehill resulted in a Royalist victory, it was the turn, for Oxford, of a Royalist occupation – and a far longer and more complete one than anyone at that time could possibly have foreseen. The King himself made a state entry into Oxford on horseback within the month, but at that moment he and the army commanders envisaged Oxford only as a stage and a stop on the way to London. However, a month later the King was back, this time in a coach, having in the meantime – after some bloody fighting in Brentford and a formidable confrontation with the Parliamentary forces at Turnham Green – realized the strength of Parliament's grip on London and so the size of the task that faced him if he was to retake his capital. Humanely, if possibly unwisely, he refused the challenge. So Oxford became and remained the centre of the Royalist war effort until it was finally shut up by siege two years later.

Aubrey returned to Oxford in February 1643, some two months after the King. On his way, near Abingdon, he passed an outpost of the Royalist troops 'perhaps a dozen or more, that kept watch and guarded themselves in a great pitt thereby: so that if an Enemie came there was nothing to be shott at but there Heads.'[10] The sight may have made him ponder what he would find at Oxford. In fact, it had changed almost out of recognition. The quiet university town he had left playing at soldiers in an academic, amateurish way had in his absence become virtually an armed camp. It was packed with troops. The garrison alone numbered some 2500 men. With their different uniforms they must have made it a colourful as well as a crowded scene. Of the four foot regiments that originally comprised it, the Life Guards wore red, Colonel Charles Gerard's regiment, blue, Sir Ralph Dutton's, white. The colour of the coats of Sir William Perryman's regiment is not known but no doubt it added to the variety of the scene. A further colour was added to the spectrum with the arrival during Aubrey's stay of the greycoats of Colonel Thomas Pinchbeck's regiment.

In addition to the garrison inside, there was also the cavalry, all of whom, with the exception of the King's Lifeguard of Horse, were deployed outside and around Oxford, but who for one reason or another were always coming in and out. Other bodies of troops too, were frequently moving through, or collecting for a particular purpose, such as Prince Rupert's attack on Cirencester, which took place early in February 1643, just about the time of Aubrey's return, which resulted in a thousand prisoners being brought in to add to the congestion. Most of the university buildings had, of course, also been taken over. The Law and Logic Schools were used as granaries, the Music and Astronomy Schools as Quartermasters' stores, the Rhetoric School was requisitioned for the construction of drawbridges, which must have given them something to talk about, New College Cloisters and Tower became the main arsenal, although arms were also stored on the top floor of Schools Tower. Magdalen Grove became the artillery park. Wood was very cross when 'his Majestie caused his magazine to be put into the New college cloister and tower, etc. whereupon the master of the school there, with his scholars (amongst whom A. Wood was one) [like Aubrey, Wood sometimes wrote of himself in the third person] were removed to the choristers chamber at the east end of the common hall of the said college. It was then a dark nasty room and very unfit for such a purpose.'[11]

How full the Oxford streets normally were with the activity of the army, how heavy the air with its sound, shows by implication in Wood's description of the startling quiet that fell on the city when, early in April, all available troops were moved out, in a vain attempt to prevent the surrender of Reading: 'there was not so much as a drumme heard to beate all the morninge (as usually they did) nor any tramplinge of horses etc. but everything hush and silent.'[12] Everything hush and silent – there can not have been many moments of such comparative peace in Oxford at that time. For it was not only the army that caused the congestion. With the King came the court, and with the court came families and servants. Soon all the colleges and houses were filled to bursting point. It was often a drastic and dramatic change. Ann Harrison, the daughter of a Royalist baronet who had made his fortune farming the Customs, only to have to return the greater part of it to the King when war broke out, gave a vivid description of what the change had meant to her and many others like her:

> 'my father commanded my sister and myself to come to him to Oxford
> where the Court then was . . . we, that had till that hour, lived in great
> plenty found ourselves like fishes out of the water . . . for from as
> good a house as any gentleman of England had, we came to a baker's
> house in an obscure street . . . no money, for we were as poor as Job;

nor clothes more than a man or two brought in their cloak bags: we had the perpetual discourse of losing and gaining towns and men; at the windows the sad spectacle of war, sometimes plague, sometimes sicknesses of other kinds, by reason of so many people being packed together.'[13]

How many were packed together shows clearly in a remarkable study by two distinguished historians, Margaret Toynbee and Peter Young, of a survey made by Edward Heath, in June 1643, at the King's behest, of those billeted and lodged in a single district, St Aldates. *Strangers at Oxford* is one of those few books which seem to open a window on to an earlier age. St Aldates, the district opposite Christ Church, where the King himself lodged, was of special use for those guarding, serving, attending or advising him. 'The strangers' came from every social level. At one extreme there were grandees, such as the Earl of Forth, the Lord General and the Earl of Lindsay, the Lord High Chamberlain; also the Earls of Bath and Carlisle, a French nobleman, the Vicomte de Saint Paul, who was later to conduct a gallant defence of Chester as its Governor, and several Members of Parliament. At the other, St Aldates also lodged many of the Royal servants – the King's barber, his apothecary, his sempstress, one of his poulterers, his candlestick-maker, and a Samuel Nurse, who had the grand sounding, but possibly exhausting, position of 'coal-carrier to the Court'. Curiously, one of the many soldiers also billeted in the area was another Aubrey – Anthony, an officer in the Life Guards, killed that autumn in the first battle of Newbury – possibly a Herefordshire cousin. The overall impression created by the authors' sympathetic survey is one of total congestion: 'practically every house in St Aldates was requisitioned . . . the houses most generally have been full to bursting, literally crammed from cellar to attic. Even the tiniest, which we know had only one room up and one room down, were forced to hold several soldiers at need; they must have slept packed like sardines.'[14]

On his return, Aubrey was quick to get to the centre of things, which was, of course, the King's presence. 'I was wont to go to Christ-church to see King Charles I at supper. Where I once heard him say "That as he was hawking in Scotland, he rode into the Quarry, and found the Covey of Partridge falling upon the Hawk" . . . When I came to my Chamber I told this story to my tutor . . . said he, That Covey was London.'[15] Aubrey's story brings a vivid picture before the mind's eye – the King dining with his court in Wolsey's splendid hall while students and other onlookers mingled with those serving the tables.

By the time Aubrey returned, Trinity, like other colleges, had its lodgers, and one of these, curiously, was the Ann Harrison who by her own account had found the first weeks of her stay in Oxford so difficult and depressing, but now clearly had recovered her spirits. This was probably because she had found her true love in Richard Fanshawe, a scholarly courtier who acted as Secretary to the King over several periods, and whom she was to marry at Oxford in 1644. But in Aubrey's time she and her great friend Isabella Thynne, who lodged at Balliol next door, used to frequent Trinity Gardens to the admiration of the court gallants and the distraction of the Trinity students. They were 'wont', writes Aubrey, 'to come to our Chapell, mornings, half-dressed like angels'. On one occasion they 'would have a frolick to make a visit to the President. The old Doctor quickly perceived that they had come to abuse him: he addresses his discourse to Mistress Fenshawe [across the gap of forty years Aubrey had obviously forgotten that she did not marry until the following year and so was still then Ann Harrison] saying "Madam . . . I knew your grandfather, I know you to be a gentle-woman, I will not say you are a whore; but gett you gonne for a very woman." The dissoluteness of the times grieved the good old Doctor, his dayes were shortened, and he dyed'.[16]

Aubrey's second taste of Oxford life was even shorter than the first. Having arrived back in February, in April he caught smallpox. So although he was to remain in Oxford for a further two months before he returned home, while the disease ran its course, he was in circulation for only a matter of weeks. Yet these were sufficient for him, as always, to make friends. William Radford, who had his hair cut by Dr Kettell with the bread-knife while at table, must have been a particularly close one for he was brave enough to run the risk of infection and keep Aubrey company in his sick-room. For this Aubrey was particularly grateful, reckoning that without these visits 'melancholy would have spoyled a scurvey antiquary'.[17] They were to remain friends until Radford's death in 1673. There was also, of course, Ralph Bathurst. John Hoskyns, of the high-pitched treble, was unlikely to have been a close friend in these early days at Trinity because of the disparity in age, but certainly became one later on. But the two friends of those Aubrey made at Trinity at this time for whom he seems to have cared the most were John Lydall and Anthony Ettrick. John Lydall, a scholar of Trinity, went on to become a Fellow. In 1653, Aubrey invited him to accompany him on the Grand Tour which his mother was to thwart, but Lydall excused himself on the grounds of his 'crazy and sickly constitution of body'. That this was no false excuse was shown by his early death three years later at the age of thirty-two. Aubrey never forgot him and he was on the select list of fourteen particularly valued 'Amici' that Aubrey made forty years later. Anthony Ettrick was older than Aubrey but outlived him. Like Aubrey, he was by nature an antiquarian. Like Aubrey, he studied at the Middle Temple as well as Oxford, but, unlike Aubrey, he went on from there to pursue a successful career, mainly in law, being Recorder of Poole for twenty years.

Later he was a Member of Parliament. But he still managed to keep up his antiquarian interests. The results of his research were to play their part in recording the features and buildings of his home county Dorset, in much the same way that Aubrey's *North Wiltshire Collections* preserved for posterity a record of his. He and Aubrey made a tour of Ireland together in 1660. Aubrey made a draft of a will when he was thinking of making his Grand Tour. Bathurst, Lydall and Ettrick all figure in it. Bathurst and Lydall were to be left 'a ring of the value of 50s. with a stone in it'. But on these Ettrick seems to have had the edge, being left 'ten pounds to buy a piece of plate, my saphire ring, Sir Walter Raleigh's history and my Philip* Comineus'.[18]

But in these two periods in Trinity before and during the war, Aubrey was not too busy with his friends or his studies, or too absorbed in the observation of this unique moment in Oxford's history when it was the capital of Royalist England, to follow his own bent, which was to explore the old buildings of Oxford itself and of the surrounding countryside. Early in August 1642, just before he was recalled to Broadchalke, he made a visit to Woodstock to see Rosamund's Bower. He was very distressed when his notes, and probably drawings, were lost when his belongings, as well as he himself, were moved from his rooms when he caught smallpox. He was also greatly struck by the ruins of Osney Abbey on its island in the Isis, close to Folly Bridge. Osney Abbey had been one of the largest monasteries in England until the Dissolution, its tower supposedly the third tallest, and its church Oxford's cathedral. But at the Dissolution it was partially demolished, its bells, notably the famous Great Tom – still sounding over Oxford – removed to Christ Church. By Aubrey's time it was in total disrepair and liable at any moment finally to fall, or be pulled, down. Aubrey was so impressed by it, and at the same time appalled by its state, that he arranged for a pupil of William Dobson, the leading court painter, to make drawings of it. In the margin of an autobiographical passage headed 'Phansie', in his 'Lives', Aubrey wrote: 'I got Mr. Hesketh, a priest, Mr. Dobson's man, to draw the ruines of Osney 2 or 3 ways.'[19] One of these drawings he passed on to Sir William Dugdale seventeen years later for his *Monasticon Anglicanum*. It is the only record of the Abbey's appearance, for it was finally demolished, or fell down, shortly after Aubrey's visits. It was a remarkable effort for an undergraduate of seventeen that he should go to the trouble and expense, in such exceptionally difficult and distracting circumstances, to provide and preserve the record of an old building that was clearly soon to disappear. It shows that 'the love of antiquities' to which Aubrey as he wrote 'was inclined by my Genius from my childhood' was already a deep one.

*It is curious that Aubrey seems to have been mistaken over Cominius' Christian name. His Christian names were John Amos.

Prospectus Ruinarum Abbatiæ de OSNEY, juxta Oxon:

136.

An engraving of Osney Abbey, taken from a drawing commissioned by
Aubrey when still an undergraduate, from one of Dobson's drawing staff.
This is all that survives to give us a picture of old Osney.

But the incident also showed something of the other side of the coin. Aubrey paid twenty shillings, in those days a sizeable sum, for the drawings. He was an adequate artist in his own right and could perfectly well have done them himself. Clearly, already, money was a matter of little or no account. In this episode, one can see emerging the two traits of his character which more than any others were to shape the course of his later life.

'Consumption' at Broadchalke
1643–6

After his return from Oxford in June 1643, Aubrey spent the rest of the Civil War with his parents at Broadchalke, now his main home, although one would doubt if it ever supplanted Easton Piers as the focal point of his affection. Broad Chalke lies south of the main expanse of Salisbury Plain, some six miles south-west of Salisbury itself and four from Wilton, but in an area that is still predominantly downland, although here the undulations between the downs broaden into vales, most of which are wooded. Aubrey measured the proportion of down to vale, his method exact but eccentric, by cutting up a map and weighing the hill against the vale. 'To find the proportions of the downs of the Country to the vales I did divide Speeds Mappe of Wiltshire with a pair of cizars, according to the respective hundreds of downes and vale, and I weighed them in a curious ballance of a goldsmith, and the proportion is . . . about ¾.'[1] By contrast with the emptiness of the Plain itself, villages are frequent and full of beautiful houses, most of which were built with money that came from sheep. For this is perfect sheep country. Few weeds grow on the chalk, the close cropping of the flocks thickens the sward and there is a wide area over which to roam, which suits all grazing animals.

Nor did, or does, the downland turf suit only sheep. Salisbury Races are still run officially at Broad Chalke, although the actual course is a mile or so distant from the village. Already in Aubrey's day there was an annual Salisbury Race, instituted by an Earl of Pembroke in Elizabethan times of which the start was 'on the edge of the north downe' – on Aubrey's farm. The race was run over a distance of four miles and ended at the Hare Warren 'built by William, Earl of Pembroke', which is in the grounds of Wilton, just below and to the north of the present race-course. Aubrey described it as 'since very famous . . . and beneficiall to the city', the prize was 'a silver bell . . . about 1630 turned into a cup of the same value'. Aubrey had inherited some of the sporting instincts of his father and was greatly

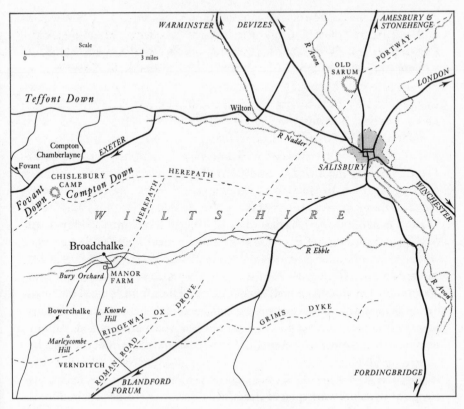

Broadchalke and its neighbourhood

interested in the Salisbury Race and the horses who ran in it. He particularly admired one of them called Peacock who 'used to run the four mile course in five minutes and a little more . . . Peacock was first Sir Thomas Thynne's of Long-Leate, who valued him at £1000. Philip, Earle of Pembroke gave 5£ but to have a sight of him: at last his lordship had him; I think by gift. Peacock was a bastard barb. He was the most beautifull horse ever seen in this last age, and was as fleet as handsome. He dyed about 1650'.[2]

Aubrey believed that the local people of north and south Wiltshire were just as different as the areas on which they lived. Curiously – for of his two homes, his affection always seems to have been drawn more towards Easton Piers rather than Broadchalke – he appears from his descriptions in his *Natural History* to have preferred those who lived in the south to those of the north. Those of the north he describes as being 'phlegmatique, skins pale and livid, slow and dull, heavy of spirit: hereabout is but little Tillage, or hard labour, they only milke the Cows and make cheese: they feed chiefly on Milk-meates which cools their Brains too much, and hurts their Inventions. These circumstances make them melancholy, contemplative and malicious . . . they are generally apt to be fanatiques: their persons are plump and feggy [spotted]; gallipot [the colour of earthenware] eyes and some black; but they are generally handsome enough'. But by contrast, around Broadchalke 'where 'tis all upon tillage or shepherds', the more active life seems to have shaped a more active type of character that Aubrey preferred. They 'labour hard, their flesh is hard, their bodies strong'.[3]

*   *   *

The village of Broad Chalke lies in a shallow valley between the downs, close to the source of the small river Ebble, a chalk stream with all the attractions that implies – crystal-clear water, abundant trout, beds of water-cress, many duck – which runs its short course to join the Hampshire Avon some four miles below Salisbury. The downs on either side rise to a height of some six hundred feet. Those to the north, towards Wilton, rise, however, in a more uniform spread until they reach the ridge formed by Fovant and Compton Downs. From this they topple down an escarpment so steep that the Wiltshire Regiment, among others, have been able to cut out the sods of the turf, exposing the chalk beneath in the design of a gigantic regimental badge in the same way as the white horses at Cherhill – which Aubrey could see in the distance from Easton Piers – Warminster, Beckington and elsewhere, were cut. The downs to the south of Broad Chalke are much more rounded and individual. Aubrey catches their character well when he writes of them as 'remains of the smooth primitive world, when all lay under water'. They do, indeed, look like gigantic pebbles, smoothed and shaped by the surge of the sea. The road over one of the most remarkable of these – Knowle Hill, or as Aubrey spelt it 'Naule Hill' – passes in front of Manor Farm before it starts its climb. It is a strikingly beautiful road not only for the view from the top, over a wide spread of woodland, which Aubrey called 'boscage', and valley, but also for the plantations along it, several of beech and one, more recent, mixed, with a preponderance of sycamore. The beech plantation nearest to Aubrey's house, covering the twist in the road as it starts its climb up the hill, is magnificent, the trees being of a size (some of them rising to a height of sixty feet) and of an apparent age, which makes one wonder whether they could possibly have been standing in Aubrey's time. Being a down the hill has no particular summit but the road runs for some three miles along its crest, crossing at one point a farm track that follows the line of the ancient Ox Drove and ridge way, and further on, crossing a lane which once was a Roman road leading from Salisbury to Dorchester. Most of Knowle Hill would in their day have been farmed by Aubrey and his father.

The downs themselves, in summer, pleased Aubrey to the point of lyricism. 'The Turfe is of a short sweet grasse, good for sheep and delightful to the eie for its smoothnesse like a Bowling-green. About Wilton and Chalke the downes are intermixt with Boscages . . . nothing can be more pleasant and in summer-time do excell Arcadia in verdant and rich turfe and moderate aire . . . The plaines doe abound with Hares, Fallow deer, Partridges and Bustards.' Aubrey delighted in the magnificent views that could but seen from the tops of many downs, particularly from Vernditch, which adjoined his land: 'from where you may see, over the New Forest, the French Sea, and ships sayling; you may behold the Isle of Wight from one end to the other and but turning your eie a little forward you may see the promontory of Portland'. In a flight of fancy back to the previous century, Aubrey imagines Sir Philip Sydney riding over these downs where he now farmed, finding in them the inspiration for his poems: 'These Romancy plaines and Boscages did no doubt conduce to the heightening of Sir Philip Sydneys phansie; he lived . . . in these parts and the most masterly touches of his pastoralls he wrote here upon the spot where they were conceived.' However, the muses which attended Sidney never favoured Aubrey: 'they are never so kind as to appear to me although I am the usufructuary.' Aubrey adds above in humorous regret 'I could never meet with them.'[4]

At times, Aubrey found the climate tiresome, particularly in what he described as 'Feaverish Autumnes' when 'the Mists doe lie more on the Hills than in the Vales. My books at Chalke all white with mouldinesse, when those at Easton Piers are not at all toucht with it.' This is surprising, for when we lived only a mile or so from Easton Piercy our books suffered severely from mould, which suggests that its presence depends more on the dampness or dryness of the house rather than the outside climate. Nor does Aubrey seem to have liked living on a chalky soil any more than in a misty climate: 'Chalk-ie (Marly) Soiles doe abound with Nitre, which . . . causeth Dampishnesse, and condenseth the aire, hurts the Nerves, and gives Aches.' Nearby Salisbury seems at that time, by Aubrey's description, to have been an appalling place in which to live: 'At the city of Salisbury doe range the Consumption, Dropsy, Scurvy and Gowte. It is an exceeding dampish place'.[5]

$$* \qquad * \qquad *$$

Manor Farm was by far the largest in Broadchalke, occupying the land over half the parish. Before the Dissolution it had belonged to the Abbey of Wilton, which in fact was a nunnery. Aubrey tells us that the last Lady Abbess, and probably some of her predecessors also, had taken a personal interest in the farm, and retained some of the land, otherwise let to produce the revenue on which the Abbey subsisted, on which they ran their own flock of sheep. Sold to the Wilton estate at the time of the Dissolution, the Broadchalke land was subsequently let out in two tenancies, separated by the river Ebble, throughout most of the sixteenth century. That on the north bank consisted of 30 acres of river meadows, 200 acres of permanent pasture on the downs, and 670 acres of arable, a surprisingly large amount for those days when the only fertilizer was muck of some sort or another. This was probably what was known as 'in and out' land, land on which a year of tillage alternated with a year of grass. On the south bank of the Ebble there were 200 acres of 'shared' land – which probably means common land – and 1000 acres of downland grazing. By the end of the sixteenth century, the two blocks of land had come together again under the tenancy of the Penruddocks. When Manor Farm was handed over to Aubrey's father in 1637, it must have carried with it about 2000 acres of land, clearly not only a sizeable but, even in those days, a very viable farming unit. According to the *Victoria History*, the increase of size of tenanted farms was common at this time throughout the corn and sheep country of south Wiltshire, but not in the north, where the most economical way of running a dairy farm, which most of them were, was as a family business. So manors tended to be on the decline in the north, but flourishing in the south. There the large and profitable tenancies led also 'to the rise of the gentleman farmer, a man of . . . education and leisure' who could 'mix and deal with cultivated squires and minor landowners on equal terms'. The *Victoria History* then names four families who exemplified this trend, among them 'the Aubreys of Chalke', a mistaken identification in an otherwise clear-sighted and convincing analysis which would surely have made the aristocratically connected and snobbishly inclined Aubrey speechless with indignation.

The river-meadows by the Ebble, most of which belonged to Manor Farm, were undoubtedly the pick of the parish. This must have been particularly so at that time. For it was here, and in the neighbouring river valleys of the Wylye and the Nadder, all of which flowed into the Avon just above or below Salisbury, that just at the time of the Aubreys' move to Broadchalke in the 1630s, the practice of the floated water-meadow originated. This the *Victoria* historians regard as at this time 'technically the crowning glory of English agriculture. A floated water-meadow was a hot-bed for grass. When floated the meadow was covered by an evenly distributed sheet of flowing water about one inch deep. In addition to the warmth provided, all the chalky sediment of the stream passed through the grass and was deposited amongst its blades and stalks. Floated water-meadows provided an early bite for ewes and lambs and yielded a much greater and better hay crop, besides being an excellent method of creating meadowland from marsh and arable'.[6]

Broadchalke would have been a particularly suitable site for such water-meadows not only because the fields beside the Ebble are little above it, and so easily floodable, but because the source of much of its water was a three-acre lake 'at a place called Naule'. This was on the extremity of Aubrey's land, on the edge of the neighbouring village of Bower Chalke, 'where are a great many springs that issue out of the Chalkie ground' and where 'there are no better Trout in the Kingdom of England',[7] for which James I when he visited Wilton had a particular liking. Now the lake is, suitably, a trout-farm, in a place called Knowle, fed by springs, of which the temperature now, and so presumably then, varies little from a constant of fifty-three degrees. So it never comes close to freezing, even in the hardest of winters. An abundant supply of warm water throughout the winter was an ideal source for floating water-meadows and it can be no surprise that the farmers in the Chalke and Wylye valleys were among the first to use them. That his father was one of these Aubrey confirms in his *Natural History*: 'the improving of watering meadows began at Wylye in 1635, about which time I remember we began to use them at Chalke.'[8] The Aubreys, of course, only came to Broadchalke about 1637, but no doubt the process of the move was a gradual one, particularly since they were taking over the lease from such close friends as the Penruddocks. The spring water with its constant temperature, so warm in winter, was of course cool, even cold in summer; too cold for some crayfish which Aubrey introduced into the lake at Naule: 'but they would not live there – the water is too cold for them'. It was too cold also for 'the North Wilts horses', presumably in the main those that came from Easton Piers, 'and other stranger horses [who] when they come to drinke of the water of Chalke river [and here Aubrey inadvertently breaks into rhyme] will sniff and snort, it is so cold and tort'.[9]

The house and buildings of Manor Farm stand in the centre of Broad Chalke close to the church, which is close to the river. It is a very old church, mainly of the thirteenth and fourteenth centuries, which impressed Aubrey in his day, Pevsner in ours. Aubrey admired its immense cross-beam. It 'hath no Pillar, and the breadth is thirty and two feet and two inches. Hereabouts are no trees (now) growing that would be long enough to make the cross-beames'.[10] The church also had 'one of the tunablest ring of Bells in Wiltshire, which hang advantageously, the river running near the church-yard, which meliorates the sound'.[11] Outside, the church is built of faced stone of a very light, almost silvery colour. In spite of which Aubrey wrote that 'the walls of the Church at Broadchalke, and of the Buttery at the farme there – doe shoot out, besides nitre, a beautiful red; lighter than scarlet; an oriental horse-flesh colour,'[12] presumably when they caught the rays of the setting sun.

From Aubrey's house one looks down on the church, only 100 yards distant, but at an angle. But immediately opposite, on the other side of the road which leads up Knowle Hill, was, and is, a curious feature, a rectangular ridge some three feet high, enclosing, according to Aubrey, an area of five acres, called Bury Orchard, although nowadays it has no apple trees in it, only some grazing horses. Aubrey thought it to have been a Roman swimming pool. 'Just by the Farme near the River side, south of the Church, between the Farme and the Vicar's house is a ground called Bury Orchard, containing five acres. It is encompassed with a bank of great breadth, not now very high, at the square, and hath great convenience for Aquation, which (as Livy sayeth) the Romans did ever principally respect.' If Aubrey was probably right about its Roman origin it seems much more likely, in that dry downland area, that its intended use was as a reservoir of water rather than as a swimming pool. Aubrey concludes his note on it in his *Monumenta Britannica* by commenting in surprise: 'nobody hath taken notice of it before though obvious enough.'[13] But then both in south and north Wiltshire there was, at that time, so much of interest 'obvious enough' waiting for someone like Aubrey to come along.

The front part of the house in which Aubrey lived still stands, easy enough to distinguish from the later additions or replacements, since these are in brick, whereas the old part of the house is in stone, of much the same colour, and possibly of the same provenance, as that of the church. It is in the shape of a small L, the front forming the shorter bottom stroke. The long stroke, covering outhouses as well as the back rooms, stretches out for some fifty yards to terminate in a circular dovecot standing some ten feet high to its eaves, built of small stone with a conical stone tiled roof. This would certainly have been there in Aubrey's day. The dovecot, as outstanding when Aubrey knew it as it is today, still terminates the range of buildings. So that one gets the feeling that even if some of the buildings are not the same, one is looking at much the same layout that Aubrey knew, particularly since the farmyard and buildings built mainly of brick and flint, which lie below the house, have not been greatly extended. One would think they cover much the same area as they did in Aubrey's time, when they were serving a much larger farm. The general impression, when one stands, where Aubrey must have stood many times, at the gateway to the drive which serves both house and farm, is that time has been kind, and that not nearly as much has changed as one would have expected. Outside. Inside, the whole of the interior has been gutted relatively recently, not by the present owner. Only some of the beams and the timber side to the staircase might possibly have been there when Aubrey was.

The garden lies above the house. Aubrey wrote that in it 'by my Parlour-window at Chalke grows a Bon Chretien Peare-tree against the wall.' A pear-tree of a great age, although it could hardly be the one that Aubrey remembered, still grows up to the eaves of the house in what one could fairly think was the same place, close to the corner of the L. Aubrey in the margin of his *Natural History* drew a small coloured sketch of the original tree, presumably to show a curious loop in its trunk. In the garden grew also 'a Warden peare, near to a Ewe-tree – that is to say within a yard or less; the Pear-tree reclines from the Ewe-tree, as by an antipathy and looks as if it were shorne that way'. Aubrey was proud that 'our orchards . . . doe beare the best and most poignant fruit.' [14] House, garden and setting add up to a most attractive home. One would think that over the centuries many families have been happy there.

*   *   *

Not however, Aubrey, during the three wartime years which followed his return from Oxford recuperating from smallpox. Both his stays in Oxford had been short, particularly the second one; for during his attack of smallpox he must have been kept in virtual isolation save for the visits of the odd courageous friend such as Radford. But short and in part necessarily secluded as they were, they had been long enough to introduce him to the delights of both a scholarly and a social life. They had shown him too, that he had a talent and a taste for both. It is much more difficult to abstain when one has had a taste of whatever it is one likes than when one still does not know what one is missing. Coming back to his quiet country home, Aubrey found it hard to adapt to a life without his friends, without – or at any rate with very few – books; without conversation or such as he would have deemed conversation; without the excitement of great events going on around him. Here, back at Broadchalke for a long three years, Aubrey was able, by his account, to converse with 'none but servants and rustiques (to my great griefe, for in those day fathers were not acquainted with their children) and soldiers quartered . . . It was a most sad life to me in the prime of my youth not to have the benefit of ingeniose conversation and scarce any books. Almost a consumption'.[15]

One can understand Aubrey's frustration at being virtually imprisoned by the circumstances of war in his home over this long period. It is more difficult to understand his father's indifference and lack of interest. Yet it may be that ill-health lay at the root of it. Aubrey tells us that his father suffered from what Aubrey calls 'a pinne and webbe in the Eie (a pearle)', which must surely be cataract. 'My father', wrote Aubrey in his *Natural History* 'laboured under this infirmity; and one learned man of Salisbury could do him no good; at last one good wife Holly, a poore woman of Chalke cured him in a little time: my father gave her a piece of gold for the recipe.'[16] If it really was cataract, one cannot believe that 'good wife Holly's' recipe could bring more than temporary relief.

It would seem, too, that there was already something more generally and more seriously wrong with Richard Aubrey's health. When Aubrey, after his return to Oxford after the war, had completed his studies and taken his degree, at the end of 1648, he was immediately called back to Broadchalke to help his father run his various estates. Less than four years after that his father died, in October 1652, at the premature age of forty-nine. For a man such as Richard Aubrey, seemingly with few inner reserves or resources, only interested in sport, ill health must have been hard to bear. This may have been the main reason why he seems to have been particularly distant and difficult during the war-time years of Aubrey's exile from Oxford. From his mother Aubrey would hardly have expected much attention, for this was the period when her two younger sons were born, William in 1643 and Thomas in 1645. Aubrey does not give any reason for the long gap between the death at Easton Piers of the second Isaac in infancy and the birth of his brother William at Broadchalke.

Yet, in spite of his father's lack of interest and his mother's preoccupation, one cannot help thinking that Aubrey was exaggerating the severity of his situation when he wrote that over these years he led 'a most sad life . . . almost a consumption'. Certainly, it was bad luck, for a person as sociably inclined as he evidently was, that near-by Wilton, the most likely place in the neighbourhood where he would have found 'ingeniose conversation', was closed to him and one would think to most of the neighbourhood for the duration by the surprising fact that the Earl of Pembroke, despite his family's long association with both James I and Charles I and his own position as Lord Chancellor from 1626 to 1641, had declared for Parliament. It must have been a strange situation to have landlord and tenants technically at war with each other.

Yet there was an alternative source both of intelligent conversation and of books much closer to hand than Wilton. The living of Broadchalke was in the gift of King's College, Cambridge, and both the incumbents in Aubrey's time were scholars of the two sister foundations, Eton and King's. The Aubreys seem to have been on good terms with both of them. Robert Peyton, who was there when the Aubreys took over Manor Farm, had a brother-in-law Theophilus Wodenote, who had been a Scholar at Eton and a Fellow at King's, becoming subsequently a doctor of divinity and vicar of a Cornish parish, Linkinghorne, some six miles south of Launceston. Wodenote seems to have stayed for long periods at Broadchalke. Aubrey tells us that 'when I was a schoolboy he lived 2 years with his brother[in-law] Peyton . . . He did me much good in opening of my understanding: advised me to read Ld. Bacon's Essayes, and a book of Proverbs Eng. Answered my Q[ueries] of Antiq.[uities] . . . He wrote in his Solitude of Chalke, a little manual called Good thoughts in bad times (I had it)'.[17] With such scholarly occupants one can not believe that the library in the vicarage, which stood on the other side of the church from Manor Farm, was not well stocked. Peyton was within a year of his death when Aubrey returned from Oxford, and so may have been too old and ill to supply any of the 'ingeniose conversation' Aubrey so much sought. We do not know whether Wodenote was staying in the vicarage at this time, but it seems likely that he was, for as a Royalist divine his writings would soon have got him into trouble with the Parliamentarian authorities. His parish was later to be sequestered. Broadchalke, so long as his brother-in-law lived, was an obvious refuge. This may have been the time of his 'solitude at Chalke', when he wrote his very aptly-named manual. It is a curious crossing of life-lines, that of the erudite divine from Cornwall with that of the scholarly schoolboy whom, in all probability, he later met as a disgruntled undergraduate. But it was one which probably had considerable influence on Aubrey at a time when, in his home, he was getting little intellectual encouragement or stimulus. Peyton's successor John Sloper – nephew of John Hales, a Fellow of Eton, a Canon of Windsor in Royalist times, and an acquaintance of Aubrey's – clearly became a close friend, for Aubrey was to be godfather to his first child. Aubrey later referred to his godson in his *Collectio Geniturarum*, a notebook of astrological information: 'Jo. Sloper, my god son baptised 1649', and also to his sister, 'Mistress Abigail Sloper. 1648. Pride and lechery – ungrateful to her father – and then, one would think to the relief of all concerned – married'.[18]

It is also possible that in spite of the war Aubrey paid the occasional visit to his grandparents at Easton Piers. In his *Monumenta Britannica* he refers to a find in the churchyard of Langley Burrell, a parish on the eastern outskirts of Chippenham. 'At Langley Burrell, about 1644, digging in the west part of the churchyard were found coffins of freestone; which whereupon the then Rector caused to be digged all over for the stone, with which he paved his Hall (to my knowledge).''[19] It may have been, of course, that Aubrey acquired his knowledge later but it is much more likely that he heard it through local gossip at the time and so must have been at Easton Piers. This was the rectory in which, in the late nineteenth century, Francis Kilvert spent the later part of his youth and the early years of his manhood, which included two spells as curate to his father, the then rector. It would have been in this house that Kilvert wrote the Wiltshire part of his diary. During that period he must every day have trodden on the tiles which his father's seventeenth-century predecessor had stolen from the churchyard. One wonders if Kilvert knew where they came from.

So, all in all, Aubrey's sojourn was probably not as confined, nor as solitary, nor books, borrowable books at any rate, as scarce as he made out. The depth of Aubrey's depression during this undoubtedly dull period of his life can really only be understood when weighed in the balance against the pleasure and promise that he had found in his two short stays at Oxford. Yet war is war, and anyone that comes through without injury to himself or his family must count himself lucky. In Aubrey's vicinity one had only to travel three miles north to Compton Chamberlayne, the home of the Penruddocks, the previous tenants of Manor Farm, to hear a very different story. Two of the sons of Sir John Penruddock, the then head of the family, who had himself fought in the Civil War, had been killed in it. A third, Colonel John Penruddock, had fought and survived but was to be executed in 1655 after the gallant but mistimed Royalist rising, which bears his name, had failed. Aubrey in his relatively safe, but dull, existence had more reason over this period to think himself fortunate than sadly maltreated, as he obviously did. It is an intriguing thought that in a modern war anyone of Aubrey's age would have been called up.

*   *   *

As luck would have it, there was no serious fighting close to Broadchalke. The nearest battles of any importance were the Royalist victory at Roundway Down, close to Devizes, in 1643, and Fairfax's first major victory in his devastating and decisive campaign through the West, at Langport in 1645. Both battles were bravely and bitterly fought, but Devizes is some twenty miles to the north-west, and Langport some thirty miles to the west. In both cases the routes of the victorious armies led them away from rather than towards Broadchalke.

Yet there was always the danger of marauding, or simply travelling, troops. Pembroke, and so Wilton, might have sided with Parliament, yet the area round Broadchalke was still predominantly Royalist. But there was no safety in this. It was such a mobile war. The numbers involved were relatively so small, that neither side, outside certain fortress towns, could establish a permanent defensive screen that would be effective against enemy forces brought more likely by chance than by plan. This showed even in the early years of the Royalist ascendancy when, as Aubrey tells us, a Major John Morgan of Wells 'marching with the Kings army into the West, fell sick of a Malignant Fever at Salisbury . . . and was brought dangerously ill to my Father's in Broad-chalke'. Here, for fear of the sudden, unexpected arrival of Parliament-ary troops he had 'to be lodged secretly in a Garret'.[20] The major remained at Broadchalke for a month, but all Aubrey could tell us about his stay was that he had acquired a pet sparrow, who would peck at the window until he was fed crumbs from the major's plate.

But if the Civil War barely seems to have touched Aubrey it yet held, and was increasingly to assume, great importance for him. To him, as to many, it became the watershed between the old and the new. It was not that Aubrey was out to show the superiority of the one to the other. In fact his allegiance seems to have been split between them. On the one hand, as he showed in his preface to his *North Wiltshire Collections* he hankered after a Golden Age, long before the Civil War, before even the Dissolution, when the Church ruled the land and more particularly the road until 'by the selling of the Church landes is the Balance of the Government quite altered, and put into the hands of the common people. No Ale house nor yet Innes then, unless upon the Great Roades. When they had a minde to drinke, they went to the Friaries, and when they travelled they had entertainment at the Religious Houses for 3 days, if occasion so long required. The Meeting of the Gentry was not held at tippling howses; but in the Fields and Forests with their Horses and Howndes . . . This part very much abounded with Forests and Parkes. Thus were good spirits kept up.'[21]

But on the other hand in his *Natural History* Aubrey deplored the general apathy towards innovation or new ideas which existed before the Civil War: 'Till about the year 1649 'twas held a strange presumption for a man to attempt an Innovation in Learning: and not to be good Manners to be more knowing than his neighbours and forefathers; even to attempt an Improve-ment in Husbandry (though it succeeded with profit) was looked upon with an ill Eie . . . 'Twas held a sinne to make a Scrutinie into the waies of Nature.'[22] Aubrey was equally scathing about the scholars and teachers of those earlier times. 'From the time of Erasmus till about 20 years past [1536–1650] the learning was downright pedantry. The conversation and habits of those times were as starch as their bands and square beards; and Gravity was then taken for Wisdom.'[23]

Aubrey also saw the Civil War as the centre-piece of a sequence of destruction. The two spans, on either side, were of very unequal length, the one stretching back to the Dissolution, the other covering the Puritan purge, the immediate consequence of the Parliamentary victory. But time meant little to Aubrey. It was the interconnection of all things, even those separated by centuries, that fascinated him. And so the manuscripts of the great abbeys around Easton Piers, which had been flying around 'like butterflies' in the days of his youth, were just as much a part of a general process of destruction as the damaged and desecrated church of Slaughterford – 'the most miserably handled that ever I saw'. The Civil War, coming when it did at a very formative period of Aubrey's life, played a powerful part in hardening the resolve forming around his 'natural inclination to antiquity' – to record as much of the past as had survived into the present, and as much of the present as seemed worth recording, before they too disappeared. 'I was from my Childhood', he was to write in his *Natural History* 'affected with the view of things rare, which is the beginning of Philosophy.'[24] It was the beginning, too, of one of the main interests and occupations of his life.

'The Greatest Felicity of my Life'
Oxford 1646–8

In the early life of many young there is often someone – not necessarily of family nor necessarily otherwise intimately involved – who yet seems to be standing at each crossroads they come to, pointing the way they are to take. Such a one for Aubrey was William Browne, the master at the school at Blandford, to which he was sent when his parents moved to Broadchalke. It was William Browne who there and then encouraged him along the paths of learning, which previously he had little opportunity to explore either at home or under his various tutors and schoolmasters, with the single, sadly short-lived exception of Latimer. It was William Browne who, when the time came for Aubrey to move on to university, arranged for him to go to Trinity, his own college – and with Dr Kettell still in fine form and fettle, despite his considerable age, it could not have proved a better choice. By then William Browne himself was back at Trinity as a Fellow and was to be Aubrey's tutor. Now again, when for two and a half war-time years Aubrey had been mentally mouldering in the country, it was William Browne, still in Oxford although it was by then under siege, seeing clearly that the Civil War was at last coming to an end, who wrote to him showing the options open to him and suggesting which of them he should take.

Browne's letter was dated 9 September 1645 and addressed to his 'loving friende, Mr. John Aubrey, at his father's house in Broadchalke'. It was not the first he had sent there; over the period of Aubrey's seclusion he had sent him three letters in Latin, written in a meticulous regular script, of which the main object, one would think, was to exercise his pupil's increasingly rusty powers of translation. But this later letter one can see at a glance, as no doubt did Aubrey, was quite a different matter and missive. It was for one thing written in English in Browne's everyday, looping, rather untidy hand. For another, although certain passages were clearly those of a tutor writing to his pupil – he sent with it two books Aubrey had evidently asked for and regretted the inevitable loss of Aubrey's Latin 'notwithstanding your hard studies, for want of schollar companions' – for the greater part of his letter he is clearly writing as a personal friend concerned to advise Aubrey as to the best course of action in a difficult and still dangerous situation.

Browne first suggests that Aubrey might come back to Oxford – rather surprisingly for the siege was not to end for a further ten months. But the siege was in reality a loose-knit investment rather than an impenetrable barrier around Oxford, with the Parliamentary forces concerned to contain the military and not bothering over much about the civilians. Browne writes: 'I should think it would not be amisse for you to come up next lent and take your degree, which I doubt not but to crown [you with] notwithstanding your long absence.' But then he offers a clearly more sensible and considerable alternative: 'If you think not fitt to come to Oxon (where to speak truly the soldier spoyles the scholar for the most part) I doe seriously advise you to go to London.' This is clearly the alternative that Browne prefers: 'If you can by any means procur your fathers good will you may live . . . as at Oxon – and more safe . . . besides your advancing your ability in learninge you will much better your understanding in the worlde.' Browne foresaw that Aubrey would have to overcome family opposition before he regained his freedom, surprisingly not only from his father: – 'I doubt your mother and grandfather will stoppe all good motions.' Although surely this would only have been natural concern at the thought of a loved one venturing away from home into a rough outside world that was still at war. Browne ends his letter: 'Your most affectionate and loving tutor . . . "[1] – as indeed he had once again shown himself to be.

Aubrey followed his advice and opted for London, stringing his desire to go there on the excuse of reading law, for which considering his later liking for litigation, and also his descent from Elisabeth's distinguished 'little doctor', he might well have had both taste and talent. But as Browne forecast, he did not gain his freedom without a struggle. Looking back over this period in later life Aubrey remembered and recorded: 'This sad life I did lead in the country till 1646, at which time I got (with much adoe) . . . leave of my father to let me goe to the M. Temple. April 16, 1646 admitted.'[2] One does not know the particular reason for the 'much adoe', but one suspects that at the root of it lay his father's failing health. Did the constraint and burden of illness make Richard Aubrey regret that he had not used these war years, when his eldest son was forcibly at home, to overcome the barrier which not only their different ages but their different attitudes imposed between them? Aubrey had, of course, had 'much adoe' getting his father to allow him, in February 1643, to return to an Oxford that was no longer simply a university town but had become the centre of the Royalist war effort. That on both occasions he succeeded in getting his own way, in spite of his father's opposition, surely shows a strength of character surprising in the apparently mild and gentle youth who had become a scholarly, if sociable, young man.

So Aubrey went off to eat his dinners and read not a great deal of law in the Middle Temple, while the father remained at Broadchalke facing not only increasing ill health but increasing financial difficulty, difficulty which can not have been helped by the payment on 8 January 1646 of the fine imposed by a penurious if victorious Parliament on all Royalist landowners. In his case it amounted to '£33 in sixty fat sheep, and £60 in money accepted for the fine here and in Herefordshire'.[3] In coming to this figure the Parliamentary committee, sitting at Falstone House, near Wilton, had taken into account '£7 already paid . . . in North Wilts towards his five and twentieth part there'. This is interesting since it implies that Isaac Lyte had at some date in the past handed over a part, if a very small part, of Easton Piers, possibly to his daughter, more probably to his eldest grandson. On Aubrey's grandfather's death seven years after his father's, Easton Piers was to become totally Aubrey's. But since at the time of the Parliamentary fine Aubrey was only nineteen, and so legally under age, his father would have been liable for his son's small share in it.

In London, Aubrey probably lodged from the start close to the Middle Temple. A letter from William Browne in the early autumn of 1646 was sent to 'his most loving friend Mr. John Aubrey – student of the Middle Temple – at Mr. Birde's Howse . . . by the Middle Temple gate'. We do not know when he left 'Mr. Birde's Howse' but from 1651 onwards we know from the address of letters to him in London that he lodged in a room or rooms above a stationer's in Fleet Street 'at the signe of the Rainbow' near Temple Bar. From the continuing flow of letters to the same address over the years one knows, also, that he lived there when he was in London well into the sixties and probably until the stationers, together with the greater part of Fleet Street, was burnt down in the Great Fire of 1666. Both 'Mr. Birde's Howse' and the rooms above the Rainbow were not only convenient for his so-called study of law, but very central in a London still so delightfully small that one could walk from one side to another in a couple of hours.

Some two months after Aubrey's admission to the Middle Temple 'Oxon was surrendered and there came to London many of the King's party with whom I grew acquainted (many of them I knew before)', probably from his school days at Blandford as well as his two terms at Oxford. It was company that in normal times Aubrey might not have chosen since 'I loved not debauches.' But it was company and 'company a man must have' (provided it was socially suitable). Also he liked their 'martiall conversation even if it was not fitt for the messe'. One would imagine that many mornings of these first months of joyous release from the restraints of the prison that clearly

Broadchalke had become for him during the war years, saw him with a sore head, or more probably a sick stomach, for by his later admissions his was a 'stomach so tender that I could not drinke claret without sugar – nor white wine but would disgorge. Not well ordered till 1670'. But much as no doubt Aubrey enjoyed himself with his roistering Royalist friends, one can not believe there was much intellectual content in their talk, without which for him even their 'martiall conversation' might have begun to pall. By the end of the year, however, he was back where he most wanted to be, among his friends in Oxford, where he could have all the intellectual conversation he wanted. 'November 6 I returned to Trin. Coll. in Oxon againe to my great joy: was much made of by the fellows, had their learned conversation, look't on books, musique. Here and at M.T. (off and on)' – and one would think more off than on – 'I enjoyed the greatest felicity of my life . . . Dec. 1648 (Xmas eve) I was sent for home from Oxon to my sick father who never recovered.'[4]

At the start of the siege, Anthony Wood had, for safety, and to avoid the various infections and epidemics then rife in Oxford, been sent to stay with the vicar of Thame, to whose wife his mother was related, and to go to school there. Coincidentally, he was to return to Oxford at much the same time as Aubrey. Wood was very loth to leave Thame – as he tells us in his *Life and Times*, still writing of himself in the third person – 'where he was well and warme . . . had good companie, and seemed to have a fixed love for the place, so much so that he did never afterwards care to hear of New Coll. School to have given him scholastical education but applied all that he had to that of Thame . . . But go . . . he must'.[5] His mother was no longer able to afford to keep him there, having lost two houses, which she had previously let out, as well as the stables and the back premises of the Fleur de Luce, in a bad fire 'occasioned by a foot-soldier's roasting a pigg he had stolen'.

On his return home Wood 'found Oxford empty as to scholars, but pretty well replenish'd with Parliamentarian soldiers. Many of the inhabitants had gained great store of wealth from the Court and royalists; . . . but as for the young men of the city and university he found many of them to have been debauched by bearing armes, and doing the duties belonging to soldiers, as marching, warding and sitting in tipling houses for whole nights together'. Wood was now sent 'once or twice in a day . . . to receive instruction from his brother Edward, of Trinity College' – a friend, but not a very close one, of Aubrey's – 'in his chamber, which was a cockleloft over the common gate of that college'.[5] So, once again, Aubrey's and Wood's lifelines crossed. So surely must their paths – Wood's on his way to or from his brother's cockleloft, Aubrey on his way to pursue his studies, see friends or buy books.

Joyous though Aubrey was to return to Oxford there were some things he was sad to see. He was, in particular, distressed that much of the stained glass in the colleges, not only in the chapel, had by his return been partially, and was soon to be completely, destroyed. 'When I came to Oxford crucifixes were common in the studies-windows; and in the chamber-windows were canonised saints (e.g. in my chamber-window St. Gregorie the Great)' – particularly appropriate for Aubrey since he had been born on St Gregory's day – 'but after 1647 they were all broken – no religion to be found.'[6] But it could have been worse, and often it was the victorious Parliamentarians that Oxford had to thank that it was not. Aubrey believed that Fairfax had saved the Bodleian, if not from destruction, at the least from disastrous despolia-tion. 'When Oxford was surrendred (24 June 1646) the first thing General Fairfax did was to sett a good Guard of Soldiers to preserve the Bodleian Library. 'Tis said their was more hurt donne by the Cavaliers (during their garrison) by way of Embezilling, and cutting off chaines of books than there was since. He was a lover of learning and had he not taken this speciall care, that noble Library had been utterly destroyed – for there were ignorant Senators enough, who would have been contented to have had it so . . . This I doe assure you from an ocular witnesse, E. W., Esq.'[7] 'E. W., Esq.' was Edmund Wyld, a rich, scientifically-minded eccentric who adopted Aubrey, in his penurious days, as his drinking and talking companion. Over a period of some twenty-five years they were constantly to grow 'lethargique' together.

Among the Fellows who made much of Aubrey on his return to Trinity were, of course, William Browne, who, while remaining a resident Fellow at Trinity throughout the war, had also enlisted in the Royalist cavalry and taken part in several sorties round about Oxford; and Ralph Bathurst, who by generously opening his library to Aubrey on his two earlier visits had in so doing opened his mind to the love of books. Bathurst's elder brother Edward, also a Fellow, had, like William Browne, joined the Royalist cavalry as a part-time participant, but had been killed in the siege of Faringdon. His loss was great not only to his brother, but also to Trinity for he was one of the most forward-looking Fellows and had been a close friend of William Harvey, with whom he had conducted experiments. William Radford, Aubrey's courage-ous companion during the period of his smallpox, and John Lydall were not yet Fellows, but were to become so during the period of his residence. Lydall, when Aubrey had reluctantly to leave Oxford on Christmas Eve 1648, because of his father's illness, was to be his most faithful correspondent and his most useful link with Oxford. In these later letters Lydall would often pass on the good wishes of the friends Aubrey had left behind him. Thus in a letter dated 'February 21st 48/49' he wrote: 'Mr. How, Mr. Bathurst, Mr. Hawes, Mr. Highmore present their love and service to you.'[8] Absent friends then, but clearly among Aubrey's close friends when he was at Oxford. 'Mr. How' was Josiah Howe (the missing 'e' means nothing since Lydall could never make up his mind even about the spelling of his own name – sometimes using a 'y' and sometimes an 'i' – nor, for that matter, could Aubrey), a Senior Fellow who was an ardent Royalist, and so to lose his Fellowship after the Parliamentary Visitation of 1648. He was to continue to live in or around Oxford – his home was at Grendon Underwood, some twelve miles distant – until the Restoration when he was reinstated. Both Bathurst and Hawes in due course were to become Presidents of Trinity, but under different regimes and holding the position for vastly different lengths of time. Hawes, appointed in 1658, died suddenly a year later of a lung haemorrhage; while Bathurst, who became President in 1664, held his position until his death in 1701. Nathaniel Highmore, a physician, never became a Fellow of Trinity but seems to have remained there long after he took his medical degree, engaged in medical research. From Oxford in 1651 he published an influential *History of Generation* of which Aubrey had a copy. He, like Edward Bathurst, was a friend and protégé of William Harvey, whose work on the circulation of the blood had been a medical milestone earlier in the century. Highmore ultimately left Oxford to practise at Sherborne but seems always to have remained closely in touch, not only with Trinity, where he endowed an exhibition from Sherborne School, but with the van of medical research, ultimately achieving his immortality by having an anatomical feature – the cavity in the superior maxillary bone – named after him.

These four friends – Howe, Bathurst, Hawes and Highmore – were on average ten years older than Aubrey. But in this post-war Oxford, as throughout his life, Aubrey made friends of all ages. Among his contemporaries, as well as Lydall, Radford and Ettrick, was another old, but still young, friend, John Hoskyns. Like Aubrey, both Ettrick and Hoskyns were completing their academic studies at the same time as they were starting their legal ones. Both, like Aubrey, were up at Trinity at the same time as they were members of the Middle Temple. Unlike Aubrey, however, both were subsequently to have successful legal careers. Ettrick shared Aubrey's antiquarian interests, while Hoskyns, like Aubrey, was interested in paintings, although more as a purchaser than as a practitioner. Aubrey during this period found time, even amongst so much else, to sketch. Among his friends he clearly gained something of a reputation as a draughtsman, for Lydall in one of his letters declared: 'I more estime one piece drawne by your hand than of all the faces in the school gallery.'[9]

A new friend that Aubrey made at this time was Tom Mariet, who was up at Trinity for the first time and was in fact tutored by Lydall. Coming of a staunchly Royalist country family, Mariet was later to be involved in a premature attempt to persuade Monck to bring back the King, in which Aubrey was also involved by reason of his giving Mariet hospitality in his lodgings over the stationer's in Fleet Street during the period of the negotiations, and which Aubrey describes in his 'Life' of Monck. Now as a Trinity undergraduate in a more suitably youthful mood, Mariet was to set off in September 1647 with Radford and Ned Wood on what was deemed to be a great adventure – to walk to London, to which none of the three had yet been. They went via Windsor, and at Eton called on 'the memorable John Hales', then living in quiet retirement under the Parliamentary regime, but still a Fellow, who 'treated them well and putt into Mr. Woods hands ten shillings'.[10] One wonders whether the suggestion for this call came from Aubrey. Hales was the uncle of the vicar at Broadchalke and this was the sort of roundabout connection which would have appealed to him.

One would think that it was mainly with his older friends, most of them Fellows, that Aubrey had 'much learned conversation' but clearly and happily not all of his conversation was learned, for Howe, Bathurst, Browne and Hawes all contributed gossipy information which remained in his mind and found its way eventually into his 'Lives'. Thus Howe told him that Sir John Denham – the Royalist poet who had a considerable reputation in his own time, mainly for his poem *Coopers Hill*, when he was an undergraduate at Trinity was not only 'the dreamiest young fellow' but an incorrigible gamester who 'when he had played away all his money he would play away his Father's wrought rich gold cappes'. Later when his father died – 'who left 2000 or 1500 pounds in ready money, two houses well furnished and much plate – the money was played away first and next the plate was sold. I remember', continued Aubrey, 'about 1646 he lost 200 at New-cutt in one night.' Was Denham one of the Royalist friends who came to London after the surrender of Oxford, with whom Aubrey enjoyed his first taste of liberty from Broadchalke, before going back to Oxford? The date would fit. Denham was only saved from the total disaster which seemed perpetually imminent by the affection Charles I had for him, because of which he was granted 'the post of the Surveyor of His Majesties Buildings'. After the Restoration, Charles II honoured his father's appointment and Denham held the post until his death in 1669. From it, Aubrey writes he 'gott seven thousand pounds, as Sir Christopher Wren told me of'. Wren was Denham's 'Deputie' and one would think and hope, did most of the actual work.

Denham had two wives, the first 'the daughter and heire of Mr. Cotton of Gloucestershire by whom', Aubrey writes, showing an odd sense of priorities 'he had 500 pounds per annum, one son and two daughters'. His second wife was 'a very beautifull young lady; Sir John was ancient and limping. The Duke of York fell deeply in love with her'. Aubrey quickly assures us 'he never had any carnall knowledge of her. This occasioned Sir John's distemper of madness' which caused him to do several very odd things, of which much the oddest was to go to the King and tell him he was the Holy Ghost. 'But it pleased God he was cured of this distemper and writt excellent verses afterwards.' Aubrey's account of Denham's career and character is not only one of the most colourful of his 'Lives' but one of the most affectionate. It shows, too, how acute an observer he was of personal characteristics. 'His Eie was of a kind of light goose-gray; not big; but it had a strange piercingness . . . when he conversed with you he look't into your very thoughts.'[11] Aubrey mainly got to know Denham when he was enduring a penurious period under the Commonwealth after his return from France in 1652. He then lived for a year on the charity of the Earl of Pembroke, mainly at Wilton and so close to Broadchalke. Clearly, Denham's real strength lay in the fact that he was a most likeable character – as, of course, it was Aubrey's also.

Both Ralph Bathurst and William Hawes were friends of the charismatic Lucius Cary, Viscount Falkland, who 'lived at Tue, which is a pleasant seat and about twelve miles from Oxford'. They told Aubrey about him. Bathurst emphasized a lesser-known side of his character – that he was 'an extraordinary hard student'; while Hawes told a story which showed a softer side, in that his wife, 'a good and pious Lady' was able to get whatever she wanted out of her husband at 'the expense of a few Teares' so that from this 'great witt, the greatest master of reason and judgement of his time, being stormed by her teares (I presume there were kisses and secret embraces that were also ingredients) would this pious Lady obtain her unreasonable desires of her poor Lord'. Her 'unreasonable desires' were, in fact, nothing more heinous than doing favours to the 'maids, nurses, etc.' of the household, 'my Lady being (after the manner of women) much governed by, and indulgent to, the Nursery'. Aubrey remembered that at Tew 'in the dining room there is a picture of him at length and like him (t'was donne by Jacob de Valke, who taught me to paint)'.[12] One wonders when. Aubrey would hardly have had time during the seven terms that he studied at Oxford after the war, although one knows from the letter of Lydall's that he did do some drawing at this time. It could also, and more probably, have been during the years following his father's death, when he had more leisure and, temporarily, more money.

'My tutor, W. Browne' and also Bathurst, told Aubrey about the controversial Dr Chillingworth, a Fellow of Trinity, a great friend of Falkland; according to Aubrey he was 'his most intimate and beloved favourite'. He was also 'the readiest and nimblest Disputant of his time in the university, perhaps none have equalled him since'. But if a brilliant academic, Chillingworth was also untrustworthy and ambitious. He was the godson of Laud and 'sent his Grace weekly intelligence of what passed in the University'. This, on one occasion, included an excerpt from the letter of a close friend Dr Gill, with whom he also used to hold 'weekly intelligence', exchanging letters in which 'they used to nibble at states-matters'. In this letter Gill had referred to the then king, James I, and his son as 'the old foole and the young one'. This was passed on to Laud, thence to the King. 'The poore young Dr. Gill was seised, and a terrible storme pointed towards him,' only averted 'by the eloquent intervention of Edward, Earle of Dorset, together with the Teares of the poor old Doctor, his father and supplication on his knees to his Majestie'.

Chillingworth had hoped to succeed Dr Kettell as President of Trinity, but his main supporter, Falkland, who had been appointed Secretary of State in January, 1642, was away with the King, on the campaign which started so successfully with the taking of Bristol but continued disappointingly with the failure to take Gloucester, at the time of Kettell's death in July 1643. Falkland himself was to be killed during the First Battle of Newbury on 20 September, in a charge so courageous but rash that even the most recent historian of the Civil War, Professor Kenyon considers 'his conduct . . . so reckless as to raise suspicions of suicide'. For this most people thought the reason to be the military failure of his advice to the King, but Aubrey considered 'that it was the griefe of the death of Mrs Moray a handsome Lady at Court, who was his Mistresse, and whom he loved above all creatures that was the true cause of his being so madly guilty of his own death'.[13] So the Presidency of Trinity did not go to Chillingworth but to a formidable Fellow, Hannibal Potter, who 'whipt his scholar with the sword by his side when he came to take leave of him to go to the Innes of Court as I well remember'.[14] Potter was a friend of the Visitor of the college, the Bishop of Winchester, to whom he had been Chaplain, who appointed him without properly consulting the Fellows. Will Hawes told Aubrey that in consequence he was not 'lawfully elected'. However, even if Chillingworth had become President, there would have been another election soon, for he was to die the following year, according to Aubrey, of *morbus castrensis* (syphilis), only recently introduced into the country. 'In his sicknesse', Aubrey tells us, 'he was inhumanely treated by Dr. Cheynell, who, when he was to be buryed, threw his booke into the grave with him, saying, "Rott with the rotten, let the dead bury the dead".'[15] It is a chilling episode. Aubrey's account of it gives us an inexplicable shiver as if someone had walked over a grave. Yet Aubrey, much as he delighted in life and living, was always conscious of the imminence of disaster, disease and most particularly, death. So, in the course of conversation with his friends, the Fellows of Trinity, were sown some of the seeds which much later were to flower in the 'Lives'.

*   *   *

By his own account during the period, Aubrey had not only 'learned conversation', he also 'look'd on books, musique'. He not only 'look'd on books' but bought them. Some of those he bought are still in Oxford. In the later part of his life Aubrey gave a number of his books to Gloucester Hall, now Worcester College, seemingly to strengthen his chance of becoming the Principal. Of this he clearly had some hope for in a letter to Wood of November, 1675, he wrote 'As you were saying if I could be Principall of Gloucester Hall that were a fine way of ending my dayes in peace.' Most of these are still in Worcester Library, although their ranks were thinned during the nineteenth century in an effort to avoid duplication. Amongst those that are still there are mathematical works by Robert Recorde, the sixteenth-century Oxford mathematician, a book on trigonometry by B. Pitifous, which had belonged to William Oughtred and is annotated in his hand, a volume of Euclid inscribed 'Jo. Aubrey. Trin. Coll. Oxon 1648', and a transcription by Aubrey of Edward Davenant's *Algebra Literalis* taken from a copy that had in itself been transcribed by Davenant's daughter, whom Aubrey compliments on the cover as 'a good logist'. Davenant and Oughtred were Aubrey's main mathematical mentors. There are also astronomical works by Michaelis and Blaeu. Towards the end of his life Aubrey also gave books to the newly founded Ashmolean. Of these Denham's *Coopers Hill*, and copies of the poems of Beaumont and of Corbet would seem by their inscriptions to have been bought when Aubrey was an undergraduate. Michael Hunter, who was himself a Research Fellow at Worcester, in his scholarly and stimulating study *John Aubrey and the Realm of Learning*, places the Recorde, the Euclid, the Michaelis and the Blaeu as purchases by Aubrey 'while at Oxford in the 1640s'.[16]

The choice of these early purchases of astronomical books, now at Worcester, is particularly interesting, for if mathematics was the corner-stone of the new mood of scientific investigation and inquiry and so a common denominator to all the thoughtful groups of forward-looking young men then living in both Oxford and London, astronomy was very much for Aubrey a personal preference. In his London life it was later to become one of his main interests, but one tends to think that its use to him then was as a compensatory counterweight to his feeling of guilt for the personal disasters which had befallen him: for how could one blame oneself if it was all written in the stars anyway? Yet clearly his interest in astronomy started much earlier, for he bought these two books when he was still an undergraduate. Aubrey's love of books lasted throughout his life, and, rather more surprisingly, considering the fall in his fortunes, most of the books themselves seemed to have remained in his possession. At times he was forced to sell a few of them, although doing so was always a painful process.

'Musique'? It is exceptional to find Aubrey showing an interest in music. At the other end of his life, in his *Idea of Education*, he writes of it as one of the temptations to be guarded against, 'for it is a great thief of time'.[17] Clearly he himself was not at all musical, yet during this magical springtime it was a new experience, and enjoyable simply as such. Aubrey, describing his general state of bliss at this time, writes of himself as one of those 'ingeniose youths [who] like rosebuds, imbibe the morning dew'.[18] It was not an altogether happy choice of simile, yet it was clearly the reflection of an extremely happy man.

But if Aubrey at Oxford lived in a cocoon of content through the two years and two months that separated his return there on 6 November 1646 from his departure on Christmas Eve 1648, it was in general, on all levels, a period of uncertainty, confusion, and ultimately, change. Parliament had won the war but it was far from certain at the time of Aubrey's return that it had won the peace. There was still a surprising amount of support amongst the Parliamentarians for the retention of the monarch. Had the King been less intransigent, had he accepted the relatively reasonable 'Heads of Proposals', drawn up by Henry Ireton – himself an old Trinity man – presented to him in July 1647, after acceptance by the Army Council, and discussed by him with Cromwell and Ireton at Hampton Court throughout late summer and autumn, there can be little doubt that some form of constitutional monarchy would have emerged, and that there would not have been a Commonwealth. However, he was not, and he did not. By the end of the year, negotiations had broken down, the King had fled to Carisbrooke and events were gathering pace towards the outbreak of what is now called the Second Civil War. When it came it proved to be a series of separate uprisings, expressing as much a mood of discontent against the threat of Army and Parliamentary rule as well as loyalty to the King rather than a concerted campaign. But it was as bitterly fought as the First War, and at various times throughout the length of it the issue seemed in doubt. Even at the end, when the King was a prisoner awaiting trial there were moments when it seemed possible that an arrangement between the two sides might be patched up. But such possibilities all foundered on the single-minded, rock-like attitude of the King, and in the end he died as much from his own wish, considering that a martyr's death would serve his cause better than could his continued and constricted life, as that of his judges. He did so a month after Aubrey left Oxford.

Throughout this eventful period, Aubrey lived happily with his books and his friends in Oxford. Yet the course of university life, if fortunately it was not as directly involved in the Second Civil War as it was in the First, very much followed the political pattern elsewhere. A period of relative inaction, during which the Parliament established its authority but did not assert it, was followed by one marked by a much more militant attitude as the chances of a constitutional accommodation lessened. In May 1647, a Parliamentary Visitation was announced and appointed, consisting of twenty-four members, of whom five formed a quorum. Even so, the Visitors for some months waited on events while the King and Cromwell negotiated. But then, when clearly nothing was coming of them and the possibility of a new outbreak of war increased, they moved into action against the considerable Royalist opposition in the university. In a series of visits or purges resumed in October 1647, first the Vice-Chancellor, Dr Fell, and a particularly antagonistic head of college, the Master of Pembroke, were dismissed; then in the following spring most of the heads of houses. These were mostly removed in the course of a walk-around on 13 April 1648, by the Visitors, headed by the Chancellor, the Earl of Pembroke, Richard Aubrey's landlord at Broadchalke, in the course of which the heads of Magdalen, All Souls, Wadham, Trinity, St John's and Brasenose were all deposed, and in most cases immediately replaced. At Trinity, the fearsome Hannibal Potter proved to be fearful also and had already fled to the vicarage of his brother, Francis Potter, who was to become a close and corresponding friend of Aubrey's, at Kilmington in Somerset, before the Visitors arrived. He was replaced by one of the Visitors themselves, Dr Robert Harris, an elderly scholar and Puritan preacher who was to remain President until his death in 1658, and as such, surprisingly, to prove much more moderate and conciliatory than might have been expected. Gilbert Sheldon, who had been Warden of All Souls for over twenty years, and who was to be Archbishop of Canterbury for most of the Restoration, was found by the Visitors walking in his garden, arrested and imprisoned. On the previous day, Pembroke had evicted the family of the deposed Vice-Chancellor Dr Fell from the Deanery of Christ Church, where they had put up so spirited a resistance that troops had had to be called in. Mrs Fell and her children were finally carried out 'upon boards, as if they were going like so many pies to the oven'.[19] Clearly these were two memorable and noteworthy days. One is surprised that Aubrey makes no mention of them, but maybe he was not there, for it would have been in the middle of the Easter vacation.

Since then it would have been term-time, Aubrey was likely to have been there during the next stage of the Visitation in May, when the Fellows, scholars and students and even servants of the various colleges, were summoned in turn before a committee sitting in Merton, and asked the single and simple question: 'Do you submit to the authority of Parliament in this visitation?' Many of those summoned refused to attend. Lydall was the only Fellow from Trinity to appear, and he answered the Visitors' questions bravely but brusquely: 'My answer is that I am not satisfied how farre I may submit.' He was quickly expelled, together with twelve students and a servant. Of Aubrey's particular Fellow friends absent on the occasion, Bathurst submitted, Radford was expelled, as was Howe at the beginning of the following year, together with an obviously characterful cook who was suspended on two counts: '1. That Hee often said That the Reformation intended by the Visitors was a deformation. 2. That Hee often drinkes in the Cellar of the Colledge more than Hee puts on for in the Buttery Booke.'[20] Hawes, although absent on the occasion of the summons to Merton, seems to have submitted at some later date for he never lost his Fellowship, although over this difficult period he left Oxford to live at Woodstock with a friend, Sir William Fleetwood, who had a house 'in the park'. It was from Hawes that Aubrey heard of a most curious incident when a Parliamentary Commission sitting at Woodstock, presumably to assess the liability of landowners in the area, was attended by poltergeists, who clearly had Royalist sympathies: 'the committee which sat in the Mannour were pelted out of their chambers by stones thrown in at the windows . . . candles were continually put out, as fast as they lighted them . . . one with his sword drawn to defend a candle was with his own scabbard in the meantime well cudgelled.' In the end, the committee was forced to give in and give up and 'to remove some of them to Sir William Fleetwood's house and the rest to some other place'.[21] On the face of it then, this seems a thoroughly disruptive and divisive period which more or less split the college down the middle.

Yet the reality was very different. Most of those suspended were in fact allowed to continue living, and in some cases teaching, at the college, and the particularly needy cases were given financial support. But this was not easy for the college, which had come out of the Civil War with its finances in a disastrous state. Not only had the supply of students, from which it drew most of its income, dwindled from the normal pre-war levels of between twenty and thirty commoners a year to three in 1643, and none at all in the last two years of the war, but the royalist officers and courtiers who had been billeted on the college had rarely paid their bills. So the college had come out of the war with a massive, for those times, amount of arrears of rents and battels and as late as 1651 was still owed £1,385. Not only this, it had had to make a loan, one would think forced, of some £200 to the Royal Paymaster-General, and virtually all its plate had been requisitioned, to be melted down into money for the troops. A pathetically brief inventory at the end of the war shows that only the chalice and paten, and two flagons which served in chapel – and a small chalice that had supposedly belonged to Dr Kettell – remained.[22] No doubt the Fellows who had 'made much' of Aubrey on his return did so because of the genuine liking of him which they had formed during his two earlier visits, yet all the same, well-to-do students such as Aubrey undoubtedly was (whatever his other faults, Aubrey's father was clearly generous towards him, otherwise he would not have been able to commission the drawing of Osney as he did during his first term nor to buy the books that he did now) must have been doubly welcome, for they could help in many minor monetary matters towards the financial recovery of the college. Nor was it only in minor matters that the undergraduates personally contributed to the Fellows' finances. In those days undergraduates paid their tutors directly – as Aubrey tells us in his *Idea of Education*, complaining that by then (1684) the tutors were asking too much. 'In my time, Gentlemen Commoners gave but £6 or £8 per annum to their Tutors, £8 was high. Now the tutors are grown so high that they demand twelve guineas per annum for Tutoridge, and be payd in Guineas or els they will take it unkindly.'[23]

It seems likely that one of the ways they did so was by a gift to those who had lost their livelihood through suspension by the Visitors. John Lydall, as a close friend, would have been the obvious person for Aubrey to help. His first letter to Aubrey, written on the New Year's Day that followed Aubrey's departure home on the previous Christmas Eve, shows clearly that he did: 'Honest and loving Mr. Aubrey . . . thanke you for all, especially your last favours or rather legacies, which at your departure you so freely bequeathed.'[24] The tenor of his continuing correspondence seems, too, to be that of someone deeply indebted and deeply grateful – the two not necessarily always going together – trying to do all he could to help Aubrey in return. This included looking after the books and other possessions including his laundry, which Aubrey left behind; sending materials for the experiments with which Aubrey intended to keep up his scientific interests; simply recounting happenings and so keeping him in touch with Oxford life and thought. A later letter, in mid-March, shows Lydall anxious about a further investigation of the Visitors, and eager that Aubrey should be in Oxford at the critical time to give, one would think, financial as well as moral support: 'I do not wonder that you should heare of another purging of the university, which although it be not yet done, will in all probability be shortly. The Parliament hath indulged one favour as to stay till the 20th March for our subscriptions, after which there is no favour to be expected for those that refuse. I should be glad therefore to see you here about that time.'[25] Possibly Lydall submitted on this occasion, for the following autumn he was confirmed by the same Visitors, who a year earlier had suspended him from his Fellowship, as Tutor of Philosophy at Trinity, an appointment which otherwise seems curiously contradictory. Or it may simply have been that once the authorities had established their position, seen that their supporters were in the positions of power and responsibility throughout the university, and weeded out the more dangerous elements of the opposition, they were out to heal rather than deepen wounds. The ensuing years were marked by a surprising degree of tolerance – which extended even to religious beliefs. At Trinity, which, with a notable preacher as its President, one would have expected to have been as strict as any in the enforcement of Puritan dogma and discipline, and which did impose many and long services in chapel on its undergraduates, yet made no objection to those who held more traditional Anglican beliefs, such as Ralph Bathurst, who arranged and attended services to their own liking.

But change there was, and the wind of it was soon to blow open many doors hitherto closed. There was a new feeling of excitement, of enterprise, of experiment in the air – particularly noticeable around Oxford, perhaps because its importance during the war had established a position of prominence which carried over into the peace. New habits were forming, of thinking, teaching, even talking, for the coming age was to be a very conversational one, the age of the coffee houses rather than the taverns. Discussion groups of friends were shaping that were soon to become clubs. 'About the yeare 1649,' Aubrey was to remember and write, 'Experimental Philosophy was first cultivated by a club at Oxon.'[26] The influence and embrace of the club was soon to widen to include such subsequently famous figures as William Petty, the most entrepreneurial of academics, who became Oxford's Professor of Anatomy in 1649 and later Aubrey's 'singular friend'; and Christopher Wren who arrived in Oxford as an undergraduate in 1650, aged only nineteen, but already carrying a reputation for such mathematical brilliance that his degree course was shortened from four years to two so that he should not have to waste two unnecessary years in taking it. Robert Boyle, too wealthy to bother about university posts or degrees, but who, attracted by the sound of all that was going on in Oxford, came there in 1654 to set up a laboratory in which to carry out scientific experiments. A year later Robert Hooke arrived at Christ Church, and subsequently became Boyle's assistant. Of all of these Aubrey became a close friend: in the first place because they were friends of friends of his, and then because they were all members of this club, which met for discussion sometimes in Petty's rooms, sometimes in Boyle's, sometimes in those of Wilkins, the Wadham warden. Later, the centre of gravity was to move to London where the movement continued its development and enlargement throughout the Commonwealth, finally reaching its due place of eminence after an infusion of Royalist nobility, necessary to secure the royal patronage of Charles II. Then it became, in 1662, by Royal Charter, the Royal Society, of which Aubrey was one of the first elected members.

For Aubrey, all of this stemmed, of course, from the friendships that he made in Trinity when he returned there after the war. In reality they shaped the future course of his life. For these ever increasing circles soon carried him to a point when he was an established member of the intelligentsia – a particularly brilliant intelligentsia – first under the Commonwealth and then after the Restoration. His membership of the Royal Society was to be especially important after his financial fall, for it kept him among the leading intellectuals of the day, when he had little else by way of position or property to keep him there. Aubrey later described the post-war years at Oxford as the 'most felicitous' of his life. They could well have been the most important also. Aubrey was to put his many personal disasters down to the astrological misfortune of having been born 'in an ill howre'. But surely now the stars were kind to him. For, unquestionably, he was in the right place at the right time.

Avebury
1649 and after

In spite of his father's illness, Aubrey can not have stayed long at Broadchalke on his return from Oxford on Christmas Eve 1648, for early in the New Year we find him going on a hunting trip. This was at the invitation of his friend Charles Seymour who lived at Allington Manor which then stood a mile and a half south of Easton Piers. It was an invitation that was to lead to one of the most momentous days of Aubrey's life.

Charles Seymour was possibly Aubrey's closest local friend. He and Sir James Long of Draycot, some three miles to the east of Easton Piers, were the only two of the fourteen 'Amici' of whom Aubrey made a list late in life – with the intention it would seem of separating into a select group those whose friendship he particularly valued – who lived in the locality. The inclusion of Charles Seymour seems to show a particularly deep degree of friendship since he died relatively young at the age of forty-four, twenty years before Aubrey made his list. Charles Seymour, 'with whom' Aubrey describes himself, in the preamble to his description of the hunting trip, as having 'the honour to be intimately involved', was the eldest son of Lord Francis Seymour, who was to be made Baron Seymour of Trowbridge in his own right. Unlike most of the Seymours, who led in the main notable, sometimes notorious lives, Charles Seymour seems to have been content to live quietly and unremarkably in the country and is in consequence now chiefly known as the father of the Duke of Somerset, his eldest son inheriting in due course the main family title. He and Aubrey seem to have remained close friends throughout his life. When at the age of thirty Aubrey had his portrait painted, he gave it to Charles Seymour. One does not know whether this was a portrait possibly painted by Lely, or a miniature painted at about the same time by Samuel Cooper. But whichever it was its gift was clearly an expression of deep friendship.

Charles Seymour lived at Allington Manor because his mother had been the daughter and heiress of Sir Gilbert Prinne who owned it, but Seymour's father lived at Marlborough, in the castle situated in the centre of the grounds that now belong to the College. His estate, stretching widely around, included a considerable area of the Marlborough Downs themselves. Although one would have thought on this occasion that Aubrey might have found it convenient to stay at Easton Piers, and then join Seymour at Allington Manor before setting off together for Marlborough, it seems that he rode up from Broadchalke with 'my honoured Friend and neighbour Colonel John Penruddock of Compton Chamberlayn and that good old Gentleman Mr. Stephen Bowman, steward to the Ld. Marquisse of Hertford. We went together.' Although Aubrey knew 'Salisbury plane and Stonehenge . . . from eight years old . . . I never saw the country around Marlborough' until this time.

The following day 'the Morrow after Twelf Day, Mr. Charles Seymour and Sir William Button' (Aubrey asterisks in the margin – 'of Tokenham, Baronet') 'mett with their packs of Hounds at the Grey-weathers. These Downes looke as if they were sowen with Great stones, very thick, and in a dusky evening they looke like a flock of sheep from whence it takes its name.' Nowadays the 'Grey Weathers' are penned into small enclosures, shep-herded by the National Trust and most of the Downs have been ploughed up to grow corn, but it is easy enough to imagine them as Aubrey saw them, when the stones spread across the Downs looked in the half light like a grazing flock. Aubrey continues his account, following as yet his imagination rather than the hounds. 'One might fancy it to have been the scene where the Giants fought with huge stones against the Gods.' But now the real hunt starts. 'Twas here that our Game began; and the chase led us (at length) through the village of Auberry into the Close there – where I was wonderfully surprized at the sight of these vast stones, of which I had never heard, as also at the mighty Bank and Grasse about it. I observed in the Inclosures some Segments of rude circles, made with these stones: whence I concluded that they had been in the old time complete. I left my company a while, entertaining myselfe with a more delightful indagation [investigation] and then I steered by the cry of the hounds, overrode the company, and went with them to Kennet, where there was a good Hunting dinner provided.'

Aubrey rarely writes narrative. It is a pity that he did not do so more often, for his flowing unpretentious style carries the reader with him. One senses not only the exhilaration of the hunt, but the personal excitement at the discovery of these massive and meaningful stones. The feel, too, of a remarkable area of country, that of the Grey Weathers and the Downs as they then were, comes vividly across. It is throughout a brilliant and convincing account, which makes one feel one was there oneself, of a remarkable discovery and a truly momentous day. But the day was not yet over. 'Our

Repast was cheerfull, which being ended, we re-mounted, and beat over the Downes with our Grey-hounds: by this afternoon's diversion I happened to see Wensditch [Wansdyke], and an old Camp and two or three sepulchres. The evening put a period to our sport, and we returned to the Castle at Marlborough where we were nobly entertained.'

It was the end of the hunt but only the start of the story. Some years later, Aubrey was stimulated by the publication of a book on Stonehenge 'writt by Mr. Inigo-Jones . . . which I read with great delight'. He did not agree with the argument and explanation of the origin of the stones that Inigo Jones, who was a personal friend, put forward, but the book 'gave me an idea to make more researches' at Avebury. 'A farther opportunity was that my honoured and faithfull Friend Colonel James Long of Draycott', Aubrey notes in the margin 'since Baronet', 'was wont to spend a week or two every Autumne at Aubury in Hawking, where several times I have had the happiness to accompany him'. James Long was the first of the two local friends, Charles Seymour being the other, whom Aubrey included in his list of 'Amici'. Born some thirteen years before Aubrey, whereas Charles Seymour was only five years older, and so once they were grown up was considerable as a contemporary, Long always seems to have been treated by Aubrey with the respect due to an elder and better. Long came of one of the oldest and largest landowning families in north Wiltshire which in itself would have appealed to Aubrey. He may not have been all that good a soldier, for in 1645, returning from escorting the Prince of Wales to Bristol, he was ambushed by the Parliamentary forces and captured, a disaster which Clarendon attributed to his fault. But there may have been some animosity at the back of Clarendon's verdict, for Long's reputation remained high with his brother officers who would have been the best judges of whether he was to blame or not. However, whether or not Long was a good soldier, in every other way he seems to have been the epitome of all that a country gentleman should be – sporting, cultured, kindly, interested in nature, and in scientific experiment and investigation. He was to be a founder member of the Royal Society. He also had considerable personal charm which, according to Aubrey, subjugated even Oliver Cromwell, with whom he shared an interest in hawking. 'Oliver Cromwell, hawking at Houneslowe Heath, discoursing with him, fell in love with his company, and commanded him to wear his sword' (forbidden at that time for ex-Cavalier officers) 'and to meet him a-Hawking, which made the strict Cavalier look on him with an evill eye'. Considering their long friendship, Aubrey wrote a surprisingly brief 'Life' of Long, but it was fulsome enough. 'I should need,' Aubrey declared, 'to be both Orator and Soldier to give this honoured friend of mine, a Gentleman absolute in all his numbers, his due character.' Despite being neither Aubrey proceeded to pack a lot of praise into a short space: 'Good swordsman, horseman: admirable extempore orator, great memorie, great historian and romancer: great falkoner, for insects exceeding curious, and searching long since re natural things.'[1]

On these hawking expeditions around Avebury, the 'Colonel', as Aubrey called Long, evidently charmed Aubrey with his intelligent talk, just as he had Cromwell. As Aubrey put it: 'the Muses did accompany him with his Hawkes and his Spaniels.' Aubrey paints an idyllic picture of these days on the Downs: 'Our sport was very good: and in a Romantick country sc. the Prospects noble and vaste, the Downes stockt with numerous Flocks of Sheep: the Turfe rich and fragrant with Thyme and Burnet . . . Nor are the nut-brown Shepherdesses without their graces.' The picture portrays happiness. And Aubrey fits perfectly into the frame in the character of the cultured countryman, with enough sporting and social instinct to understand and enjoy both the pleasure of the chase and the companionship of his friends, and yet with the intelligence, when the opportunity arose, to link it to a far more important quest – that for knowledge. One can but be sad for him that because of his financial mismanagement happy days, such as these on the Marlborough Downs or on Salisbury Plain in the vicinity of Broadchalke, were already numbered.

Aubrey naturally talked about his discoveries at Avebury to his friends in London, many of whom after the Restoration were to become not only founder or original members of the Royal Society, but also friends at court. In 1663, in May of which year Aubrey himself was elected a Fellow of the Royal Society, two of the other Fellows, Lord Brounker, the first President, and Dr Walter Charleton, the King's Physician – also a keen antiquarian and archaeologist – 'discoursing one morning' with the King, 'concerning Stoneheng, they told His Majestie what they had heard me say concerning Avebury that it did as much excell Stoneheng as a Cathedral does a Parish church. His Majestie admired that none of our Chorographers had taken notice of it and commanded Dr. Charleton to bring me to him the next morning'. When Aubrey went to see the King, he took with him a drawing of Avebury 'donne by memorie only: but well enough resembling it with which his Majestie was pleased, gave me his hand to kisse and commanded me to waite on him at Marlborough when he went to Bath with the Queen (which was about a fortnight after)'.

A fortnight later, as commanded, Aubrey joined the King, the Queen, the Duke of York and the Court at Marlborough on their way to Bath. 'The next day when the Court were on their Journey his Majestie left the Queen and diverted to Aubury, where I shewed him that stupendous Antiquity, with the view whereof he and the Duke of Yorke were very well pleased. His Majestie then commanded me to write a Description of it, and present it to him: and the Duke of York commanded me to give an account of the old Camps, and Burrows on the Plaines. As his Majestie departed from Aubury to overtake the Queen he cast his eye on Silbury hill about a mile off which he had the curiosity to see, and walkt up to the top of it with the Duke of Yorke, Dr. Charleton and I attending them.' On Silbury Hill, the Duke of York spotted and picked up some snails, intending to have them cooked that evening. Then 'they went to Lacock to dinner, and that evening to Bathe; all the Gentry and Commoners of those parts waiting on them with great acclamations of joy, etc'.

Apart from Aubrey, the person who comes out of the episode the best is surely the King. Whatever else he may or may not have been, Charles was in the main an admirable patron of the arts and an intelligent supporter of scholarship. This shows clearly in his treatment of Aubrey and Avebury. Not only from the beginning did he take Aubrey's seemingly rather tall story seriously, when he could easily have disregarded it on the grounds that if it was all that Aubrey said it was it would surely have already been recorded, he made time to see Avebury in what was probably an already tightly planned and packed schedule. It was, of course, extremely fortunate that the royal Progress to Bath came so soon after Aubrey's audience, when Avebury was still fresh in the royal mind.

Throughout the visit he showed an intelligent and appreciative interest of all he saw and heard. When Aubrey later presented the plan and dissertation which the King had commanded, having 'the 11 September following surveyed that old Monument of Aubury with a plain-table', throwing in 'a Review of Stonehenge' for good measure, the King 'commanded me to digge at the bottom of the stones marked with the fig. 1 to try if I could find any human bones'. Aubrey admits sadly 'I did not do it.' Perhaps his personal worries were beginning to weigh on him – these were the years during which the Herefordshire properties he had inherited from his father had to be sold off – for he seems suddenly to have lost heart as if preoccupied with other things. On one occasion at Avebury, seeking to estimate the distance from the south entrance to the Kennet he noted 'a shower of raine hindered me from measuring it.' But it would not have needed a very determined researcher to have waited for the rain to stop, or to have come back on another and finer day. Nor did he ever print the 'Discourse' he presented to the King, as he was commanded to. For this he gave the excuse that he could not finally make up his mind about the origin of remains such as those at Avebury and Stonehenge without having seen personally the comparable ones in north Wales in the judging of which 'I was for relying on my own eyesight.' This was a reason very much in line with the Baconian doctrine of trusting to one's own eyesight as well as one's own judgement. But it was also, quite clearly, an excuse for doing nothing more about it at that time. However, in the last years of his life a later friend, 'Mr. Edward Lhwyd, custos of the Museum at Oxford' – which we now know as the Ashmolean – into whose safe keeping Aubrey was to commit the greater part of his manuscripts, 'hath made accurate Observation of Antiquities in Wales'. His acceptance of these observations enabled Aubrey to come at last to the conclusion that 'these monuments were Pagan Temples, which was not made out before, and also that they were Temples of the Druids'.

Aubrey goes on to advance his reasons for thinking so, modestly and movingly, in a passage which delineates his character quite as much as it shows the lines of his thought. 'When a Traveller rides along by the Ruines of a Monastery, he knows by the manner of a building, sc. Chapell, Cloysters, etc that it was a Convent, (but of what order sc. Benedictine, Dominican, etc it was, he cannot tell) . . . now my presumption is that the Druids, being the most eminent Priests (or order of Priests) among the Britaines: 'tis odds, but that these ancient Monuments . . . were temples of the Priests of the most eminent Order, viz Druids, and it is strongly to be presumed that Aubury, Stonehenge, etc are as ancient as those times. This Inquiry I must confess is a Gropeing in the Dark, but although I have not brought it into a cleer light yet I can affirm that I have brought it from an utter darkness to a thin Mist: and have gone farther in this Essay than anyone before me. These Antiquities are so exceeding old that no Bookes doe reach them; so that there is no way to retrieve them but by comparative antiquitie which I have writt upon the spott, from the Monuments themselves. Though this be writt as I rode, a gallop: yet the novelty of it, and the faithfulness of the delivery, may make some amends for the incorrectness of the state. The first draught was worn out with time and handling, and now, me thinkes, after many years lying dormant I come abroad like the Ghost of one of those Druids.'

Aubrey ends by begging 'the Reader's pardon for running this Preface' (a timely reminder that it was intended not to be simply an account of his association with Avebury but an introduction to his collected notes on *Monumenta Britannica*, 'into a storie', (but what a story) and 'wishes him as much pleasure in the reading them [the Monumenta] as I had in seeing them. Vale! John Aubrey.'

Aubrey's conclusions were in fact way ahead of their time, and they are little behind those of ours, but the importance of his encounter with Avebury is not whether he was correct in the conclusions he drew about the origin of the stones, but simply in that by bringing Avebury to the attention of the King, which was happily followed by all the publicity of the royal visit, he put it on the map. Thereby he halted the process of destruction whereby local farmers, and others, had been breaking up the stones to use them as material for their buildings. This had been going on for centuries. Aubrey considered that the local 'houses are built of the Frustums [fragments], for hereabouts are no other stones to be found, except Flints . . . The Church is likewise built of them; and the Mannour house . . . and also another faire House not far from that. One of the Monuments in the Street that runnes East and West is converted into a Pig-stye, or Cow-house: as is to be seen in the Roade.' Curious as ever to learn not only what had happened and why but also how, Aubrey discovered and described the means by which these massive and, one would have thought totally indestructible, slabs of stone were broken into smaller and usable pieces: 'I have verbum sacerdotis* for it that these mighty stones (as hard as marble) may be broken in what part of them you please without any great trouble – sc. make a fire on the line of the stone where you would have it crack; and after the stone is well-heated, draw over a line with cold water, and immediately give a knock with a Smyth's sledge, and it will break.'[2]

Nor were the local farmers the only predators lurking around Avebury. Aubrey transcribes a letter from a Dr Troop of Bristol, who believed that human bones had medicinal qualities, and found the area around Avebury a particularly happy hunting-ground. He describes one such find. 'In Wilts between Kynett and Overton on the lands of one Captain Walter Grubb I approached workmen (digging not far off the roade). I inquired their digging, who answered making Boundaries to inclose for French-grasse or 5 foile; said the men, we throw up many bones here, but know not of what creatures. I quickly perceived, they were humane and came the next day and dugg for them and stored myself with many Bushells of which I made a noble medicine that relieved many of my distressed neighbours . . . the bones large and almost rotten but the teeth extreme and wonderfully white, hard and sound (no tobacco taken in those day).'[3] However, happily, well meaning cranks like Dr Troop were few and far between and they did not pose anything like as serious a threat as the local farmers.

Aubrey's description of Avebury, which he presented to the King, but never printed, and which he subsequently used in *Monumenta Britannica* is, in spite of the showers of rain and his worries over his own affairs, extremely thorough. It includes four maps – of the main circle; of 'the whole view of Aubury with the Walke and the lesser Temple appendant to it; of the stones on the brow of the hill from West Kennet'; and of 'eight huge stones in a Circle [which] doe lie fall'n down in a lane from Kynet towards Marlborough . . . which could never be by chance, and (besides) they are (rudely) hewen'.

*Aubrey adds in the margin 'Parson Brunsden of Mounckton'. This would have been Winterbourne Monkton, which lies about a mile and a half to the north of Avebury.

Except in the map of 'the whole view', the individual stones in the circles are placed and counted. Thus 'on the brow of the hill East from Kynet . . . the inner circle 15 stones, outourd circle 22'. The circles themselves are measured. In the main circle 'from S.Port to N.Port, or from W.Port to E.Port is 60 perches'. The two main maps have the additional interest and charm of marginal drawings and illustrations – on that of the main circle, of a church labelled 'Shillen', of a small cluster of the stones, and a sectional drawing of the rampart. In the corner of his 'whole view' a much simplified sketch of Silbury Hill, which makes it look like a sand-castle. This map is bounded on the bottom by 'Fluvius Kynet'.

Aubrey's accompanying text is equally careful and constructive. The main circle is 'envirened with an extraordinary great vallum (or Rampart) . . . within which is a Grasse of a depth and breadth proportionate to it. Wherefore it could not be designed for a Fortification, for then the grasse would have been on the outside of the Rampart. Round about the Grasse are pitched on end huge stones, as big or rather bigger than those at Stoneheng; but rude and unhewen as if they are drawn out of the earth. Most of the stones there pitched on end are gonne: only here and there doe still remain some curvilineous segments: but by these one may boldly conclude that heretofore they stood quite round about like a Crown. From the South entrance runnes a Solemne Walke, with stones pitched on end about seven feet high which goes as far as Kynet'. In a marginal, and obviously much later, note Aubrey wrote that he was surprised that when one of these stones 'the great stone at Aubury towne's end . . . fell downe in Autumne 1684, and broke in two, or three pieces' it was found that 'it stood but two feet deep in the earth.' He learnt this 'from Mr. Walt. Sloper' – like Parson Brunsden – 'of Mounckton. Attorney'. Aubrey never had the slightest doubt of the importance of Avebury, which 'is peradventure the most eminent and most entire Monument of this kinde in the Isle of Great Britaigne'.[4] His careful and thoughtful description of it, based clearly on much painstaking observation and measurement, is a worthy introduction even to so great a subject, and served as such over the centuries.

Periodically Avebury, in the centuries that followed, relapsed into relative obscurity. Periodically, interest was rekindled – by the visits of Dr William Stukeley, at the beginning of the eighteenth century, and by Sir Richard Hoare, at the beginning of the nineteenth – both of them led to it by Aubrey's account in *Monumenta Britannica*. But it never sank back into the destructive darkness, under cover of which the farmers could break and take what they wanted for their buildings. That Avebury is such as we see it today must in some measure then be due to the astonishing chain of events set in motion when Aubrey riding with his friends into Avebury on that early January day in

1649 'was so wonderfully surprised at the sight of those vast stones' that he later broke away from the hunt to examine them; and which culminated with the royal visit some fourteen years later which set the seal on Avebury's importance. Had Aubrey not come that way then, what further destruction and depletion might not have taken place? Had anyone else other than Aubrey happened upon them at that time would they have realized the importance of their find? It is an astonishing thought that these then virtually unknown stones should now be listed among the ten most important archaeological remains in the world, their fame promising to exceed that of Stonehenge 'as a Cathedral does a Parish church'. Both their state of preservation and their fame must surely owe much to the fact that, more than three centuries ago, Aubrey was interested enough and important enough, to bring them to the royal, and so the public, eye. It was not the least of his achievements.

'Never off Horseback'
1649–57

Richard Aubrey's various properties, which his son now had to overlook, were widely spread. Apart from Broadchalke, which, of course, he held on lease from Wilton, there were the two Herefordshire properties, Burleton and Stretford, some thirty miles apart from each other on either side of Hereford itself. There was, also, an unexpected, inexplicable estate on the Kent coast, near Rye, which Aubrey tells us in his *Miscellanies*, had, on the seaward side, thirty to forty acres of 'marsh land, very conveniently flanking its upland'.[1] If one takes into account, also, that Aubrey would certainly have been making regular visits to Easton Piers, not only out of affection for his grandparents but because, as the heir of his grandfather, now in his seventies, he was bound to take an interest in the running of the estate, one can accept that he was only mildly exaggerating when he wrote 'from 1649 to 1670 was never off my horse back'.[2]

But because to him learning was not a duty but a pleasure, Aubrey managed to continue his studies, even on horseback. Throughout his life, he was always greatly interested in mathematics, although he did not have the talent to be an original thinker. Nor did he have the necessary training. This he much regretted, writing in his *Idea of Education* 'my Ignorance, and want of good early mathematicall Education, makes me write this Idea more feelingly, than a more learned man would have done.'[3] In his 'Lives' he had a separate section for mathematicians of note, and in moments of boredom, which occurred more frequently in his later penurious years, he would 'divertify' himself with mathematical problems. So it is not surprising that the studies he continued on horseback were mainly mathematical ones. In particular, he tells us he carried about with him the works of Edward Davenant and of William Oughtred. In the case of Davenant the works would have been in the form of instructional letters. Both Davenant and his son John, a contemporary of Aubrey's at Oxford and, like him a member of the Middle Temple, were close friends. Davenant, although Aubrey many years later 'heard Sir Christopher Wren say he does believe he was the best Mathematician in the world about 30 or 35+ yeares agoe', would not allow his work to be printed. This was because, as well as being a mathematician, he was Vicar of Gillingham, and Treasurer of Salisbury Cathedral, where his uncle was Bishop. 'Being a Divine [he] was unwilling to print because the world should not know how he had spent the greater part of his time.' Even so, 'he has written (in a hand as legible as print) manuscripts in quarto a foot high, at least.' Davenant, according to Aubrey, was always 'very ready to learn and instruct. He did me the favour to inform me first in Algebra'⁴ – most probably by means of the letters which Aubrey carried with him on his travels. Algebra seems to have been the side of mathematics in which Davenant was particularly interested, and in which he excelled. Evidently he passed on both his talent and his interest to his children, in particular to his second daughter, who married Aubrey's closest friend, Anthony Ettrick. She, according to Aubrey, was 'a notable Algebraist'. Aubrey might have done worse than to marry one of Davenant's other daughters, of whom there were several on offer, for he had ten children. In their spare time they would have been able to 'divertify' themselves with mathematical problems.

The long arm of the family-minded Bishop Davenant, who had helped Edward Davenant so generously, stretched even into Aubrey's home district of north Wiltshire. The living of West Kington, some three miles to the west of Easton Piers was in the gift of Salisbury. The bishop gave it to yet another Davenant. This was Robert, the brother of Sir William Davenant, the poet and dramatist. Both were the sons of a 'Vintner' at Oxford, in whose house 'Mr. William Shakespeare did commonly lye.' William Davenant 'would sometimes when he was pleasant over a glasse of wine with his most intimate friends . . . say, that it seemed to him that he writt with the very spirit that did Shakespeare, and seemed contented enough to be thought his son.'⁵ Aubrey knew well his brother Robert, the Rector of West Kington, who was also a Fellow of St John's College, Oxford, and who shared Aubrey's scholarly interests. More than a century earlier West Kington had been for five years, from 1530 to 1535, the parish of Latimer, before he became Bishop of Worcester, but who, even then, described it as 'his little Bishoprick of West Kington'. It was close to the Fosse Way, along which there was a constant flow of pilgrims. It is interesting to read in a letter from Latimer that even in those days parishes were concerned to help their finances by catering for them: 'As for pilgrimage you would wonder what juggling there is to get money withal. I dwell within half a mile of the Fossway and you would wonder to see how they come by flocks out of the west country to many images.'⁶ Some of the pilgrims would, no doubt, have found their way to the hospitable table of Aubrey's grandmother, and great-grandmother at Easton Piers, who like many other housewives in that area in that time kept open house for travellers.

The work, or works, of Oughtred that accompanied Davenant's letters would have been books published when Aubrey was a boy, of which the most famous were *Clavis Mathematicae* and *Circles of Proportion*. These had brought Oughtred international fame. They also brought many visitors from home and abroad to the Rectory at Albury, near Guildford. Oughtred, like Davenant, was a country parson. Like Davenant he had an immense family – nine sons and four daughters, but unlike Davenant he did not pass on his talent – 'none of his sonnes he could make any great scholars'. Aubrey wrote admiring and affectionate 'Lives' of both men. For Davenant he seems to have had a particular liking and respect, describing him as 'not only a man of vast learning but of great goodness and charity'. Yet as well as Aubrey's undoubtable affection and admiration for Davenant, one senses running through his 'Life' a slight strain of envy. If this is correct, it would not have been because Davenant had inherited not only the fortune of his father, a London merchant who lived at Croydon, 'in the farthest handsome great house on the left hand side as you ride to Bansted downes', but also that of his uncle the Bishop, who while he was alive had showered him with benefices that were in his gift, but because with the aid of a 'discreet and excellent housewife' Davenant managed to live just the sort of sheltered scholarly life that Aubrey sought but never found. 'He very rarely went any further than the church, which is hard by his house . . . he troubled himself about no mundane affaires, and . . . 'tis a private place . . . he was but little diverted with visitts.'

Oughtred, on the other hand, must have been constantly 'diverted with visitts'. For, Aubrey tells us 'He was more famous abroad for his learning, and more esteemed, than at home. Several great Mathematicians came over into England to converse with him. His country neighbours (though they understood not his worth) knew there must be extraordinary worth in him that he was so visited by Foreigners.' Yet from Aubrey's account many of his most eminent contemporaries also went to learn from him. 'Seth Ward . . . came to him and lived with him half a year – he would not take a farthing for his diet – and learned all his Mathmatiq of him . . . So was Christopher Wren his scholar. So Dr. Wallis.' At least three other of Aubrey's contemporary Fellows of the Royal Society had been his students also. 'Sir Jonas More. Mr . . . Smethwyck, R.S.Soc., Mr Thomas Henshawe R.S.Soc.' Of an earlier generation, but still some thirteen years younger than Oughtred, Thomas Hobbes came to learn from him, and found himself being taught not only mathematics but how to improve his handwriting. Oughtred 'could not endure to see a scholar write an ill-hand . . . Mr. T. H., who when he came to him, wrote a lamentable hand, he taught to write very well'. Not all of those who came to learn from Oughtred could survive the strain of living at so high an intellectual altitude. 'One Mr. Austin (a most ingeniose man) was his scholar, and studyed so much that he became mad, fell a laughing and so dyed – to the great grief of the old Gentleman. Mr. . . . Stokes, another Scholar, fell mad and dreamt that the good Gentleman came to him and gave him good advice; and he recovered and is still well.' In view of the facts that Oughtred taught 'all free', that his living was worth only a hundred a year, and of the immense family he had to bring up, it was as well that he had married a wife of 'an ancient Family in those parts', who probably had some money of her own – and also that she was 'penurious', understanding it in the sense that she was parsimonious rather than penniless. But at times she clearly carried her frugality too far. She 'would not allow him to burne candle after supper, by which meanes many a good notion is lost, and many a Probleme unsolved: so that Mr. Henshawe when he was there, bought candle, which was a great comfort to the old man.'

Aubrey gives a vivid description of Oughtred's appearance and habits. 'He was a little man, had black haire, and black eies (with a great deale of spirit). His head was always working; he would draw lines and diagrams in the Dust; studyed late at night . . . had his tinder-box by him, and on the tip of his Bedstaffe he had his Inke-horne fixed.' In the morning he would 'lye abed till eleven or twelve o'clock with his Doublet on'. Oughtred's genius knew no bounds. He shared Aubrey's interest in astrology and was 'a great lover of Chymistry', telling 'Jo. Evelyn of Detford Esq R.S.S. not above a year before he dyed that if he were but five yeares (or three yeares) younger he doubted not to find out the Philosopher's Stone'. Oughtred was to die in 1660, a few weeks after the Restoration, having been born more than a decade before the Armada. It was a great span of life, but clearly a great life also. Yet at the beginning he had had luck on his side. His father 'taught to write at Eaton'. In such a place his son's talent was quickly noticed. He was made a King's Scholar at Eton, and then became a Scholar at King's College, Cambridge. Everything else seems to have followed naturally after that. But would he have had so simple a start had he been born in a more obscure place? His life exemplifies two of the most attractive aspects of the age – not only its liking for learning but also its liking to learn.

After Oughtred's death Aubrey did his best to preserve his memory and reputation but was shocked to find when he later visited Albury Church in which Oughtred was buried, that 'I had much adoe to find the very place where the bones of this learned and good man lay (and twas but 16 yeares after his death).' However, Aubrey 'desired Mr. John Evelyn to speak to our Patrone the Duke of Norfolk to bestowe a decent inscription of marble on him . . .'.[7] Similarly, after Davenant's death Aubrey did all that he could to rescue his work from the oblivion which usually follows work which does not get into print. On behalf of the Royal Society he wrote to Davenant's executor to ask if they could have 'the honour and favour to conserve his manuscripts in the Library of the Royal Societie, and to print what is fitt'. But by far the best memorials to both men lie in the 'Lives' which Aubrey wrote about them.

Aubrey was twenty-two when he came back to Broadchalke and down from Oxford, the age at which his father had married, and he too at this similar age seems to have had similar thoughts. For in a later note in his *Collectio Geniturarum*, his astrological notebook, in which he made a list of his mother's 'Accidents', by which he meant 'happenings' or 'events' which might have astrological significance, he dates the breaking of 'her arme in 1649 or 1650 . . . 'twas when I was a Suitor to Mistresse Jane Codrington'.[8] Aubrey does not seem to have taken his rebuff – if rebuff there was – at all seriously, as one can see from this casual reference. Yet a socially suitable marriage such as this even at so early an age would certainly have saved him later trouble and might have even saved his inheritance.

In the same year Aubrey started a new but important friendship in the neighbourhood of Broadchalke. This was with Francis Potter, a curious character, similar in a scholarly way to both Davenant and Oughtred, but sadder, possibly because he had neither a 'discreet' nor a 'penurious' wife. Potter was much older than Aubrey. He was the younger brother of Hannibal Potter the, at that time, deposed President of Trinity, and like his brother had long been a Fellow of Trinity. When Aubrey came up in 1642, Francis Potter was already third in seniority among the Fellows, junior only to Dr Kettell and his brother. Much earlier, on 16 December 1625, before Aubrey was even born, Potter 'goeing up staires into his chamber at Trinity Coll. which was the senior Fellowes chamber there (he lay with his brother, Dr. Hannibal Potter) . . . the notion of the root of 666, for the roote of the number of the Beast in the Revelation, came into his head so he opposed 25 to 12 the roote of 144'. This 'notion' achieved considerable notoriety and Potter subsequently wrote a book about it; but he must have been very slow in so doing, for when Aubrey 'was admitted of the college' some eighteen years after Francis Potter had his revelation, 'his booke was in the presse'. However, Aubrey 'had not the honour and happinesse to be acquainted with him till 1649'. Fourteen of Potter's letters to Aubrey still survive in the Bodleian, written in a shaky hand which fits in with Aubrey's description that 'he was of a very tender constitution' – he had once in his Trinity days 'swooned in Divinity Schoole' – which makes them difficult to read. In the main they deal with technical matters which time has now passed by. Aubrey quickly developed a great admiration not so much for Potter's learning as for the originality of his way of thinking. 'He understood only common Arithmetique, and never went further in Geometrie than the first six books of Euclid: but he had such an inventive head that with this foundation he was able to do great matters in the Mechaniques and to solve phenomena in naturall philosophy.'[9]

The Potters were sons of the vicar of Kilmington, a parish in west Wiltshire close to the Somerset boundary, some twenty miles from Broadchalke as the crow flew, probably about thirty as Aubrey rode. Since 'in that darke time', by which Aubrey meant before the Civil Wars, Francis Potter failed to find at Oxford the appreciation or encouragement he needed, when his father died he took over his living at Kilmington 'worth per anno about £140'. It was there that early in January 1650 Aubrey paid the visit which was to be the first of many. Aubrey found his house 'undeckt as a Monk's cell, yet he had there so many impressive inventions that it was very delightful'. Potter himself Aubrey considered to be the most like a monk in appearance of any man he knew. 'He was pretty long visaged, and pale cleare skin, gray eie.' At the time of that first visit, Potter was mainly concerned with the idea that blood transfusion might help in the cure of certain diseases. On a later visit Aubrey helped Potter carry out an experiment with a hen, of which the results seem to have been unfortunate, particularly for the hen: 'the creature to little, and our tooles not good'. Aubrey subsequently sent Potter 'a surgeon's Lancet'. Fortunately, Potter never seems to have got to the point of experimenting on people, for in those pre-blood group days the results would almost certainly have been disastrous.

Aubrey reckoned that he learnt something every time he went to see Potter and 'always tooke notes'. In the delight of learning clearly lay much of the pleasure of these visits. But it was a very real one: 'I never have enjoyed so much pleasure nor ever so much pleased with such philosophicall and heartie entertainment as from him.' As with Hobbes, another whose intellect he greatly admired and whose friendship he correspondingly valued, Aubrey much regretted that Potter's original mind should moulder unappreciated in a remote country area. He regretted also, on Potter's behalf, that he missed the stimulus of meeting and mixing with others of comparable interests and intellects. 'Twas pitty that such a delicate inventive witt should be staked in an obscure corner from whence men rarely emerge to higher preferment, but contract a mosse on them, like an old pale in an orchard, for want of ingeniose conversation: which is a great want even to the Deepest thinking man (as Mr. Hobbes haz often sayed to me).'[10] Again, as with Hobbes, when he was in a position to do so, Aubrey did all he could to help his friend to remedy this neglect. In the year of his own election to the Royal Society, and so only in the second of its existence, he put Potter up as a candidate. He was duly elected in the same year. From 1650 on, when Aubrey was at Broadchalke his visits to Potter became a regular and valued part of his pattern of life. But however much Aubrey looked forward to them – as undoubtedly he would have done – Potter must have even more. For Aubrey provided just the sort of company and stimulus he lacked and needed. Throughout his relationship with Potter, Aubrey's gift for friendship shows at its most creative and compassionate.

Unlike many newly-fledged graduates, Aubrey continued his studies even when he had taken his degree. With his Oxford friends he kept in touch and in line by carrying out small scientific experiments at his home. Lydall's letters often contain responses, usually negative, to requests for ingredients Aubrey could not obtain at Broadchalke, but even on his travels when he was not studying Oughtred or Davenant he was looking around him: 'my head was always working, never idle . . . did gleane some observations'.[11] These observations were to be the foundation of his *Natural History of Wiltshire*. He did not seriously start putting down his notes, or collecting them, until 1654, possibly because his pace was then more leisurely since he was by then his own master and had the company and help of a personal servant. But one can be certain from his nature that throughout these early journeys on his father's behalf he would always have been looking out and around not only for anything odd or unusual, or even for something instructional, but simply at what was there. From Broadchalke, Easton Piers was conveniently on the way to the Hereford properties and one would imagine that Aubrey always broke his journey there. But over this period his pleasure at seeing his grandparents, the house in which he was born, and a property for which he was only to realize the full extent of his love when he had lost it, would have been tempered by dismay at the damage in the neighbourhood caused by the Puritan backlash. Kington St Michael itself had luckily remained in the air-bubble of safety in which it had survived the war, but in nearby Slaughterford, only a couple of miles away, a straggling village which followed the meanderings of the trout-full Box Brook, as did and does the nearby Bristol Road, the church had been stripped, savaged and all but destroyed. 'Here is a prettie small church, the most miserably handled that ever I saw, the very barres are taken out of the windows; here have been two good south windowes, and the doores are gone and the paving, and it serves for any use, viz. weavers. The font gone to make a trough.'[12] It was destruction and desecration such as this which made Aubrey come to the conclusion that the hand of man was a greater threat than either time or tempest.

It was not only the business and farming interests of his father that took Aubrey to Hereford and then on to Wales, it was also 'to solicite a law suit' which his father had started. This was, on the face of it, a totally hopeless attempt to break the entail on the will of Aubrey's great-grandfather, William Aubrey, Elizabeth's 'little doctor'. He had left the most important properties in Brecon and Monmouth, which included the Great House at Usk and

Abercynfrig, the main estate of the Aubrey family, to Edward, the eldest of his three sons. After his death it was entailed to his male descendants. Edward, or Sir Edward, as he became, had six sons, the eldest of whom had seven. The entail then skipped William Aubrey's second son and his descendants – only because they had been separately provided for – and came to Aubrey's grandfather, the third and last son. He had already been given the estates at Burleton and Stretford. By his own admission, Aubrey was only eighteenth in the remainder, and his father can have been only one link further up the chain. What possibly can have influenced Richard Aubrey and his son to pursue such an absurdly hopeless case? One can only surmise some sort of family feud. Yet Aubrey clearly believed fervently in their right and in the chance of victory. At the end of *Faber Fortunae*, a notebook in which he jotted ideas and observations which he thought might make his fortune – but, of course, never did – he inserted a slip on which he had written 'I have the Deed of Entail of the Landes in South Wales [he inserts 'Brecon and Monmouth' above], by my great grandfather Wm. Aubrey which lands now of right belong to me.'[3]

The whole affair would be laughable were not the results for Aubrey's fortunes to be so totally tragic. By the time he died, Richard Aubrey had spent a thousand pounds on the preparation of his case. Its prosecution was to cost Aubrey, by his own admission, a further twelve hundred pounds, and when it came to its inevitable and miserable end left him with nothing more than this very considerable bill. Even had Aubrey stopped proceedings after his father's death he would have saved himself a sum that would certainly have reduced his debt to manageable proportions, and might well have covered it altogether. Once his father had set the ball rolling, it may not have been easy – even after his death – to stop it, but how different Aubrey's later life might have been if he had.

Over this period, Aubrey's other connections with the law – his legal studies in London – seem to have been no more successful than proceedings in Brecon. For his failure to 'make anything of them' he, justifiably, blamed his preoccupation with his father's business, but one feels that had he felt a genuine call to the Bar he would have managed somehow to combine the two. In reality, whether at London, Broadchalke, Easton Piers or 'on his travels', Aubrey's thoughts and interests were still centred on Oxford. Lydall's letters from there span the years between his departure and his father's death. They must have been signals of hope during what was clearly otherwise a period of confusion, constraint and also concern, for despite the differences and distance between them, Aubrey was fond of his father and must have been sad to see his gradual decline towards death.

As one would expect, Lydall's earlier letters are full of domestic details as well as his constantly reiterated thanks for whatever Aubrey had given him at Oxford and his regard for Aubrey's ability. Thus a letter of 13 March 1649 tells 'honest Mr. Aubrey . . . I have according to your instructions delivered your bedding and two pairs of sheets with a pillow to the carrier. There is a towel yet behind which your laundress could not find. If anything else be wanting you must impute it to my mistake, and not to Sue Compton who now lyes in.'[14] An earlier January letter tells Aubrey that his battels* for the last weeks of his residence came to 'o–11–6' and a February one that his 'caution'† was £3. Several letters reflect Aubrey's concern about boxes of books due to be delivered to him at Oxford, which is curious, for why when Aubrey had left Oxford would he have books, presumably bought in London, sent to him there? It was in fact to be a long time before the boxes of books and other belongings reached Aubrey, mainly, it would seem, due to the vagaries of the carrier who always seemed to be arriving earlier or later than expected. It was not until three years later that in a letter of 10 February 1652 Lydall wrote to Aubrey, one imagines with immense relief, 'I have according to your order delivered to Edgerley [the carrier] the things which were in my custody. They are in five boxes corded up and superscribed with your name.'[15] Unimportant, inconsequential details of daily life, yet some years later Aubrey, angry at being criticized for going into too minute detail in his life of Hobbes, exploded ungrammatically, 'a hundred years hence that minuteness will be grateful'. In fact these details of his bedding, battels and books bring Aubrey back to us much more vividly than his demands for curious ingredients that he needed for his scientific experiments, such as *aurum fulminans*. *Aurum fulminans* had some explosive properties. One wonders whether the continuous inability of his friends to supply Aubrey with any – excuse follows excuse in Lydall's letters – was really due to a doubt whether he could handle it with safety in whatever sort of amateur laboratory he had set up for himself at Broadchalke. One of these excuses passed on by Lydall in a letter of 23 January 1649 was that 'Mr. Willis, our chymist' had been 'long absent'. 'Mr. Willis, our chymist' was Thomas Willis, a distinguished doctor as well as a chemist, to whom in 1662 Aubrey sold the estate at Burleton. In his 'Lives' Aubrey later paid due tribute to his distinction as a doctor, but seems to show something of his soreness over the sale in his personal description: 'he was of middle stature; darke-red brindle haire – like a red pig . . . stammered much.'[16]

Occasionally Lydall's letters give one a glimpse of wider horizons than those of Christ Church and Magdalen meadows, as when he writes 'My

*His personal account with the college.
†A deposit forfeit in the case of bad behaviour.

brother [William] goes with the next shippe for Barbadoss. I know he would be glad of Mr. Etterick's company.'[17] Lydall's younger brother William had been a scholar at Corpus Christi. Like Lydall, he had fallen foul of the Visitors and had been expelled. Anthony Ettrick, too, had lost the Trinity Fellowship he had only recently been awarded. One can imagine the inclination, and temptation, in such circumstances, to seek not only a new life but a new world. However, fortunately for Aubrey, since he was to remain a lifelong friend, and possibly for himself, Ettrick did not go. One does not know but one would expect that William Lydall did, for he had less, in fact very little, to lose. In the main, however, his brother's letters to Aubrey dealt with Oxford events and 'inventions – one by Dr. Petty'.

William Petty was one of the two most remarkable men – in what was to prove a brilliant generation – to come to Oxford over this period. The other was Christopher Wren. Robert Boyle would qualify as a third, but although the same age as Aubrey, being the son, if only the seventh son, of supposedly the richest man in the British Isles, the Earl of Cork, he was not subject to normal economic and educational rules. He only came to Oxford later when attracted by the presence of men like Petty, and by the exciting intellectual atmosphere. Of all Aubrey's many friends, Petty was probably the one he most respected. It is significant that Aubrey's first 'Life' was of Petty and that he was also the first of whom he made a nativity in his *Collectio Geniturarum*. In his list of 'Amici', Petty was the only one to whom he gave an additional commendation beyond the simple fact of inclusion; 'my singular friend', he was to call him, and he certainly was. The son of a clothier in Romsey, he, like Aubrey when visiting his grandmother in Bristol, when a boy, had taken particular delight in watching the work of the local 'artificers'. While still a youth Petty had worked on the boats which sailed from the local ports to and from France. At either end of these voyages he had managed to make some money, by buying and selling. With this he managed to pay for his education in the Jesuit college at Caen. Thence he moved to Paris to continue his studies, where he met Thomas Hobbes, then in exile with the future Charles II to whom he was tutor. Petty seems to have worked for a while both with and for Hobbes, surviving conditions of extreme poverty in order to complete his studies. He told Aubrey that he once had to live for a week on 'two penniworth' – Aubrey adds – '(or three I have forgott which) of walnuts'.[17] Coming to Oxford in 1648, Petty quickly took his medical degree, became a Fellow of Brasenose, then Vice-Principal, and in 1651 the University Professor of Anatomy, all in the space of four years.

Aubrey probably met him in 1648, the one year over which their time at Oxford overlapped, but only got to know him at all well on his visits to Oxford in the immediately succeeding years when they were both members of the

Experimental Philosophy 'Club' which Aubrey had declared 'we formed in 1649'. It was in Petty's rooms that some of the early meetings were held. Aubrey's enduring admiration for him was probably based on the fact that while they shared many intellectual interests, Petty complemented them with a practical ability that Aubrey totally lacked. He was efficient, inventive, assertive, and in the main successful. Perhaps nowadays one would describe him as an academic entrepreneur. Inevitably with such a forceful character, and in uncertain times, he had his downs as well as his ups. But he ended up with estates in Wiltshire, Ireland and a town house in Piccadilly, where Albany now stands. He also had a charming wife with 'browne and glorious eies', the widow of a Royalist officer killed in Ireland, with useful aristocratic connections. He had also 'very lovely children' whose descendants still live at Bowood on Derry Hill above Chippenham. He could also claim credit for an impressive list of practical achievements, of which the surveying of Ireland at Parliament's behest was the most notable. He also left on record a host of imaginative ideas which were only not realizable because they were too far ahead of their time to be so, such as a double-bottomed boat, and a primitive version of the modern tank. A 'singular friend' indeed.

Christopher Wren was only eighteen when he came up to Wadham in 1650, but already brought a reputation of mathematical brilliance with him. Having taken his degree he became a Fellow of All Souls. Earlier, Wren might easily have been a near neighbour of Aubrey's at Broadchalke, since his father at the time of his birth and during the early years of his childhood was vicar of East Knoyle, a village some sixteen miles from Salisbury. During his period of pastorship, Wren's father altered architecturally and greatly improved the village church, so it was clearly from him that Wren inherited his architectural ability – in his case genius. But for Aubrey and Wren the years of their childhood in Wiltshire did not quite overlap. The Aubreys only moved to Broadchalke in 1637 but in 1635 Wren's father had been made Dean of Windsor, and Chaplain to the King, in the place of his brother, who had been promoted to be Bishop of Norwich, subsequently becoming Bishop of Ely. As such, he was to spend a long period of imprisonment in the Tower, since over the years he refused to acknowledge the ecclesiastical authority of Parliament. This was in spite of the personal efforts of Cromwell who liked him and wished to release him if the Bishop would only give him the slightest pretext for so doing. The Bishop's two sons were to come to Oxford slightly later than Wren and there is record of the three of them together often frequenting a coffee-house near All Souls. The first coffee-house in England had, in fact, been opened a year or two earlier in Oxford, at the Angel, St Peter-in-the-East. Matthew and Thomas

Wren, as well as Christopher – and of course Aubrey – were later to be on the first list of Fellows of the Royal Society, registered on 20 May 1663.

Although Wren was not included in the 'Amici' he was to remain a close and valuable friend throughout his life. In Aubrey's penurious period nobody was to try harder to find him a job. It was through his efforts that Aubrey obtained his one and only commission – to do a survey of Surrey. On his side, Aubrey was always Wren's fervent admirer, writing to Wood when Wren made a mistake in his birthdate that it was a curious slip since Wren had made such admirable use of his life that one would not think he would want to shorten it. Luck often attends not only the brave but the brilliant. Wren – fortunately for us as well as for him – always seems to have been in the right place at the right time. In court circles, even as a boy, the clear flame of his brilliance would have been immediately obvious, but would it have been picked out so early had he remained longer in the vicarage of an unknown village in Wiltshire?

Arriving new to Oxford at this exciting and stimulating moment, exactly right for one of his inventive genius, Wren came also to the right college, Wadham. The Warden of Wadham, appointed by the Visitors after the dismissal of the previous Warden in their famous walk-about of April 1648, was the brother-in-law of Oliver Cromwell, Dr John Wilkins, a doctor of divinity, but whose main interest really lay in scientific and scholarly fields. He possessed a strong personality, progressive ideas and drive. It was he who, according to Aubrey 'began the experimental philosophical clubbe' whose early meetings were held in his rooms as well as Petty's. Lawrence Rooke, later famous as a mathematician, was also at Wadham at this time. So too was Seth Ward, who although basically a Cambridge man, became now the Oxford Professor of Astronomy, mainly through the good offices of Ralph Bathurst, of whom he was a close friend. Wren was to be one of his pupils. In a letter of 27 February 1651/52, Ward referred to 'the Clubbe' by then consisting of thirty members, chiefly concerned to investigate and to enquire into 'natural philosophy & mixt. mathematics, collecting only an history of the phenomena out of such authors as we have in our library, and sometimes trying experiments as we had occasion and opportunity'.[18] Seth Ward was to become one of Aubrey's 'Amici'. A man of considerable charm as well as ability, he was obviously destined for a distinguished career in some field or another. But the changing political climate made the course of it more serpentine than it otherwise would have been. Appointed President of Trinity in 1659, again probably through the influence of Bathurst, on the sudden and unexpected death of Aubrey's friend William Hawes, he lost the post when Hannibal Potter was reinstated at the Restoration. However, returning to the Church, he soon became Dean of Exeter, then its Bishop and finally Bishop of Salisbury. So the ripple of Aubrey's friendships spread ever wider, but that they did so was due in the main at this time to Ralph Bathurst, who by introducing Aubrey to his friends at Wadham, made him incidentally a member of this, as it was to turn out, very important and influential 'clubbe'.

In the discussions in Petty's or Wilkins's rooms and later in those of Boyle, it is unlikely that Aubrey took a leading part, or that in such brilliant company he was ever a leading light. But it is equally unlikely that he was ever regarded simply as a likeable hanger-on. Aubrey was humble about his own intellectual qualities. With the likes of Petty, Wren, Wilkins and Ward around it was only natural that he should be, but even when in less exalted company he was always out to learn rather than to teach, to enquire rather than to impress. This made him a good listener. But he was more than this. When in his autobiographical fragment in his 'Lives' Aubrey, then in his late fifties, considered what had been and was his main function in life, he gave himself the answer. He was a 'whetstone, though himself unable to cut'.[19] But the ability to bring out the best in others – to sharpen their ideas, their thought, their speech, to stimulate and suggest – is almost as valuable an ability as original thought itself. In Aubrey's character it was linked with his gift for friendship. At the back of both lay an intense interest in, and curiosity about, what other people were thinking, doing and saying.

However, Aubrey's functions as his father's health declined must have been increasingly confined to Broadchalke. Richard Aubrey died on 21 October 1652. Aubrey relates in his *Miscellanies* what he took to be a supernatural warning of his father's death. 'Three or four Days before my father died, as I was in my Bed about nine o'clock in the morning' (Aubrey, even then, was obviously not an early riser) 'perfectly awake, I did hear three distinct knocks on the Bed's head, as if it had been with a Ruler or Ferula'.[20] Curiously, and rather pathetically, for it seems to suggest that he still considered Easton Piers rather than Broadchalke as his real home, Richard Aubrey had asked to be, and was, buried at Kington St Michael. Aubrey intended 'to erect a little inscription to the Memory of my father: about an ell high or better' to commemorate Richard Aubrey as a '*vir pacificus et fidelis amicus*'. 'A peaceable man and a faithful friend' maybe – but definitely a difficult father.

* * *

There is all the difference in the world between looking after someone else's affairs – even one's father's – and one's own. Once the initial and inevitable period of grief and readjustment was over, Aubrey's life seems to have settled into a more relaxed rhythm, in which his personal pleasures, interests, desires and ambitions played a greater part. He went now frequently to Wilton, a considerable community, in which a pyramid of people served the few at the top. Aubrey reckoned 'one hundred and twenty . . . in uprising and down lying, whereof you may take out 6 or 8, and all the rest Servants and Retayners'.[21] He also estimated that 'the Revenue of this family till about 1652 was £16,000 per anno'. It was at this time that Aubrey got to know the likeable Sir John Denham, poet, gambler, Surveyor as yet designate of the royal buildings, who was staying there on his return from France where two years earlier he had escorted the two younger princes. The fourth Earl of Pembroke, who as Vice-Chancellor had headed the Parliamentary Visitation at Oxford in 1649 and led the evictive walkabout, had died a year later. This may have had something to do with Aubrey's reappearance at Wilton. The new earl was less politically minded and committed than his father, so there would no longer have been any discrimination between those who had been Parliamentarians and those who had been Royalists. In any case, he had urgent financial problems to deal with, due in the main to his father's extensive building at Wilton – and rebuilding also, for, according to Aubrey, 'the south side of this stately house . . . was burnt down 1647 or 1648, by airing of the roomes.'

To deal with the debt caused by all this building and rebuilding, the new earl was forced to sell a great part of the Wilton collections, including many of the magnificent pictures, which Aubrey considered 'the best collection of paintings of the best masters of any peer of this time in England . . . a great many pieces of Georgeon [Giorgione] and some of Titian, his scholar. His lordship was the great patron of Sir Anthony Van Dyke, and had most of his paintings of anyone in the world'. As well as family portraits of the Pembrokes and their widespreading aristocratic connections, there were royal pictures – 'a stately picture of King Henry the eighth; . . . King James the First sitting in his throne, in his royall robes, a great piece, as big as the life'; two of Charles I who, according to Aubrey, 'did love Wilton above all places, and came thither every summer': one 'on horseback, with his French riding master by him on foot . . . a copie from that at Whitehall', the other an original Van Dyke of Charles I 'on his dun horse'. In the hall 'were the pictures of the Ministers of State in Queen Elizabeth's time and some of King Henry the Eighth'. These included Wolsey, Walsingham, Essex. There were several pictures of Sir Philip Sidney, whose sister, Mary, had been the second wife of Henry Herbert, the Earl of Pembroke during the last years of Elizabeth's reign. One of Sidney's portraits carried the sadly prophetic inscription:

> Who gives himself may well his picture give
> Els were it vain, since both short times do live.

Mingled with these distinguished pictures of distinguished people were others less expected: 'the picture of Thomas Lyte of Lytes Cary', who had married, as his second wife, the widow of Philip Sidney's brother John; a portrait of 'Archey (King James's jester)'; by the side of the copied equestrian portrait of Charles I which hung at the top of the stairs 'the pictures of Peacock', the racehorse which Aubrey so much admired, 'with the groom holding him, as big as the life . . . to both Sir Anthony gave many master touches'; underneath the portrait of the first earl 'the picture of his little dog, of a kind of chestnut colour, that starved himselfe for his master's death'; a portrait of 'the last Lady Abbess of Wilton', to whose foundation the farm at Broadchalke had belonged before the Dissolution, 'a pretty, beautiful, modest Penelope' – all these and 'many others now forgotten by me and everybody else'.[22]

It was, of course, mainly Aubrey's artistic side which regretted the dispersal of what must have been, clearly, a magnificent collection, but his scholarly side made him regret almost as much the fact that so many of these portraits went unnamed. So, in many cases, they would have passed into the oblivion from which it was Aubrey's persistent effort to rescue as much as he could. 'It is a great and a generall fault that in all galleries of pictures the names are not writt underneath.' It was perhaps this feeling that made him write in such detail of the Wilton collections, when he came to do so some thirty years after their sale, putting on paper, one would think, all that he could remember of them in the hope that it might be of interest or use later in identifying the pictures. Perhaps also he was referred to at the time. He certainly should have been. For as he wrote in his section on Wilton in his *Natural History*: 'I was heretofore a good nomenclator of these pictures, which was delivered to me from a child eight years old, by old persons relating to this noble family.'

As one would expect, Aubrey was as sad to see the books of the library go as the pictures. 'Here was a noble librarie of bookes, choicely collected in the time of Mary, Countesse of Pembroke. I remember there were a great many Italian bookes . . . Here was Dame Julian Barnes of Hunting, Hawking and Heraldry, in English verses, printed temp. Edward the Fourth . . . A translation of the whole book of Psalmes, in English verse, by Sir Philip Sidney, writt curiously, and bound in crimson velvet and gilt; it is now lost. Here was a Latin poeme, a manuscript, writt in Julius Caesar's time . . . Now all these bookes are sold and dispersed as the pictures.'[22]

Yet another reason that took Aubrey to Wilton at this time was that a contemporary acquaintance of his, Christopher Wase, a former Fellow of King's College, Cambridge ejected by the Parliamentary Visitation, was tutor to Pembroke's eldest son, William. The new earl, like his father, whom the DNB rather sourly notes as being 'addicted to sport', was passionately keen on hunting. So, too, was Aubrey, although as he writes in his *Natural History* it was 'Philip 1st Earle of Pembroke that was the great Hunter . . . 'Twas after his decease that I was a Hunter'. Pembroke and Aubrey's father died within two years of each other. So it was probably at this time that Aubrey became 'a hunter', although clearly he had always been interested in it. In sport, as in other aspects of its life, Aubrey was immensely Wiltshire proud. 'It is certain that no County of England had greater variety of Games than Wiltshire, and our county hounds were as good or rather the best in England . . . Sir Charles Snell, who was my honest friend & neighbour (at Easton Piers), had till the Civil Warrs as good Hounds for the Hare as any were in England, for handsomeness – deep mouthed – and suited one another admirably well.' Aubrey was equally proud of 'the Wiltshire Greyhounds . . . also the best of England, and are still. My father and I had as good as any were in our time in Wiltshire. Our Wiltshire greyhounds are generally ox-black'.[23] At Wilton, Aubrey, presumably bringing his greyhounds with him, would often join Kit Wase and his pupil. Between Latin lessons they would hunt together on the Plain.

Like so many of Aubrey's acquaintances Kit Wase was to become and remain a life-long friend. After the Restoration he was to become Headmaster of Tonbridge School and subsequently Supervisor of the University Press at Oxford, where he was also a 'bedell'. This was a university official whose duties were largely ceremonial. As such, on one occasion, that of a state visit by James II, Wase was to earn Anthony Wood's all-too-ready derision. This was for drinking too much and in consequence having such shaking hands that he could not get on to his horse without being helped up, nor hold his staff of office straight when he got there. Aubrey later was to assist Wase with an 'Inquiry into the Free Schools of England'. The last on the list, arranged chronologically, of the books which Aubrey possessed at the time of his death, was one written by Wase, given to him by Wase's son only a year earlier. Wase had died six years before Aubrey. On it Aubrey had written 'The author . . . was of my oldest acquaintance, and my singular friend.'

*   *   *

Under the terms of his father's will, Aubrey had been left all his father's properties – the two Herefordshire estates, Burleton and Stretford, and the tract of land on the Kent coast near Rye. He had also been left the tenancy of Manor Farm. This was in the form of a three-person lease, under which his father had been the first tenant, Aubrey himself would be the second, and he would have the right to nominate the third, after which the farm reverted to the Wilton estate. Aubrey had to give each of his two very much younger brothers, William and Thomas, aged nine and seven at the time of their father's death, £500. He also had to look after his mother who, although she probably had some money of her own – as the only child of her Lyte parents – may also in some way have been linked to the lease at Broadchalke. Aubrey did not consider selling it until after her death, although in her later years she did not live there but in Bridgwater.

On the face of it then, Aubrey was now a man of considerable means, yet of considerable responsibilities also, and with, from the start, considerable debts, which he had also inherited from his father. By Aubrey's account these amounted to '£1,800 lib'. If one adds to them the £1000 he had to pay to his two brothers, it obviously increases his initial debt to an amount which seems to have been about three times the income he and his mother enjoyed. In a letter of 1671 to Anthony Wood, he was to write 'I was left £600 per ann. or better, my mother and I together,' adding pathetically 'I should have been glad to have kept it.' He could probably have raised the money he needed to pay off his debt and his brothers' legacies by the sale of the two Herefordshire properties, for this was roughly the amount that he was to get for them some ten years later. But in those days selling a property was not the relatively simple matter of putting it on a house agent's list that it is today. A buyer had to be found personally. This took time, and it was entirely natural, understandable and forgivable that Aubrey should have preferred to spend that time savouring the pleasure and pride of possession. He, no doubt, also enjoyed spending some of the money that was readily available to him, even if he had already a background of debt, for who would have refused to lend money to someone who could offer such substantial security at, no doubt, high rates of interest.

But not always. In his 'Life' of Edward Davenant, he expressed his 'very great gratitude' to him as 'my singular good friend: and to whom I have been more beholding than to anyone beside for I borrowed five hundred pounds of him for a yeare and a halfe; and I could not foster any interest on him'.[24] One does not know the date of the loan, but 'John Davenant of the Middle Temple', Edward Davenant's son, was mentioned in the will which Aubrey made in 1653, when he intended to go abroad. Like Hawes, Lydall and Bathurst, he was left 'a ring of the value of 50s, with a stone in it'. This suggests that his inclusion in the will may have been intended as a token of gratitude to the family as a whole, and the father in particular. In which case Aubrey must have taken the loan soon after his father's death, perhaps to help pay the legacies to his brothers or perhaps to deal with some particularly demanding debtors.

As well as allowing him to spend much more time with his friends at Wilton and elsewhere, his father's death freed and financed Aubrey at least to consider and plan for the Grand Tour, for which his plans had once already been thwarted by his mother's understandable opposition during the period of his father's illness. This was an obvious and natural ambition for someone with his antiquarian interests. It had long been one of his keenest desires, and might have enabled him to bring back much more in the way of extended experience and widened horizons than was customary in the case of many other well-born and wealthy young men, whose leisurely amble round southern Europe was accepted as the habitual prelude to their settling on their estates for the rest of their lives.

Aubrey was not long in starting to make the arrangements for such a tour, for which a primary requisite was to find a congenial companion. A letter from Lydall, dated 5 April 1653 – and so little more than five months after the death of Richard Aubrey – is clearly the reply to one sounding out his various friends at Oxford as to whether they would, and could, come with him. But either they would not or could not. These were still precarious and penurious times, in which few would have wanted, or have been able to afford, to travel abroad. This was particularly so among those who were Aubrey's obvious choice as companions, as we see from Lydall's letter: 'I acquainted Mr. Bathurst with your designe of travelling and of your desire of his company . . . he is not minded at all to travel, and he knows Mr. Willis is of the same resolution. Neither can I yet heare of any other. As for mine own parte there is no man living with whom I would rather go than yourself . . . but there are two great impediments . . . the charge of the journey – the other a crazy and sickly construction of body.' Lydall's plea of ill-health was no excuse but sadly all too true, and he was to die four years later.

Bathurst, too, was going through a period of particular difficulty, but in his case financial. As one of a vast family – supposedly of fifteen sons – he can have had little or no money of his own, and a Fellow's salary was woefully inadequate. He had been forced to abandon his studies for a doctorate of divinity in favour of those for a doctorate of medicine. Qualifying in 1654, he thereafter served for two years as a surgeon in Cromwell's navy, a surprising appointment for one who was an ardent Royalist and who was later to be appointed Chaplain to Charles II. Willis, 'our chymist' in one of Lydall's earlier letters, although nine years later well enough off to buy Aubrey's Burleton estate, was at this time very much a working doctor. So clearly for practical reasons none of the friends whom Aubrey approached could have come with him even if they had wanted to, which clearly they did not. However, they were still friendly and concerned. 'Your friends would be extremely glad to see you before your departure. Mr. Bathurst says you must not scruple to take physic.'[25] Aubrey seems not to have been at all deterred by their refusal and determined if need be to travel alone. This was the time when he made the will in which he left bequests to his closest friends and by his own account 'settled my estate as trustees intending to have seen the antiquities of Rome and Italy, and then to have returned and married'.

It was a curious will in many ways: he left £50 to each of his 'loving' grandparents in order to erect 'a decent inscription of white marble for my father and the like for myselfe; the Epitaph to be made by Mr. A. Ettrick'. It was odd that someone of his age should have cared so much to leave his memorial behind him. It was curious, too, that there was no mention in his will of his mother or brothers. It was only natural that Trinity should be left 'a colledge pott of the value of ten pounds with my armes thereon inscribed, and ten pounds which I shll desire my honoured friends Mr. Ralph Bathurst of Trinity Coll. and Mr. Jo. Lydall to outlay only upon Mathematicall and philosophical books', but it was odd that Jesus, a college with which he had no personal connection, save that it had been the college of 'the little doctor', should have been left 'all the rest of my bookes that are fitt for a Library'. But most curious, and intriguing of all was the final item: 'I leave to Mistr. Mary Wiseman of Westminster my best diamond ring.'[26]

However, all Aubrey's preparations and precautions were to come to nothing because 'my mother to my inexpressible grief and ruine, hindred this designe, which was my ruine.' [27] It is easily acceptable that Aubrey's mother, with two small sons to look after, should have objected to being left also to look after their far-flung possessions, and to deal with all the protracted complications that inevitably follow a family death. But what one finds difficult to understand is why its abandonment should have been so catastrophic for Aubrey – a disappointment surely but how could it have been the cause of 'my ruine'? One can only guess that something disastrous happened during the next year or so – which would not, or might not, have if he had been abroad, as he intended. There is perhaps a clue, but only to various possibilities, in the last thought-provoking item in his will, the bequest of the best diamond ring to 'Mistr. Mary Wiseman of Westminster'.

It seems that two years earlier, in April 1651, Aubrey had fallen in love for the first, and so far as we know, only time in his life. It was in London that 'I saw that incomparable good-conditioned gentlewoman Mistress M. Wiseman with whom at first sight I was in love.' 'Mistress M. Wiseman' was Mary Wiseman, the daughter of a wealthy merchant, who had a town house in Westminster, a country one at Felsted in Essex, and who had been a 'Groom of the Privy Council of Charles I'. She was extremely young when Aubrey first saw her. If his date of their first meeting, and the age given in the marriage licence in 1661, when Mary Wiseman was married – not to Aubrey – of twenty, are correct, then she would only have been eleven when he first saw her, and thirteen when he made the will in which he left her his diamond ring. Yet it must be remembered that Aubrey's mother had only been fifteen when she married, and this would have been Mary Wiseman's age on Aubrey's return from his Grand Tour if it had taken the couple of years or so that he seems to have envisaged. It was a pleasing prospect – an instructive and entertaining couple of years wandering around Italy and the south of France, adding to his experience, his knowledge and his enjoyment – and then at the end coming back to marry his 'good-conditioned gentlewoman'. Even if his mother had stopped him going abroad, he could pass the time while he was waiting for Mary Wiseman to grow up, pleasantly and profitably – learning how to run his estates, eating his dinners at the Middle Temple, seeing his friends there and in Oxford, and through them keeping in touch with what was already proving to be, intellectually, an excitingly inventive and innovative period. This was in fact very much how the pattern of Aubrey's life was to form over the years which would have been those of his Grand Tour had his plans come to fruition. But at the end of it all, so far as Mary Wiseman was concerned, it seems somehow to have gone wrong. Why?

In an emotional situation of this sort, at this distance of time, and in the absence of any surviving correspondence, facts are few and far between and even the most plausible explanation can be but surmise. But such as they are the few facts are these. In view of Aubrey's recorded reaction to his first meeting with Mary Wiseman and the bequest of the 'diamond ring', there can be little doubt of his devotion or of his intent to marry her. But in his later list of 'Accidents' under the year 1656 and the month December is a mystifying entry. It consists of the astrological sign for Venus, and the abbreviation '*morb.*' – which must stand for '*morbus*' – disease or sickness. This suggests that Aubrey may have contracted some venereal infection. It can not have been all that severe an infection or serious a problem for Aubrey was to live to a considerable age, in very reasonable health. But it could have been serious enough to prevent him marrying at this time. It would, too, if Mary Wiseman had come to hear of it, have been only natural and understandable that it should have turned her against him. Yet there is an alternative interpretation of this worrying entry. Aubrey might simply have meant that his love for Mary Wiseman was not prospering, that it was sick, perhaps dying or dead. Mary Wiseman was eventually to marry John Saintloe, whose family were near neighbours of Aubrey at Broadchalke, living at Knighton Manor, which still stands in a fold of the downs, about a mile to the west. Did she, in the course of a visit to Aubrey, which it was only normal that she should make, meet John Saintloe and later decide she liked him the better of the two?

In practical terms Saintloe may have seemed the better prospect. He was born wealthy, the son of a rich merchant – he was to become one himself – and well connected. His grandmother was the aunt of Edward Hyde, Earl of

Clarendon, Lord Chancellor to Charles II. In support of this more acceptable supposition is the fact that in the course of the year that followed Aubrey was to become engaged to someone else, Katherine Ryves. It is hard to believe that he would have been irresponsible enough to do this if he was still infected. Yet, particularly in those days, it was a very short time in which to be cured. Whatever the truth of the matter, Aubrey's luck in his love affairs was clearly totally out at this time. At the end of 1657, only eleven months after his '*morb.*' entry, he noted 'November 27, *obiit* Kather. Ryves, with whom I was to marry, to my great losse'.[28]

It was, indeed, a great loss. Katherine Ryves sounds to have been just the sort of wife Aubrey sought and needed. She was well-to-do, well connected, living at the time of Aubrey's courtship with two aunts in one of the loveliest of the many lovely houses in Salisbury, the King's House in the Cathedral Close. Her will gave confirmation of an intimate and affectionate relationship. To 'my deare ffriende Mr. John Aubrey' she left £350, and to 'Mrs. Aubrey, his mother, a mourning ring'. On the strength of this, one can not doubt that had she lived, Katherine Ryves and Aubrey would have married. She would have fitted easily into Aubrey's family circle. The bequest of the mourning ring shows that she and his mother were already friends. She had known the area around Broadchalke all her life, her own home being near Blandford, where, of course, Aubrey had been at school. There was a possibility, too, that the house in the Cathedral Close might eventually have become hers, for the fact that she was living there with her aunts rather than at home with her father suggests that she might have been their heiress. Aubrey would have loved having a house there, particularly when his friend Seth Ward became Bishop. More importantly than all this, she seems from the terms of the will, and the language in which it is couched, to have been a nice woman who might well have made Aubrey a 'discreet' wife – another such as Edward Davenant's, whom Aubrey so much admired – running her family and her household pleasantly and well, doing her best to free her husband from mundane worries, so that he could follow his intellectual interests. However, sadly, perhaps tragically for Aubrey, the stars decreed otherwise.

One can see then that these were eventful and fateful years for Aubrey – and accept that they influenced critically the course of his life – without ever being able to put one's finger with certainty on the precise event, or run of events, to which he attributed 'his ruine'. But, otherwise over this period, everything seemed to promise well for him. The early death of his father had left him in a position of exceptional independence. He had his responsibilities certainly, but provided he showed even a modicum of common sense in running his affairs these need have imposed only lightly on whatever pattern of life he chose to make for himself. And, in fact, he hardly had to make a choice. With on the one hand Broadchalke, and to an ever-increasing extent as his grandfather aged, Easton Piers, to satisfy his country interests, and on the other, frequent sojourns in London and Oxford, where he had already made for himself many friends among the most intelligent and interesting men of his time, he seemed to have to hand a combination that perfectly suited the duality of his character. Before him seemed to lie the prospect of a successful, interesting, influential and, with any luck, happy life. Yet the path of life is rarely as smooth as it may look in the light of a promising dawn. Aubrey, looking back from the other end of his long life, was to consider, humorously and humanely, but with absolute truth, that he had been 'much tumbled up and down'[29] in the course of it.

Enjoying Life
c. 1655–9

Aubrey described the division of his time over these years of the mid and late fifties, which followed the death of his father, in the autobiographical fragment he inserted into his 'Lives'. He was in one of his impersonal moods '– J.A. lived most at Broad-Chalke . . . , sometimes at Easton Piers: at London every terme – much of his time spent in journeying to S. Wales ['entaile' inserted above] and Herefordshire.'[1]

At Broadchalke Aubrey now had responsibility for the farm. In a landlordly sort of way, although in fact he was the tenant, he seems to have taken a considerable interest in it. It was a farm worth taking an interest in. The land round Broadchalke had probably always been good stock country. As early as the thirteenth century the tenants were recorded as holding, on the demesne land 1000 sheep, thirty-three oxen and forty-two cows which for that time must have been a high stocking rate. Aubrey ran only sheep on Manor Farm. He was highly conscious of their commercial value, writing in *Monumenta Britannica* that they were 'the greatest benefit' of the farm, and seems to have had a particular liking for the shepherds themselves, whom he saw as survivors from an earlier 'Golden Age', when life in his opinion was simpler and saner. It seems to have been not only the simplicity and hardiness of their lives which appealed to him, but also their distinctive dress: 'They wore a long, white cloak with a very deep Cape (which comes down halfe the way of their backe; made of the locks of their sheep); their Armature was a sheep-crook, a sling, a scrip, their tar box and their dog.'[2] Nor, of course, as Aubrey admitted in his account of the Avebury hunt were 'nut-brown shepherdesses without their graces'. In his time, in Wiltshire at any rate, it was customary not to pay shepherds wages, but to allow them to keep a number of their own sheep with the flock. This system had the advantage that money did not have to be found to pay the shepherds' wages before the sheep produced their profit. It had, however, the disadvantage that it was virtually impossible over a large area to check not only the number of sheep on the farm but those which belonged to the shepherds. So it was easy for them to take more than their due. Aubrey hinted at this when he wrote 'the shepherds lambs doe never get scurvy.'

Aubrey ran his farm through the agency of 'Geo. Lawes, my Bayley'. 'Geo. Lawes' undoubtedly organized the day-to-day running of the farm and one would think decided also, but possibly after discussion with Aubrey, the general lines and direction of farming policy. Yet one can not doubt after reading the sections of the *Natural History* concerned with general aspects of farming, that Aubrey's interest was genuine, and that he was conscious of commercial realities as well as the phenomena and features of climate and countryside. Thus one finds him very concerned that the fall in the price of wool, due he believed, in part, to the loss of the profitable Turkey trade and also to changing fashion – to 'our Woemans wearing of much silk and Indian ware'[3] in place of wool – meant that his income was reduced by some sixty pounds a year. Also in his *Natural History* he transcribes a cure for the 'smutt of wheate' sent him by Sir Walter Long which might have helped to improve the poor returns of the cornfields at Broadchalke where, one reads in *Monumenta Britannica*, 'the corne does but little more than pay the corne-rent.' By contrast 'about Burleton' – this is one of the rare occasions when Aubrey mentions his Aubrey grandfather's Herefordshire home, which had become his on the death of his father – 'the arable land grows very good Corne (wheat and rye) . . . but the fallowes do beare a very poor coate of grasse – worse than the mountains of Wales. The soile is compounded of sand and clay.'[4] As well as recording general characteristics of land, Aubrey recognized that individual fields could have identities and idiosyncrasies: 'It is found by experience that Holtgore (belonging to Chalke Farm) must not be sown for Barley before our Lady-Day, nor after St. George-tyde, for if before our Lady-Day it will be red-legged and sterile; if after St. George's tyde but three days it will not ripen.'[5]

All of this would seem to show that Aubrey could have been a good farmer on a proprietorial level if he had had time. But did he have time? In those days when travelling was slow and wearisome how could he possibly manage to keep abreast of affairs in his Herefordshire properties, spend a suitable amount of time with his ageing grandparents at Easton Piers, continue his legal studies in London (which would not however probably have taken up much of his time), follow up the social and intellectual pursuits essential to his satisfaction, and combine all this with the competent care of his farm at Broadchalke? It was not possible. Yet in spite of this one gets the strong impression that the vortex of debt which in the end was to swallow all that Aubrey owned was not created by farming failure but by financial misman-agement elsewhere, in particular by Aubrey's inability to cope with the problems created by his father's debts, and the expenses of the law suit over the entail. His father's debts, which Aubrey assessed at £1800, were still not totally cleared more than thirty years after his death. Among the correspondence which Aubrey kept is a pathetic letter – pathetic in that it shows how desperately short of money Aubrey was to become – from a Welsh cousin, Thomas Price, who evidently acted in Wales as debt settler and debt collector on Aubrey's behalf, dated 30 November 1684: 'Dear Cousin – Your fathers debts grow so fast upon me that like Hydra's heads I no sooner satisfie one but two or three new ones start up in place of it – which has made me so bare of money that I had much adoe to get this £5 which I have sent you.'[6] If there was still a dribble of debts coming in thirty years after Richard Aubrey's death, surely in the years immediately following it there must have been a flood, which even a more experienced and competent person than Aubrey might well have found difficult to withstand.

The dispute over the entail finally came to court in 1656. Aubrey dates it not only in his 'Accidents', the list of personal events which might have astrological significance (often providing incidentally a useful source of autobiograpical information) but also in his *Natural History*. This was in the course of a lengthy and detailed account of a peculiar practice of a distinguished judge, Rumsey, who cleared his throat of phlegm by pushing down it a stick of whalebone. This 'instrument . . . he carried along with him on the Circuit . . . He was my Councill Learned in the Lawe'. At this point, Aubrey inserts above '1656 in Brecknockshire'. He goes on: 'a servant of mine (Mk.C)' – this was Mark Collins, who seems to have entered Aubrey's service at Easton Piers – 'a brisk young fellow that would adventure at anything, seeing the Judge use it, when the Judge turned his back he wipes a little the whale bone, and after 2 or 3 tryalls gott it down to the bottome of his Stomach . . . When I came to Oxford, Dr. Willis, Dr. Ralph Bathurst and several others sawe my servant doe this tricke . . . if there be Wind in the stomach it does immediately give it vent with a blast as when a Bottle is unstopped'. Aubrey had a try at it himself. 'I was very desirous to have mastered it but could not; I could never swallow a pill.'[7]

It is typical of Aubrey's taste for the trivial – sometimes interesting, sometimes infuriating – that he should go into great detail about this unattractive party trick but tell us nothing about the court case itself. He included Judge Rumsey in his 'Lives', from which one learns that he was but 'one of my Councill'. Despite the outcome of the case, and the extent of the bill which followed it, Aubrey seems to have regarded Judge Rumsey with considerable affection and admiration. 'He was so excellent a lawyer that he was called the Pick-Lock of the Lawe . . . He was an ingeniose man, and had a philosophicall head; he was most curious for grafting, inocculating and planting and ponds . . . he had a kindnesse for me and invited me to his house, and told me a great many fine things both natural and antiquarian.'[8] Aubrey obviously enjoyed his visits to Wales, and one is glad that he did. It was all that he was to get out of his lawsuit, other than a bill for £1200 in costs, in addition to the £1000 which his father had paid to start proceedings. Judge Rumsey, the other counsel, the solicitors and all the other busy bees surrounding the honeypot may not have actually cheated Aubrey, but they undoubtedly 'cozened' him into proceeding with an obviously hopeless case.

*   *   *

Aubrey was thirty in 1656, the year of the court case and in that year he had his portrait painted, possibly by Lely. Aubrey's purpose in so doing was probably twofold: to leave a record of himself (he had already shown in the making of his will a surprising concern in a young man to make sure that he left a memorial behind him), and also to cement his increasingly strong friendship with Charles Seymour, to whom he gave either the portrait itself, or a miniature by Samuel Cooper painted at much the same time. The full-scale portrait has not survived, but an engraving of it has, which, together with a portrait drawn by William Faithorne ten years later, now in the Bodleian, intended to be the frontispiece for *Monumenta Britannica*, are the only visual records of Aubrey's appearance that remain. Of the two, the earlier one is much the more likeable and, one would think, truer to life. Apart from the inappropriate studio prop of a grinning negro boy on whose head Aubrey is resting his right hand, it fits very well with the impression one forms of Aubrey from his writing – keen, kindly, observant eyes, a full mouth, an expression that looks as if it is about to break into a smile, generally a surprisingly boyish appearance considering his age.

Aubrey was frequently in London over these years pursuing, although at a considerable distance and without any hope at all of catching them up, his legal studies. He was 'at London every terme' but one feels that learning law was no longer, if it ever had been, the reason but rather the pretext for his visits to London. Altogether, Aubrey supposedly studied law over a period of ten years, writing in a letter to Wood 'I was a student of the Middle Temple 1646–56.' It was probably towards the end of this period that the curious and indirectly dangerous episode occurred when Aubrey gave hospitality to Tom Mariet, a younger friend from Trinity, in his lodgings at the sign of the Rainbow in Fleet Street. Tom Mariet, an ardent Royalist, was in London in company with Major-General Massey, who had fought on the Parliamentary side in the war, but subsequently changed his mind and side, and joined Prince Charles in France. They were there as the emissaries of the exiled King-to-be, to sound opinion as to whether or not it would be favourable to his return. They carried letters of authority from Charles. In particular, Mariet and Massey were to approach General Monck, a key figure in any Restoration, as he was to prove later, because of his control of the army. 'Colonel Massey and Tho. Marriett of Whitchurch in Warwick, Esq, held correspondence with His Majesty, who wrote them letters with his owne-hand which I have seen. Both these were now in London privately. Tom Mariet layd with me (I was then at the M. Temple). Col Massey and T. Mariett every day were tampering with G.M. . . . they could not find any inclination or propensity in G.M. for their purpose sc. to be instrumentall to bring in the K. – every night late I had an account of all these transactions abed, which like a sott which I was I did not while fresh in memorie committ to writing – as neither haz T.M. – but I remember in the maine that they were satisfied he no more intended or designed the K's restauration when he came into England or first came into London, than his Horse did.'[9] These were dangerous waters in which to paddle, even at the very shallow depths to which Aubrey ventured. But he never seems to have appreciated the risk he was taking simply in giving Tom Mariet a bed while he was engaged on this perilous mission. It was probably as well for all concerned that the prudent and pragmatic General not only did not respond in any way to Mariet's and Massey's overtures but also kept his mouth shut.

Aubrey's fringe involvement in this episode seems to have sparked off an interest in Monck, which led to one of the longest, most vivid and most interesting of his 'Lives'. As with Sir William Petty, whose entrepreneurial, opportunist character Aubrey so much admired, it was really the attraction of opposites – for nobody could have been more unlike the gentle, credulous, scholarly Aubrey than the vigorous, shrewd, hard-bitten soldier. Aubrey describes Monck as a young man as 'a strong, lusty, well sett young fellow and in his youth happened to slay a man. This was the occasion of his flying into the Low Countries where he learned to be a soldier. At the beginning of the late Civill-warres he came over to the Kings side . . . Ao . . . he was prisoner in the Tower . . . where his semstress was Nan Cl[arges] . . . (a Black-smiths daughter)'. An asterisk above 'Blacksmiths' leads to the marginal information that 'the shop is still of that trade, the corner shop, the first turning on the right hand as you come out of the Strand into Drury Lane: the howse is now built of brick.' According to Aubrey the blacksmith's seamstress daughter was kind to Monck 'in a double capacity; it must be remembered that he was then in want, and she assisted him: here she was gott with child. She was not at all handsome nor cleanly . . . I have forgott by what meanes he gott his libertie and Employment under Oliver (I thinke) at Sea against the Dutch where he did good service; he had courage enough. But I remember the Seamen would laugh that instead of crying "Tack about", he would say "wheele to the right or left". While he was at sea, Monk's seamstress had her child. Her brother 'T. Cl[arges] . . . came shipboard to G.M. and told him his sister was brought to bed. "Of what", sayd he? "Of a Son." "Why then", sayd he, "she is my wife": he had only this child'.

Monck had in fact served under Cromwell in Ireland and Scotland before going to sea, and when he came back on to land 'he had command in Scotland, where he was well beloved by his Soldiers.' Aubrey tells that Monck had other overtures from the Royalists than those from Massey and Mariet – but always managed to avoid committing himself. On one occasion after dining with a Royalist, who suggested that 'God had put a good opportunity into his hands . . . he gave an indefinite answer and sayd he hoped he should doe like an honest man'. On a later occasion, when the tide was clearly beginning to turn, 'some months before G.M.s coming into England, the King sent Sir Richard Grenvill to him, to negotiate with him . . . and to correspond with him: said he – if opportunity be I will doe him service but I will not by any means have or hold any correspondence with him – and he did like a wiseman in it: for if he had, he would certainly have been betrayed.'⁹ Aubrey obviously enjoyed being for once if not quite at the centre of the stage, at least in the wings. When the Restoration eventually came, he used Monck's 'Life' to give a vivid and valuable eye-witness account of it.

But, as Aubrey put it, 'long before these dayes' he was clearly beginning to spread his wings in the warmth of London life. An invitation, which seems to have found its way into Aubrey's collected correspondence only because of some notes he had written on the back, came from a friend 'Jo. Yate'. 'Sir. Your company is much desired by Mr. Squib, Mr. Radford' – the Trinity friend who had courageously kept him company when he had smallpox – 'and others between 12 and one. If you enquire at Mr. Dalby's (a fishmonger at the hither end of old Fish St) by him you will find us.' One would imagine there were many more invitations of this sort, not preserved because they were not used as scrap paper for Aubrey's notes. Those on the back of Yates's invitation were dated 'June, 1655' and were queries for Dr Harvey who by now was Aubrey's physician –

> If Epshom or Tunbridge Water be good for me
> This Spring felt a touch once or twice of the catchy pains in my thigh.
> If whey be good for me in the spring time
> The reason why in fainting fits people do recover lying on their faces.¹⁰

Clearly even at this early age, twenty-nine, Aubrey was something of a valetudinarian, but also, as the last entry shows, impersonally and intently interested in the oddities of human behaviour.

Harvey by this time was much more to Aubrey than simply his doctor. Despite the disparity in age – Harvey was old enough to be Aubrey's grandfather – they had become close friends, Aubrey recognizing as he always did true distinction and rewarding it with his regard and interest, as he did with Hobbes, Petty, and Francis Potter among others. Harvey on his side too may have been glad not only of Aubrey's custom but his company, for despite his fame as the discoverer of the circulation of the blood, in these, which were to prove his last, years both his position and his practice had deteriorated. This was partly because as the Royal doctor he was now out of favour with the authorities, and partly because, perversely, his patients were wary of his fame. Aubrey 'heard him say that after his Booke of the Circulation of the Blood came out he fell mightily in his Practice, and that 'twas befeered by the vulgar that he was crackbrained'.

Aubrey first saw Harvey 'at Oxford, 1642, after Edgehill fight, but I was then too young to be acquainted with so great a doctor'. It was not until 1651 that Aubrey became 'acquainted with him being my she coz. Montague's pysician and friend'. At that time, Aubrey was preparing for his abortive trip to Italy and Harvey being 'very communicative and willing to instruct any that were modest and respectful to him. And in order to my journey dictated to me what to see, what company to keepe, what books to read, how to manage my studies: in short he bid me goe to the fountain head and read Aristotle, Cicero, Avicenna and did call the neoteriques shitt-breeches'. Aubrey gives a good description of Harvey's appearance: 'he was not tall; but of the lowest stature, round face, olivaster complexion like manuscript, Eie little, round, very Black, full of spirit. His haire was black as a Raven, but quite white 20 yeares before he dyed.' In his youth, Harvey had been an angry young man: 'He was as all the rest of the Brothers very cholerique and in his younger days wore a dagger (as the fashion then was – nay I remember my old schoolmaster Mr. Latimer wore a Dudgeon [a wooden shafted dagger] as my old grandfather Lyte and Alderman Whitson of Bristowe [Aubrey's step-grandfather]). This Dr. would be apt to draw out his dagger upon every slight occasion.'

After the war, Harvey – whom the King had made Warden of Merton as a reward for his services, but who had had it taken away from him before he was able to 'receive or enjoy any benefit by it' – moved to London and lived with his brother Eliab, a rich merchant, in Cockaine House. Aubrey dates his account by adding 'now (1680) the Excise Office . . . a noble house where the Doctor was wont to contemplate on the leads of the house and had his several stations in regard of the sun and the wind: he did delight to be in the darke and told me he could then best contemplate. He had a house heretofore at Combe in Surrey . . . where he had caves made in the earth in which in summer time he delighted to meditate'. Fortunately for Aubrey, there were meditating apartments within Cockaine House as well as the various 'stations on the roof' where Harvey also took himself to ease his gout. He would sit 'with his legs bare if it were frost, putt them into a payle of water, till he was almost dead with cold, and betake himselfe to his stove, and so 'twas gone'. There he made Aubrey 'sitt by him 2 or 3 hours together discoursing'. Aubrey remembered that 'he kept a pretty young wench to waite on him, whom I guessed he made use of for warmth-sake, as King David did and took care of her in his will.'

Sadly their friendship was a short one as Harvey was to die only six years after he and Aubrey first became acquainted 'at my she coz. Montagues', but even in that time it seems to have become both firm and warm. Aubrey was one of Harvey's coffin-bearers – 'I helpt carry him into the Vault.'[11] One feels that Aubrey's attitude to the truly great men of his time, of whom Harvey was undoubtedly one, was similar to that in which he approached Avebury, or one of the beautiful north Wiltshire houses which he was to describe in his *North Wiltshire Collections*. He was intent on recording as much as he could, the apparently trivial as well as the obviously important, and by so doing hoping to outwit the erosion of time.

In 1651, the year in which he first became acquainted with Harvey, Aubrey had also started an unusual but, as it was to prove, influential friendship with Samuel Hartlib, the Protestant philosopher who was by origin a Polish Prussian, in other words a Prussian who came from the part of Poland then occupied by Prussia. His father was a wealthy merchant living at Elbing on the Baltic coast, who had sent him to study at Cambridge, where he had become an ardent Baconian. Returning to Elbing at the end of his studies, he left it after the Catholic invasion of 1628, and thereafter made England his home. The core of his belief, and his life's work which he based on that belief, was the spread of knowledge. Within the ideological framework of a Protestant society, he considered that this could be the panacea for all ills. In particular he was concerned with the improvement of education and husbandry. This appealed to the English landed gentry, disenchanted in the pre-war years by the increasing centralization of their lives, to the extent that the Long Parliament in 1641 granted Hartlib a pension. His influence quickly grew, greatly aided by his close association with another central European figure, Jan Comenius, the last of the Moravian Bishops, who had also fled before the conquering Catholic forces, but who had found not only sanctuary on the estate of a Polish nobleman at Leszno but also the works of Bacon, by which he too was immediately conquered. In the following years, still at Leszno, he wrote works on education based on Bacon's ideas but to which he gave his own mystical slant. These were pirated and printed in England, where they were read by Hartlib who, recognizing not only a kindred spirit but a useful ally, wrote to Comenius and became what amounted to his English agent, arranging and paying for the printing of his subsequent works. These had such success that the triumvirate of Hartlib, Comenius and the son of an exiled Scottish minister, John Dury, who also came from Elbing, became what Professor Trevor-Roper calls 'the intellectual cement of the English country party'. Their supporters were widespread and included Pembroke, Petty and Pym.

'By command of Parliament' Dury and Comenius were invited to England. Comenius came in October 1641, leaving behind the community of Pansophists – as his followers were then called – he had founded in Leszno, and having so terrible a sea journey that once he was safely back in Leszno he refused ever to repeat it. He stayed in England until the following summer, by which time the outbreak of war had ended the chance of a widespreading reform of the education and social system, emanating from a central college of knowledge. However, they were to get a second chance under the Commonwealth. Cromwell himself, very much in earlier days a member of 'the country party', came back to these three foreign philosophers for his political inspiration. Hartlib became a close adviser and saw some of his ideas implemented in Cromwell's reforms, of which the most notable was the establishment of a new college at Durham, although nothing approaching the Utopian clean sweep he had wished and worked for. Comenius, who had become once again a refugee when Catholic forces razed Leszno to the ground, was invited to bring the whole of his community and set it up in Cromwell's newly conquered Ireland. But by the time Cromwell's invitation reached him, Comenius had found a much more comfortable refuge under the protection and in the home of the Amsterdam industrialist Louis de Geer and his son Laurence. The de Geers controlled the whole of the Swedish copper and iron industries, and from there supplied the armies and fleets of most European countries. Possibly the idea of another rough crossing, and an even rougher life in Ireland at the end of it, did not appeal either. So Comenius made a sensible but possibly cowardly refusal to Cromwell's offer.[12]

Aubrey probably first met Hartlib in 1651 through the agency of either Robert Boyle, Petty or Wren, all of whom were strong supporters of these foreign philosophers. The design of a house for Hartlib in London was the first of Wren's architectural commissions. Aubrey's friendship with Hartlib was never to acquire the warmth of that with Harvey, but even so they were soon writing to each other. A surviving letter from Hartlib, written from 'my house near Charing Cross, over against Angel Court', on 16 March 1652, was clearly in reply to one from Aubrey asking, as he had of Harvey, for advice about his projected tour abroad. He had also, as he seems to have done whenever he had the opportunity, been putting forward Francis Potter's claims to fame and to help, for Hartlib replies rather pompously by assuring Aubrey, 'I shall very heartily join with you, in all your wishes, prayers and endeavours for the advancement of sciences, so called.'[13] Hartlib admired Aubrey's wit, and his enthusiastic support of new ideas. Aubrey was too young to have seen Comenius during his stay in England over the winter of 1641–42, but he was undoubtedly a student and supporter of his work, for in the will that he made in 1653 in preparation for his Grand Tour that never came off, he took the trouble to itemize his 'Comenius' which he left to his closest friend Anthony Ettrick.

The Restoration, of course, ended the influence of Hartlib and his friends. Most of the Cromwellian creations and reforms which had owed something to their ideas were quickly renounced and reversed. Hartlib himself died in 1662, the year in which the Royal Society received its royal charter. Comenius was later to claim that the Royal Society was the materialization of 'the invisible college' which he and his co-believers had earlier formed. In fact it was a much more strictly scientific society and for its intellectual origins went directly back to the ideas of Bacon, missing out the curious detour round which Hartlib and Comenius had led their followers. Yet on the minds of the distinguished members of the Royal Society who had followed this route – Boyle, Wren, Wilkins among others – the experience would have left its mark. In this lay the real achievement of this benevolent but hopelessly Utopian movement. Aubrey's participation in it had one long-lasting effect on him. It encouraged and widened his interest in education which led, with other more personal motives, to the writing of his own *Idea* some twenty-five years later. It is in a letter from Samuel Hartlib, not to Aubrey but to Dr John Worthington, Master of Jesus College, Cambridge, that one learns that in 1655 Aubrey had plans to write a life of Bacon – the first sign he had shown of any literary ambition or aspiration. It was also about this time that he started taking notes on his journeys between Broadchalke and Easton Piers. The two together seem to show that his interests and inclinations were converging to point the way he should go if he sought to find self-expression and satisfaction.

In the following year, 1656 (he puts the date in the text) Aubrey paid a visit to Bacon's two houses, Verulam and Gorhambury, which stood within a mile of each other close to St Albans. In so doing he was following a method of which his subject would have entirely approved, and of which he had adopted the precept: that whenever possible one should think and look for oneself.

Gorhambury, which Aubrey describes as a 'large, well-built Gothique house', had been built by Bacon's father, and came to him via his childless elder brother Anthony, but Bacon had built Verulam House himself.

It was in fact part of a larger ambition which, however, even Bacon's excessive and needless extravagance could not achieve, to rebuild the ancient Roman town of Verulam in the centre of whose site his house stood. Aubrey's description of both houses is clearly based on careful observation and examination. But over Verulam House he was to regret he had not taken even more trouble. In the building of it Bacon's architectural assistant had been 'Mr. Dobson . . . a very ingeniose person but in spending his estate upon woeman, necessity forced his son Will Dobson to be the most excellent Painter that England hath yet bred. The howse did cost nine or ten thousand the building and was sold about 1665 or 1666 . . . to two carpenters for fower hundred pounds . . . I am sorry I measured not the front and breadth; but I little suspected it would be pulled downe for the sake of the Materials'. Even so, it is only due to Aubrey that we know that the rooms were 'very loftie and very well wainscotted'; that there was 'a delicate Staire-case of wood which was curiously carved, and on the posts of every interstice was some prettie figure, as of a grave Divine with his booke and spectacles, a Mendicant Friar, etc, not one thing twice'; that 'from the Leads was a lovely Prospect to the Ponds . . . also over that Long Walke of Trees, whose topps afford a most pleasant variegated verdure, resembling the works in Irish stitch'; and that 'on the dores of the upper storie on the outside (which were painted darke Umber) were the figures of the gods . . . larger than the life, and donne by an excellent hand; the heightnings were of hatchings of gold, which when the Sun shone on them made a most glorious shew.' On the back panel of one of the doors on the top floor, was a trick mirror, which caught the reflection coming through the house to simulate the view out of a window. According to Aubrey, Verulam House was 'his Lordship's Summer-house' – Gorhambury presumably being his winter one – 'for he sayes (in his essay) one should have seates for Summer and Winter as well as Cloathes'. The unexpected destruction of such a relatively new house must have shocked Aubrey and strengthened his resolve to record what he could, while he could.

Aubrey himself, of course, had no first-hand remembrance or recollection of Bacon, who died in the year in which Aubrey was born, but he had two first-class second-hand sources of information – Harvey and Hobbes. William Harvey told him that Bacon had 'a delicate, lively hazel Eie . . . like the Eie of a viper'. Thomas Hobbes, according to Aubrey, 'was beloved by his Lordship, who was wont to have him walke with him in his delicate groves where he did meditate: and when a notion darted into his mind, Mr. Hobbs was presently to write it downe, and his Lordship was wont to say that he did it

Easton Piers, Aubrey's birthplace and inheritance in north Wiltshire.

Kington St. Michael Church, with spire and manor house which no longer
exist. From the *North Wiltshire Collections.*

Aubrey's drawing of St. Mary's, a hundred yards from his birthplace at Easton Piers. From the *North Wiltshire Collections.*

better than anyone else around him: for that many times, when he read their notes he scarce understood what they writt, because they understood it not clearly themselves'. It was also Hobbes who told Aubrey the curious cause and manner of Bacon's death. 'He was taiking the aire in a coach with Dr. Witherborne, (a Scotsman, Physitian to the King) towards High-gate, snow lay on the ground, and it came into my Lords thoughts, why flesh might not be preserved in snow, as in Salt. They were resolved they would try the Experiment presently. They alighted out of the Coach and went into a poore woman's house at the bottom of Highgate hill, and bought a Hen, and made the woman extenuate it, and then stuffed the body with snow, and my Lord did help to do it himself. The snow so chilled him that he immediately fell extremely ill . . . in 2 or 3 days as I remember Mr. Hobbes told me he dyed of suffocation.' In fact, by Hobbes's and Aubrey's account it was surprising that something of the sort had not happened to Bacon before. For 'in April and in the Springtime his Lordship would, when it rayned, take his Coach (open) to receive the benefit of Irrigation, which he was wont to say was very wholesome because of the Nitre in the Aire.'[14]

Back at Broadchalke, enjoying what one hopes was the peace of the countryside but which because of the pressure of business – in a later letter to Wood he was to write 'never was man so plagued with an Estate' – may well have been less peaceful than his apparently highly occupied London life, he must have much mourned and missed the presence of his near neighbour and 'honoured friend', his companion on the Avebury hunt, Colonel John Penruddock. In 1655 Penruddock had been executed for his part in the Royalist rising, which briefly occupied Salisbury, a rising which at first burnt with the brilliant flame of kindling wood, but then quickly died away for lack of the solid fuel of general support. Penruddock seems to have been the victim of his virtues, for the West Country rising was intended to be but one of six regional uprisings which were to erupt simultaneously throughout the country. But he was the only leader who, when it came to the point and the day, had the courage and the loyalty to risk, and lose, his head. It was a tragedy of mistiming. For had Penruddock but waited a few years he would in all probability have been among those watching the chain of bonfires which spread like wildfire – from 'Salisbury to Chalke where they made a great Bonfire on the top of the hill; from home to Blandford and Shaftesbury and so to the Lands End'[15] – in celebration of the return of the King. So, once again as he had several times during the Civil War, Aubrey avoided involvement in fighting which took place dangerously close to his home. One wonders whether he thanked his stars that he had been 'inclined by my Genius from childhood to the love of Antiquities' and other peaceable pursuits rather than being a man of action and adventure, such as

Penruddock undoubtedly was. In those days it was undoubtedly safer to be a scholar rather than a soldier.

But some scholars suffered, if in a different and less drastic way. A sequence of letters from Francis Potter covers this period, mainly thanking Aubrey for the gift or loan of books. At this time, Francis Potter had his elder brother Hannibal, the deposed President of Trinity, living with him. But the two brothers clearly got on each other's nerves as is evident from letters which both of them wrote to Aubrey within the space of a few days in May 1653. Francis Potter wrote first on the 23rd, 'Thanks for more books – which I would have sent [back] earlier had I not bin continually vexed . . . with bitter and sharpe contentions in my owne house between my brother and myselfe. It hath bin my hard fortune, not only to impoverish my selfe to do others good, but to be deeply upbraided for covetousness by him who spends more of my money than I do myselfe.'[16] This was followed (one would think by the next post, for although it is dated three days later, deliveries in those days can hardly have been daily) by a riposte from Hannibal Potter, who obviously saw or knew that his brother was writing to Aubrey, and guessed the contents of his letter: 'I have another request to you concerning my brother. You do often commend him too highly to his face . . . you cannot go a speedier way to ruine him. He hath a wonderful opinion of himself . . . The scripture doth not speake in vaine – Let he be proud fall in condemnation. I consider him to be erroneous in many of his notions, not to say ridiculous. Concerning myselfe, I am (as I have been for a long time) in a sad rage, my life passeth and I can do no good for want of employment – my books, which were my comforts, kept from me for debts, and like to be sold for half their worth . . . no man will stir for me. What to do I know not, God help me, and us all in this woefull time. I am, Sir, your poor ffriend, Hannibal Potter.'[17] It was an obvious cry for help but one which the generally generous and responsive Aubrey did not answer. Maybe he remembered the formidable President who, when his students came to take their leave of him to go to the Inns of Court, 'used to beat them with his sword scabbard, as I well know'. Hannibal Potter was eventually to get his Presidency back at the Restoration, and to live 'to enjoy its benefits' for a further four years. But it must have been a long wait – for both brothers.

*   *   *

Aubrey had a great admiration for Inigo Jones, whom he met at Wilton. Inigo Jones had a long association with the Pembroke family, dating back to William, the third Earl, his contemporary, with whom, and at whose expense, he travelled widely in Europe as a young man. He thereby extended not only the range of his knowledge but the range of his contacts also, being subsequently commissioned by continental courts as well as the English one.

Throughout the rest of his life he was the architectural and artistic adviser at Wilton. Although he was not personally in charge either of the extensive additions, instigated by Philip, the fourth Earl, in the 1630s, because he was busy building the Queen's House at Greenwich for Charles I, nor of the rebuilding after the fire, because he was then too old, he was the overseer of both works and responsible for much of their design.

Inigo Jones seems to have had, like Aubrey, a keen sense of the tragic inpermanence of buildings, even of substantial ones such as castles. He regretted, as Aubrey did, that in so many cases they disappeared without record and he did his best, like Aubrey, to rescue what he could from oblivion. 'Mr. Inigo Jones (Architect to King James and to King Charles I) was wont to waite upon their Majesties, when they went their Progress. He designed admirably well, and in these Progresses he drew a great many Prospects of the old Gothick or eminent Castles in sheets of paper.' In 1656, four years after the death of Inigo Jones, Aubrey found time in what must have been a very busy year – what with Mary Wiseman, the entail, and all his other occupations and preoccupations – to visit 'the Mannour of Burley, near Glastonbury (once belonging to it but very unfortunate to the late possessors)' which Inigo Jones had bought, and then bought back with a fine when his estates were confiscated at the end of the Civil War. There 'in a large Parlour I saw the Draughts of those Castles; they did furnish the Roome round; one of them was fallen downe and in a childs hands, which I rescued and hung it up myselfe.' Remembering and recording the visit some thirty years later in *Monumenta Britannica*, Aubrey added sadly 'Of these once stately Castles there is not now a stone left upon a stone except that of Windsore.'[18] 'Not a stone left upon a stone' – Aubrey's telling phrase shows how needed were the efforts of those like Inigo Jones and himself to record what was there, while it was.

The year before Aubrey's visit to the manor at Burley, the notes on Stonehenge which Inigo Jones had made as a result of various visits, were posthumously published under the title *Stonehenge Restored*, having been collated and edited by his son-in-law John Webb, who had also dealt with the repairs and rebuilding at Wilton after the fire. It was this book which rekindled Aubrey's interest in Avebury, which he was able to follow up with individual visits in the course of his hawking and hunting trips with his friend James Long. It may also have been the spur which pricked him into making the visit to Burley, wondering what had happened to the drawings of castles which he knew Inigo Jones had made. It was not, however, until the September following the momentous royal visit to Avebury in 1663 that Aubrey 'surveyed that old Monument of Aubury with a plain table and afterwards took a Review of Stonehenge' – which led him to conclusions quite different from those of Inigo Jones – and which were to show him at his innovative best.

The stones at Stonehenge Aubrey believed to have had the same origin as those at Avebury. 'They are certainly the Stones of the Gray Weathers distant from here not above fourteen miles where there are thousands of such stones to be drawn out of the earth.'[19] Like the stones at Avebury Aubrey believed those at Stonehenge to be the remains of 'Temples of the Druids'. In the course of his examination of Stonehenge Aubrey also came across a circle of fifty-six holes on the inner side of the main bank, in which subsequent investigations have found fragments of cremated human remains. They are still known as the Aubrey holes. This important find, coupled with his rediscovery of Avebury completed an impressive archaeological achievement which by itself should ensure that Aubrey's fame is enduring.

Around Broadchalke itself, Aubrey never seems to have made the most of what a glance at the map suggests might have been an area rich in rewards for both archaeologist and historian. Every down or rise seems to have its tumulus, and often an 'earthworks' upon it. Part of what had been the Roman road from Old Salisbury to Dorchester crossed the far end of what was Aubrey's farm. So too does Grims Ditch. Nearer at hand an ancient drovers' way called Ox Drove, connecting Salisbury and Shaftesbury, known to have been in use in the eleventh century, and still well used in the nineteenth, crosses Knowle Hill. Close to where it does, the site of a settlement has been found, since Aubrey's time, thought to date back to the Iron Age. On Marleycombe Hill, next to Knowle Hill and probably at that time part of Aubrey's farm, stands a group of barrows. Little over a mile to the west on Woodminton Down fifty burials of the late Bronze Age have been identified. In front of Manor Farm itself in Bury Orchard, which Aubrey thought probably rightly to have been of Roman origin, but probably wrongly to have been some sort of swimming-pool, remains of a pagan cemetery have been found. There can be no doubt that it was, and is, an area of intense interest to the archaeologist and historian – and so one would have thought to Aubrey.

Yet, apart from the mention of Bury Orchard, which Aubrey could hardly have missed since it was opposite his front door, very little in the area seems to have interested him enough to find a place in *Monumenta Britannica*. If it does it is generally given little more than its geographical location – 'In the Parish of Broad-chalke in the county of Wilts, upon the North Downe is a Campe called Chiselbury; it is situated on the brow of the hill near the Rode from Salisbury to Shaftesbury; not far from the Start.'[20] The 'Start', of course, was the start of the race for the Salisbury Bell. Almost as an afterthought and in a tone of some disinterest, Aubrey adds 'it seemes to be a Danish fortification.' Chiselbury Camp was on the northern boundary of his farm. On the southern edge 'near Vernditch in the Tenants-downe is an old Work; which see'. But did he? It might well have been the site of the Iron Age settlement, which was later identified in that area. In the one lengthy entry 'on the south downe of the farme of Broad-chalke, on the top of the plaine is a little Barrow (not very high) called by the name of Gawen's Barrow', Aubrey seems more interested in Gawen than his barrow, suggesting that the family might descend from the Knight of the Round Table of that name. He tells us also that in his time '1648, this family (old John Gawen, Esq) had in Wiltshire and Somersetshire £1800 per annum'.[21] He also digressed even further to tell us about the Abbess of Wilton keeping her own flock of sheep on part of the farm, and that he in his time and tenure found that sheep paid much better than corn. Does this suggest that Aubrey was really more of a historian than an archaeologist, that except when he was dealing with a subject as immensely important as Avebury or Stonehenge, when the excitement of discovery overcame all other feelings or inclinations, he was basically interested in people, and buildings lived in by people, works put up by people, rather than simply the tombs in which they were buried?

Aubrey's own very proper feelings of respect towards the dead may also have hampered him, for in the next entry to that on Gawen's Barrow, he writes 'I never was so sacrelegious as to disturbe or rob the urne; Let his Ashes rest in peace – but I have oftentimes wisht, that my Corps might be interred by it: but the Lawes Ecclesiastick denie it. Our bones, in Consecrated ground, never lie quiet; and in London once in ten years (or thereabout) the Earth is carried to the Dung-Wharfe.'[22] It is a macabre entry, but one which links with later entries at the time of the excavation of St Paul's graveyard after the Great Fire. Did Aubrey see and fear impermanence – even in death?

The Restoration and
the North Wiltshire Collections
1659–60

The end of 1657 must have been a sad time for Aubrey. Katherine Ryves, 'with whom I was to marry', died in November, Aubrey thereby losing not only the possibility of finding just the sort of 'discrete' wife he wanted, but also his best chance of securing and steadying his already shaky finances. A month earlier, John Lydall's 'crazy and sickly constitution of body' had given up its struggle for survival. Lydall's death was mourned deeply by Aubrey, but it was a greater loss to Trinity for he had proved himself an exceptionally gifted tutor and a very well-loved Fellow. Ralph Bathurst, acting in his role as Trinity Librarian, used a bequest from Lydall, for which his name was added to the list of College benefactors, as a pretext for eulogizing his lost colleague, commending his integrity, his tutorial ability and his experimental work in anatomy, botany and chemistry. He was missed throughout Oxford, and even the usually disparaging Anthony Wood paid for once generous tribute: 'He was an ingenious man, an excellent philosopher, a great tutor, and might have honoured the world with his learning had his life been longer spared.'[1]

It may in part have been because of Lydall's absence that Aubrey's visits to Oxford over the next few years seem to have become less frequent. But a more probable reason was that the centre of intellectual gravity was over these years moving to London; the centre of hilarity also, for the habit of 'coffee-housing', which had started in Oxford, was also to spread there during these years. Some of the members of the 'Club', of which Aubrey was so pleased and proud to be a member, would have said it was a move back. For it was a disputed point where it had all started. There had been meetings of intellectually inquisitive men in London from as early as 1645, whereas the group of like-minded men in Oxford, originally meeting, according to the first historian of the Royal Society, Thomas Sprat, for 'the satisfaction of breathing a freer air, and of conversing in quiet with one another',[2] had started doing so a year or two later and only formed itself into a club in 1649. Yet it was from the Oxford group that most of those who were particularly to distinguish themselves in later life were to come. In reality, both groups were the product of a happy combination of a freer intellectual climate with an exceptionally gifted crop of intelligent men.

There was much movement, too, between the groups. John Wallis, one of the earliest members of the group who met weekly in London, became in 1649 Savilian Professor of Geometry in Oxford, where he became a leading member of the club there. Thus at different times Wallis was a member of both groups. He has left an account which shows something of the proceedings in both places and how gradually they merged into the nucleus of what was to become the Royal Society. 'Early attendants [in London] included Dr. Wilkins, Sir George Ent, and Dr. Goddard.'[3] Dr Wilkins was Cromwell's brother-in-law. During the period 1648–59, when he was Warden of Wadham, he is considered by Professor Trevor-Roper to have been 'effective ruler of Oxford University'. According to Aubrey, who wrote his 'Life', he was the son of a goldsmith in Oxford, and 'was no great read man but one of much and deepe-thinking and of a working head'.[4] Sir George Ent, a distinguished physician, later to be President of the College of Physicians, was for long a close friend of Aubrey's. Dr Goddard was Cromwell's physician-in-chief, and accompanied him on his campaigns in Scotland. Aubrey tells us in his 'Life' of Goddard, that Cromwell, in Scotland, became 'dangerously ill of a kind of high fever which made him mad . . . he pistolled one or two of his commanders that came to visit him'.[5] Goddard subsequently became Warden of Merton, and was 'a Fellow of the Royal Society and a zealous member for the improvement of medical knowledge amongst them. They made him Drudge for when any curious taske was to be donne they would lay the Taske on him. He loved wine . . . [Aubrey inserts above "most hospitable"] but dranke not to excesse'.[5]

These three men, Wallis goes on, 'with myself met weekly – sometimes at Dr. Goddard's lodgings, sometimes at the Mitre in Wood St – we made a weekly contribution for the charge of experiments . . . we barred all Discourse of Divinity, of State Affairs and of News, confining ourselves to Philosophical Enquiries. These meetings we removed soon after to the Bull's Head in Cheapside and in Term time to Gresham College. About the years 1648, 1649 some of our company were removed to Oxford (first Dr. Wilkins, then I and soon after Dr. Goddard); whereupon our company divided. Those at London (and we, when we had occasions to be there) met as before. Those of us at Oxford with Dr. Ward, Dr. Petty, Dr. Bathurst, Dr. Willis, and many others of the most inquisitive persons in Oxford, met weekly (for some years) at Dr. Petty's lodgings (so long as Dr. Petty continued in Oxford and for some while after because of the Convenience we had there – to view, and make use of, Drugs and other like matters). Our meetings there were very numerous and very considerable. We did afterwards (Dr. Petty being gone for Ireland and our numbers growing less) meet at Dr. Wilkins Lodgings in Wadham. Eventually these set meetings ceased in Oxford and were held in London. Where we continued to meet at Gresham College. Being much increased by the accession of divers Eminent Noble Persons upon His Majestie's Return we were about 1662 Incorporated by the name of The Royal Society'.[6] And so the Royal Society, which was to play so important a part in Aubrey's later life, was born.

Gresham College, the first home of the Society, was in its own right and way quite as remarkable as the members who met there. It had been founded as a centre of adult education in the sixteenth century by a wealthy merchant, Sir Thomas Gresham, who had also started the Royal Exchange, from which it was financed. It had no resident students but seven professorial chairs, whose occupants, perforce from Oxford or Cambridge, had to give weekly lectures, on music, geometry, astronomy, divinity, law, rhetoric, and physics. Many of Aubrey's friends held these professorial posts at various times. Wren was Professor of Astronomy from 1657 to 1661, William Petty, Professor of Music from 1650 to 1660, (one wonders how many lectures he in fact gave, for over much of this period he was in Ireland); Lawrence Rooke, at Wadham when Aubrey was at Trinity and a leading member of 'the club', was first Professor of Astronomy from 1652 to 1657, and then of Geometry from 1657 to 1662. Robert Hooke, who came late into Aubrey's life (but he was nine years younger) via a period in Oxford as assistant to Robert Boyle, and who was to prove as inventive and versatile a genius as Wren and Petty, was appointed Curator of Experiments to the Royal Society in the year of its foundation, with the additional role of caretaking the College itself. He was to live there for the rest of his long life, which was to take him into the next century.

The college building had been Gresham's town house, standing on what was then the edge of the city, in Bishopsgate. It was an impressive building with an arcade, standing around a quadrangle with a lawn and trees. By a matter of a few hundred yards it was to escape destruction in the Great Fire of 1666. In the later penurious period of Aubrey's life, Gresham College was to play as important a part as the Royal Society. Together they were to provide the framework and the stimulus for much of his work.

Aubrey's social life in London, over these last years of the Protectorate and the uncertain period of the Interregnum which culminated in the Restoration, seems to have been ever widening. There were not only constant meetings with the Oxford friends who had now come to London but attendance at *salons* such as that of Catherine Ranelagh, a sister of Robert Boyle who had a house in Pall Mall. It may have been here that Aubrey first met John Milton, who lived just across the Park in Petty France. Aubrey's acquaintance – it never developed into a full friendship – with Milton lasted until Milton's death in 1674. It led some ten years later to an informative, much of the information coming from Milton's brother Christopher, and sympathetic 'Life'. From this we learn that his 'harmonicall & ingeniose soul did lodge in a beautifull and well-proportioned body. He was a spare man. He was scarce so tall as I am (quaere, quot fut I am high; resp., of middle stature)' – in which answer Aubrey seems to have been flattering himself, for by all other accounts he was small. 'He had abroune hayre. His complexion exceeding faire . . . His eie a darke grey.' Milton, according to Aubrey, was writing *Paradise Lost* in the period over the Restoration, but only in the winter: 'All the time of writing Paradise Lost, his veine began at the Autumnal Ecquinoctial and ceased at the Vernall or thereabouts (I believe about May) and this was 4 or 5 years of his doeing it. He began about 2 years before the K[ing] came in and finished about three yeares after the K[ings] Restauracion.'[7]

Robert Boyle was one of an immense brood, totalling fifteen. Aubrey clearly found the bevy of sisters, who formed the nucleus of the *salon* in the house in Pall Mall, somewhat formidable, for he queried whether it was lawful to refer to 'the female branches' of the Boyle family 'because their virtues were so masculine, souls knowing no difference of sex'. No doubt intended as a compliment, one wonders whether it was accepted as such. But Catherine Ranelagh herself, although strong and serious minded – typical of the intellectual calibre of her entourage was Peter du Moulin, a French theologian who was also a prebendary at Canterbury – was also charitable, greatly concerned to alleviate in any way she could the sufferings of the sick, and charming. Milton became devoted to her. She was always Robert Boyle's favourite sister. After she became estranged from her husband Boyle, since he had never married, went to live with her. He died a week after she did.

Although such social circles were high enough, Aubrey at times moved in even higher ones. At that particular period there were none higher. For 'in 1657 or 8' Aubrey 'heard Oliver Cromwell, Protector, at dinner at Hampton Court tell the Lord Arundell of Wardour and the Lord Fitzwilliam that he had been in all the counties of England, and that the Devon husbandry was the best', an opinion which Aubrey used in the chapter on Agriculture in his *Natural History* to support his contention that the 'Devonshire men were the earliest improvers'.[8] One does not know whether Cromwell then (just as fifteen years earlier Charles I had in Christ Church) kept not so much open house as open court, or whether Aubrey was himself dining as a guest. One would in fact think the latter. But either way Aubrey was clearly well enough known to be allowed into the immediate presence of the man who at that time ruled England. Another scrap of evidence endorsing Aubrey's movement in high Parliamentary circles at this time comes in the few lines that he wrote about Richard Lovelace in a very brief 'Life'. 'He dyed at Whitehall . . . went out like a spent candle, dyed before Dr. Holder could come to him with the Sacrament.' Aubrey inserts in brackets, 'I was then there.'[9] Lovelace died in 1658.

Such occasions and associations had their political risks in a time that was far from settled and sure. They have since led to Aubrey being condemned by some as a supporter of the Parliamentary regime. David Masson, the biographer of Milton, included him in a list of Parliamentarians in the literary and intellectual world, in the very distinguished company of Milton, Boyle, Dryden, and John Locke, among others. Aubrey was later to inveigh strongly against the Parliamentarians: 'the greatest part of the Parliament-men were cursed tyrants.' One would think the main reason for this untypically violent outburst was to clear his name of any surviving strain of Parliamentary sympathy. In reality Aubrey seems to have been apolitical. 'A pox on all Parties', he was to write in a later letter to Anthony Wood. But since he was an intensely inquisitive and sociable man, interested in all that was going on, whatever it was, and the people who were causing it so to do, whoever they were, it was only natural that he should take advantage of any opportunities or occasions that presented themselves which would enable him to see for himself.

And yet in so doing Aubrey did in fact run very real risks to which he remained dangerously impervious. Had that earlier secret approach to Monck been discovered it was quite possible that Aubrey would have found himself in the Tower along with Mariet and Massey. Again, in the closing months of Parliamentary rule, Aubrey regularly attended meetings of the Rota club. This was a political debating group formed around the person and the ideas of James Harrington, a political theorist whose Utopian and Republican theories were not to the liking of either the Royalists or the Parliamentarians but who personally seemed to be greatly liked by both, particularly by Charles I, who made him a Groom of the Bedchamber. According to Aubrey, 'Mr Harrington and the King often disputed about Government. The King loved his company; only he would not endure to heare of a Commonwealth: and Mr. Harrington passionately loved his Majestie. He was on the Scaffold with the King when he was beheaded.'[10] In the middle of the actual Commonwealth in 1656, Harrington published his *Oceana*, a picture of an ideal Commonwealth in which land and wealth were distributed and limited, and in which Government was by rotation, so that no one person or party could ever hold power for long. Hence the name of the

Rota club, which met from November 1659 onwards 'every night . . . at the Turke's head in the New Pallace Yard, where was made purposely a large ovall-table, with a passage in the middle for Miles to deliver his Coffee. About it sate his Disciples, and the Virtuosi . . . The room was every evening as full as it could be crammed'.[11] Aubrey never became either a 'Disciple' or one of 'the Virtuosi'. He and Anthony Ettrick, who accompanied him throughout, remained simply 'auditors', but as such took part in the ballots by which everything was decided. Aubrey admitted in his 'Life' of Harrington that he found 'the Doctrine very taking, and (as an alternative to the Parliamentary rule) the more because, as to human foresight, there was no possibility of the King's returne' which is interesting since the Restoration was, in fact, but a few months away. Yet, undoubtedly, for Aubrey, the main attraction was the brilliance of the debate: 'The Discourses . . . were the most ingeniose and smart, that ever I heard, or expect to heare, and bandied with great eagernesse. The Arguments in the Parliament house were but flatt to it.'[11]

In retrospect, Aubrey seems to have realized something of the risk he had been running, for he wrote ''twas not fitt, nay Treason, to have donne such', but in fact the incoming Royalist exiles, all too glad to be safely home, proved neither vengeful nor vindictive. Although Harrington was briefly imprisoned, no action was taken against the disciples, the virtuosi, or the auditors. Harrington's period of imprisonment seems to have turned him mildly mad. For he had an obsession that his perspiration turned into flies, or, on occasion, bees. When there were flies in his room 'he would crye out, "Doe not you see it these come from me?" Twas the strangest sort of madness that ever I found in anyone: talke of anything els, his discourse would be very ingeniose and pleasant.' Harrington lived until 1677 in 'Little Ambry (a faire house on the left hand) which lookes into the Deanes-yard in Westminster. In the upper story he had a pretty gallery, which looked into the yard, where he commonly dined, and meditated, and took his Tobacco'.[11]

Aubrey remained a friend, although never a close one, throughout Harrington's life. A letter survives in the Bodleian from Harrington, written on 16 February 1669 getting out of some engagement he had made with Aubrey in the nicest possible, although not at all convincing, way. 'Honoured Sir, It is very much against my nature to fayle in anything that might please a friend to whom I have an hearty affection but something not worth giving account of is nevertheless the reason why I can not waite on you according to my promise on Wed night.'[12] Like so many others, Aubrey seems to have become genuinely fond of Harrington. In the last year of his life when Harrington was losing both his mind and his memory, he found it 'a sad sight to see such a sample of mortality, in one whom I lately knew as a brisque, lively, cavalier.'

Over the midwinter of 1659–60, when Aubrey was attending, and obviously greatly enjoying, the meetings of the Rota, most people in London, even staunch Royalists, would have shared his view that in the foreseeable future 'there was no possibility of the King's returne.' Yet as winter turned to spring, the political climate changed even more dramatically. On 4 April, the King made the Declaration of Breda, and wrote to the Speaker of the House of Commons, protesting his Protestantism and declaring his belief in constitutional partnership between King and Parliament in which each was 'best preserved by preserving the other'. The Declaration of Breda dotted the i's and crossed the t's of the letter to the Speaker, promising no retribution, except against the regicides, and religious liberty; also, not of least importance, that all arrears of army pay would be settled. Taking the letter and the Declaration together there can have been few in England that were not reassured in one way or another. So they were able to give free rein to their feelings that it was time for a change and to their hopes that the return of the monarchy would be a change for the better. On 1 May, the Commons passed a resolution inviting Charles to return to England and the throne. On the 26th, he landed in Dover.

As Aubrey clearly saw – and there was much that at this time he personally saw, for he seems to have been in London throughout the crucial period that led up to the Commons' invitation – the key to the incredibly swift transformation was the presence in London of Monck and his army. Monck had brought his troops down on their famous march from Coldstream in early January, ostensibly at the request of Parliament in order to enforce the disbandment of Lambert's army, but there can be little doubt the personal purpose close-closeted in Monck's mind was to ease the return of the King. But being by nature and experience cautious, he might have taken longer to achieve this purpose had his hand not been forced by the City crowd, tired of Parliamentary rule in general, and in particular of that of the much hated Rump Parliament. According to Aubrey, at that time 'Threadneedle Street was all day long, and late at night crammed with multitudes, crying out 'A Free Parliament, a free Parliament... One evening, he [Monck] coming out on horseback, they were so violent that he was almost afrayd of himselfe, and so, to satisfie them (as they used to doe to importunate children) "Pray be quiet, ye shall have a free Parliament". This about 7 or rather 8, as I remember, at night. Immediately a Loud Holla and shout was given, all the Bells in Citie ringing and the whole Citie looked as if it had been in a flame by the Bonfires, which were prestigiously great and frequent and ran like a Traine over the Citie, and I saw some Balcones that began to be kindled."[13] It was good luck that the Great Fire was not started then rather than six years later, particularly for Charles, for a personal disaster on such a scale might well have distracted people's minds from the political business in hand.

Aubrey seems to have enjoyed to the full the excitement of that moment, the detail of his description showing that like many of the crowd he probably got little if any sleep that night. 'They made little Gibbetts and roasted Rumpes of mutton; nay I sawe some very good Rumpes of Beefe. Healths to the King Charles 2 were drunk in the streets by the Bonfires, even on their knees . . . So that the return of his most gracious Majestie was by the hand of God, but as by this person [Monck] meerly accidental, whatever the pompous history in 8vo. sayes.' However the 'pompous history in 8vo' might in this instance have been right, for if it was certainly fortuitous that the Restoration came when it did, and that Monck's fright at the hands of the crowd precipitated it, yet the ground swell of discontent at Parliamentary rule was such that one can but think the recall of the King was merely a question of time. But it was very much a part of Aubrey's creed that great events can turn on chance circumstances – and who, in general would gainsay that?

Important though the Restoration was for Aubrey – and all other Englishmen – an event of a year earlier was of a much greater personal moment. This was the death of his grandfather Isaac Lyte at the age of eighty-two. As a result of this he became – as he had probably long known he was going to be (three years before his grandfather's death his book-plate had proclaimed 'Sum John Aubrey de Easton Piers 1656') – the owner of Easton Piers. So he became the latest in the long line of Lytes or their descendants who had lived there over the centuries, for some 250 years as tenants, for the last 85 as owners. His was the house which his grandfather had built 'on the brow of the Hill above the brook' when he and his brother had split the estate between them; his the house in which he himself had been born, where he had lived through his childhood, and whose 'prospect is the best between Mars[h]field and Burford'; his a charming and characterful small estate or large farm, whichever one chooses to call it, a happy mixture of south-facing fields and woods, full of 'breakes and good ground objects' that also (if one accepts the figure that he gave as the income he lost when he was forced to sell) produced a very useful £700 a year – '500L + 200L Timber' – enough, one would have thought, to have shored up the tottering edifice of the Aubrey finances. And yet, within twelve years it was all gone – Easton Piers, the Herefordshire properties, the land near Rye – all save Broad-chalke, which happily not being his was not his to lose. Aubrey, the latest in the long line of Lyte descendants to live at Easton Piers was, sadly, also to be the last.

*   *   *

In March 1660,* a year after his grandfather's death and some two months before the return of the King, Aubrey attended a meeting in Devizes, 'a meeting of Gentlemen', i.e. landowners, 'for choosing of Knights for the Shire' – in other words the Members of Parliament. It was an occasion that for Aubrey was to have quite unforeseeable consequences, which were to provide the main thrust of his activity, throughout the years that he owned, and lived at, Easton Piers. On that, as it was to turn out for Aubrey, momentous day in Devizes, once the main business was done, attention turned to other matters of local interest. In the course of the subsequent discussion 'it was wished by some that this County (wherein are many observeable Antiquities) were surveyed in imitation of Mr. Dugdale's Illustration of Warwickshire: but it being too great a taske for one man, Mr. Wm. Yorke (Counsellor of Lawe and a Lover of this kind of Learning) advised to have the Labour divided. He himselfe would undertake the middle Division. I would undertake the North. T. Gore, Esq., Jeffrey Daniel, Esq and Sir Jo. Erneley would be assistants.' One wonders whether it was Aubrey who conceived the idea. He was a friend of William Dugdale, to whom he had sent the drawings of Osney Abbey which, as an undergraduate, he had commissioned from William Dobson. Aubrey goes on: 'Judge Nicholas [who was clearly amongst those present at the meeting] was the greatest Antiquary as to Evidences that this County hath had in memory of man: and had taken Notes in his *Adversaria*, of all the ancient Deedes that came to his hands. Mr. Yorke had taken some memdums in this kind, too.' By the time Aubrey came to write the preface to his *North Wiltshire Collections*, the result of his researches over some ten years, both these men were dead. Aubrey much regretted that these 'Notes' and 'Memdums' 'shoulde fall into the mercilesse hands of woemen and be put under pies'.[14]

The meeting at Devizes took place in a period of particular political uncertainty– after the death of Cromwell and before the Restoration of the King. So it was natural that the 'Gentlemen' should be drawn from both sides of the political divide. Judge Nicholas, for example, was a Commonwealth judge who had come near to being hanged himself when, on circuit in Salisbury in 1655, he was one of two judges caught up in the brief flare-up of the Penruddock rising. Sir John Erneley was an ardent Royalist who

---

*Aubrey himself gives the date of this meeting as March 1659, but according as to whether he was using the old or the new calendar this could mean 1659 or 1660. I incline to the later date mainly for two reasons. If it had been the earlier one it would have been only a month after his grandfather's death. It seems too short a time for Aubrey to have found his feet and his place in local society as the new owner of Easton Piers to warrant his inclusion amongst 'the country gentlemen'. Also the earlier date would have placed the meeting only some seven months after the death of Cromwell, at which time one would have expected its composition to be still predominantly Parliamentarian.

eventually was to become James II's Chancellor of the Exchequer. In the meantime, in 1672, he had married the widow of Aubrey's close friend Charles Seymour. But whatever their political loyalties and connections those at the meeting who shared Aubrey's antiquarian and archaeological interests and his love of the county in which they all lived must also have shared, if to a lesser extent, the sense of urgency which he felt about the task they had set themselves.

Yet times change quickly. The Restoration was soon to be achieved swiftly and smoothly, in a more peaceable manner than even the most ardent Royalists can ever have hoped for. In its wake the country settled back into its old monarchical ways. In consequence, with the exception of Aubrey, the 'Gentlemen' of Devizes turned their thoughts to tending their estates, or putting their personal affairs in order, setting aside any thought of the Survey and the labour that, obviously, it would have involved. As Aubrey himself put it, 'this good design vanished in fumo Tabaci, (over their tobacco pipes) and was never thought of since.' Except by Aubrey. He was the only one of the Devizes 'Gentlemen' to make any attempt to achieve the task they had set themselves on that March day in 1659 – and a very considerable attempt it was. Looking through the manuscript now one can have no doubt of the time it must have consumed, and the trouble that Aubrey must have taken over it.

So, over the next ten years, Aubrey spent much of the time he was at Easton Piers riding round the villages of north Wiltshire, visiting the churches, noting the monuments and the inscriptions, the coats of arms on the tombs and in the windows, describing any interesting houses, sometimes in detail, when it was a friend's house, which it often was, and he had access; sometimes simply their general appearance, when he had not, pointing out on the way any archaeological or architectural features he came across, and generally relating any items of interest – the character of the countryside, a local custom, an item of history, a piece of gossip – anything that came to his attention or into his mind.

It was a tremendous task for Aubrey to tackle by himself, and the result was in many ways a remarkable achievement. Yet it never reached the audience it deserved, and never has, mainly because of Aubrey's perennial disinclination or inability to shape his notes into some sort of publishable form. So the notes remained notes. The excellent editor that Aubrey eventually found, or rather who found Aubrey, two centuries later – Canon J. E. Jackson – a distinguished antiquarian and scholar, vicar of Leigh Delamere, where Latimer had taught Aubrey, also realized this. He wrote in his introduction that Aubrey's manuscript 'makes no sort of pretension to the dignity of a County History. It is literally nothing more than the rough original notebook of a somewhat miscellaneous Collector'.[15] Yet what a notebook. For in it Aubrey has sought and found expression not only for his scholarly side but for his artistic instincts as well. Most readers would find the preponderance of heraldic items – there are illustrations of over 400 coats of arms, crests, shields, armorial bearings of one sort or another – tedious in the long run, save that the majority of them are not only carefully drawn, but caringly painted. Their bright colours give a gaiety to the pages which lightens the load of the heraldry. Nor was Aubrey concerned only to draw and to paint armorial bearings. Statues on the wall, designs in the windows, brasses on the floor, figures on tombs, sometimes the tombs themselves, are all drawn and sometimes painted. In the text is generally a careful description to accompany and explain them, of which that in North Wraxall Church is typical. Aubrey's drawing shows a knight, totally clad in chainmail, apparently standing on his prostrate lady: 'In the Church, North Aisle, East Windowe, is the picture of a man, head and shoulders mailed. He weares or beares a coate of arms, as also a scutcheon, which is Ermine 2 barres G. He hath a loose flying coate comes below the knee, his legges are mailed and heeles spurred; in his hand he holds a kind of staffe, like a pilgrims, as high as the eare. Underneath his feet lies a lady all along.'[16]

Sometimes Aubrey lets his choice of subject be swayed by personal feeling, as when, in the same church, he remembered Sir William Button, who had brought his pack of hounds to join that of Charles Seymour on the Avebury hunt, and who had built 'a vault in the N. Aisle, where he and his sonnes lie buried. There is no Monument set up for them, but the pennons, which are now dropping; and though nothing of antiquitie, yet for pitie, and for they were my very worthy friends I will here sett them downe'.[17] Aubrey proceeds to describe and draw crests in a row of six Buttons. In general, Aubrey was more concerned with the inside rather than the outside of the churches, although he did a detailed drawing of the tower of Kington St Michael church (but mainly, one would think, to show the cracks which warned of its impending collapse). However, he did several drawings, usually lightly touched up with water-colour, of some of the more important and impressive houses. These, since few of them still stand, are of particular interest, such as those of Draycot and the manor at Kington St Michael. There is also a particularly pleasing prospect of one that, in part, still does – St Mary's Priory.

Aubrey, of course, was mainly writing to record, and without much thought of possible readers. Yet quite clearly he took both pleasure and pride in much of his work. Towards the end of his time at Easton Piers he became disheartened, writing at the end of the preface, 'This searching after Antiquities is a wearisome Taske . . . nobody els hereabouts hardly cares for it, but rather makes a scorn of it'.[18] But this was probably because what he

called his 'worries' were then coming upon him. The apparently unapprecia-
tive attitude of the neighbourhood may, too, simply have been the feeling –
since it was common knowledge that he was in financial straits, because of
various lawsuits in which he was involved – that for his own good it would
have been better had he stayed at home and tried to sort out his own affairs, as
the other landowners did, rather than wandering about the countryside on
this unrewarding and apparently interminable task. Most of the time,
however, the work reflects his endless interest in all that he saw. Yet it is never
a work for the general reader but rather for the particular person who lives or
has lived in Wiltshire, and who taking his home as a central point, can draw a
circle round the immediate neighbourhood and see what comes up in
Aubrey's net. It invariably produces a rich and varied haul.

Take our own house for example – but in the radius round it leaving out
Kington St Michael, which was in fact our parish, but about which, since it
was his too, Aubrey naturally enough wrote a disproportionate amount. Our
small but widespread hamlet Allington – which consists now of little more
than six farms and their cottages but which would have been a more
important entity in Aubrey's day while the manor house, the home of
Charles Seymour, was still standing – surprisingly gets a mention, although
a brief and not very informative one: 'Quaere [ask] J. Milsham, about the
Chapell, or then perhaps Church, where the pidgeon-house stands now,
the pidgeon house being part of it.' This chapel was still standing and in use
during our day, known locally as the Bull Pen since this had been one of its
several uses in the interim. Aubrey also tells us that 'the Manour belonged
to the Monks, at Mounkton Farleigh, given by . . . I guess, Cotel,' for which
he gets rapped over the knuckles by Jackson in his appending footnote: 'A
bad guess. Allington was given by King Stephen to the Nuns of Martigny in
the Valais, and by them transferred, temp Edw. I, to Monkton Farley
Priory.'[19]

Crossing the Bristol Road and carrying on for a mile and a half one comes
to Biddestone, a copybook village with a pond, a wide green, and a semi-
circle of mostly beautiful houses looking on to it. But it is not of these that
Aubrey writes. There is a well here the water whereof is so diuretique that
it makes one urine shortly after the drinking of it. I have known some troubled
by the stone go often for that reason.

         The Virtues attested by the Neighbourhood –
            For the Stone.
            the Spleen
            Fitts of the Mother. The woman of the house was
much troubled by Fitts of the mother . . . found herself much mended. Also
her mother troubled by that infirmity found good by it.' By the sound of it one

would think that 'Fitts of the Mother' was a local name for epilepsy. Showing the proper scientific spirit of the time, Aubrey tested the water: 'I had not time to try it by Evaporation, but by Precipitation it yields a yellowish nitre.'[20] In Chippenham parish, near Sheldon, Aubrey tested the water of 'a spring called Holywell . . . The name of this well made me curious to try it, and by precipitation of one third of a pint of it with a strong Lixivivium in 12 hours space I found a sediment of about the quantity of a small nut shell somewhat turning to yellow, the particles as big as powder of freestone pounded for scowering. By evaporation a pottle [a half-gallon measure] of the said water yielded a sediment of the colour of Cullen earth.'[18] By 'Cullen earth' one would think Aubrey meant the colour of the earth at Colerne, locally pronounced as 'Cullen', an upland parish some two miles nearer Bath. Colerne, besides earth of a remarkable colour, had according to Aubrey, 'a most noble prospect', and on its church 'a stately, high, well-built tower, which, when the bells, which are new cast, ring, shakes much. . . . Colerne down is the place so famous and frequented for stoball playing. The turfe is very fine, and the rock is within an inch and a half of the surface, which gives the ball so quick a rebound'. At this point, rather surprisingly, Jackson inserts into Aubrey's text a description of the 'staff, commonly made of withy about three and a half feet long', with which the ball was hit, which is not in the manuscript. But the description of the 'stoball' definitely is. It was 'about four inches diameter, stuffed very hard with quills, sowed into soale leather and as hard as stone'.[21] In his notes Jackson quotes Strutt, the author of a book called *Sports and Pastimes*, who describes stoball 'as a variety of the game more commonly known as "Goff"'.

Circling north, one passes through Slaughterford where Aubrey had been shocked to find his 'prettie small Church, the most miserably handled ever I saw', by the Puritan purge, but somewhat comforted by the knowledge that 'in the Gravelly stream are excellent trout.'[22] There still are. About a mile north-east of Slaughterford is Yatton Keynell, in whose church Aubrey found a pulpit of stone, 'the most curious carving in our country'. The screen between the church and the chancel was, too, 'of a very curious gothique worke in freestone'.[23] The pulpit had gone by Jackson's time, but the screen was still there to please Pevsner when he inspected it for his *Wiltshire*, as did the greater part of the mainly Perpendicular church, despite 'being drastically restored in 1868'. The soil at Yatton Aubrey found to be 'clay and stony', and as one would expect, the plants were 'sowre . . . Centaury, wood sorrell, etc. Lady's bedstrawe'.[24] On the slopes of West Yatton leading down to the Box Brook Aubrey found 'almost at the lower end of the Conigere [rabbit-warren] the ruine of a Chapell . . . a pleasanter, [more] romancy place I knowe not where to find'.[25] Completing the circle, on the return to our house, from which over the fields it was less than a mile away, was Fowleswick 'an ancient howse with a faire mote about, and with cross-barred windows . . . The retayners here, well-fed and led an idle, lazie life'.[26] In our day Fowleswick still had the semblance of a moat, but few, if any, retainers. It had lost most of its land. The only archaeological feature which Aubrey came across in our area was a barrow at Lanhill at the opposite end of Allington from our house, which he thought to be the tomb of a Danish leader called Hubba. By Jackson's day it had become simply 'a heap of stone about sixty paces in length, covered with turf. For the convenience of obtaining road materials it has been much injured'. In our day it virtually disappeared when it was ploughed up.

Thus our neighbourhood. Those who live in other parts of north Wiltshire will find a circle of similar interest around them. But the real charm of Aubrey's work lies in the combination of his text with his very detailed illustrations and decorations. It is only those who have the chance to penetrate into the altitudinous atmosphere of Duke Humfrey's Library who will realize, as they turn over the pages of the manuscript, that they have before them a small but singular work of art.

Social and intellectual success
1662–5

As soon as Aubrey had realized, in the early months of 1660, that the Restoration was no longer simply a possibility, but a probability, he had written a letter to Hobbes, who had spent the winter of 1659–60 at Chatsworth, 'to advise him of the good news'. In his letter Aubrey 'desired him by all means to be in London by his Arrival'. Both Hobbes and Aubrey had been painted by Samuel Cooper – in Aubrey's opinion 'the Prince of Limners of this last age' – and it occurred to Aubrey that 'knowing . . . his Majesty was a good lover of good painting I must needs assume he could not but see Mr. Cowpers curious pictures, of whose fame he had so much heard abroad . . . and that he would sitt to him for his Picture, at which place he [Hobbes] would have the best opportunity of winning his Majesties grace to him.'

It all turned out much as Aubrey planned, although by chance Hobbes was to have an earlier encounter with the King than that in Cooper's studio. Following Aubrey's advice, Hobbes 'came to London in May following. It happened about 2 or 3 days after his Majesties happy return that he was passing in his coach through the Strand. Mr. Hobbes was standing at Little Salisbury House Gate (where his Lord then lived). The King espied him, putt off his hatt [Aubrey adds 'very kindly' above] and asked him how he did. About a week after he had orall conference with his Majesty and Mr. S. Cowper, where as he sate for his picture, he was diverted by Mr. Hobbes' pleasant discourse. Here his Majesties favours were reintegrated to him, and order was given that he should have free access to his Majestie'.[1] Charles II always seems to have liked Hobbes, who in the early days of his exile had been his tutor, as also that of the future James II, but the publication of *De Cive* and then *Leviathan*, had angered many in court and Catholic circles. Even Charles was momentarily displeased but as Aubrey tells us 'not very long . . . his Majestie had a good opinion of him and said openly that he thought Mr. Hobbes never meant him hurt'.[2] All the same after the Restoration it was vitally important for Hobbes to be openly and quickly reinstated in the King's favour before his many enemies could strike against him. This Aubrey's brilliant stratagem achieved. Thereafter Charles gave Hobbes not only his protection but a pension, and was always glad to see him at court where he 'very much delighted in his witt and smart repartee: the witts at Court were wont to bayte him; he would make his part good and feared none of them. The King would call him the Beare. "Here comes the Beare to be bayted." He was marvellous happy and ready in his replies; and that without rancour (except provoked)'. Aubrey marks this passage with a cross and comments on the opposite page 'This is too low witt to be published.'[3] But, of course, it is not. It is, in fact, the sort of gossipy but relevant story with which others might not have bothered yet which in Aubrey's hands brings the picture to life. Aubrey considered the portrait of Hobbes which Cooper painted before the Restoration to be one of the best pieces he ever did. So too did Charles II who 'on his returne bought [it] of him and conserved as one of the great rarities in his Closet at Whitehall'.[4] Aubrey himself valued greatly the miniature for which he sat to Cooper, and which towards the end of his life he gave to the Ashmolean for safe keeping, only for it very shortly afterwards to be stolen. Perhaps one of these years, or centuries, it will surface again.

The episode of Hobbes's rehabilitation – only one of a series of revealing and interesting incidents strung along the line of their long relationship – shows that Aubrey would do anything in his power to help his friends, particularly those such as Hobbes whose intellectual powers he held in high esteem. Yet as one reads his account one finds oneself thinking that if Aubrey was prepared to spend so much time, trouble and thought helping his friends why was he seemingly never prepared to do anything to help himself? One gets this feeling particularly strongly in the years immediately following his inheritance of Easton Piers. Now, with the cup of his considerable inheritance from his father and his grandfather full to the brim, was surely the moment for Aubrey to make a determined effort to put his affairs in order, to decide what he had to sell, and what he could keep. If he had immediately sold Burleton and Stretford, as in fact he should have done when he first inherited them from his father – and as he was to have to do in a few years' time – he still might have had enough with his new found income from Easton Piers to continue to live there. One can be virtually certain, knowing the character and circumstances of his grandfather, that, unlike his father's estate, Easton Piers was unencumbered. Yet, even if the sale of his Herefordshire properties was not enough to cancel his debt, and Easton Piers had to go as well, surely the money from all three sales would have been more than enough to secure his fortunes at Broadchalke, of which admittedly he was not the owner, but of which the farm was of a size to be both valuable and viable, even to a tenant. Adequately funded, Manor Farm would have provided a secure and pleasant base for the sociable scholarly life that Aubrey obviously wanted to lead. Burleton and Stretford were together to bring him roughly three thousand pounds but Easton Piers would surely have produced much more. At the time of the Stretford sale the Bishop of Hereford, the eventual purchaser, made his offer to Aubrey in a letter which is still in the Bodleian, in which he quoted what one would think was then an accepted formula for evaluation. After what he calls 'diligent enquiry' the Bishop considers 'the uttermost' worth of the property to be 'a hundred pounds per anno' – surely on the low side? But the Bishop gave as his reason the poor state of the property, which may have been so. He then comes to what he calls 'the Sum state of the business . . . 18 years purchase will be in this country the full value, and this I shall give'.[5] If one applies this formula to Easton Piers, where one knows the annual income to have been £500, not counting the timber, then its worth comes out at £9000. Anything approaching this would, of course, have been an immense sum for those days – and surely enough to keep even an Aubrey in comfort for the rest of his days.

However, at this vital moment, Aubrey never seems to have considered any of these options. Instead, he seems simply to have let things drift, while pondering the, at this stage, exciting prospect of his survey of north Wiltshire. This was an ideal occupation for someone of his interests, but surely the worst possible distraction at this particular moment. He also went on holiday for a couple of months, in July and August 1660, with his friend Anthony Ettrick, to Ireland. It can not have been a good moment to visit Ireland, with the memories of Cromwell's conquest and resettlement still fresh and bitter. Even Aubrey's 'singular friend', the resilient and, one would have thought, impenetrably thick-skinned Sir William Petty – intimately concerned, in one way or another, with Ireland from the early fifties onwards – found living there depressing and dispiriting. In a letter to Aubrey he wrote: 'I begin to be afraid of living in a place where we have ten exasperated enemies for one friend.'[6] Aubrey, even on so short a visit, seems to have felt much the same. For in a letter to Hobbes describing his holiday he wrote 'the animosities between the English and Irish are very great and will, ere long, I am confident, break into war.' In general, however, Aubrey seems to have been sympathetic to what he saw as the Irish 'manner of living . . . scorning industry and luxury, contenting themselves only with things necessary'.[7] He and Ettrick mainly amused themselves by drawing sketches of the country-side from horseback 'symbolically' (the best way one would have thought to draw anything from horseback) but had a bad crossing on the way back which prompted an entry in his list of 'Accidents': '1660. July, Aug. I accompanied A. Ettrick into Ireland for a month, and returning, were like to be shipwreckt at Holyhead, but no hurt done.'[8] No doubt at the time it had been an alarming experience but once it was safely over, they were still both young enough – Aubrey was thirty-four, Ettrick four years older – to look back on it, no doubt with amusement, as a great adventure, of which Aubrey in his life was to have few.

At Easton Piers, for the two years following his grandfather's death, Aubrey had the company of his grandmother who, one year younger than her husband, outlived him by two. Probably by then Israel Lyte was too old to be the 'excellent menagere' who kept open house and open table and delighted in so doing but even so he must have greatly mourned his 'dear grandmother' when she, too, died. However, Aubrey still had two of his 'Amici' close at hand, although Charles Seymour not for much longer. When he inherited the title of Lord Seymour of Trowbridge in 1664, he moved from Allington to his father's home, the castle at Marlborough, where he was to die the following year. But James Long was to live at Draycot for the rest of his life, and so to be there throughout, and long after, Aubrey's time at Easton Piers.

Aubrey seems also to have been close friends of the Tyndales who lived on the other side of the brook, in St Mary's Priory, only a matter of a few hundred yards or so distant from Aubrey's house. But the closeness of their friendship may in the main have been due to proximity. Aubrey seems to have genuinely liked the parents, but they were a good generation older than he was. Although in many cases disparity of age seems for Aubrey to have been no barrier to friendship – Thomas Tyndale was approximately of the same age as Hobbes – yet Tyndale seems particularly to have prided himself on his old-fashioned ways, which by itself put a distance between them. Nor had he the mental distinction which so appealed to Aubrey in other elderly friends such as Harvey, Hobbes or Potter. However, both Tyndale and his wife Dorothy were great gossips which not only amused Aubrey but was to give him useful, if sometimes scandalous, material for his 'Lives', some of which he was later to cross out when he found himself in trouble for suggesting to Anthony Wood that Clarendon as Lord Chancellor took bribes when considering the appointment of his judges. However, Aubrey's crossings out are always light, and one can not but feel that if he intended them to prevent or at least deter publication in his lifetime, yet he wanted them to be legible for posterity. One such – Aubrey cites in the margin as his source 'Old Sr. Wr. Long of Draycot and old Mr. Tyndale' – concerned the incestuous relationship between Sir Philip Sidney and his sister Mary, Countess of Pembroke. 'Sir Philip Sydney was much here and there was so great love between him and his faire sister that I have heard old Gentlemen say that they lay together and it was thought that the first Philip Earle of P. was begot by him.' Another later habit after her husband's death of this 'very salacious' countess was to watch her stallions cover their mares in the courtyard below 'and then act the like with *her* stallions. One of her great Gallants was Crooke-backed Cecill, Earl of Salisbury'. Aubrey attempts to balance this very scandalous portrait (as well he might) by writing that 'she was the greatest patronesse of witt and learning of any Lady in her time; she was a great Chymist and spent yearly a great deale in that study.'[9] He also thought she was part author of Sidney's *Arcadia*, and that it was none the worse for that.

However, it was Dorothy Tyndale who told Aubrey of the wayward wife of John Overall, the Dean of St Paul's. Aubrey always had a weakness for truly beautiful women, however wanton, as shows in his portraits of other famous beauties such as Venetia Stanley and Bess Broughton. But he wrote no more charming portrait that that of the Dean's wife, 'who was the greatest Beautie of her time in England . . . She was not more beautiful than she was obligeing and kind, and was so tender-hearted that (truly) she would scarce denie anyone. She had (they told me) the loveliest Eies that were ever seen, but wondrous wanton . . . The good old Deane, notwithstanding he knew well enough he was horned, loved her infinitely: in so much that he wished she should enjoy what she had a mind to . . . Old Mistress Tyndale (who knew her) remembers a song made of her and Sir John [Selby: one of her many lovers] part whereof was this . . .

> The Deane of Paule's did search for his Wife,
> and where d'ye think he found her?
> Ev'n upon Sir John Selby's bed
> as flatte as any flounder.'[10]*

As well as their daughter Frances, the Tyndales had three sons, of whom the eldest, Stafford, could have been Aubrey's contemporary, or even a little older, for his parents had married in 1621. However, from the effusive, supplicatory and very much subordinate tone of his letters to Aubrey, one would think he was in fact some years younger. He and Aubrey seem not to have known each other during Aubrey's childhood years in Easton Piers, which also suggests, since they lived so close to each other, that Stafford Tyndale was that much younger, for a few years makes all the difference at that age but very little later on. Yet clearly they saw a lot of each other – now that Aubrey was once again living at Easton Piers – and not only in Wiltshire but in London also. They might well have gone on a Grand Tour together if

---

*It was also Mrs Tyndale who told Aubrey that her daughter 'Mistress Fr. Tynedale' early in her life had 'voyded a lumbricious biceps', a phrase and an event which at first reading seems beyond imagination or comprehension. However, after recourse to the Oxford dictionary, one finds that 'a lumbricious biceps' proves to be a two-headed worm. Very odd all the same.

Aubrey had accepted the invitation which Stafford Tyndale, who had already started on his travels, sent from Alençon in a letter dated July 24th/Aug 7 59 – 'Allow yourself but two hundred pounds a year and in the company I'll bring you acquainted with you may live and travel like a Prince.' As a bait to induce Aubrey to come Stafford Tyndale held out the prospect of being in Paris at the time when the French King was to bring back his Spanish bride, when they would see 'all the glory of the Spanish and French court . . . which will be a sight for my neighbours eyes and his remarckes'.[11] One wonders why Aubrey did not accept so enticing an invitation, which promised a much more interesting and companionable journey than the solitary and very short-lived one on which he was to set out some five years later. Tyndale's affection and admiration for Aubrey showed clearly at the beginning of the letter when he wrote, 'I can not think myself completely happy without Mr. John Aubrey's company.'[11]

Some ten months later Tyndale, now on his way home, wrote to Aubrey from Angers, very reproachfully (for clearly Aubrey had answered few of his letters): 'If I had less esteem for you I should not make my complaints that you neglect me, nor after so many letters that I have wrote you seek to prise one from your hands with so many entreaties.'[12] However, it had been arranged that Tyndale on his way back should in Paris meet John Hoskyns, Aubrey's Trinity and Middle Temple friend, who was setting forth in his turn on his Grand Tour. One hopes that Hoskyns brought out the long-awaited letter. Aubrey seems to have been a better correspondent to Hoskyns than to Tyndale, perhaps because he liked him more, and Hoskyns's letters from Dijon in September 1660, Rome in December, Venice in July of the following year, then finally on his way back, from Paris in August 1661, were mostly in answer to those from Aubrey. One can see from these two itineraries that these journeys lived up to their name – and were indeed 'Grand Tours'. But they took time, and one is surprised that John Hoskyns, a budding barrister, the son and grandson of lawyers famous in their time, and who was in due course himself to become a Master in Chancery, could spare so large a chunk out of his life. With Tyndale, who seems to have aspired to nothing more than becoming a country gentleman like his father, and in the meantime to enjoy himself in London, often with Aubrey, it seems less surprising.

At home, seeing much of each other, there was little need of letters between Aubrey and Tyndale, but occasionally like ships in the night they seem to have passed close-by without seeing each other. One such near-miss prompted a letter of 21 August 1661, from Tyndale – still, needless to say, reproachful – which interestingly reveals several aspects of Aubrey's less well-known London life. Clearly, as well as the men of letters, and the men of eminence in the Royal Society, Aubrey frequented the society of the better known artists of the time. Samuel Cooper's studio seems to have been the centre of this circle. In this letter, Tyndale writes 'Alexander the Pictor [this was probably Alexander the elder brother of Samuel Cooper] is now dying. You may be sure the Club is spoiled by it.'[13] So evidently attendance by Tyndale and Aubrey, among others, was so regular that this circle had assumed the shape of a club. Aubrey was evidently feeling foot-loose at this moment for he was contemplating joining Jean-Baptiste Caspars, sometime assistant to Lely and Kneller and a well-known portraitist in his own right, who was planning a visit to the Low Countries, or William Faithorne, who was thinking of going to Paris. Faithorne was the best-known engraver of the time, generally of the portraits of leading artists such as Van Dyke, Lely or Dobson, but sometimes of his own carefully executed drawings. Aubrey was to sit to him five years later, when he was seeking a portrait that he could use as a frontispiece to *Monumenta Britannica*.

Aubrey had also, according to Tyndale, been thinking of asking for inclusion in the entourage of Sir Richard Fanshawe, the courtier poet, then English Ambassador to Portugal, who was shortly embarking on a mission to woo Catherine of Braganza for his royal master. Tyndale, when he wrote to Aubrey, clearly thought he was already too late for inclusion on what surely would have been a fascinating journey and experience – for 'some vessels are gone already to Portugal . . . if you intend that journey you must hasten.' So it must have proved, for Aubrey did not go on it. From Tyndale's letter one learns that Aubrey not only liked looking at pictures, he enjoyed buying them as well. He had evidently commissioned a portrait of Hobbes which Caspars was slow in executing, for Tyndale adds as a postscript to his letter 'I have been urgent with Mr Caspar, but Mr. Hobs his picture is not yet done.' Aubrey had also evidently fancied 'a couple of Landskips' but 'Mr. Anderson' – one would think a dealer – 'not imagining you would come to his price . . . put them off to the next commer.' As well as all this, Tyndale in this interesting letter – although possibly more to us than to Aubrey – gives us a piece of more intimate information: 'I saw your mistress the other day in the Street so that I can tell you that she is well, though I spake not to her. She simpered . . . and I must tell you (to her advantage) that I esteem her prettier than she was in Spring garden or at Cowpers.'[13] So probably, Aubrey's simpering mistress was also a habituée of the Cooper circle. In the next letter, dated 15 May 1662, from Tyndale in London, 'where we are not able to live without your company', Aubrey's 'Queen' had been very ill. As also had been 'our good friend Mr. Hoskins – sadly vexed with a violent and almost continual fever'. This was probably not Aubrey's Trinity friend, but a more elderly John Hoskins, the leading miniaturist of the period preceding the

Civil War, and the uncle and teacher of both the Coopers. This time Tyndale, who obviously had a taste for the pageantry of state occasions, tried to lure Aubrey to London with the promise of Royal festivity, just as he had three years earlier when to entice Aubrey to join him on his Grand Tour he had dangled the carrot of seeing the French king bring his Infanta bride back to Paris. This time it was the prospect of seeing the arrival 'which cannot now pass many days' of Charles II's bride, Catherine of Braganza – 'the last fine sight that is liable to happen in yours and my time'.[14]

Tyndale always ends his letters to Aubrey when he is writing to him at Easton Piers with a request to be remembered to 'all our good friends, of Easton and Keinton'. It is pleasant to think of Aubrey over these years as a liked and respected member of this quiet country society. It makes a comforting counterbalance to his London life which with his buying of pictures and books, and a seemingly endless social round, was clearly both crowded and costly. Before reading Tyndale's letters one would have thought that Aubrey placed physical love low in his list of priorities, certainly way beneath affection and friendship. But one might have been wrong, at this time at any rate. For in a letter of 12 January 1663, sent to Salisbury (so Aubrey was evidently at Broadchalke), John Hoskyns the barrister, not the painter, addressing him for once by his Christian name even if he put a 'Mr' before it, wrote 'Dear Mr. John – Some of your intimate acquaintance have late told me how extremely amorous you are by nature, and I am much inclined to credit that opinion when I take notice that the suddeness of your departure from us, and the ill-pretended ground of your melancholy when you last wrote could not proceed from anything but from the violent passion, the first of a hopefull, the last of an unsuccessful amour. Alas, is she froward? Let her goe, you can do well enough without 'em.'[15] Hoskyns was a notoriously ugly man, and this jaundiced view of women may well have been occasioned by his lack of success with them. In due course he was to marry, seemingly happily, so no doubt by then he had sensibly changed his mind.

One would think, too, that Aubrey's abrupt departure and the melancholy tone of his letter were much more likely to have been caused by financial worry than amorous anxiety for this was the time when having sold Stretford the previous autumn, he was now contemplating the sale of Burleton. Having come up against a hard-headed bishop as his purchaser in his first sale, Aubrey seems to have come up against an equally hard-headed doctor in his second. This was Thomas Willis, an old acquaintance from Oxford days, where he had been 'our chymist Dr. Willis' in Lydall's letters, who had sensibly procrastinated over the delivery of the *aureum fulminans*, the explosive substance with which Aubrey wished to experiment. Subsequently he had run a successful medical practice in the vicinity of Oxford. An able, as well as an ambitious man, Willis contributed to medicine as much as he took out, the most important of his achievements being the identification of diabetes mellitus. At the end of his highly successful life Willis was given the ultimate accolade of being buried in Westminster Abbey. Like Aubrey he was an FRS and had earlier been a member of the club at Oxford. Two letters in the Bodleian, in a highly illegible, typical busy doctor's scrawl, concerned with the sale, show that he was as skilled, and successful a bargainer as he was everything else. Aubrey was asking £1 500: 'I can not possibly do it, unless you will take 300£. in Hereford & Clun.'[16] So Willis acquired an estate fully stocked with beef cattle and sheep for the price that Aubrey was asking for the estate alone. In spite of some soreness over the sale, Aubrey would, no doubt, have been delighted had he been able to foresee that Willis's grandson who inherited Burleton, Browne Willis, was to become one of the most distinguished antiquarians of his day.

The sale of Burleton and Stretford must surely have eased, if only temporarily, the financial pressure on Aubrey. In consequence one would hope and think that the years which followed were the happiest and most carefree of his time at Easton Piers. They were years of considerable personal triumph. Aubrey was elected to the Royal Society at the first autumn meeting of the Society, which thereafter was to become its main one of the year. He was elected in November and was admitted on 21 January 1663. He was thus included in the first list made in May of those to be officially registered as members, so while not being a founder member he was one of the original members, as those on this first list were to be called. Also on this list were Elias Ashmole, the founder of the Ashmolean, to whom Aubrey was to be greatly indebted at the end of his life for help in the safeguarding of his manuscripts; Robert Boyle, proposed to be first president, but who refused, disliking the wording of the oath he was required to take; Sir John Denham, Dryden, Seth Ward, at that time Bishop of Exeter, John Evelyn, Robert Hooke, Sir William Petty, Edmund Wyld, Aubrey's eccentric and wealthy friend, and three Wrens – Christopher and his two contemporary cousins Matthew and Thomas. Pepys, together with Ralph Bathurst, was among those elected the following year.

Aubrey was proposed by Dr Walter Charleton, at that time Physician to the King, but also an ardent antiquarian whence a long-standing friendship with Aubrey. In a later letter dated 27 January 1671, to Wood, when Charleton was falling out of favour at court, Aubrey referred to him as 'my old and faithful friend. It is a pity such a man is not valued at Court as he deserves. He hath 100 times more learning than . . . Dr. Fr. [Fraser]'.[17] From the moment of his election Aubrey played a considerable part in the Society's discussions. But the quality of his early contributions makes one wonder what the very distinguished audience really thought of their new member. Thus it is recorded that on the day of his admission 'Mr. Aubrey presented the Society with the scheme of a cart with legs instead of wheels.' On 18 March 1663, 'Mr. Aubrey mentioned he had heard the Duke of Orleans had a way of producing animals by the putrifaction of vegetables.' On 29 April, 'Mr. Aubrey mentioned that holly-berries after they have lain five or six hours at the bottom of a vessel with water will rise and swim in the middle thereof.' In May, 'Following an enquiry by Sir Robert Moray whether manuring the ground with lime makes wheat more wholesome, Mr. Aubrey mentioned that liming the ground altered the wool for the worse.' However, none of this seems to have altered his fellow members' opinion that Aubrey was a man of practical experience and financial acumen, for in November that year Aubrey was appointed to the Committee to audit the Treasurer's accounts. In the spring of 1664 Aubrey offered to introduce the Society to what sounds like ginger beer: 'Mr. Aubrey mentioned a new way of brewing good and lasting beer with ginger without hops, and promised to produce some bottles of such beer as proof.'[18]

These, in the main, not very sensible suggestions seem to show that Aubrey, in what was primarily a scientifically orientated Society, was not so much out of his depth, as out of his element. In the years after his departure from Trinity he had followed the fashionable practice of carrying out small amateur experiments but neither by nature nor experience was he a scientist. His friends, the other Fellows, accepted him for what they knew him to be, an excellent observer of all that went on round him, with a passionate interest in the past that made him into a good antiquarian and historian, and a lively curiosity about all aspects of the present that made him into an intelligent and stimulating companion. The official meetings of the Society were but the tip of the iceberg of their activity. The Society's real value lay in its constant bringing together of distinguished men from diverse fields, and in the informal discussions which followed. In these Aubrey's talent, which he himself with considerable humility recognized as a whetstone for sharpening the talent of others, must constantly have been in use, and consequently valued.

In his own neighbourhood Aubrey's standing and reputation can, surely, never have been higher. His election to the Royal Society clearly placed him in the company of the most distinguished intellectual figures of his time, although it must be remembered that the Royal Society took some time to establish its position of scientific supremacy and that it had in these early days of its official existence its opponents as well as its admirers. The royal visit to Avebury, throughout which Aubrey was the King's main and chosen guide, must have impressed all the Royalist supporters in the locality, and there can have been few at that time who were not. This was just as it should have been, and how it should have remained. One cannot but feel sad for Aubrey that the tightening grip of debt should have pulled from under his feet the rug on which all this – as well as he himself – stood.

But not quite yet. In the midsummer of 1664, Aubrey at last seemed on the point of achieving what he had so long wished and planned for, and no doubt dreamed about – his Grand Tour. In June, he crossed to Calais, seemingly by himself. But sadly his Tour was to prove not very grand, and not much of a tour either. He got no further than Orleans, where in August he had so severe an attack 'of the spleen and piles' that he later entered it in his 'Accidents', and turned for home. He crossed back in October. He did, however, spend some time in Paris on his way to Orleans and while he was there received two letters which have survived, one from Hobbes and one from Hoskyns: that from Hobbes posted on 30 June 1664 was sent to 'Monsieur Jean Aubry, gentilhomme anglais chez M. de Houtte dans la cloître de St. Julian le pauvre, devant la fontaine de St. Severin'. That from Hoskyns was addressed identically, save for the addition 'au charge Royale d'Angleterre', so there was obviously some Embassy connection. Both are little more than messages of affection and friendship, but that from Hobbes is also interesting in that it shows Aubrey was intending a much wider ranging tour than he in fact achieved. Hobbes did not, personally, write the letter. His sight was obviously already going and it is in the careful copperplate hand of a professional scribe: 'I approve of your designe to see the Loyer, and the country of Britanny, and that about Geneva. For though you assigne your selfe less time, perhaps, than these Journeys require yet I see you meane to husband all your time to your best advantage. I have nothing to add but my wishes for your safety, and the continuance of your health, which is not to be despaired of in one that can temper himselfe from excesses, and especially in fruit, as you can.'[9] Little of interest remains in Hoskyns's letter, beyond an obvious affection for Aubrey, save that he suggests that Aubrey on his way back should call in and see him at Tunbridge Wells, where he was undergoing a three-week cure 'if your way to London lay by Rye'. Evidently Aubrey still owned the property on the coast near Rye, which is surprising, for one would have thought it would have been the first to go. It was now getting on for two years since Burleton and Stretford were sold. Any letter that Aubrey sent to Hoskyns was to be sent to The Artichoke in Lombard Street.

One would have thought, too, that Paris had much to offer that would have interested and pleased Aubrey but he is remarkably silent about the whole of his French trip, which is a bad sign in someone generally so forthcoming. All that he seems to have brought out of France was a tapestry, for which a customs note survives, 'Jean Aubre un tableau de tapisserie a bordure doree.

Estant dans une caisse',[20] and indirectly, a good servant to whom, during the few years that he was able to afford him, he was to become devoted. This was Robert Proudhomme, or perhaps Robert Wiseman – Aubrey refers to him so often as one or the other that one does not know which is the surname, which the nickname – who came to him through the intermediacy of George Ent, the son of Sir George Ent, the distinguished physician who had been one of the earliest members of the select group that some twenty years earlier had met weekly in London to pursue 'philosophical inquiries'. The elder Ent was the close friend of Hobbes and Harvey and of Aubrey also. He had, in fact, sent his son to the school run by Aubrey's friend William Radford, possibly on Aubrey's recommendation. The younger George Ent seems to have been in Paris at the same time as Aubrey but to have remained there after his departure, for in a letter dated October 1664, the month that Aubrey returned to England, he wrote, 'I have enquired after Robert and it seems his Master has taken another servant much worse than himselfe, and the poor rogue is at present quite destitute of a service. I have not seen him since, but I doe intend, since it is your desire, to bring him with me to London, which will be God Willing next Wednesday come seven night.' Aubrey had evidently during his stay in Paris acquired some other servant who had not proved satisfactory, for 'Mr. Dicas,' who seems to have been their landlord, 'is very willing to defray the charges of this boy to England, condemning very much the rashness of them here in advising you the other.' Aubrey seems to have been feeling so seedy with his 'attack of the spleen and the piles', and possibly also suffering from an attack of home sickness, that he went straight back to England without returning to Paris, where he had left some belongings. These he had no doubt intended to pick up on the way back, for in his letter George Ent wrote that 'Mr. Dicas has sent away your clothes . . . I have sent Palladia's *Architecture* away . . . with your linen . . . Your hat case is not to be found.'[21] The clothes, the linen, and the book were all sent to the Rainbow, still Aubrey's London base, although, sadly, as it was to prove, not for much longer.

Robert Wiseman spoke Italian as well as his native French, and was of use to Aubrey for the translation of works in both languages. During the years they were together, Aubrey seems to have developed a deep affection for 'Robinet'. When he could no longer afford to keep him he did his best to find him a good job elsewhere. As this turned out to be in Oxford, Aubrey's later letters to Wood frequently carried messages of remembrance and affection to 'Robin' or 'Robinet', such as that in a letter of 20 December 1671 – 'My love to Robinet. I sent him a letter and the Italian Book of Fencing and Pinching of Napkins. It is a rare piece.'[22] An odd one also, one would have thought, from the strange title. Such gifts were swiftly to cease as Aubrey ran through the small store of cash that he seems to have salvaged out of the wreckage of his bankruptcy, or possibly held at Broadchalke but the messages of affection continued for many years.

Wiseman would certainly have been the servant that Anthony Wood describes in his account of his first meeting with Aubrey. 'Mr. Aubrey was then in sparkish garb, came to town with his man and two horses, spent high, and flung out A.W. at all reckinings [i.e. would not let Wood pay his share of the bills].' Surely only someone determined to find fault would have criticized Aubrey for his generosity. There is some doubt about the date of the meeting. Wood dates his entry 31 August 1667, but he clearly wrote it in distant retrospect. The spitefully malicious description of Aubrey with which he ends seems conclusively to place the writing of it at the end of his life when they had fallen out. In this entry Wood describes Aubrey as 'a shiftless person, roving and magotie headed, and sometimes little better than crazed. And being exceeding credulous, would stuff his many letters to A.W. with fooleries and misinformation, which sometimes would guide him into the paths of errour'.[23] Wood must surely have written this during the final period of failing friendship, that is to say more than twenty-five years after their first meeting, for until then they had been close friends. At so great a distance of time it would be easy for Wood to make a mistake of the date. What suggests that he did is a passage in an early letter from Aubrey to Wood, possibly the first after their meeting, giving him details of the barrow at Lanhill which he thought to be the burial place of a Danish chieftain, in which he refers to 'my hond. friend the Honble Charles Seymour of Allington (since his fathers death) Lord Seymour'. But Charles Seymour was only Lord Seymour for the year between his father's death and his own in August 1665. Surely Aubrey would not have referred to him in the way he did had he already died – which suggests that Aubrey and Wood first met in the summer of 1665 rather than 1667. This earlier date is endorsed beyond reasonable doubt by the fact that in the list of 'Amici' after the name 'Anthony Wood' Aubrey puts the date '1665'.

However, there can be little doubt of the accuracy of Wood's account of their meeting, and of the occasion for it: 'John Aubrey of Easton Piers in the parish of Kington St. Michael in Wilts was in Oxon with Edward Frost, a bookseller, living against Alls. college, to buy books. He then saw *Notitia Academiae Oxoniensis*, and asking who the author of that book was, he answered the report was that one Mr. Anthony Wood, of Merton College, was the author, but was not. Whereupon Mr. Aubrey, a pretender to antiquities, having been contemporary with A. Woods elder brother in Trin. Coll. and well acquainted with him, he thought he might as well be acquainted with A.W. himself. Whereupon repairing to his lodgings, and

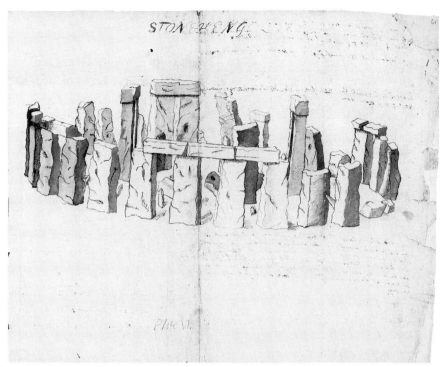

Aubrey's drawing of Stonehenge, from the *Monumenta Britannica*.

'Sir James Long of Draycot and J. Aubrey hawking.' Drawn by Aubrey from horseback.

59

Mem my Father & mother are buried in the South east angle of the chancell here.

(est,) ...yd in the chancell windowe over my fathers grav; was when I was a boy the greatr part remayning of the picture of the Ladie Bodenham in her Cope & robes: who gave that windowe. in the Limb Orate p[ro] [a]nia ... ... bono statu) domine Cecilie Bodenham. Priorisse, q[ue] hanc fenestr . . .

Alexander Brome has an Elegie on him in his Poems who made at y[e] request of the ... next neighbour & friend m[r] Isaac Lyte Afterm[a]n of Londo[n] my kinsman: to which ... ... my fathers Christian na[me].

RICARD AWBND   P. M.

※ He was a Justice of Peace tpe [Caroli primi]

I would have a blanke of two lines for my Mother.

I doe hope to live so long & erect a little Inscription of white marble to the memory of my Fa- ther: about an Ell high or better.

P. M.
RICARDI AWBREY Armig. filij unici JOHANNIS AWBREY de Burlton in agro Heref. filij tertij Gulielmi AWBREY LL. D[octo]r[i]s et e Supplicum libellis Eliz. Reg. Mag[is]t[r]i. Viri pacifici, fidelis amici. / Uxorem duxit DEBORAH Filiam et heredem Isaaci Lyte de Easton-Pierse, per quam suscepit tres Filios superstites. Johannem, Guliel- -mum et Thomam filios. Obijt XXI° die Octobr. Año (D[omi]ni: 1652 (Ætat. 49.

B. if for Abbot Bere.

Jesus puer.
In the Windowe over my grandmother Lytes Pease.

telling him who he was, he got into his acquaintance, talked to him about his studies, and offered him what assistance he could make, in order to the completion of the work that he was in hand with.' After describing Aubrey's 'sparkish garb' and 'high spending' Wood goes on, 'But his estate of 700li. per an being afterwards sold and he reserved nothing of it to himself, lived afterwards in a very sorry condition, and at length made shift to rub out by hanging on Edmund Wyld, Esq, living in Bloomsbury near London, on James Bertie earle of Abingdon whose first wife was related to him, and on Sir John Aubrey, his kinsman, living sometime in Glamorgan, and sometimes at Borstall near Brill in Bucks.'[23] But the beginning is not necessarily as the end. Although the relationship between Wood and Aubrey was to end on a sour note it was for years the mainstay of both men. So the meeting that marked the start of it is an occasion of great personal importance.

But an event of even greater personal moment occurred in 1665, the year in which Aubrey first met Wood. This was when on 1 November, 'in an ill howre,' he made his 'first address to Joane Sumner'.[24]

'Under an ill-tongue'
1666–9

Joan Sumner was a member of a wealthy clothier family, who had relatively recently moved to Seend, near Melksham, where she now lived in the house of her brother John Sumner, her father having died when she was in her teens. When Aubrey paid his 'first address' she was at least twenty-nine, possibly thirty, an age which then, when considered in terms of marriageability, corresponded with the mid or late thirties today. Previously the Sumners had lived in Sutton Benger, which is only three miles to the east, slightly north-east, of Easton Piers. So that it is probable that the two families – the Aubreys and the Sumners – at least knew of each other and, possibly, actually knew each other, for the Draycot estate, the home of the Longs, and in particular of Aubrey's close friend James Long, was near-by. Seend is further away from Easton Piers, some eleven miles to the south, but it would have been only just off Aubrey's route between Easton Piers and Broad-chalke. So if they were already acquainted, it would have been a likely stopping-off or calling-in point for the sociable Aubrey, whose journeys between his two houses – as one can see from the numbers of observations in his *Natural History* which clearly originated in the course of them – must have been very slow and meandering.

Seend is remarkable not only for its position – Aubrey describes it as 'a very well-built village on a sandy hill', whence, he believed, it took its name – but also because, as Pevsner comments, it is 'full of good houses'. Seend had long been a favourite place of residence for wealthy clothiers, mainly because of its proximity to Bradford and Bath, and to the river, the Avon, which runs to Bristol. Two memorial brasses to one of them, John Stokys, who died in 1498, and his wife, are still there. John Stokys built the north aisle of the church, and, as it were, signed his work by having a set of sheep-shears carved on the inset of one of the windows, thus indicating the source of his wealth, and at the same time thanking God for it. They continue to do so. But most of these 'good houses' were built in the late seventeenth or eighteenth centuries. So in some small measure they possibly owe their existence to Aubrey, who discovered and promoted the medicinal qualities of the local water. This led to the establishment of Seend Spa which had a brief flare of fame and fashion at the end of the seventeenth and the beginning of the eighteenth centuries. Aubrey describes the occasion of his discovery in his *Natural History*: 'Come there on a certain occasion [he adds in a note "At the Revell there Anno. D. 1666"] it rained at twelve or one of the clock very impetuously, so that it had washed away the sand from the oare: and walking out to see the country, about 3 p.m, the sun shining bright reflected itself from the oare to my eies. Being surprised at so many spangles, I took up the stones with a great deal of admiration. I went to the smythe, Geo. Newton, an ingeniose man, who from a blacksmith turned clockmaker and fiddlemaker, and he assured me he has melted of the oare in the forge . . . Finding this plenty of rich iron-oare, I was confident that I should find in the village some spring or springs impregnated with its virtue; so I sent my servant to the Devizes for some galles to try it; and first began at J. Sumner's, where I lay, with the water of the draught-well in the court within the house, which by infusion of a little of the powder of the galles became immediately as black as nitre. I proceeded and tried other wells but my ingeniose faithfull servant Robert Wiseman tryed all the wells in the village, and found that all the wells of the south side doe turne with galles more or lesse, but the wells of the north side turne not with them at all.'[1] Aubrey was subsequently, in June 1667, 'to send some bottles to the R.S. . . which were tryed with Galles before a great Assembly there . . . and did there after so long a carriage turn as deepe as a deepe claret.'

By the time Aubrey made this discovery, he was engaged to be married to Joan Sumner (which was obviously the reason for his presence at the Revel), a licence for their marriage being taken out on 11 April 1666, at Salisbury. The previous year Joan Sumner had been a party to another marriage licence, this time to a Samuel Gayford, described on it as a yeoman. The proximity of these two engagements suggests not only that she was desperate to get married – as well she might have been at her age if she wished to have her children without undue difficulty – but that her marriage to Aubrey would have been purely one of convenience. The well-connected Aubrey would have provided her with a social status she would not have had as a member of a clothier family. She, on her side, would have provided the money that would, at least temporarily, have got him out of financial trouble. Marriages of convenience can, and often do, work out happily, but only if the two characters are reasonably compatible, which one would doubt whether Aubrey and Joan Sumner were, or ever could have been. On the little evidence that Aubrey provides she appears as a strong-minded but unreliable

woman, capable of courageously backing her own opinion – as when she tried
to get the drowned body of a pregnant girl opened because she believed the
baby inside was still alive – but capable also of breaking her word when it
suited her, even of juggling dishonestly with her financial claims and
commitments, which it would seem she did with Aubrey and several others.
Aubrey by his own account lived in the 'howse'with her – one does not know
which house but one imagines her brother's at Seend – for a year and two
months, as had earlier the brother of Dr Joliffe, an acquaintance of Aubrey's,
for three years, during which time 'he contracted to her and then she left him
in the lurch.' Thus this 'unlucky woman' – Aubrey was writing in March
1673, by which time Joan Sumner was dead (she had eventually married a
Robert Pope in March 1671 and died nine months later, probably in
childbirth) – 'undid the Dr's eldest brother; . . . amongst severall others
besides yours J.A'.[2] During the course of the engagement a marriage
settlement between Aubrey and Joan Sumner had been signed and sealed.
Joan Sumner was to bring with her a dowry of £2000, while Aubrey was to
settle on her, as her jointure, the farm at Easton Piers 'with other lands'.

Some time early in 1667 Joan Sumner broke off the engagement. One does
not know for certain the reason for this sudden change of heart. When she
was contesting the suit for breach of promise which Aubrey and his mother
were to bring against her at the end of the year, she said that it was because
Aubrey's estate had proved to be heavily mortgaged and because in the
course of their engagement he had used rough language to her. But she had
clearly known from the beginning at least of the mortgage of £500 to John
Scrope, who owned, and lived in, the Manor at nearby Castle Combe, for in
the marriage settlement it was agreed that £500 of the £2000 which she was
bringing as her dowry should be made immediately available in order to pay
this off. The second charge, of using rough and hurtful language, is totally
out of character with the mild, scholarly and generally gentle Aubrey which
his many friends knew, and which we know through his letters and
manuscripts. Aubrey himself seems to have believed that the rift was caused
by the malicious intervention of a Captain Robert Chaloner, an ex-army
officer who had subsequently become a Herald – first Bluemantle, and then
Lancaster Herald. He was a well-known local figure, and had leased the
estate of Roundway near Devizes from Judge Nicholas, with whom he was
connected by marriage, his sister having married the Judge's brother. Judge
Nicholas had, in 1657, gone to live at Seend. So there was every reason for
Chaloner to be a familiar of the Sumner circle, Roundway itself being only a
matter of some three miles distant. Aubrey's resentment towards Chaloner
shows in a letter to Wood dated 5 December 1668. Aubrey, as always doing
his best to help his friends, had approached his antiquarian friend William

Dugdale, who was himself a Herald and who eventually was to become Garter King-of-Arms, about the possibility of a vacancy for Wood. However, 'There is not yet any vacancy; but he supposes one I know that is not fitt for the place will be contented for money and resigne. He is Lancaster Herald and one that the office (and I think everybody) hates, or ought to doe, if they knew him as well as I doe: for he hath been the boutefeu [firelighter] to set my dame and me at Variance.'[3] One does not know, and cannot even guess, what Chaloner told Joan Sumner about Aubrey – there is plenty of ill that can be said about anybody – but from the anger of Aubrey's tone one can have no doubt that he held Chaloner responsible.

The break up of his engagement to Joan Sumner seems to have been financially disastrous for Aubrey. In those days when there were no bank statements, when loans were personal matters, generally between friends, and in particular because Aubrey seems to have kept no financial records, although he made notes about virtually everything else, it is difficult to chart in detail his progress to the brink of financial failure, the position in which he now seemed to stand. One can see from his Welsh cousin Thomas Price's note of eighteen years later that his father's debts had, even then, not been cleared. Their accumulation, the expense of the entail, Aubrey's extravagance and financial mismanagement, would certainly have already led to a crisis but for the sale of Burleton and Stretford. But even the considerable amount of money they raised seems only to have been enough to delay disaster for a few years. Now Aubrey described 1666 as a year in which 'all my business and affairs ran kim-kam, nothing tooke effect, as if I had been under an ill-tongue.'[4] Marriage with Joan Sumner must then have seemed the best, and possibly his last, hope of saving Easton Piers.

From the fact that Aubrey first paid court to Joan Sumner in November 1665, and in his letter to Wood wrote that he had lived in her brother's house at Seend for a year and two months, it would seem that the period of their engagement ran throughout the length of 1666. But even then word seems to have got around that all was not well. To his note in which he wrote that in that year all his affairs 'ran kim-kam' Aubrey added 'Treacheries and enmities in abundance against me'. It is hard to imagine that so obviously likeable a character as Aubrey had an enemy in the world, yet it may be that he had offended some in the neighbourhood, as he did Anthony Wood, at their first meeting by 'his sparkish garb' and 'high spending'. There may have been others who sensed the end of an era, the end of the centuries-old Lyte occupation of Easton Piers, and wanted some of the pickings. Others too may simply have wanted to be sure of their money, for quite apart from his mortgage to John Scrope, it is likely that Aubrey had spread a mantle of small debts to his various suppliers around him. But whatever the reason or reasons, the unfortunate course of the year clearly induced in Aubrey a sense of impending doom. He was to be proved right.

The break-off of Aubrey's engagement to Joan Sumner, probably at the beginning of 1667, was followed, after an interval of some months during which both sides marshalled their forces and checked their ammunition, with a sad sequence of litigation. It began in November with the presentation of *The Bill of Complaint of John Aubrey and his Mother Deborah against Joan Sumner* (their complaint being that Joan Sumner had failed to fulfil the conditions of her written engagement to Aubrey) and was followed in December by Aubrey's arrest 'in Chancery Lane at Mistress Sumner's suite', presumably for debt. This was obviously a counter-attack but it may have been more than that – an attempt at intimidation, aimed at persuading Aubrey to drop the case – as it probably would have been sensible for him to do. It would have been even more sensible for him never to have begun it even if it meant accepting the loss of Joan Sumner, and the hope of saving Easton Piers with her dowry. For even if he won the case, he was bound in the end to be the loser. Someone in his position, with a still reasonably high reputation locally – he was after all an FRS and the friend of the famous in distant London – could still borrow time when he could no longer borrow money. In such a situation time can be just as valuable. At the end of the case whatever the verdict, his reputation was bound to be in shreds. Was it the same fatal liking for litigation that eleven years earlier had led him to proceed against his great-grandfather's entail with such disastrously costly results that brought him again into the courts?

To Aubrey his arrest in Chancery Lane must have been both a shock and a humiliation but he seems to have had no difficulty in securing his release. Not quite three months later his *Complaint against Joan Sumner* was heard in Salisbury. Aubrey is exact not only to the day but to the hour – which of course was important for it was essential to know if the stars were on his side: 'Feb. 24, A.M., about 8 or 9. Triall with her at Sarum: Victory and £600 damage[s]; though devilish opposition against me.'[5] In such a case there can be little conclusive evidence, and much of it is bound to be contradictory. It is more a question of whom the judge chooses to believe. On this occasion the judge evidently and emphatically, as one sees from the size of the damages, chose to believe Aubrey rather than Joan Sumner, as most of us would.

But that was not the end of the case. Joan Sumner appealed. The hearing of her appeal was to have been on 8 July in Winton (Winchester) but the day before Aubrey was arrested for the second time – this time by 'Peter Gales malicious contrivance'. Gale is a well-known name in and around Kington St Michael, and no doubt Aubrey owed him money, yet one can but wonder if this too was at Joan Sumner's instigation. There is no direct evidence that it was. Yet there is a slight link, for in John Sumner's will there is reference to some land he bought from Peter Gale. If it was an opening shot from Joan Sumner this time it fell not far from the mark. For though 'it did not retard me above two hours' yet an obviously disheartened and dispirited Aubrey 'did not then go to the Triall'.[5] It was not until nine months later that the appeal was heard, and the case closed. '1669 March 5th was my trial at Winton from eight to nine. The Judge being exceedingly made against me by my Lady Hungerford' (of several Lady Hungerfords in existence this was probably the one who owned property at Stanton St Quinton, only a mile from Easton Piers). With 'much adoe, got the moiety of Sarum verdict is £300'.[5]

Aubrey had now won two hard legal battles, but there can be no doubt that he had lost the war. He no longer had either credit or credibility. He had no other option but to sell Easton Piers for whatever price he could get.

Over the period of his engagement to Joan Sumner, and the years of litigation that followed the breaking of it, Aubrey seems to have managed to follow the pattern of life that one must now consider as normal for him. Thus he spent some of his time in London with his friends, a great deal of it in Wiltshire making notes and sketches for his *North Wiltshire Collections* – now also following the track of an even more ambitious undertaking, that of making a collection of *Monumenta Britannica*, an obvious development from his discoveries at Avebury and Stonehenge – and very little of his time trying to straighten out his hopelessly entangled affairs.

Over the years of his courtship of, and then court proceedings with, Joan Sumner, Aubrey's London had been irrevocably changed by an event of great general importance, and indirectly of particular personal consequence to himself. This was the Great Fire of London, which started on 2 September 1665 and raged for the greater part of a week. In the course of this catastrophic week, thirteen thousand houses were burnt and a hundred thousand people were made homeless. Luckily for Aubrey, he was not in London at the time of the Fire, although if he had been we might have another eyewitness account to rival that of Pepys. But, unluckily, the stationers' shop at the sign of the Rainbow in Fleet Street, in the room or rooms above which he had lodged for over a decade when he was in London, was just the wrong side of Temple Bar, which marked the northern limit of the Fire.

Aubrey, however, must have found some compensation for the loss of his lodgings in the numerous finds of historical and antiquarian interest unearthed in the subsequent excavations. A macabre letter to Wood describes some of those discovered in the area of the now ruined St Paul's. 'When the Rubbish was cleared in St. Faith's church (which was ruined by the fall of the St. Pauls Choire in the great Conflagration 1666) when the

Labourers tooke up the Leaden Coffin of William Herbert Earle of Pembroke (whose sumptuous Monument was among others tumbled into the Church underneath) the stinke of the Corps so abominable that they protested to me they did hardly recover themselves in a week.'

Most people would have been put off at this point, and would not wished to go further. However, not Aubrey. 'About the same time in digging the Rubbish there, they found the Body of Bp. Braybroke tumbled dwn (which I saw and it was publiquely shown for 2d a person) which was uncorrupted . . . was dry, stiff and would stand on end. It was never embalmed for his belly and stomach were untoucht; unless on one side by the fall was a hole, wherein I might put in my hand, whereby I could see his lungs dried.'

Even before the fire Aubrey's friend Edmund Wyld had been nosing around St Paul's, not with Aubrey, but with 'Ralph Graham (Mathem. Instrumt Maker)' and came on the coffin containing Dean Colet's body, which lay below his monument. This was visible because 'it happened a little before the Conflagration that a piece of the Monument being broken, one might discern the lead coffin; somebody made a little hole towards the upper edge.' Through this Wyld and his instrument-maker friend poked 'the body with a piece of Iron Roof that accidentally lay thereby: they found the body did lye in a liquor and they could feel the body like boyld Brawne: the liquor was clear and insipid: they both tasted it. E. W. Esq. favoured it had the taste of iron but that might proceed from the rest of the iron curtain roof. This was a strange and rare way of conserving a corpse: perhaps it was a Pickle, as for Beefe'.[6] Clearly it was not a squeamish age, but that Aubrey shared to the full the general taste for the gruesome showed in a late minute of a Royal Society meeting: 'Mr. Aubrey related that dogs licking the sanies* of one hanged in chains near Kensington were poisoned and died; and that a man wearing the shoes that had been taken off a malefactor's feet had his feet rotted off.'[7]

Aubrey kept also a less nauseating source of material, a record covering some twenty-three years, but only three pages, of some of the finds that Wren and Hooke came across in the course of their work in surveying and planning the rebuilding of the burnt City. The earlier entries came from Wren, the later ones from Hooke.

The first entry, dated 1667, tells that 'the Roman Highway lies nineteen feet under Cheapside as it now lies . . . Opening the Foundations in old Fish St. in St. Nicholas Cole abbey church were found walles of Roman brick lined with stucko, painted red with fresco . . . The wharfing, which wharfed up the old Bankes of the River of Thames, was found an hundred foot distant from the present wharfing of the river on Thames St. near the Bridge. This must be long before the building of the Bridge (sc. 400 years ago) and the

*'A thin feted pus', according to the Oxford Dictionary.

oake was entire: and Beds of Oyster-shells were petrified into lumps of stone.'

The later information from Hooke was very similar. 'Under Chanon Street about twenty-foot deep was found a pavement of Mosaic worke . . . Roman bricks were found by Algate, seventeen inches long: eleven Inches broad: thick one inch and a quarter . . . In digging the foundation of Fleet Bridge they found Thresholds of Doors lying lower than now the high-water mark . . . Mr. Hooke asserts that the whole City of London is raysed since the time of the Romans near twenty-foot; it has been raysed (now 1689) since the fire two foot.' All of this is pleasantly prosaic after the details of the exploration around St Pauls until the last entry, which is more chilling than any – 'In digging for foundations they found at St. Martin's le grand, in a little kind of Vault, in which were all the bones of a skeleton! and on the walls were staples (or manacles) for the hands and feet; where he suffered death by immuring.'[8]

In spite of the suffering it caused, the fire presented a wonderful opportunity for improving the layout of London, and for influencing its future development. Several of Aubrey's friends put forward schemes for the royal approval. Wren was the first to do so, and had a plan on the King's table only a week after the fire was finally extinguished. Petty, Hooke and Evelyn were other of Aubrey's friends to put in alternative schemes. Petty's and Hooke's plans featured wide thoroughfares which might have eased future traffic problems. But Evelyn's for a garden city was the most interesting alternative. In the end the Crown accepted none of them, but chose in the main to keep the old street plan, while laying down standards of building. This may have been a missed opportunity. Yet in spite of it, Wren built the Cathedral and his churches; Hooke, whose best buildings were outside the City – the Royal College of Physicians on the corner of Pall Mall (east) and Montagu House, which stood on the site of the present British Museum – built inside it Bethlehem Hospital ['Bedlam'] near London Wall, and designed the Monument. Perhaps this mixture of old and new enabled the City to retain its character in a way that wholesale acceptance of one of the proposed schemes might not. Aubrey was not in a position nor qualified to put forward a scheme, but through his conversations with his friends at the Royal Society and elsewhere he must undoubtedly have felt himself involved.

In London, as usual, Aubrey saw Hobbes: '1665. This year he told me he was willing to do some good to the Towne where he was borne: that his Majestie loved him well, and if I could find out something in our Country that was in his Guift, he did believe he could beg it of him, and since he was bred a scholar he thought it most proper to found a Free school there . . . After enquiry I found a piece of land in Braden forest, that was in his Majesties Possession, of about £125 per annum, value which he designed to have obtained of his Majestie for a salary for a schoolmaster: but the Queen's priests smelling out the Designe; and hateing him, prevented this publique and charitable Intention.'

According to Aubrey, Hobbes was very charitable by nature, particularly to his relations in or around Malmesbury, but also to the man, or rather the beggar, in the street. 'One time, I remember, goeing in the Strand, a poor and infirme old man craved his Almes. He beholding him with eies of pitty and compassion, putt his hand in his pocket and gave him 6d. Sayd a Divine that stood by, would you have done this if it had not been Christ's command? Yea, sayd he. Why, quoth the other. Because, sayd he, I was in paine to consider the miserable condition of the old man; and now my almes, giving him some reliefe, doth also ease me.' In view of his constant charity Aubrey was surprised that Hobbes 'dyed worth neer 1000 pounds'. Unlike Aubrey, Hobbes was clearly not only charitable but careful with his money.

Aubrey was obviously fascinated by Hobbes not only as a remarkable man, but as a possible subject for a biography, and his close observation brings him vividly back to us: 'he had two kindes of Lookes . . . when he laught, was witty, and in a merry humour one could scarce see his Eyes: by and by when he was serious and positive he opened his eie round . . . he had middling eies, not very big, nor very little.' Although Hobbes left Wiltshire at fourteen he never lost his brogue just as 'Sir W. Ralegh spoke broad Devonshire to dying day.' In his youth he had 'been sent up and down to borrow for his Lord and as a result he took colds, being wett in his feet, and trod both his shoes inside the same way'. In his old age he 'worked indoors with bald head bare – never caught cold but great trouble in keeping flies from putting on it'.[9]

It would seem that Aubrey had at last obtained his portrait of Hobbes, which he had commissioned from 'Jean Baptiste Caspars, an excellent Painter, and 'tis a good piece' for which earlier Stafford Tyndale had been badgering Caspars on his behalf. Aubrey was ultimately to give his portrait to the Royal Society, but before he did so he had it engraved by Wenceslaus Hollar. A letter from Hollar to Aubrey, dated August 1665, seems to refer to this. But it is one of the few letters in Aubrey's collection which has suffered with the passage of time and part of it has faded away. However, the main message is clear. Hollar thanks Aubrey for sending 'the Principall', presumably the main payment, and had 'halve a dozen copies for you'.[10] But from what one can make out of the mainly invisible rest Hollar was disgruntled by the lack of response from other clients or their failure to pay.

Aubrey was clearly interested in Wenceslaus (or Wenzel) Hollar both as a man and as an artist, and made him the subject of one of his 'Lives'. Hollar, a Bohemian, the son of a 'Knight of the Empire' had always liked drawing, particularly of 'mappes . . . which draughts he kept, and they were pretty; but had been designed to be a lawyer, until his father's troubles' – he had forfeited the estate because he was a Protestant – 'together with the warres, forced him to leave his countrey. So that what he did for his delight and recreation only when a boy, proved to be his livelihood when a man'. He was lucky enough to impress the Earl of Arundel, an English diplomat as well as the Earl Marshal, and a keen connoisseur of painting, with his work when they met in Cologne in 1636. Arundel subsequently went as 'Ambassador to Vienna . . . and amongst others Mr Hollar went with him (very well clad) to take viewes, landskapes, buildings, etc'. Returning with Arundel to Arundel he married 'my Lady's waiting woman'. Subsequently he became well known for his drawings and engravings of topographical scenes, many of which were of the London that was burnt in the Great Fire, including several of Old St Paul's, and so have historical as well as artistic value. According to Aubrey, 'He was very short-sighted and did work so curiously that the curiosity of his worke is not to be judged without a magnifying glass.' It was perhaps his short-sight that made him delight and excel in details of ships, one of his favourite subjects, as well as buildings. 'He was a very friendly, good-natured man . . . but shiftlesse as to the world and dyed not worth much.'[11] But who was Aubrey to talk or to judge?

In his *North Wiltshire Collections*, when he came to consider Malmesbury, Aubrey planned for 'Mr Hollar to draw a Mappe of the Towne, with the names of the Rivers that imbrace it, the Avon and (Newton Water), the Prospect of it, the Abbey Church, and K. Athelstan's Monument'. And maybe he did, for a map of the neighbourhood is included in the treasure trove that is still to be found between the somewhat battered covers of the volume that can only be seen in Duke Humfrey's Library, but it is more concerned with roads than rivers, and suggests the work of a talented amateur, rather than that of a skilled professional. So it is more likely to be Aubrey's own work than that of Hollar.

One would think that Aubrey made most of his notes on Malmesbury, for his *Collections*, in which the same year as he positioned and dated Latimer's first school at Westport (which to all intents and purposes was, and is, a part of Malmesbury) as being 'next to the Smyths shop as is now, 1666, opposite the Three Crowns, an Inne'. Aubrey had an associative mind, and while he was thinking of Hobbes – which he very much was at this time – it was likely that he was thinking of Malmesbury also. His interest in Hobbes, as it turned out, obscures his account of this ancient, interesting and beautiful borough, so that there is too much about Hobbes and too little about Malmesbury; but two incidents illustrate how well founded was his constant fear of destruction and at the same time how difficult it was either to predict or prevent it. All one could do was to record. Caught in the cross-fire of the Civil War, Malmesbury was militarily occupied and reoccupied seven times between

1642 and 1644. In March 1643 it was recaptured by Parliamentary forces under Sir William Waller. Westport had 'before the late Warres . . . a prettie church . . . reported to be more ancient than the Abbey . . . there were very good windows and a fair steeple . . . which much adorned the Towne of Malmesbury; in it were five tuneable bells, whom Sir Wm. Waller melted into Ordnance, or rather sold; and the church was pulled down, that the enemie might not shelter themselves against the garrison of Malmesbury'. It was a perfectly understandable military precaution, and not at all malevolent, yet it was destruction all the same. Waller's troops committed another much less important but more despicable act of destruction when they 'broke the head of the figure' of Athelstan in 'a handsome Gothique monument . . . to pieces'.

The other incident would seem comic were it not so obviously disastrous. 'The Abbey Church was build per crucem, in the middle whereof was the Tower, on which, no doubt, as everywhere else almost in this Champagne [level and open] Country was a steeple. Here was a great Bell, called St. Aldhelms's Bell, which was rung when it did thunder and lighten, to send the Tempest from the Town into the Country. When the great rejoicing was on the King's birthday, 1660, for the return of King Charles 2d., viz 29th May, here were so many and so great vollies of shot, by the inhabitants of the Hundred, that the noise so shook the pillars of the Tower, that one pillar and the two parts above fell down that night. Where the Choir was, now grass grows, where anciently were buried Kings and great men.'[12] Jackson in his turn adds 'The site of King Athelstan's grave is now [i.e. in mid-Victorian times] under an asparagus bed.'

Aubrey refers in the course of his notes on Malmesbury to 'the wealthy clothier Stump', of whom 'Parson Stump', the Rector of Yatton Keynell, where Aubrey went at the age of six 'to be entered in my Grammar and the Latin', was one of the descendants. Aubrey even in his childhood had thought him 'a proper man and good fellow' even though he had the deplorable habit of stopping the bung-hole of the barrels of his 'Special Ale' with sheets of the manuscripts that had probably come from the library of the Abbey at the time of the Dissolution. 'About 1647' Aubrey went to see Parson Stump to see whether he still had any of the manuscripts which in Aubrey's childhood used to 'fly about like butterflies' and which could have provided useful material for the *North Wiltshire Collections*. He tells us about his visit at the end of what he calls 'A Digression' in his *Natural History*. 'I went to see Parson Stump out of curiosity to see his MS whereof I had seen some in my childhood, but by that time they were lost and dispersed; his sons were Gunners . . . and scoured their gunnes (with them) . . .'

If Aubrey's visit to Parson Stump produced no manuscripts it did provide a pretext for a remarkable story about Captain Thomas Stump, one of the sons that were 'Gunners' – who had been 'a boy of most daring spirit . . . too much to be a scholar and about sixteen he went on a voyage with his uncle, since Sir Thomas Ivy, to Guyana in anno 1633 or 1632. When the ship put in some where there, four or five straggled into the country too far, and in the interim the wind changed, and the sailes were hoist, and the stragglers left behind. It was not long before the wild people seized on them and strip't them, and those that had beards they knocked their braines out, and (as I remember) did eat them. But, the queen saved T. Stump, and the other boy . . . [who] shortly died. He lived with them until 1636 or 1637. He says there is incomparable fruite there and that it may be termed the paradise of the world. He says that the spondyles of the backbones of the huge serpents there are used to sit on, as our women sitt upon butts. He taught them to build hovills, and to thatch and wattle . . . A ship then sayling by, a Portugese, he swam to it; and they took him up and made use of him for a sea-boy. As he was sayling near Cornwall he stole out of a port-hole and swam to shore; and so legged to his father's in Wiltshire. When he came home, nobody knew him, and they would not own him: only Jo. Harris the carpenter knew him. At last he recounted so many circumstance that he was owned, and in 1642 had a commission for a Captain of Foot in King Charles the First's army'.[13] It is a remarkable story well worth recounting, not only for itself but for Aubrey's telling of it.

With so much of his *North Wiltshire Collections* still to do – of which a considerable part because of the way events turned out never was to be done – one would think that over his last years at Easton Piers, Aubrey, after he had completed the section of it on Templa Druidum which he placed and dated 'Broadchalke [Easton Piers crossed out] 1665', would have concerned himself little with extending the range of *Monumenta Britannica*. But in 1666 he sat for a portrait by Faithorne, which he intended to use as a frontispiece for it, presumably only for the first part. Faithorne's ink-drawing, lightly touched up with colour, is less appealing than the supposed Lely portrait of ten years earlier, but partly because Aubrey is wearing a long wig, and also an elaborately embroidered collar which fits close up to his chin. Aubrey's face peering out between them looks constricted, uncomfortable – as no doubt he was – but the humour lurking in the eyes of the Lely portrait has gone and the full mouth, which had seemed to be on the point of breaking out in a smile, is now set in a petulant pout. The eyes, earlier watchfl, are now wary. The overall feeling of the Faithorne portrait is that Aubrey is now on the defensive, whereas in the Lely portrait he looked young, hopeful and confident. Simply on the evidence of these two portraits Aubrey seems to have aged more in the period between them than the ten year gap justifies.

However, if for the moment Aubrey had more to think about than further

investigation of *Monumenta Britannica* he did in 1667 pay a visit to friends in
north Hampshire, of which the object one would think was partly the pleasure
of an enjoyable visit but partly also to see nearby Silchester. At what must
have been a particularly worrying time for Aubrey, with his engagement to
Joan Sumner broken off and his law-suit pending, one is glad that he had a
few days of the happiness that is clearly reflected in the brief account of his
visit: 'for the year 1667 I was invited to Bramshill by Sir Andrew Henley, with
his brother Sr Robert Henley and his Lady (whose friendship I must ever
remember with respect) and besides my good entertainment at that Noble
Seat, they did me the favour to carry me out to see these eminent Ruines.'[14]

Nor, over these undoubtedly difficult years did he miss many, if any, of the
meetings of the Royal Society, as he clearly never would unless he had to. In
November 1666 he made the seemingly sensible suggestion 'to recommend
the observation of the tides to the deputy-governor of Chepstow in
Monmouthshire'.[15] In the same month but not at the same meeting he was
reappointed as one of the five Fellows to audit the accounts. In December
1667 he was 'desired to give an account of the measure of time produced by
him, being a watch to go with a pair of bellows instead of wheels'. In April
1668 'Mr Aubrey produced some mineral water from Milsom in Wiltshire,
about 80 miles from London which kept its strength so well that when a little
dust of galls was poured onto it, and stirred, it was presently tinged with a
dark red colour.' At the end of 1669 he was rather pathetically presenting the
Society with small treasures from his soon-to-be-sold home: in November
'an old printed book in the ancient British tongue', in December 'a piece of
Roman antiquity, which was a pot found in Week-field, in the parish of
Hedington in Wiltshire'.[16] Then came a long silence. It is not until February
1674 that his name reappears in the Records of the Royal Society. A piece of
news that must have added considerably to his many sorrows at this time was
that of the unexpected death of William Browne, his schoolmaster at
Blandford, his tutor at Trinity and his friend throughout the early, formative,
vitally important years of his youth. William Browne had left Trinity to
become Vicar of Farnham, and there he died on 21 October 1669, of smallpox caught from a corpse that he was burying.

Among Aubrey's many notebooks is one which is amongst the smallest and
shortest and which Aubrey called *Faber Fortunae*. It is a personal notebook of
a sort that one would not expect Aubrey to make. In it over the years Aubrey
jotted down ideas, and observations, which he thought could be profitable –
and he meant profitable in a money-making rather than a benevolent
sense. Because the colour of the ink and the qualities of the quill seem not to
vary, as surely they would if these were the original notes which Aubrey had
taken over the years, because of its formal title page, over which Aubrey

had clearly taken considerable trouble, and because throughout it is clearly, carefully, neatly written, this must surely be a fair copy made by Aubrey late in life of the pocket book, or books, which he kept for everyday use. He rarely dates his entries, but some of them date themselves, and quite a number clearly stem from his Wiltshire days. Many of them deal with mineral or metal deposits – 'Nitreous Springs be found at Minety, Wilts, 1665; [this is one of the few entries Aubrey actually dates] where is good Fuller's earth – in this Sr. Edward Hungerford will be engaged, and help me to get the ground from our friend George Pitt, Esq; Copper oare in Flint-shire, Shropshire and Foxhanger in Devises; Antimenie in Somerset and Amesbury near Bristol; the curious blew, azure clay – at Verknall for Potteries and Porcellaine and casting; in Somerset Mrs Hucker advised me to purchase a barren ground four miles from her estate, wherein a wondrous rich oare of Antimonie and lead, unknown to the Owner . . . The owner is a poor man and would (not knowing this) sell it for a small matter.'[17]

But not all Aubrey's ideas are for the exploitation of metals, minerals and poor ignorant owners. Despite his sorry experience at Seend, Aubrey obviously remained fascinated by its possibilities. 'It would be a prudent way of laying out money to build a handsome convenient House of entertainment for the water drinkers at Send and to make a fine bowling green.'[18] The most grandiose of all Aubrey's schemes was to widen the Bristol Channel, which would entail blowing up an island and 'making obtuse' the rock at St Vincent's.[19] Aubrey also refers to this scheme in *Monumenta Britannica*: 'I did acquaint Sir Thomas Langton,* one of the Aldermen of Bristowe of my Designe to remove the Lidds etc and he did impart it to the Council of the Citie; and it was very well received by them: but presently hereupon Troubles and Debts came upon me, so that I could not emerge and so it lies.'[20]

As the pages turn, and the years pass, the entries from Wiltshire dwindle, but still there are possibilities of silver in Flintshire, Cardiganshire and Yorkshire; copper in Derbyshire; lead on the Duke of Buckingham's estate and in Surrey; antimony in Somerset, Cornwall and near Bristol; in Scotland lapis lazuli and gold dust – also more mundanely 'Pitch and Tarre [with which] we may be furnished without being beholding to the Swedes'.[21] As late as February 1688, Aubrey was noting that Mr Cole of Bristol had told the Royal Society 'of Curious things to be observed along the Devon and Cornwall coast'.

There are also suggestions which, one would think, were more in Aubrey's line: 'to procure an Artist in Holland for the melting and working of copper',

---

*The Langtons had bought Easton Piers Manor, when Charles Snell had been forced to sell it after his unwise involvement in 'The Archangel Gabriel'. So they were Aubrey's near neighbours, although one does not know if Sir Thomas himself lived there.

and to find out the details of a German method 'of casting Statues in Metall, which will be applicable to our Copper worke'. There are too, some personal entries of considerable interest: 'William Penn, Lord Proprietor of Pennsylvania did give me a Grant under his seale of six hundred Acres in Pennsylvania, without my seeking or dreaming of it. He advises me to plant it with French Protestants.' This must have been an entry of the early 1680s, for Penn did not get the grant by royal charter of the territory 'that his Majesty was pleased to name Pennsylvania'[22] until 1681. At this time Penn was obviously doing his best to entice Aubrey and other members of the Royal Society, of which he was himself a Fellow, to go with him to Pennsylvania or to join him there. Elsewhere in Aubrey's notebook there is evidence of ground-bait that Penn had spread around: 'Penn showed excellent copper from P-ia'; also antimony – 'W. Penn says lots in P-ia.' Another entry of personal interest concerns the realization of his *Idea of Education*: 'The Instruction of my Idea for the Education of young Gentlemen of quality sc. from 9 to 18 yeares of age, in Derbyshire, or Cheshire, London, etc.'[23]

It is an extraordinary notebook to find in Aubrey's pocket. One wonders particularly at his persistence over the years with schemes that he knew would never be carried out, and ideas that would never be implemented. Yet one senses that this was how he wanted it. His fertile and inquisitive mind enjoyed the ferreting out of such information, the devising of such schemes. But it all ended there. It did not seem to matter to Aubrey that without money or backers there was virtually no chance of putting his ideas into practice. It is an obvious paradox which one finds not only in this notebook but in many of his manuscripts also. So much energy and time and work go into the preparation. Yet Aubrey will not complete his work by ordering it into at least a readable and possibly a publishable shape – until the last years of his life, when he seems to have decided to give posterity the chance that he denied his contemporaries. But by then, of course, he would not have been alive to be hurt yet again if their response did not come up to his expectations.

XII

The absconding
1670

After the hearing of Joan Sumner's appeal against the first judgement of Aubrey's claim against her in February 1669, there seems to have been a peaceful period in Aubrey's hitherto very agitated affairs. It was not so much the lull before the storm, as the lull after the storm. The essentials were now settled. Easton Piers had to be sold. It was merely a question of whether Aubrey could squeeze enough out of the sale to satisfy his creditors, yet, at the same time, to provide enough for him to live on. It was a protracted process. In his 'Accidents' he wrote, '1669 & 1670. I sold all my estate in Wilts.' But Easton Piers was not actually handed over to the new owner. 'Mr Robert Sherwin', until 21 March 1671.

Meanwhile, Aubrey took his mind off the sad state of his affairs by writing the Preface to his *North Wiltshire Collections* and by drawing and painting a description of the home he was soon to leave, which he called 'Designatio de Easton Piers'. This he intended to be in two slim volumes – the one of his sketches, which he completed at Easton Piers, the other an accompanying text which he seems not to have had time to do before he moved out. By his word, which there seems no reason to doubt, he wrote it in 1671 while again staying with his friends the Henleys on their estate near Silchester. Sadly, this verbal description of Easton Piers has been lost.

By itself, the Preface to his *Collections* would seem a big enough task to fill in such time as he had left at Easton Piers, for in it Aubrey surveyed the course of north Wiltshire history from as far back as the ancient Britons. As one would expect, it is a highly individualistic, somewhat simplistic account, intermingling a surprising amount of scholarly knowledge – considering the sources then available – much intelligent guesswork, some personal reminiscences and a lot of local information. Above all else it has, to us, the great interest that it is three centuries nearer the events Aubrey was describing than we are. It has both impersonal interest as an intelligent seventeenth-century gentleman's view of the country's, as well as the county's, social history; and as always, the charm of Aubrey's very individual viewpoint and way of writing.

He starts with a long leap of the imagination: 'Let us imagine what kind of countrie this was in the time of the Ancient Britons. By the nature of the soil, which is sour woodsere land, very natural for the production of oake especially, one may conclude that this North Division was shady dismal wood: and the inhabitants almost as savage as the Beasts whose skins were their only rayment . . . They were, 2 or 3 degrees less salvage I suppose than the Americans.' Aubrey was obviously thinking of the South American tribe who had eaten Thomas Stump's companions when they were left behind after the wind had changed and their ship had sailed off without them. 'Their priests were the Druids; some of their Temples I pretend to have restored, as Avebury, Stonehenge, etc. The Romans subdued and civilized them. At Lackham, Mr. Camden saith was a Colonie of them . . . About 1654 in Week-field in the Parish of Heddington digging up the ground deeper than the plough went, they found for a great way together, foundations of howses, hearthes, coles, and a great deal of Romane Coine, silver and brasse; whereof I had a pint . . . The pott in which a good deal was found, I had.' This was the pot that Aubrey gave to the Royal Society in December 1669. These two entries were to appear almost word for word in *Monumenta Britannica*, or maybe Aubrey transposed them from there – one does not know which he wrote first. 'The Britons received the knowledge of husbandrie from the Romans: the foot and acre which we yet use is the nearest to them. In our west country they give no wages to the shepherd, but he has the keeping of so many sheep with his Master's flock.' It was not an entirely admirable system, as Aubrey had found to his cost at Broadchalke.

'The Saxons succeeded them . . . Here was a mist of ignorance for 600 yeares. They were so far from knowing Arts that they could not build wall with stone. The Church of Glaston was thatched. They lived sluttishly in poor howses, where they ate a great deale of beefe and mutton, and drank good Ale in a brown mazard [a bowl made out of wood]. . . . Their very kings were but a sort of Farmers.' Interested though he was in farming, Aubrey clearly put farmers low in the social scale. 'The Normans then came and taught them civility and building; which though it was Gothique, as also their Policy, yet they were magnificent. The Government . . . was like a Nest of Boxes' – a neat description – 'for Copy-holders held of the Lords of the Manor, who held of a superior Lord, who held perhaps of a superior Lord or Duke, who held of the King . . . A great part of this Division held of the Honour of Trowbridge, where is a ruinated castle of the Dukes of Lancaster. No younger brothers then were . . . to betake themselves to Trade: but were churchmen, or retayners and servants to great men: [they] rid good horses . . . and their Blood . . . was upon every occasion lett out in their quarells . . . The Lords lived like petty Kings: had Gallows within their Liberties where they would try, condemne, hang and drawe.' Aubrey adds in a bracket that 'at [Castle] Combe, a Gallows were still standing within these 50 years.' They 'never went to London but in Parliament time, or once a yeare to do their Homage, and duty to the King. The Lords of Mannors kept good howses in their countries, did eate in their great Gothique Halls . . . The beds of the servants and retayners were in the great Halls . . . The hearth was commonly in the middle . . . Aunciently, till about the Reformation, ordinary men's houses had no chimneys, but Flues, like Louver holes; some of them were in being when I was a boy.' So Aubrey completes the chain which linked his time to the Ancient Britons. It makes us realize how far that time is from ours.

Aubrey much regretted the 'destroying of petty Manors' which 'began in H.7. . . . whereby the meane people lived lawlesse, nobody to govern them, they cared for nobody, having on nobody any dependence'. He regretted also the Reformation, and the selling of the 'Church landes', which altered 'the Ballance of the Government'. He regretted the decline in horsemanship – 'the Gentry of the Nation is so effeminated by Coaches . . . that they know not how to ride hunting horses.' But most of all he regretted the change in the countryside and in country practices wrought by enclosures. Until his grandfather's time the country round Easton Piers was 'a lovely campania. Very few enclosures, unless near howses . . . all between Cromhall's [the westernmost farm in Easton Piers] and Castle Combe was so'; at this time 'Easton, Yatton and Combe did intercommon together. In my remembrance much hath been enclosed, and every year more and more is taken in. Anciently pastures were noble large grounds as yet the Demesne lands at Castle Combe are. So likewise was . . . all between Kington St. Michael and Draycot Cerne common field. Then were a world of labouring people maintayned by the plough . . . Since the Reformation and Inclosures these parts have swarmed with poore people . . . Inclosures are for the private, not for the public good. For a shepherd and his dogge, or a milk mayd, can manage that land, that upon arable employed the hands of severall scores of labourers.' Aubrey's social compassion is unexpected. Being, or having been, a landowner himself, one would have expected him to side with the local landowners, many of whom were, or had been, his friends. But one warms to him for it. Aubrey also regretted the lost habit of hospitality. 'I have heard my grandfather say [that] in his grandmother's time . . . the Tablecloath was on the board all day long ready for all that was to sett thereon for Strangers, Travellers, Fryars, Pilgrims, etc. . . . and my honoured grandmother Mrs. Israel Lyte was also of this hospitable nature.'

Yet all these regrets never turn to self-pity. Aubrey had lost his money, his land, and, locally, his social position, yet he had not lost his most precious possessions – his interest in his work and his belief in it. Concerned with the past as the main subject of his work, Aubrey himself always looked to the future, to the work it would bring. One can all too well understand that at this particular point of time he felt weary and ill rewarded for all that he had done. Yet although disheartened he was still determined to continue his self-imposed task 'methinks I am carried on with a kind of divine Oestrum . . . methinks it showes a kind of gratitude and good nature to revise the memories and memorialls of the pious and charitable Benefactors since dead and gonne.'[1] Indeed it does.

Aubrey was surprisingly methodical in the planning of his work. In his *Collections* each parish of any size has its separate page with its name written on top in red ink. The smaller ones share a page but here again their particular space is allotted to them. Whatever church or house or archaeological feature he was visiting, he was always, too, very thorough in his examination of it. Yet there was always some madness in his method and never more so than in the Preface. He wrote it in a few pages at the beginning of his vellum-covered notebook. These he quickly filled. Then his writing goes every which way – up and down the margins, sometimes from top to bottom, sometimes from bottom to top, along the top, back upside-down along the bottom, in between the lines, filling every available inch of space, including the inside of the cover, sometimes going backwards to an earlier page where a glimmer of space beckons. And all without any indication of the order, so that it is only by the sense that one can make out the sequence. It is altogether an appalling mess and may be the reason why Aubrey had to wait two centuries to find an editor. There may, in fact, have been a particular and practical reason for this disorder and disarray. If he was short of paper, he was also short of credit, and may not have been able to obtain any of either locally. Yet, in fact, there are many blank entries in the manuscript, of parishes that he had not yet visited – sometimes blank pages. Could he not have used these? Perhaps he hesitated to intrude upon them because it would upset the overall design. There could possibly yet be another reason, that he was writing primarily for himself, rather than the reader. Perhaps he had lost his self-confidence, and so could not face the final, practical steps of working on the manuscript in preparation for publication. Perhaps in the face of his personal disaster he was retreating into himself – even considering retreating from the world altogether, for his letters to Wood in the years immediately following the sale of Easton Piers show that he was seriously contemplating the possibility of becoming a monk. Whatever the reason, the extreme disorder of the Preface, exceptional even for Aubrey, must surely be taken as some sort of sign or signal of his distress at this time.

Designatio de Easton Piers also poses its own problem. It was entirely to be expected that as artistic and affectionate a person as Aubrey should want to make a record of the home where he was born, which he had eventually inherited, and where he had lived for the past eleven years, but which he now had to lose and leave. In part, his *Designatio* is very much what one would anticipate. There are two wide-lensed sketches of the house in its setting drawn from the top of the slope across the brook. These show that Aubrey still had something to learn about perspective, for the front and the side of the house seem to run into one another. One is that in which a red cross marks 'My Grandfather Lyte's chamber wherein I drew my first breath'. The other, a prettier picture, drawn from further up the brook, shows relatively little of the house itself but a great deal of the surrounding trees. Then there are several sketches, some carefully drawn and lightly painted, simply of trees. But trees in the end are only trees. One would have much preferred to have had some close-up detail of the house itself. There is also a pleasing, if distant, drawing of Kington St Michael, showing that the village then was much more concentrated round the church than it is now.

All of this was to be expected but not the drawings of an imaginary house, which, possibly, Aubrey had planned to build in place of the existing one, but more probably was simply using as the means of an escapist exercise. It was an extraordinary house even to contemplate building in a Wiltshire climate. For its style was that of a large Italianate villa, with wide windows that might have kept it cool in summer, but would have made it bitterly cold in winter. It was seemingly intended to be on the site of the existing house, with below it an elaborate terraced garden on three levels, with fountains, an arched alcove and a quantity of what appear to be Lombardy poplars, leading down to the brook. To the side was a subsidiary house, of similar style, only slightly smaller in size, intended, no doubt, for servants and stables. Aubrey made three careful drawings of this house, two from below and one from above. There are also two charming vignettes, presumably from the imaginary house, for one is over a balustrade that did not exist in the real one, and one a view to the Priory, showing two nuns working in the intervening field. He also made a drawing of a beautiful stone bridge he intended for the brook with his monogrammed initials in stone on the side. Through its arch one looked up a long avenue of pollarded poplars. A lightly sketched-in swan floats below the bridge. It is all very much a dream world. Perhaps, at that time, it was for Aubrey a pleasanter one to inhabit than the real one.

However, Aubrey could not indefinitely stay in make-believe. Eventually he had to face reality, and it was not a pleasant prospect. He was in an extremely bad bargaining position, and, knowing Aubrey, one would think he probably made the worst of it. But one knows few of the facts of the sale.

Aubrey never disclosed either the amount he was in debt, or the sum for which Easton Piers was finally sold. All one knows definitely is that Aubrey was by his own admission 'disappointed . . . of moneys';[2] that he did not make enough out of the sale to satisfy all his creditors, let alone to leave himself something to live on; and that in the end, Easton Piers was sold, and handed over in March 1671, to 'Mr. Robert Sherwin', about whom one knows little except that he was also to buy the Priory, after the death of Thomas Tyndale, from the third son, another Thomas Tyndale. One wonders what happened to Stafford Tyndale, Aubrey's demanding, but undoubtedly devoted, friend.

There was also some disagreement with his brother William over a mysterious £500 from the sale, seemingly ambushed by him when on its way to Aubrey. Two years later Aubrey was still feeling sore about this, writing to Wood on 14 April 1673, 'had I not been persuaded* by my brother William to lose £500 of which I shall never see a farthing I could have been in the happiest condition I was in my life.'[3] It does look, on the face of it, as if William, who stayed at Easton Piers longer than Aubrey, had pocketed the pathetically small sum of money, considering the value of the estate, that was all that was left over when Aubrey's main creditors had taken their due. Yet in William's defence, one does also wonder whether Aubrey had ever paid him the £500 he was owed under their father's will. William had been only seven when Richard Aubrey died. So probably Aubrey would have held it for him until he came of age, as he would the similar sum due to his two years younger brother Thomas. But when the due date arrived Aubrey may have found it difficult to deepen the pit of debt already yawning under him. One cannot believe that Aubrey would ever have been deliberately dishonest with his brothers' money. But paying them their inheritance may simply have been one of those things – of which there were many – that Aubrey never got around to doing. One has no evidence to confirm this, except that the sums of money involved were the same. Also for this or another reason, the brothers were undoubtedly on bad terms after the sale, Wood writing in November 1671, and so only five months after Easton Piers was handed over, evidently in reply to a letter from Aubrey, 'I am sorry there is so bad an understanding between you and your brother. I am confident 'tis not on your part, but rather his, he is sickly and peevish as I heare.'[4]

In the end, Aubrey was forced, as he put it, to 'abscond'. Nowadays we might describe it as 'to flit' – in other words to depart suddenly and secretly, leaving unpaid debts behind him. One would think that the sums still owed by Aubrey in the locality of Easton Piers would have been small, for had a man of substance such as Scrope not been fully paid it is likely he would have had

*An ink blot unfortunately obscures most of this word but it starts with a 'p' and ends in 'ed', and is of the right length.

Aubrey arrested for debt in London, as Joan Sumner had had no difficulty in doing. But a small shopkeeper or local tradesman would have thought twice about starting proceedings in a town as distant as London, the procedures of which he probably knew little about, and of which he would fear the expense. But if the debts were small they would easily have been cleared by the £500 that never came. As it was, however, Aubrey had to live for some time in fear of arrest, and even at Broadchalke, which he continued periodically to visit, had to keep in hiding. So if it is correct to surmise that his brother did pocket the money, for whatever reason, Aubrey had good grounds to be sore with him.

Aubrey seems to have absconded some time before the hand-over. A long letter to Wood, dated 17 November 1670 – now difficult to read because the ink has run – and so over four months before he formally signed away Easton Piers, shows that he was already at Broadchalke, and in hiding, for he asks Wood 'to save me the paines of a double letter to send to my brother Wm. (for I can not send from hence) to bring a MS . . . And also desire him to see the shields I told him of in Langley Burrell window. He is as slow as Fabian.' The letter to Wood also shows that if he had to leave much that he valued behind him at Easton Piers, he had yet brought with him his most precious possessions – the notes for his work. Of his *North Wiltshire Collections* he tells Wood 'I have now donne 3 parts of 4 of Wilts. I hope the next spring in a fortnight or 3 weeks to (invisibly) doe the remaynder.' He then gives a rare glimpse of the driving force behind him. 'I know not how or why . . . but I have a kind of divine impulse to have it donne; nobody else will doe it, and when t'is donne none of these parts will value it . . . And I do also believe that you are, as it were, driven by the like impulse for your worke. I would faine, methinks, doe some good in the world, if I could, before I dye. But the next generation I hope will be lesse brutish.' This shows clearly the best and wholly admirable side of Aubrey – his belief in himself and his work – and his determination to do it, in defiance of adversity, indifference and, often, of common sense.

Aubrey also had with him much of the material that was to become *Monumenta Britannica*. 'I have a quire of Chorographica Antiquaria . . . Nothing is in it yet that hath been donne already. I have surveyed the camps; found out the places of the battles by the Barrows . . . and pretend to tell where Boadicca's battle was. Mr. Hoskyns & Dr. Bell say it is the best thing I have donne; but 'tis but drie meate . . .'[5] Although he does not mention them, Aubrey must also have had with him the numerous notes he had made, mainly on his journeys between Easton Piers and Broadchalke, to which he was to turn fifteen years later, to make into his *Natural History*. So, against appearances, Aubrey had not left Easton Piers empty-handed. But one can also see from this important and interesting, if illegible, letter, that Aubrey had been badly hurt in the process of so doing.

In the autobiographical fragment which Aubrey includes in his 'Lives', he briefly chronicled the course of his life. As one comes to the divide, marked by the sale of Easton Piers, which separates the two very different parts of his manhood, it forms a convenient way of looking back over the first nineteen years of his adult life when he was a man of considerable means and considerable opportunities. When he wrote it, Aubrey seems to have been in a particularly forgetful mood, for he seems unable to remember even the most obvious and important dates, such as that of his father's death. There are, in consequence, many blanks in his narrative but this, in a way, seems to suit and to express the chequered course of the years that he is describing. 'Ao. 165-, Octob-, my father dyed, leaving me debts 1800 lib., and law proceeds. 1000 lib. Ao. 16– I began my law suite on the entaile in Brecon, which lasted till - , and it cost me 1200 lib. Ao. - , I was to have married Mistress K. Ryves, who dyed when to be married. 2000 lib., besides counting one of her brothers 1000 lib. p. ann. Ao. . . . I made my will, and settled my estate on trustees, intending to have seen the antiq. of Rome and Italy, but . . . (my mother), to my inexpressible griefe and ruine, hindered the designe. But notwithstanding all these embarrassments, I did . . . (as they occurred) tooke notes of antiq., and having a quick draught, have drawn landskips on horseback symbolically. Then debts and law suites . . . borrowing of money, and perpetuall riding . . . Ao. - sold manor of Burleton, in Heref. to Dr. Willis. Ao. - , sold the manor of Stretford to Herbert, Ld. Bishop of Hereford . . . Then Joan Sumner . . . then law suit with her, then sold Easton Piers. Lost 500£. + 200£. goods and timber. Absconded as a banished man. I was in as much affliction as a mortall could be, and never quiet till all was gone.'[6]

But was it really as bad as that? What about the friendship with Charles Seymour, the hawking and hunting trips with James Long, the excitement and exhilaration with which he must have started on the great venture of his *North Wiltshire Collections*, the pleasure of owning and living in the much loved house with the lovely view in which he was born, the amusement of dressing in 'sparkish garb' and of 'spending high' on the things he liked such as books and pictures, the satisfaction of not only seeing but being on terms of friendship with many of the greatest men of his time – Hobbes, Harvey, Wren, Hooke, Boyle, many more – the pleasure of the companionship of as sympathetic a servant as Robinet? If one is remembering a route to disaster, one tends to forget the good moments, but for Aubrey there must have been many of these along the way.

Looking impersonally at this very personal story, Aubrey's predicament all through these years seems to have been that of a man who hated responsibility, and who was ill-equipped to deal with it, placed by unavoidable circumstances in a position where he was surrounded by the responsibilities that possessions always bring, but which to many people are a part of the pleasure as well as the price. Yet, at the same time as he hated the responsibility that possessions bring, he liked many of the possessions themselves, particularly Easton Piers. Alas, he could not keep the one without the other. Until the last years, by which time it was too late, Aubrey made little or no effort to solve his particular problems. Yet it was perhaps unfortunate that his father did not live longer. Had Richard Aubrey seen out his three score years and ten he would have comfortably outlived Isaac Lyte. Then Aubrey would have inherited his grandfather's unencumbered estate before his father's very encumbered inheritance, and possibly would have had time to learn how to run it. This should not have been too difficult, for by the regularity of the farm income it would seem that the greater part of his farm was let out. Aubrey might have had to deal himself with the '200£. of goods and timber', but even so he should have been able to distance his practical activities to a peripheral position which allowed him plenty of freedom and time to do his own work. He might then have had sufficient experience to cope, when the time came, with the undoubtedly difficult problem posed by his father's debt-ridden inheritance. At the very least he might have had the sense not to proceed with the lawsuit over the entail. Bearing in mind Anthony Powell's apt, and almost certainly true, description of Richard Aubrey as 'the victim of a long minority', should one consider his son as the victim of too early an inheritance?

XIII

Delitescent
1671–2

The second half of Aubrey's adult life was so drastically different from the first that as one follows its course one unavoidably finds oneself not only pondering the causes and consequences of his downfall but formulating more general questions which arise out of it. What, for example, is the reality of freedom? Aubrey had liberated himself from what, to him, was the burden of responsibility, only to find himself shackled by the constrained circumstances of his new life. Without money, without a home, Aubrey was from now on virtually dependent on the goodwill of his friends, which rarely failed him. In one sense he had gained his freedom; in another he had lost his independence. Again, as a scholarly, observant, yet innovative writer, mainly about the countryside, had he unwittingly cut himself off from his material? Of four main works he was to undertake during the second part of his life, three of them – *North Wiltshire Collections*, his *Natural History* and *Monumenta Britannica* – were mainly based on the notes he had already taken. Happily, much of the material for the fourth – his 'Lives' – was all around him in London. Even so it would be difficult for him in the future to continue to follow the Baconian principle which he had adapted for his own use, of seeing and judging for himself, and in Wiltshire, the area in which he had done most of his previous work, the area he best knew, impossible. Had he been admirably true to his own self in following, at whatever the cost, the paths to which his temperament beckoned – or simply foolish? Such are the complex questions that surface in one's mind as one follows Aubrey's progress through the later part of his life. Yet in the end the two which seem of paramount importance are simple enough. Were the very changed conditions of his later life more, or less, conducive to the flowering of his talent? Was he more, or less, happy under them?

Yet, all these questions might have been swiftly answered, in fact might never have arisen, if Aubrey had followed through a most unexpected course of action which he seems to have been seriously considering in the months before, and for at least a year after, the sale of Easton Piers. This was to become a Jesuit monk. Realizing this from his letters to Wood over this period, one can see that this was what he was referring to in his autobiographical fragment when he followed his sad summary of his final months as the owner of Easton Piers – 'never quiet till all was gone' – by writing 'submitted myselfe to God's will; wholly cast my selfe on God's providence. I wished Monasteries had not been put downe, that the Reformers would have been more moderate as to that point . . . fitt there should be receptacles – for contemplative men'.¹ This general feeling seems to have crystallized, at the time of his 'absconding', into a particular wish to join the Society of Jesus. At the end of his letter of 17 November 1670, in which he tells Wood of his intentions and the impulse behind them he asks, 'Pray consider were you in my case whether you would chase the advantages I may make in Maryland' – an alternative but, to Aubrey at that particular moment, much less attractive possibility – 'or I.H.S.' (the Jesuits).² Over the ensuing year, as the difficulties and disadvantages of his position became more apparent, his resolve seems to have hardened to the point when he was on the brink of making a definite decision to forsake the world and join the Jesuits. On 21 October 1671, back at Broadchalke, he wrote to Wood. 'Where could a man better withdraw himself than into a learned society as that of I.H.S. I am well acquainted with them and always reserved that designe as the ultimate refugium. To goe to reconcile the differences of the two churches I leave to those that have nothing els to do . . . This is certaine to my knowledge – to every one that has been amongst 'em – that no virtuous person shall want – and for promoting any public business they will try and turn every stone.'³

Aubrey had even picked his particular place of retreat. This was across the Channel, 'a pretty little cell of Novices at a pleasant place (Watton) near Dunkirke', run by a Father Thimelby, who, needless to say, was well connected – 'he is brother to Sir Thos. Th. of Yorkshire . . . He hath invited me over to him above this 12 months, and stay as long as I will – i.e. sojourn, and after 40 what better life could a man take. Is it not better than when one comes to be old to be scorned by his brother's cook-mayd, which I have seen to be done to a nice old gentleman at London . . . though worth at that time £60,000.'⁴ This slight has a personal ring about it. One wonders whether a nice not so old gentleman at Broadchalke had been scorned by his brother's 'cook-mayd'. Having been so long lord and master Aubrey would have found it very humiliating to have been treated with disrespect by his servants.

It seems likely that at some stage in his deliberations Aubrey went to have a look at Watton. In the difficult year after his absconding, when he went in constant 'feare of crocodiles i.e. catchpoles', in other words bailiffs, the safest place for Aubrey was in the country houses of his friends and relations. We know that he spent some time in 1671 with his friends the Henleys at Bramshill near Basingstoke and Silchester – because he refers to it in a later letter to Wood as the time and the place where he wrote the text of his *Designatio de Easton Piers* – 'a trifle of mine writt 1671 in my solitude at Sir R. Henley's in Hants'.[5] It seems possible that he also spent some time with the Earl of Abingdon, whose wife was a distant connection of Aubrey's through the Danvers, the family of his Aubrey grandmother, on his estate at Lavington. They were to be frequent hosts in later years, but maybe on this occasion Aubrey was put off by the presence of his brother William, with whom he was then on such bad terms, for Wood, in his letter in which he described William as 'sickly and peevish', went on to say 'I heare . . . that Salisbury aire doth so ill agree with him that he is going to live at Lavington.' But in fact Aubrey was to find his main refuge during the two difficult years which followed his absconding in a totally unexpected quarter, in the home of a man who hardly, if at all, seems to have entered Aubrey's life up to that point, although they must surely have met in the relatively small social circle which revolved round the Restoration court. This was Nicholas Tufton, the Earl of Thanet, an ardent Royalist, who had been twice imprisoned in the Tower by Parliament, but who had not otherwise distinguished himself. Why he should have now come to Aubrey's aid remains a mystery. He had certainly some small personal jobs he wanted done such as sorting through family papers. To deal with documents and deeds of this sort and antiquity would have needed someone of considerable learning, such as Aubrey, yet this seems an unconvincing reason for stays as long and frequent as those which Aubrey was to make during the remaining eight years of Thanet's life. Aubrey regarded Thanet's intervention at this crucial moment as he did that of Edmund Wyld, his constant host and crony in London, as the work of Providence: 'divested of all 1670, 1671 at what time Providence raysed me (unexpectedly) good friends, the Right Hon. Nicholas E. of Th., with whom I was delitescent* neer a year . . . Then Edm. Wyld . . . took me into his armes.'[6] And maybe it was the hand of Providence, but it was much more likely, in the case of Thanet, to have been the hand of Robert Boyle, whose niece was Thanet's wife.

Thanet's country estate was at Hothfield near the Kent coast. Sometimes when he went there Aubrey would go down by boat to Gravesend, and be met by a groom with horses and a 'portmanteau' for his clothes and belongings. From Hothfield it would have been easy for Aubrey to take ship from Gravesend, or any other of the Kent ports, across the Channel and so see

*The Oxford Dictionary explains delitescent as 'lying hid' which exactly describes Aubrey's situation at that moment.

Watton, the site of the 'pretty little cell of novices' run by Father Thimelby. One can not be sure whether he actually did or not, mainly because of the confusion caused by his irritating habit of referring to Hothfield in his letters as 'France'. Whenever he went to Hothfield in his letters he had gone to 'France', which makes it much more difficult to make out whether or not he ever actually crossed the Channel. But in one of his letters to Wood he writes 'I am now in Flanders' and goes on to describe the sort of insignificant, but in this case convincing, detail such as he often picks upon: 'Beyond sea the canons of Churches, when they go to Church and are there, weare things of white furre over their left armes as large as a Towille.'[7] Also, if he had not been there, how did he know that Watton was 'a pleasant place'?

But whether he had been there before or not, a later paragraph in his letter to Wood on 27 October 1671, seems to indicate that he had, in fact, taken the decision to abandon his life in England and to join the novices at Watton: 'I would willingly before I leave England finishe my Perambulation of Wilts; which is more than half done' (rather than growing, his manuscript with time seems to be diminishing, for a year earlier he had done '3 parts of 4') 'I think I must leave the finishing to you . . . when you are at leisure. About March or April I hope to . . . leave it with you. I heartily wish I were at Father Thimelby's . . . No life would like me better. For, cui bono, should I now make myself a slave to be rich. Riches and Honours . . are fine things for 25 or 30; but I vowe to God I would not be Bishop of Sarum for the trouble on't.'[8] Poor Aubrey, it is the bravado of a defeated man, and from this letter one would think it certain that he had decided to seek sanctuary at Watton.

Certainly, Wood seems to have read the letter and Aubrey's intention in such a way. For in his sympathetic reply of 11 November he wrote 'If I were in your condition I should take the same course as you have, or are like to do.' He then goes on to reveal himself as a much more admirable character than one had hitherto thought him: 'There be three things I strive to follow, these are (1) to be above the desire of riches . . . (2) above the feare of death . . . (3) to be mine own judge.' However his acceptance of Aubrey's commission to look after his work shows a return of the usual self-conceit. 'I think no person fitter than myself to keep your collections in case you leave us.'[9]

But Aubrey never did leave them, never became a monk, and did not again go to Watton – that is if he ever had been there before. As usual, he does not tell us the reason for this change of heart, but one would think that it was in the main the old inability to take decisions until they were forced upon him that had worked to his detriment during his time at Easton Piers.

But less so now. For one can not really see Aubrey as a monk. If he was undoubtedly one of those 'contemplative men' for whom 'there should be receptacles', yet he was also an extremely sociable one who would soon have missed his friends, missed being a Fellow of the Royal Society, missed all sorts of sociable things.

It may also have been a sign that he was getting over the shock of losing his money and his home. His letter to Wood in which he seemed to be announcing his intention to become a monk also declared that in the three months during which he had then been at Broadchalke 'I have more enjoyed myself than I have this 19 years since my Father dyed.' The mood of happiness seems to have followed him to Hothfield where a month later he wrote his next letter to Wood. 'I have not enjoyed myself so much these 20 years as here.'¹⁰ If there were such moments of happiness even in the proscribed and penurious life that Aubrey was now forced to lead, why leave it?

*   *   *

Aubrey seems to have liked his younger brother Thomas, now aged twenty-four and running the farm at Broadchalke, as much as he disliked his other brother, William. Perhaps out of gratitude for the happiness that Aubrey now found at Broadchalke on his perforce very limited visits, Thomas seems to have been very much in his mind at this time. In his letter to Wood in which he seemed to be announcing his intention to become a monk he regretted he no longer had the '£600 a year and better' that he and his mother together had been left. 'I should have been glad to have kept it, or at least turned it to my brother.' The brother that he might have turned it to would, of course, have been Thomas not William. Again, in the next letter to Wood he comes back to the problem of how to set up his younger brother for a happy and secure life: 'I have a great desire to see my honest brother Tom well-settled – i.e. married to a good discrete wife with about 800 £ or £1,000, which his estate [Aubrey inserts above 'Chalke Farm, 250 £ per anno'] does very well deserve. I would you could find another as your sister-in-law or sister is if she were big enough. My gr. gr. m. was of Oxfordshire. I like the people mighty well. About Chalke are no wives nearer than Salisbury' – some ten miles away, not after all a great distance to go shopping for a wife – 'proud and all gamesters and unknowing and unfit for a country gents turn; and in N. Wilts they will be drunke.' Wood, an inveterate misogynist who was soon to row with the sister-in-law whom Aubrey seems to have so much liked – to the point when she would no longer allow him to join in the family meals which she provided in the house in Merton Street which Wood and his brother shared – seems an odd person to turn to for this sort of help. Even Aubrey realized it: 'Is it not an odd thing to send to a monk and an antiquary about such a querie?'[11]

In spite of Aubrey's reference to Chalke Farm as his brother's estate, its lease must have stayed in Aubrey's name. Had Aubrey handed it over to Thomas it would on his sudden and untimely death, still single, in 1681, have completed its three name tenure and reverted to the Wilton Estate. As it was, however, after his brother Tom's death, the running of the farm reverted to Aubrey, with the foreseeable disastrous results. At some time, although it is difficult to make out exactly when, Aubrey seems to have allowed his brother William to run it for a couple of years in the hope that he might make it pay. But when he, too, failed, Aubrey sold the remaining third of the lease, in return for the clearance of his creditors and a small annuity for himself. At that time Aubrey explained the reason for ousting his brother William as that he 'never received of him for all that time for that estate but 12s 6d'. This suggests that during the earlier years when Tom was running the farm, Aubrey was regularly taking a small proportion of the farm income for his personal use, most probably collected during his visits to Broadchalke and so unobservable and untraceable by other creditors. He could, also, on occasion – such as when he needed it for the survey of Surrey that he was to make in 1673 – call on a horse to be sent up to him at London, for his use.

However, Tom's death was still a decade away at the time of Aubrey's happy stay with him at Broadchalke in the autumn of 1671. By then he seems to have completed such work on his *North Wiltshire Collections* as he could do without returning to the locality, which of course would have meant walking straight into the jaws of the crocodiles. Instead he seems to have decided to try his hand at play-writing. For he tells Wood 'I am writing a comedy for Tho. Shadwell, which I have almost finished since I came here, and I shall fitt him with another, Country Revell, both humours hitherto untoucht which in my tumbling up and down [I] have collected . . . but of this mum for t'is very satiricall against some of my mischevious enemies.'[12] There was, however, little need for Wood to keep silent. On the evidence of Aubrey's notes for the Country Revel, which are all that have survived of these two attempts at comedy, there was little to shout about. One does not know whether Aubrey's first comedy ever got to Thomas Shadwell, a successful producer and playwright, who curiously ended up as Poet Laureate.*

But whether it did or not, one regrets that Aubrey should ever have thought of, let alone attempted, anything as alien to his naturally scholarly temperament as a bawdy Restoration comedy, which is clearly what he intended *The Country Revel*, and no doubt the 'almost finished' first comedy,

*Shadwell is chiefly now remembered for being satirized by Dryden, his arch-rival and enemy, as 'MacFlecknoe, the True-Blew Protestant Poet, T.S.'

to be. His 'Dramatis Personae' sets the tone:

> 'Courtoise, Knight of the Bath, a Protector and Servant of distressed
> Ladies.
> Lady Euphrasia, wife to Sir Libidinious Gourman
> Lady Flommel, wife to Sir Surly Chagrin
> Mistress Salacious
> Ralph the Groome or the Footman her husband
> Mistress Cockain
> Ralph the Footman, her husband. [Aubrey seems to have forgotten that
>   he was already the husband of Mistress Salacious]
> Justice Wagstaff
> Squire Fitz-ale
> Sir Fastidious Overween
> Capt Exceptious Quarrelsome'

– and so on. There was a chorus of country fellows and wenches, among them
'Squeaker – a shee ballad-singer'. Aubrey's idea – one can hardly call it plot –
seems to have been to show what went on during the night, supposedly of
vigil, that traditionally preceded St Peter's Feast, and the day of the Revel
itself. Something of the Aubrey we have got to know shows here and there –
in, for example, a long speech by 'T.T.' (Thomas Tyndale? But how does he
wander into this?) 'an old Gent that remembers Q. Eliz. reigne [and] with
much choler inveighs against things now', regretting as Aubrey did in his
Preface to his *North Wiltshire Collections* that 'the Gentry' were no longer the
good horsemen they were; that they met not in the hunting field but in 'a poor
blind sordid alehouse'; and that they no longer 'kept their tenants in their due
respects to them'. 'T.T.' also shared Aubrey's dislike of enclosures: 'We had
not depopulated in those days.' Out of his own mouth, not 'T.T.'s', Aubrey
regretted that the old charitable and religious character of the Revel had gone
– of which the proceeds had been used to maintain the poor throughout the
rest of the year – and the vigil was a night of prayer and contemplation, and
not the drunken frolic that made 'Squire Fitz-Ale' declare at the end of it, 'I
believe, since the Conquest St. Peter had never a meryer Vigil observed.'
There is the odd good real-life remark such as that of Lady Harley,
'Respect . . . God help that women should be respected. Why a man should
love his wife'; and the odd good story which also from its provenance one
would think true: 'Sir Wm. Petty had a boy that whistled incomparably well:
he often wayted on a Lady, a widowe of Good fortune; every night this boy
was to whistle his Lady a sleep after she was abed. At last she could hold out
no longer; but bid the chambermayd withdraw, and bids him come to bed,
and setts him to worke, and marries him the next day.'[13] But, otherwise, this

curious rambling mixture of remarks and reminiscence, of caricatures more than characterizations, all written on the back of some immense deed or document cut up into smaller sheets, seems to show a bitter dislike of the crudity and cruelty of country life and country society, which is distasteful in Aubrey, who, if he had to blame anyone for his misfortunes, had in the main to blame himself. Happily, he seems to have got bored with his 'Revel' almost as quickly as we do, and returned, one imagines with considerable relief, to *Monumenta Britannica*, or whatever, and to searching out information for Wood.

Aubrey's friendship, and consequent correspondence with Wood, was a lifeline to him over these difficult years. Without it he would in all probability have sunk into the state of apathy to which he admitted he was prone. 'A man's spirit rises and falls with his fortunes – makes me lethargique,' Aubrey was to jot towards the end of his autobiographical fragment. But as it was, Wood's commissions gave him the nudge he needed. Wood was a hard taskmaster. On the backs of Aubrey's letters, sent in response to his queries, Wood would jot, for future reference, the names of those about whom Aubrey had written in them. To take at random that of 9 August 1671, written from 'Chalke', Wood has noted down twenty names, which included Hooke, Raleigh, Cartwright, Jo. Hoskyns and Wren. Not many of Aubrey's letters to Wood dealt with so many and diverse characters as this, yet virtually all contain some information that Wood has asked for. Obviously, collecting this information for Wood was a continuing process, and as such invaluable to Aubrey at this time when he had so little to hang on to. Curiously – for Aubrey seems to have kept almost all the letters that anybody else wrote to him – relatively few of these from Wood have survived, although one knows from the acknowledgements at the start of most of Aubrey's letters that it was a two-way flow. One regrets the loss of this part of the picture, although if it had been the other way round it would have been a greater one.

In the early years of their partnership – although not later when the solitary and sordid conditions in which he lived had soured his character – Wood was generous in his thanks and tributes to Aubrey, writing in his letter of 10 November 1671, 'I am verie glad that you have satisfied me in so many things and cease not to send into divers parts for further information of other men. I have had more from you as to these things than all others besides.' Wood then referred to the letter in which Aubrey had sent him details of William Cartwright, the Caroline dramatist who had died when still only in his early thirties, in one of the numerous epidemics that swept through Oxford during the period of Royalist residence. Aubrey had reminded Wood that at the news of his death 'King Charles I dropped a teare.' Wood went on, 'If I could give as true an account of all my writers as of him (for I have made a collection of 500 or above) I may safely say that my book would have been the best to these things that ever was printed.'[14]

But if the constant correspondence with Wood was a lifeline for Aubrey over several years it is also a useful line of communication to us. Without it we would not know where he was during the period of his 'delitescence'. One wonders, for example, where he was at the time of the hand-over of Easton Piers, on 26 March 1671. But here there is a significant gap in the letters – of some six months, on either side of the date of the hand-over, which was, of course, also the date when Aubrey's creditors knew definitely whether or not they were going to be paid. It seems that Aubrey, sensibly, did not even want Wood to know where he was over this period. Most probably this was the time when he stayed with the Henleys in the safety of their home in Hampshire, writing the text for his *Designatio de Easton Piers*, for we know that it was 'writt 1671 in my solitude at Sir R. Henleys amongst the beeches'. It is difficult to fit in this visit elsewhere in this year, which otherwise is fully occupied and documented. But on the 'Wednesday in Whitsuntide' Aubrey was back in London sending Wood details of Hobbes in Latin, and enjoining him 'by that sacred friendship between us that you send details of birth, etc'. Aubrey had decided to collect the nativities of eminent men – 'I have and shall get 30 Nativities exactly, many of them of men famous in Learning, Wealth and valour, etc.' This was probably at the instigation, and possibly with the help, of Henry Coley, an astrologer of whose professional qualities Aubrey had a high opinion, but who also proved to be a very loyal personal friend. Aubrey often stayed with him in his house in Westminster and probably was doing so now. Aubrey went on to tell Wood about him: 'My friend Mr. Henry Coley was born in Magdalen parish in the city of Oxon October 18, 1633. He is a man of admirable parts . . . His father was a joyner over against the Theater[15] [recently built by Wren].'

Aubrey was not long in missing Easton Piers, not only the place itself, but the social status which possession of it implied. One can see this from the letter to Wood written at Broadchalke, on 9 August 1671, in which he is thanking him for promising to make acknowledgement in his forthcoming book of Aubrey's help: 'I am much beholding to you that you are pleased to make my name live: pray putt in my beloved Eston Pierse, where I was borne; if Heaven had pleased I might have enjoyed it.' To emphasize the importance he attached to this he adds in the margin 'Mr. Dugdale in Monast. . . . sets me downe as J. A. de Eston Pierse.'[16] Again, less than a month later, on 2 September, writing from Hereford, he repeats his thanks and his regrets: 'I humbly thank you for the honour that you intend me by inserting my name in your living and lasting History. I desire you to name me of Easton Pierse, to contradistinguish me from other John Aubreys, it being the place where I was born and my mother's inheritance which a cruel fate enforced me to part with, a most lovely seate it is.'[17]

The other John Aubreys that Aubrey was likely to have had in mind were Sir John Aubrey, now the head of the branch of the family which descended from the 'little doctor's' second son – and his son, also called John. The first Sir John had been made a baronet at the Restoration, and since he had not been involved in the lawsuit over the entail – which had only concerned the descendants of the eldest son – he had always been on friendly terms with Aubrey, who had often stayed with him on his estate in Glamorgan, Llantrythid. It was while staying at Llantrythid in 1654 that Aubrey had started the habit of note-taking that was to form the backbone of much of his later work. Both the first Sir John and the second, who succeeded to his title and Llantrythid in 1679, were to be generous to Aubrey in adversity. The second Sir John was to be particularly so, notably in Aubrey's later years, when he would often take Aubrey with him on visits, not only to Llantrythid but to the estate at Boarstall in Buckinghamshire that had come to him through his second marriage. 'My she coz. Montague' through whom Aubrey had got to know William Harvey, was this Sir John's sister; as was 'my cosen Freeman', married to Ralph Freeman, a wealthy country-gentleman who lived in Hertfordshire next to the living of Dr William Holder, married to Wren's sister Susanna. The Holders were to prove to be among the most constant and kindest of Aubrey's friends. Several times in his last years Aubrey was to take 'the fresh aire and good entertainment in Hartfordshire', staying with the Freemans or the Holders.

Probably on the visit to Hereford in September 1671, Aubrey stayed at John Hoskyns's family home at Harewood, only a few miles south of the city, although he does not tell us as much. But he was there primarily on business, apologizing to Wood for not being able to spend more time on his affairs: 'I wish I could serve you better which I should were I less encumbred by business.' One imagines that there may have been the odd piece of property still to sell, left over from the sales of Burleton and Stretford, for his great-grandfather's empire had been widespread. There was too, surprisingly but certainly, the odd debt to collect: 'Here one owes me £100 of which I yet doubt I shall get 20.'[18] Even so, Aubrey found time to examine and explore Hereford Cathedral and send Wood his results, which included an excellent sketch of a statue of a prelate kneeling before his prie-dieu with his prayer-book open before him. He also included information about Lord Herbert, Dr Featley, Francis Potter, William Cartwright, even Owen Glendower, and a Welsh relation of Aubrey's – Robert Vaughan. Aubrey was later to refer again to his Vaughan relations, obviously at Wood's request, in his letter of 14 March 1672. 'There were 2 Vaughans (Twinnes) both very ingeniose and writers . . . Their grandmother was an Aubrey, their father a coxcombe, and no honester than he should be, he cozened me of £50 once.'[19] After Hereford came, of course, his 'happy' visits to Broadchalke and Hothfield. But for the final weeks of this dramatic and difficult year, which had seen in March the sale of Easton Piers, Aubrey was in London as letters to Wood of 20 and 30 December show.

In London, the mood of happiness which characterized Aubrey's autumnal stays in Broadchalke and Hothfield seems to have been quickly dissipated. It was replaced, not surprisingly, by one of apprehension and anxiety. Or such one must think lay behind Aubrey's commissioning from Coley of a detailed forecast for the month of January 1672, and then a later and longer one covering the whole of the forthcoming year. In the January forecast the prospects for each day are briefly analysed. Thus the '2nd, 3rd, and 4th are Badd for the most part'. However the 5th 'promises well, good to Converse with great Persons'. In general however, the outlook was depressing – as indeed it was at that very fraught time for Aubrey. By the 15th Coley is apologizing for his lack of encouragement: 'I am sorry I have not any good grounds to predict a pleasant time to the Native yet.' But by the 18th the outlook was better, in fact 'good now till the 21st day. Let the Native be cheerfull for there may neer this time be some hopes of preferment.' However, on the 21st 'now I fear the Tide is turned. Be carefull.' Towards the end of this, on the whole, gloomy month, Coley obviously feels Aubrey needs cheering up, as no doubt he did. 'Be not in the least discouraged for I have great hopes of an Amendment, and that you may live comfortably, and in peace to your great Content.'[20]

Coley's forecast for the following year, from March 1672 to March 1673, was inevitably couched in more general terms. Over this period Coley considered that the portents 'may denote this much that the Native may Gaine by an Active Industry' – probably a very necessary prod, for Aubrey was inclined to be apathetic in adversity. Throughout the year Coley urged extreme caution for Aubrey – or rather 'the Native . . . for he is not yet free from the influence of ill Directions.' Coley saw 'but little Incouragement to Travel or to enter a R.H. [religious house? Coley probably knew of Aubrey's inclination at this time towards joining Father Thimelby's "band of novices" at Watton] for there is no success portended in such an undertaking'. Coley also saw 'no Encouragement to the Native to seeke either a wife or anything like it'. Aubrey was hardly a marriageable proposition at this time so it can only be of the 'anything like it' that he can have had any hopes. But these he seems to have had – for a later prediction in the same forecast seems to be in answer to a specific request – 'As to the Election of time to visit a female friend to be kindly received . . . such a time you will finde the last weeke in January.'

In general, Coley forecast a difficult year ahead for Aubrey through which 'I know no better course than for the Native to solicit friends to provide an Employment or place that may be fitt for him and may suit with his Genius, and thereby (as much as may be) protect him from the Attempts of his Creditors which I feare may be too busy to molest his peace. However, let him not wholly confide in these Astrologicall Conjectures and rather strive to baffle a Bad Fate.'[21] One likes Coley for going against the grain of his own argument and encouraging Aubrey to fight for his future, whatever the stars predict. Coley may, or may not, have been the good astrologer that Aubrey thought he was, but he was undoubtedly a good friend.

Over the period which covered the turn of the year, Aubrey 'lay at the Blackamore Inn in Stanhope St., justa Newmarket'. The point of this was that it was next to the town house of Edmund Wyld, 'with whom I most commonly take my diet and sweet otiums [leisure]'. Aubrey had probably got to know Wyld through the Royal Society of which Wyld was, like Aubrey, an 'original Fellow'. Wyld shared, however, not only Aubrey's scientific and antiquarian interests but also his sociable tastes. The two became not only close friends but cronies for the rest of their lives. Wyld generally took Aubrey with him when he sought company in the town, whether in the relatively austere assemblies of the Royal Society, among the convivial chatter of the coffee-houses, or amid the alcoholic atmosphere of the taverns. The habit remained even when Aubrey was no longer 'lying' at the Blackamore Inn but was much more suitably settled in, or around, Gresham College. Wyld was both able and wealthy, having estates in Shropshire, Bedfordshire and Essex. His intelligence and wealth never seem, however, to have combined into much in the way of worldly achievement. He had been called to the Bar and had been a member of the Long Parliament, but thereafter had chosen to spend his life amusing and interesting himself – pursuing his various hobbies, mainly scientific and horticultural, on his various estates, entertaining his numerous friends, and being entertained by them.

Roger North, a man of many parts and posts – lawyer, historian, member of parliament, sometime Solicitor-General to the Duke of York, and author of *Lives of the Norths*, a very personal biography of his family – had been to Wyld's house in Bloomsbury, next to the Blackamore Inn, and described it as a 'knick-knackery'. It was here that Wyld provided an unusual form of entertainment for a dinner-party that Aubrey describes: 'my ever honoured friend Edmund Wyld did, just before he sate down to dinner, sow in an earthen porringer of prepared earth, seeds of Parsley, Perslane, Balme, etc. The porringer was set on a chafing dish of coales; and by the time we had ended dinner (which was about an hour and a halfe) seeds sprang visibly up.'[22] Wyld never married, but lived for the greater and later part of his life with his mistress Jane Smyth, of whom Aubrey made a nativity in which he describes her as having come to London 'half a year before the great plague 1665, born 1649', She and Aubrey obviously got on well together, Aubrey ending a late letter, 1689, to Wood 'with our earnest Request . . . to enquire for a College Lease . . . it is for that obliging body Mistress Smith . . . I owe most of Mr Wyld's civility to her goodness',[23] It is an odd enquiry, but by then Edmund Wyld's health was failing, and perhaps Jane Smith, or Smyth, was looking to her future.

Wyld was the son of a distinguished judge, Sir Edmund Wyld, who in Aubrey's time was remembered less for his legal achievements than for having been the first lover of Venetia Stanley, the greatest beauty of the day, of whom Aubrey wrote a 'Life'. 'Venetia Stanley was (first) a Miss to Sir Edm. Wyld, who had her picture . . . she was sanguine and tractable and of much *suavity.*' Aubrey underlines this in the margin by adding 'sweetness, pleasantness . . . She had a most lovely sweet-turned face, delicate dark-browne haire . . . Her face, a short ovall: dark browne eie-brows about which much sweetness, as also in the opening of her eie-lidds. The colour of her cheekes was just that of the Damask rose, which is neither too hott nor too pale', One would have said that Aubrey was himself in love with Venetia Stanley, did one not know that he was only seven at the time of her death, at the early age of 33, according to Aubrey, poisoned by her jealous husband, Sir Kenelm Digby. Possibly Aubrey had taken his description from a portrait that Edmund Wyld had inherited from his father – or more probably, since otherwise why would he have mentioned it, from 'an excellent piece, at Mr. Rose's, a jeweller in Convent Garden, drawn after she was newly dead'.[24]

*   *   *

In his first letter of the new year, 1672, Aubrey sent Wood information that twenty years later was to prove fateful for both of them and for their relationship. This concerned yet another of Aubrey's relations, a distinguished judge, David Jenkins, who, clearly, was also a remarkably brave man: 'He was one of the Judges of the Circuit of Carmarthen, Cardigan & Pembrokeshire. In the wars he was taken prisoner at Hereford – long-time prisoner in the Tower, Newgate, Wallingford & Windsore. Never submitted to the usurping power (I thinke the only man). All his estate was confiscated . . . The Parliament intended to have hanged him and he expected no less but resolved to be hanged with the Bible under one arme and Magna Carta under another . . . T'was pitty he was not made one of the Judges of Westminster Hall for his long suffering, and he might have been (he told me) if he would have given money to the Chancellor; but he scorned it.' Aubrey adds, somewhat enviously, 'He needed it not for he had his estate £1500 per an.' It was, of course, the uncorroborated charge of corruption which Aubrey thoughtlessly levelled against Chancellor Clarendon, and which Wood repeated and printed in his *Athenae*, that caused the later trouble. All of this was, of course, a long way from that letter of 1672, but it is thought-provoking how unwittingly the seeds of future trouble can be sown.

In that same letter of 16 January 1672, Aubrey was telling Wood that he would 'have you the epitaph of Sir Tho. More (his house was where the 2 pyramids are at the gate)'; that 'Sir Christopher Wren tells me he was born at ---- 20 October, 1631 . . . [that] Sir Jo. Denham [was] buried March 23rd 1668 near Sir Geoffrey Chaucer's monument and grave, if not in it . . . [that] Sir Wm. Davenant [was] buried April 19' and that 'James Harrington, Esq. Author of Oceania, etc, [was] born the first fryday in January 1611. So goodnight and a good New Yeare. My love to Robin Wiseman'.[25] Clearly, Aubrey was giving Wood good value, but in return was receiving an invaluable sense of purpose. In his next letter to him he told Wood that he would be able to get him a Thomas More manuscript; also one of Sir Thomas Browne's 'to whose son I spoke to get it', and one of Inigo Jones's 'in a ch. [est] in London, yet legible notwithstanding the fire'.[26] These, if he did manage to get all three, would have been a remarkable haul.

'On Tues. next I shall goe into Somerset.' Aubrey gave an address in Wells for Wood to write to. This was yet another 'cosen', who was to lose a letter which Wood sent to Wells, by which Aubrey was much irritated, as he was when he got to Broadchalke by his brother, presumably Thomas, taking a letter of his to post in Salisbury, meeting company, forgetting about the letter and bringing it back to Broadchalke. However, Aubrey was still in London on 1 February and 12 February, the dates of his next letters to Wood, but the later letter was written 'in haste . . . hoping on Wednesday to leave for Welles'. He had evidently acquired a piece of information which pleased him greatly for 'Surely my starres impelled me to be an Antiquary. I have the strangest luck at it that things drop into my mouth. Sir Walter Raleigh lies interred at St. Marie's church at Exon, not the cathedr.'[27] On 14 March he was at Broadchalke, presumably having paid his visit to Wells on the way, but he was 'to-morrow going towards Somerset' and possibly on to the Hoskyns' home at Harewood in Herefordshire, for in one of his February letters he had spoken of so doing at the beginning of March. Having left London late, it may have been that the connections ran late all along the line. In this letter he apologized to Wood for not having been to Allington, as Wood had required in his letter of 10 November 1671, to find out details about Sir Nicholas Fuller, who had been a prebendary at Salisbury. 'I am sorry that I dare not call at Allington. I think I wrote you that I lay at Mr. Kelsey's, minister of Newton

Toney, but a mile off. I would have gone but he would not let me, but told me
he would send the extract of the Register'[28] – which shows how careful
Aubrey still had to be when he was in the West Country for fear of bailiffs. At
the beginning of May he was back at Broadchalke, at the end of it in London,
but about to depart on a lightning tour around East Anglia. 'On Monday, God
willing I goe into Essex, and life being short and uncertain I goe from thence
to Norfolk, Suffolk, Cambridge and so London in about 10 dayes.'[29] In Essex
he would probably have stayed with Wyld; in Norfolk possibly with Sir
Thomas Browne, who lived near Norwich. Maybe at Cambridge he would
have stayed with the Holders who had a house in the vicinity, Holder still
being a Fellow of Pembroke Hall. We know that in Suffolk he 'was at
Harwich with Capt. Taylor' because he says so in a letter to Wood written on
his return to London of 18 June. Silas Taylor was an antiquary, and an old
friend of Aubrey's both in Oxford and Herefordshire, where he had been a
fair-minded and tolerant sequestrator for Parliament after the Civil War,
having been a captain in the Parliamentary army during it. At the Restoration
he had fled the country, but obviously had now returned, although, possibly
because he believed like Aubrey that life was short and uncertain, seemed to
prefer to remain in a port, whence he could make a speedy exit if need be.
From London on 6 July he was sending Wood details of Sir Kenelm Digby
who was 'buried in a vault which he built for his fair lady Venetia, over which
was a sumptious monument of marble . . . her bust on the alter in copper
gilt'.[30]

Following Aubrey's course through 1672 by means of his letters shows not
only the amount of work he was doing for Wood at this time, but also the very
varied itinerary that he followed. Perhaps he genuinely felt at risk from the
bailiffs if he stayed too long in any one place, or perhaps the dramatically
changed circumstances of his life, which had left him for the first time
without a home, had induced in him a feeling of restlessness which he could
allay only by keeping on the move. Whichever it was, one feels however that
he must by midsummer have felt the need of a haven in which he could rest,
recuperate and recover his spirits and self-confidence. Happily, he had
already found it, as he told Wood in a letter of 10 May: 'I shall take the
invitation of a delitescence in Kent for some time.' The offer of an indefinite
stay came from Thanet, who undoubtedly had his use for Aubrey's services –
in a letter at the beginning of the year he had written to Aubrey 'If the serving
of my writings be suitable to your inclination you shall not lose your time in
taking the trouble' – but who, one feels sure, made his offer mainly out of a
desire to help someone he both liked and respected, and whom he was sad to
see in so sorry a situation. This was to be the long delitescence of 'neer a
year', to which Aubrey referred in his autobiography. His stay at Hothfield

was, in fact, not to be all that 'neer a year', but it was to cover the greater part of one and so to be a very long stay indeed – from the end of August 1672 until the beginning of May in the following year.

Aubrey went to Hothfield on 19 August, writing a parting note to Wood, on his day of departure, from the Houses of Parliament. Westminster would, of course, have been a convenient point of embarkation for the voyage to Gravesend. Here he was lunching with the recently knighted Sir Llewellyn Jenkins, who in his youth had been tutor to the son of Sir John Aubrey at Llantrithyd, and subsequently had had a distinguished legal and political career. The course of it was the mirror image of Aubrey's. Starting with little, he had worked hard, taken every chance that came his way, and ended up with much. 'His father (whom I knew) was a good plaine Countryman, a copyholder of Sir John Aubrey.' He was a distant relation of Judge David Jenkins 'that was prisoner in the Tower', who, learning of his ability, had helped to pay for his education. He studied at Jesus College, Oxford, of which he in due course became a Fellow. Meantime he had tutored Sir John Aubrey's son, together with other sons of local gentry at Llantrithyd. Sir John Aubrey was a contemporary and close friend of Gilbert Sheldon, the deposed Warden of All Souls, who spent some time of his exile from Oxford with him at Llantrithyd 'where he took notice of the vertue and assiduity of the young man'. When after the Restoration Sheldon, as Aubrey puts it, became 'A.B.C.' (Archbishop of Canterbury), he made Jenkins Judge of his Prerogative Court at Canterbury. Subsequently he came to the King's notice who used him as his emissary on several missions abroad, and finally made him the Principal Secretary of State. He was several years short of this final honour when Aubrey lunched with him on his way to Hothfield, but he had already been knighted. Aubrey rejoiced in his success, as he always would in that of a friend or relation – Jenkins was in fact both – and concluded his 'Life': 'He haz a strong body for study, indefatigable, temperate and vertuous. God blesse him.' One would warm with Aubrey to Jenkins the more readily were it not for his remark when Aubrey went to congratulate him on his appointment as Secretary of State: 'He received me with his usual courtesie, and sayd that "it had pleased God to rayse-up a poor worme to doe his Majesty humble Service."'[31]

Aubrey's lunch with Jenkins would have given him a good send-off on his journey to Gravesend, where he would have been met by the groom with the horses and portmanteau, as he was on his return from a short visit to London a month later. But on this occasion he had the disagreeable task of making the groom walk home as punishment for spending most of a day, when he should have been working, in a pub. Thanet wrote in his note of instruction to Aubrey, 'Of this keep him in ignorance until you are on horseback else disgusted at his penance he may neglect looking to the horses as he ought.' Knowing the kindly and easygoing Aubrey one would doubt whether he would have inflicted the full sentence. It seems more likely that the two would have ridden together until they were in sight of Hothfield, where Aubrey would have made the groom dismount and finish the journey on foot.

Aubrey had meant to go to Hothfield earlier but had been delayed by news which obviously greatly excited him. This came in a letter from Christopher Wren, who had tried as hard as any of Aubrey's friends to find him a suitable job, and so a means of support. Now it seems that he had. It would only be a temporary task, but one likely it seemed to lead to a succession of similar ones. His job, in the first instance, would be to survey Surrey, but this was intended to be part of a grand design to survey the whole of England and Wales. It was, of course, a perfect task for Aubrey. He would be doing much the same work as he had for his *North Wiltshire Collections* but with the advantage of a royal warrant, which not only would open all doors to him, but would keep him free of the danger of arrest. It would have, too, a particular importance for Aubrey himself in that although he would be doing the survey in the royal name, it was bound to be in reality his own work. At this time Aubrey had great need to do something of his own. Wood's work was important to give him an occupation but in its nature it was limited and made little use of the skills of observation and description which Aubrey had developed in the course of gathering his *North Wiltshire Collections*. Perambulating round Surrey they would, once more, be brought into full play. This was important for Aubrey – for talents, like machines, grow rusty with disuse.

The appointment was in the gift of John Ogilby, a curious and colourful character, then approaching seventy, who in his youth had been a dancing-master, then master of revels for Strafford in Ireland, in charge of 'the poetical part' of Charles II's coronation, a bookseller and publisher. Now in his old age he was rewarded for his loyalty and his constant attendance at, or on the fringes of, the court, by being made the 'Kings Cosmographer'. In his letter to Wood, telling him the good news, Aubrey wrote that his friends had told him that Ogilby was 'a cunning Scot', and that he 'must deale warily with him' in which advice, as events were to prove, they were perfectly right. Wren, having spoken to Ogilby on Aubrey's behalf, had assured him that his appointment 'would be no very great matter', but that he must make up his mind whether he wanted it or not by 'Michaelmas Terme'. In fact, Aubrey was only actually appointed by Ogilby to do the job in the following May, after his return to London. Throughout the winter at Hothfield the thought of 'the Perambulation of Surrey' – as the product of Aubrey's tour came to be called – must have been an exciting, pleasant and hopeful prospect.

Rescue and rehabilitation
1672–3

Life at Hothfield seems to have been comfortable but quiet. Aubrey, not basically a countryman although he was interested in many aspects of country life, seems to have spent most of his time indoors – during periods of bad weather all of it. As early as October he was writing to Wood, 'The ways are so bad and aire so ill I stir not out of dore, but divertise myselfe very pleasantly with Algebra.'[1] Aubrey seems not to have taken any of his own work with him which seems a pity, for there was so much material from his Wiltshire jottings waiting to be sorted into shape, and this would have been an ideal opportunity to start on it. But going through Thanet's deeds and documents must have taken up most of his time, and in them he managed to find several personal points of interest, such as the difference in the style of the handwriting over the ages. At the end of *Monumenta Britannica* Aubrey included a section of miscellaneous papers. Among these is one headed '1672 – Extracts out of the old Deeds of Nich., Earle of Thanet.' However, Aubrey's interest was not in the information the Deeds contained but in the varying styles of handwriting in which they were written, which he characterizes:

> 'tempore Edw. I – a blackhand and difficult for the crinkum-crankums [loops] – it is a not very large hand.
> Edw. 2 – like it but not so enveloped with crinkums: not so good as Edw. 3 though like it but rawe and interfering.
> Edw. 3 – free from crinkums and a fine small legible kind of court hand.
> Hen. Sixth, an ugly scraggling hand like a blockheaded schoolboy.'[2]

Necessarily, for there was little to write about, Aubrey's letters to Wood over this period of hibernation seem to have been few and far between. During the period of bleak midwinter he does not appear to have written at all. But such letters as he did write show that he was still doing his best to glean such information as he could for Wood from the very limited opportunities which local society provided: 'Last night here supped an ancient gentleman 85 years old and able to walk 8 miles forward and back in a morning. He knows Dr. Jourdan . . . What strange luck I have in such things being to all other things unlucky.'[3] A more interesting acquaintance met earlier at Hothfield was 'my Lady Wyatt' whom Aubrey persuaded to send directly to Wood information about her father Sir Edwin Sandys – a prominent politician over the turn of the century, subsequently a successful manager and treasurer of the Virginia Company, which at that time under royal charter, effectively governed Virginia; of her uncle George Sandys – a poet, mainly known for his poetic translations of Ovid, but who also was involved in Virginia, and who was to be appointed 'a gentleman of the privy Chamber' to Charles I; and of her grandfather Edwin Sandys, Archbishop of York.

Aubrey also made contact on Wood's behalf with Peter du Moulin, a theologian, chaplain to Charles II, and now a prebendary at Canterbury – as had been his father, a French Protestant divine who had come over to advise James I. Aubrey might well have met him before, as both had frequented the Pall Mall *salon* of Catherine Ranelagh, Richard Boyle's sister, in the early years of Parliamentary rule. Now he approached du Moulin at the suggestion of Lady Thanet, Richard Boyle's niece. He received in reply 'an extraordinarily civil gentleman-like letter', not only giving the information on a Dr Jacob that Wood sought, but also offering to seek, on Wood's behalf, information about Oxonian archbishops buried at Canterbury. In the course of his stay Aubrey seems to have become as close a friend of Lady Thanet's as of her husband, and as usual with Aubrey's friendships it was to be long-lasting. Nearly twenty years later we find Aubrey writing to Wood, in a letter dated 29 April 1691: 'tomorrow [I] will goe to the good Countess of Thanet about the Earl of Clarendon.'[4] The son of the Lord Chancellor, Clarendon was at this time in the Tower because of his opposition to William and Mary. Aubrey was concerned that 'so few make visits to so great a person'.

In his hibernation at Hothfield Aubrey did not forget Robert Wiseman who seems to have been on the point of an unsatisfactory marriage which had cost him his job with the Bathursts. In an early autumnal letter Aubrey wrote 'If Robinet's marriage does not goe on I could recommend him to my Lords service here, £XX per anno wages, and all his cast clothes, hatts, stockings, etc.'[5] In an early spring letter of 7 April 1673 – from the other side of the winter divide – Aubrey was again complaining of his brother William, and again one would think with reason: 'I had 3 other draughts of several views of Osney in my trunke at Kington by Easton Piers, but dare not trust my brother with my key, for my bookes would be like butterflies and fly about all over the country; but if you shall have ought to make use of them, I shall send for my trunke to Chalke.'[6] It is surprising to find William still at Kington, but in due course he was to end his days, and a considerable number of years, living in Kington St Michael House – which no longer exists, but which shows as a sizeable building adjacent to the Manor in a drawing of Aubrey's for his *North Wiltshire Collections*.

*   *   *

Depending on one's temperament and tastes, a long stay in the country can be either a period of pleasant, restful quiet or one of depressing dullness. One would think that for Aubrey it was the latter. By the start of the spring he was obviously longing to be back in London, but was prevented by bad weather, a delay which provoked an untypical burst of universally directed bad temper. 'I think the world is besotted.'[7] However, by 14 May he was in London. 'Hither about a week since', he wrote to Wood, but staying as he was to do until he set forth on his perambulation, no longer at the Blackamore's Head, but with Henry Coley, his astrologer friend, in his house in Westminster. This may, in part, have accounted for his continuing depression, for appreciative though he always was of Coley's kindness as well as of his astrological ability, Coley was a man of modest means, and as such must have had a modest house, in which it must have been much less enjoyable for Aubrey to 'take his diet and sweet otiums' than in Wyld's 'knick-knackery' in Bloomsbury Square – although, no doubt, Wyld still took him with him when he set out to be 'merry' of an evening. Alternatively, it might simply have been that Aubrey had at long last realized that it was not much fun having little or no money. Whatever it was, it was clear from this mid-May letter to Wood that London air had not dissipated the Hothfield gloom: 'I could wish myselfe with you this month for 2 or 3 days to reshape and revive my dull dejected spirit. We are governed by the planets.'[8] At this time Aubrey was apt to put responsibility for his many misfortunes on 'the planets' or 'the stars'. For psychological as well as practical reasons it may not have been good for him to live in an astrologer's house.

However, there were no serious complications in his plans to survey Surrey. Sometime in May John Ogilby confirmed Aubrey's appointment and gave him the necessary licence as evidence of his authority, a formidable document in which Ogilby required 'all justices of the Peace, Mayors, Bailiffs, Sheriffs, Parsons, Vicars, Churchwardens, High Constables, Con-stables, Headborows, and all other his Majesty's officers, Ministers and subjects' to aid and assist Aubrey, who must have been relieved to see that bailiffs were included in the list of those required to help him. Aubrey was now officially authorized to carry out his survey, and so free to start on it whenever he liked. But inevitably there were delays. One was due to the late arrival of his horse from Broadchalke, which he needed for his journey, about which he wrote to Wood on 17 June, as 'My candid friend, I shall not begin my journey till this day or to-morrow fortnight, for the horse will not come up till next Saturday – and my brother (I thank him) has laimed my horse just as I have occasion for him, and a good handsome horse to doe me credit, so that I shall be forced to ride on my brother's little nagge.'⁹ Aubrey's spirits had not yet lifted even at the thought of the perambulation ahead, although he hoped the change and interest it should provide would raise them. 'The delicate aire and diversion of Surrey will cure my lassitude of spirit (I hope).' He still seems not to have managed to get to Oxford and to see Wood. 'I long as it were with a woman's longing to see you and Oxford.'¹⁰

Two other unforeseeable and unfortunate events delayed his departure still further. One he recorded and related in his 'Accidents': 'Midsummer. St. John's night, 1673, in danger of being run through with a sword by a young reveler at Mr. Burges' Chamber, in the M. Temple.'¹¹ One feels that Aubrey would not have recorded this as an 'accident' unless he suffered some hurt, but one wishes he had told us more about it for it is unlike Aubrey to get involved in a drunken quarrel, which this sounds to have been. The other delay was caused by the death of an old, valued and valuable friend, Sir Robert Moray, an important member of the courts of both Charles I and II, advising the first Charles to surrender to the Scots and then, when this arrangement did not work out as he had wished, attempting to rescue him from them. Subsequently he shared Charles II's exile in France; and some three years after the Restoration was appointed Lord of the Exchequer for Scotland. Although by profession a soldier – he had served in the French army before the Civil War, returning to fight for his King at its outbreak and for some years of his exile in France had commanded the Scots Regiment – he was by Aubrey's description 'very well read' and 'one of the first Contrivors and Institutors of the Royal Society . . . He was my most honoured and obliging friend, and I was more obliged to him than to all the Courtiers besides. I have a great losse in his death, for, had he lived, he would have got some employment or other for me before this time. He had the King's eare as much as anyone . . . I was often with him. I was with him three houres the morning he dyed'. Since to Aubrey friendship was paramount, one can surmise with some certainty that he would have stayed in London to attend Moray's funeral in Westminster Abbey where 'he lies next to Sir William Davenant.'¹²

But at last Aubrey, sometime in mid July, did set forth on his brother's 'little nagge', which presumably on occasion had to carry also 'the pretty youth' that Aubrey had 'found to wayte on me that can write and reade and loves ingeniose things and will be adroit for my service'.[13] Then there was a long silence. One imagines Aubrey busy with his notes and sketchings. His drawings were much fewer than in his *North Wiltshire Collections*, confined in the main to notable buildings and only in pen and ink – but carefully and cleverly done, so that one gets a feel of the atmosphere as well as an idea of the appearance, and none, happily, drawn 'symbolically' on horseback. Even if Aubrey had had time to write a letter it would have been difficult under the constantly moving conditions which his task imposed to find a carrier by whom to send it. But at length, about a month later, he surfaced, not by now in Surrey at all, but in 'an adjacent part' at Stanstrete Causeway in Sussex. He came back into circulation with a gasp of delight, 'the delicate aire and diversion of Surrey' having clearly, as he had hoped, worked wonders. 'I have had the pleasantest pilgrimage that ever any man has had since the Reformation, and found many strangers very civill to me, much more than I did in Wilts, and am now accidentally fell upon a Countryman – the curate of this place, who is exceeding humane to me.'[13] To be fair to Aubrey's Wilt-shire countrymen, they, too would probably have been very civil to him had he come to them armed with the Royal authority as he now was. Aubrey was so carried away by the delight he had found in his journey that he was already planning another one – 'I intend before Xmas to perambulate Berks.' Some five weeks later he was writing to Wood again but by this time back in London: 'I returned here 2 or 3 days since and read yours . . . at honest H. Coley's. I have a weekes worke or better left yet to do, on the other side of the Thames, which I reserved to the last. I have taken a great swab of papers but of great delight . . . If Mr. O[gilby] will be ruled by me it will be a pretty piece.'[14]

On the 'Morrow after St. Matthews Day' [22 September], Aubrey was preparing to set forth on the next day to complete this final segment of his task, intending 'to returne in a fortnight'. He had in the meantime evidently been to see Ogilby for there was an ominous comment – 'Never had a man to deale with so fickle and subtile a man as J.O' – although Aubrey does not give his reasons for this suddenly severe judgement. Aubrey seems to have had another meeting with Ogilby before he set off. For an entry in the laconic diary of Robert Hooke, dated 'Sept. 30th 1673', runs 'Met Ogilby and Aubrey at Garraways' (a popular coffee-house). This final phase of his perambulation seems to have mirrored the change in his fortunes which his comment on Ogilby suggests. It was dogged not so much by disaster as by mishap. On his return, in a letter dated 11 October he started to tell Wood about it. After the first day 'my horse broke out of a ground, or else was stolen. I have been in quest after him, and cannot yet hear of him, and yesterday came from Richmond on foot – were it not for some criticall coxcombes I would as soon doe this worke in such a way. About the middle of next week I shall either buy or have a horse lent me by a friend.'

Somebody or something interrupted Aubrey at this point for he only completes his letter five days later: 'Oct 16th . . . I was interrupted from going on any further . . . On Sunday last was sent me one of these horses I wrote you about, on which I went to Kingston on Monday and came back last night. His feed etc, came to 8s., but I should have told you that on Sunday night Mr. Og. told me he had altered his mind and would now make no more use of me. I asked him for some consideration for all my time spent on his account, and for sending down my horse – by Lord God not he a shilling . . . God deliver me from such men.' It must have been a bitter blow to Aubrey, just when he had at last found work that seemed perfectly suited to his talents and temperament, that he greatly enjoyed and which promised to keep him happily occupied for many years to come. But he took it remarkably well. In the letter in which he told Wood, who had been one of those who had warned him about Ogilby, of his dismissal, he went on, 'Mr. Hooke says he will by next spring bring him about again but I do not much care, though I should have been glad to have surveyed Sussex' – and also Berkshire, and also anywhere else that offered, for clearly it was work that he loved doing. 'Dear friende, all happiness attend you. I am resolved to lie as concealled as I can and try for some preferment be it but indifferent, for I have friends to divert me. God bless us both.'[15]

It is a sad letter and in it one senses the depth of Aubrey's disappointment. What seems, to us, so unfair is that of all Aubrey's disasters and disappointments, this is about the only one for which he seems to have been in no way to blame. One doubts whether, in fact, Ogilby would even have seen Aubrey's work before he dismissed him. It was far too short a time, a matter only of a few days between Aubrey's return and their meeting for anyone to shape his notes into a presentable form, although in the letter to Wood written on the 'Morrow after St. Matthews Day', Aubrey had told him he was already 'extremely busy in transcribing'. In reality Ogilby's decision seems to have been, as Aubrey's friends feared it might prove, a matter of money. He had another Deputy working for him, covering Essex, as Aubrey was Surrey. This was an able, ambitious young man of twenty-five, Gregory King, who had started his career as clerk to Aubrey's antiquarian friend Sir William Dugdale. In the course of his survey he held at one point a lottery of books, which made Ogilby some money. A choice between an assistant who made him money, and another whom he had to pay, even the small amount which initially he gave to Aubrey – who was subsequently out of pocket – was to someone of Ogilby's character one which made itself. The motive behind Aubrey's dismissal seems to have been as simple as this. Yet one wonders why there was need to make a choice. This was a large-scale undertaking, in which there was ample room for two assistants. Aubrey would have asked little and given much in return – if not in money.

Aubrey's dismissal was not only personally disappointing, it must have been impersonally frustrating as well, for he no longer had the incentive to complete the work, on which he had not only worked hard but well. One can see from his notes that these with a little work would have made 'the pretty piece' of which he had hopes 'if Mr. O. will be ruled by me'. Inevitably his *Perambulation* lacks some of the hidden charms of the *Collections*, for Aubrey had not the time nor the facilities to produce the paintings which give the *Collections* not only their colour but also much of their character, nor does it have the feeling of familiarity which comes from Aubrey's long acquaintance with north Wiltshire. Yet in two months Aubrey manages to extract almost as much information as he did out of his ten-year search of the countryside around Easton Piers. His observations are wide-ranging covering an area from the Thames to the Sussex coast. They also deal with a wide spread of subjects which includes pieces of historical hearsay such as that Cardinal Wolsey lived in Esher House while he was building Hampton Court; of agricultural information, such as that 'clover grass and sanfoin much in use . . . agreeing very well with the soyle . . .', that 'the kine and cattle in the sandy country are weak and of a sandy colour . . .', that 'Sussex wheat is as good as any in England . . .', that 'the mutton here is as sweet as any in England.' This was 'on Bansted-downes' where 'the aire . . . is admirable . . . the London doctors do send their patients hither as the ultimate refugium.' There was also an occasional event such as 'the Horse-race [which] is much frequented: it is four miles long'. Needless to say Aubrey was now near Epsom. There is also much miscellaneous information that is unclassifiable – on nearby Boxhill 'the great quantity and thicknesse of the Boxwood yields a convenient privacy for lovers . . . they often export hither from Epsom.' There were several ecclesiastical 'Peculiars', by which Aubrey did not mean local clergymen but parishes which came under the jurisdiction of a diocese other than the one in which they were situated. 'On the South Downes . . . are the biggest snails of any I saw . . . Elias Ashmole tells me that the Lord Marshall brought them from Italie and scattered them on the Downs.' Throughout Aubrey makes his usual careful examination of churches and noteworthy buildings, and in the background attempts a general scenic description which at times he over simplifies: 'From this hill (Boxhill) southward over the Wyld of Surrey (which runs about seven miles) to the Downs in Sussex. This hill runs continuously from Lewes to Kent and so to Dover; It is interrupted by a little valley and so round by Guildford town.' In this short circuit Aubrey manages to cover not only Surrey, but much of Sussex and Kent as well.

Amid the run of, at this stage, necessarily disconnected jottings, there is the occasional set piece such as an idyllic sounding estate 'Nr. Dorking [where] the Hon. Charles Howard hath very ingeniosely contrived a long slope into the most delightful solitude for House, Garden, Orchards, Boscages, etc that I have seen in England . . . The South side of the slope is connected into a vineyard . . . Above the hill on the west side is a thicket of Black Cherrie trees; the ground abounds with strawberries. The pleasure of the garden was so ---- [in his delight, Aubrey was clearly at a loss for words] that I cannot expect any enjoyment beyond it than that of the Kingdom of Heaven. Mr. Newman (his steward) entertained me very kindly, according to his Master's order.'[16] All in all his perambulation seems to show the Aubrey mix of knowledge, gossip, observation and entertainment at its best. It clearly provided a welcome interval that brought a breath of fresh air into the stuffy confines of his work for Wood, and into his London life.

At a time when Aubrey must have already been in low spirits, after the collapse of all his hopes and dreams of further perambulations, he was further saddened by news of the death of William Radford, the Trinity friend, who had been so remarkably courageous in keeping him company when he had smallpox, and who had for some time now been running his own school in Richmond, the school to which had gone the younger George Ent, and no doubt several other sons of Aubrey's friends. Aubrey never forgot Radford's altruistic action, as he showed in his letter to Wood of 28 October in which he told him of Radford's death. 'Will Radford my good friende ended his days at Richmond where he taught . . . when I was sick of the small-pox at Trin. Coll. Oxon he was so kind as to come to me every day and spend severall hours . . . He was recounting not many days before he dyed your brother Ned's voyage and Mr. Marriett's to London on foote.'[17] This was the 'great adventure' when the three undergraduates had walked from Oxford to London, where none of them had ever been before, calling in at Eton on the way. Aubrey's reminder of their escapade must however have given Wood a prick of pain for his 'brother Ned' had died of consumption some eighteen years earlier, shortly after becoming a Fellow of Merton. However, 'on Sunday I dined with my honest friend Mr. Ashmole' which must have cheered Aubrey up. It is interesting to learn that Aubrey was already on terms of friendship with Ashmole – although both being 'original members' of the Royal Society they were bound to be already well acquainted – since in the last years of Aubrey's life this friendship was to be of paramount importance in securing the preservation of his work.

Now, however, although there was more reason for it, Aubrey's depression seems to have cleared more quickly than the miasma which overlaid his spirits over the period between his return from Hothfield and his departure for Surrey. His letters to Wood are increasingly cheerful. He was obviously much touched, as his letter of 15 November showed, when Wood at last sent him, via his brother, a small gift as a token of gratitude. 'H. Coley delivered me your kind token [£5] which came in a very acceptable time, and I sacrificed ½ pint of sack to you. Dear John, I return you many thanks and would not have you put yourself to any further charges. You have abundantly obliged me severall ways already and your exemplary friendship is never to be forgotten by your assured and most affectionate friend – JA.'[18] Wood's gift was long overdue but Aubrey seems to have been greatly moved by it, for he thanks him again in his next letter, of 9 December. 'I thank you for your kind token by your brother.' To show his affection as well as his gratitude he now appended a verse he had 'transcribed out of a window in the Townhall at Kingston-super-Thames' – in the last, unfortunate, stage of his perambulation –

> 'Who gives the greatest gives but of his Love,
> And he that gives the least can give no lesse,
> The smallest gift my great Affection prove.
> Tis not the Guift that can the Heart express.'[19]

Aubrey added his own endorsement 'methinks 'tis well said', obviously aimed at Wood. In his next letter there was a wistful reminder of what had been and what, but for Ogilby, might have been. 'I can make friends to serve you in Sussex.' A Christmas Day letter carried little more than Christmas greetings to Wood and his Oxford friends. But one written on New Year's Day ended with the postscript 'My service and good wishes to the merry Gang, Dr. Levins, Dr. Lamphire. Mr. Browne.' They were an oddly assorted trio. While the Doctors Levins and Lamphire were senior University figures – Dr Levins being President of St John's, and Dr Lamphire President of Hart Hall – Mr Browne, the son of the Rector of Minety, and Aubrey's assistant in his researches for his *North Wiltshire Collections*, was at this time still an undergraduate. With Wood and 'the merry Gang' in Oxford, and his many friends in London, Aubrey was obviously reasonably happy again.

But if Aubrey seems, on the surface at any rate, to have ceased worrying unduly about his future, and to have been concerned mainly with enjoying the present, his eminent Royal Society friends were by contrast increasingly worried both for, and about, him. A later letter to Wood, written on 23 February 1674, refers retrospectively to their efforts on his behalf at this time. 'I have several good friends, who are great men – this afternoon they chid me, saying, have you found any good place yet, but find it out and your Businesse will be done. So I have layd Queries in the Customs House, Tower, etc.' One would think that Aubrey's timing of the sequence of events in this letter is, for convenience in the writing, foreshortened. Reading between the lines, it seems likely that the 'several good friends who are great men' had some time previously suggested that he should find out whether there was a possible job going, and that if there was they would try and get it for him. It seems probable that this suggestion came at the time in the previous October when he wrote Wood that he would try for some 'preferment be it but indifferent'. Nothing, however, having come of his 'Queries', when his friends met him on the afternoon of his letter they had 'chid' him for not finding such a job, suspecting no doubt – and possibly with good reason – that Aubrey had made no great effort to do so. So they now suggested a further option, which had thrown Aubrey's thoughts into turmoil: 'I am stormed anew. They would have me turne Parson and keepe an honest Curate, and I shall have a parsonage of £200 a yeare. What do you think of this? Is it honorable or prudent. Lord, how I should looke in a Cassoq. . . . Pray advise me by the next post for I am so importuned that I could scarce sleep last night.' Again, there is an obvious but totally unimportant discrepancy in the telling, for clearly the sleepless night must have come between the 'chiding' and the writing of the letter, and so could not have been 'this afternoon'.

At the beginning of this revealing letter, Aubrey had asked Wood whether he had become a Roman Catholic: 'Now let me take you to scrutiny. Are you turned Rom. Cath. or no? You know what I am, no enemie to them, unless Irish Biggotts. That you are so, was reported at the Vice Chancellor's table and that by the Deane [Aubrey writes "Dr. Bathurst" above] . . . Amongst the Clergy, Humility and Charity very rare, except you come to an honest, poore, old bachelor parson.' One wonders why Aubrey was concerned whether Wood was Catholic or not, until one realizes that this was the time when Catholic influence was increasing at court, and that with an ardent Catholic heir to the throne, there was widespread fear of a return of Catholic power. This gave Aubrey the excuse he was looking for. For if the country became Catholic again, what point would there be in his becoming a parson? 'In this case I shall take no paines, enjoy my friends at London and Oxon; on this account have a gentle competence.'[20] Wood seems to have agreed. For in a letter written on 'March the last' 1674, Aubrey thanks him 'for your advice concerning the Cassock; and it will be better for me to accept of £50 or £60 per. ann., which will serve my turne'.[21]

Had Aubrey's eminent friends been more determined to push him into a parsonage, as well they might have been for at that time it was the conventional solution for impoverished men of intellectual ability, they would have been sensible not to have made the arrangements which Aubrey had announced, with obvious delight, in the letter which preceded, by a month, that in which he told Wood of the offer of a 'benefice'. On 'Jan. the last' he wrote to Wood: 'The Royal Society have been pleased to lay their commands upon me to keepe a correspondance with my numerous company of ingeniose virtuosi in severall countries and will pay the expenses of Letters, etc, and allow me something of an honorarium besides.'[22] This was, of course, an arrangement that suited Aubrey perfectly. For he liked writing letters, liked feeling that he was expanding the web of knowledge, and liked, now, having the authority of the Royal Society behind him. Once again the several 'great men' had showed themselves to be Aubrey's true friends, for while among themselves they might have considered that the sensible course would have been for Aubrey to take the parsonage, which would have given him security as well as a salary, yet clearly they did not wish to force him into a way of life that did not appeal to him. So they offered an alternative – the '£50 or £60 per. ann. which will serve my turne'. Had he not had it in mind when the offer of the parsonage of £200 a year was made to him, he might have felt he had no option but to put on the cassock, the thought of which quite clearly appalled him.

For the moment then, having seemingly refused the parsonage, and having certainly accepted the Royal Society's 'commands' to deal with their correspondence, the rough passage through which Aubrey's life had been travelling seemed to be coming to an end, and the prospect of smooth water to lie ahead. This seemed to be confirmed by Aubrey's reappearance in the records of the Royal Society meetings, his first meeting since 1670. 'Feb 5th 1673/4 – Mr. Aubrey presented some written observations concerning winds, their blowing down many hundreds of oakes at once, their blowing very differently in places little distant from one another.'[23]

It is, however, just at such moments of relaxed optimism that one tends to be struck by an unexpected squall of ill-fortune. This is what seems now to have happened to Aubrey, as his next letter to Wood, written at the end of March tells: 'I am sorry I have been so long silent' (in replying to an early March letter of Wood's) 'but when it came I was in some trouble under an Arrest.' This seems to have occurred at Gresham College for Hooke noted briefly in his entry for 5 March, 'Aubrey arrested, £200 debt', and to have been instigated by creditors, not in Wiltshire but in Brecon. One would think from its provenance that this was a debt that went back as far as the entail. Aubrey was in custody for four days – which must have been for him an unpleasant, worrying and humiliating time – yet at the end he emerged surprisingly cheerful and obviously relieved. 'Thanke God [it] happened very well . . . for Providence provided better for me than I could have done for myselfe or imagined – for I have a friend will undertake to manage my concern in Brecon and I shall pay my debts.'[24] The 'friend' obviously wished to remain anonymous, but far the most likely person to have helped Aubrey in such a situation in such a place was Aubrey's namesake, the second Sir John Aubrey who had recently inherited the title and Llantrithyd, the estate in Glamorgan, from his father. The second Sir John would have been about Aubrey's age, and it is more than likely that they had become good friends during Aubrey's many stays at Llantrithyd in his more prosperous past. Nor for the sake of the family name may the second Sir John have liked the thought of a close relation languishing in a debtors' prison.

One would think that the resolution of this Brecon debt cleared the air of serious creditors, although one knows through a complaint that Aubrey was later to make of his brother William that there was at least one long-standing local debt still owed in Wiltshire, although fortunately to a person who was unlikely to take him to court. This was Captain Thomas Stump, who as a youth had had the amazing adventure in Guiana when he had been left behind by his ship. 'I desired him (brother William) to pay Captain Stumpe of Malmesbury a debt of 20 li. upon Bond borrowed in 1660, and he was so civill as to accept of the principall, and my brother never did it.'[25] It is extraordinary to think that Aubrey had never repaid this relatively small debt, after the sale of Burleton and Stretford in 1662 and 1663 which between them brought in £3000. It shows the amount that Aubrey at that time must have owed elsewhere. Where there was one such debt there may have been others one does not know about, yet Aubrey felt safe enough the following year to stay for several months with his friends the Longs at Draycot Cerne, only a few miles from Easton Piers.

Relaxed, and for the moment relieved of worry about impending debts, Aubrey returned in April to his work at Gresham College, where he told Wood in the same letter in which he recounted his arrest, he was 'engaged in writing the Catalogue of Repository for the Royal Society, which will hardly be finished by the begining of May'. But in the same month another possibility was to open before him, which, had he taken it, would have radically altered the shape of his life. This was to go to Jamaica on the staff of the newly-appointed Governor, Lord Vaughan, 'an old acquaintance and ingeniose friend'. Aubrey had long played with the idea of emigrating either to America or to the West Indies. In the year of his absconding he had written to Wood, 'Now if I would be rich I could be a Prince. I could go into Maryland which is one of the finest countries in the world [Aubrey inserts above "same climate as in France"] I can have all by favour of my Lord Baltimore, I could wish. His brother is Lieutenant there and is a very good-natured gent – plenty of all things. Ground there is 2,000 miles westward . . . I could be able, I believe, to carry a colony of rogues, another of ingeniose artificers, and I doubt not but one might make a shift to have 5 or 6 ingeniose companions, which is enough.'[26] Later Thanet was keen for him to go to Bermuda where he had an estate.

One feels that Aubrey was quite right to refuse such offers. One can not see him as a settler. He was neither practical nor purposeful enough. If he had not been able to run efficiently the small estate at Easton Piers, what hope was there that he could control a colony of 'rogues and artificers', even with the help of 'ingeniose friends'. But the offer of a job on the staff of the Governor of Jamaica was quite a different matter. As such he would have been looked after, protected and privileged. In this still little known island his knowledge of natural history and his powers of observation might well have made him genuinely useful to the Governor. There would, too, almost certainly have been some financial pickings to be gathered in the course of his stay which might have made all the difference to the conditions of his later life. Possibly most important of all, it was an appointment and an adventure of definite duration, not the indefinite exile which emigration must have seemed – and might have been.

Aubrey first told Wood about the possibility in a letter of 9 April: 'I am like to be spirited away to Jamaica by my Lord Vaughan who is newly-made Gouvnor there and mighty earnest to have me goe with him and will look at some employment worthy a Gent. for me.' He then goes on, rather surprisingly, but no doubt remembering the narrow and recent escape from becoming a parson, 'Fough! The cassock stinks. It would be ridiculous.' Reverting to the Jamaican possibility Aubrey tells Wood that 'I can send into England every month or six weeks.'[27] A fortnight later he is still sounding excited and enthusiastic: 'I have been very busy lately and chiefly with my Lord Vaughan who has promised me to looke out some place suitable to the quality of a gentleman.'[28] The loss of his money and of Easton Piers seems to have made Aubrey unduly touchy about the respect due to his birth. In fact other than menial jobs it is difficult to think what place in the Governor's entourage would not suit a gentleman, although one can think of several which would not have suited Aubrey. However, by mid May it sounds as if his enthusiasm was beginning to flag: 'I doe think it will be my fate to goe to America this summer.'[29] When Aubrey starts talking about his fate one knows he is beginning to back-track. Ten days later, again writing to Wood, he tells him he has 'a wonderful longing to see you before I go to Jamaica as I know I shall.' However, summer came and went. Lord Vaughan also went, although possibly not until the autumn, for an August letter to Wood seems to presage a final farewell: 'I hope to see you once more.' But, of course, Aubrey never went. It might have been that Lord Vaughan had failed to find a job 'suitable for a gentleman' or that he had changed his mind about Aubrey's suitability as a companion. But both of these possibilities seem most unlikely. It is clear from Aubrey's early remarks that Lord Vaughan had made a definite even if unspecified offer of a post, and as an 'old acquaintance and

ingeniose friend' he would have known that he would be unlikely to find
anyone more knowledgeable or who would be better company than Aubrey. It
is far more likely that Aubrey could not bring himself to take the final plunge
and accept the offer, partly because he always found important decisions of
this sort difficult, if not impossible, to make, but mainly because he could not
bear to leave his friends. Yet if one can not really see Aubrey either as a priest
or a parson, this surely was a missed opportunity. One regrets it for our sakes
as well as his, for a 'Perambulation round Jamaica' might have been well
worth reading. On the other hand, the health hazards in the West Indies were
such at that time that Aubrey might never have returned.

Other than deciding whether or not to go to Jamaica, a decision which in the
end, like so many of Aubrey's, seems to have been a decision by default,
Aubrey's main concern and interest throughout the summer of 1674 was the
publication of Wood's book which appeared first in a Latin version under the
title of *Historia et Antiquitates Univ. Oxon* in July, the work to which he had
himself contributed much, as Wood acknowledged in it, although his contributions were confined to the more biographical details of eminent Oxonians
and he had little to do with the main body of work. This was divided into two
parts, the history of the university from its foundation to 1649; and then that of
the various colleges and halls from foundation to 1668, which included
detailed lists of benefactors and the variously styled heads of colleges, as well as
lists of those Fellows who happened to be buried in the college chapels. It was a
monumental work of which Wood could be justifiably proud. But even before
publication it ran into trouble. This was mainly because of the clash of the two
powerful but prickly personalities – Wood himself, who had given most of his
life to its researching and writing and who in consequence cared more for it
than for anything or anybody else, and the autocratic Dean of Christ Church,
Dr Fell, of whom many others including Hobbes had already fallen foul.

As in most controversies, there was right and wrong on both sides. Dr Fell
on behalf of the University Press had bought the manuscript from Wood for
£100, and intended to publish it at his own expense. This on the face of it
clearly gave him the right to do what he liked with it. Yet what he did with it
was inconsiderate of Wood and the fact that this was his life's work. Wood
had written it in a sturdy, sensible English style that if it lacked the flare and
flash of Aubrey's often striking phraseology yet was an admirable medium in
which to present the enormous amount of knowledge he had accumulated in
his years of research. The result was a convincing and thorough picture of the
development of the university and its colleges. Dr Fell decided to have the
manuscript of the first part translated into Latin. The thought behind this
was both practical and flattering to Wood – that it would make it more
accessible to international scholars, since the universal language of learning

was still Latin. However, in reality it removed the personal element which lay in Wood's style and choice of his English, and so stole the book from him.

Another contentious issue arose between the sensitive scholar and the autocratic Dean in the course of the book's preparation for publication. Wood intended to add to the first part the brief biographies of eminent Oxford writers and scholars, for many of which Aubrey had provided much of the information. Many of them were produced during the process of the preparation for publication of Wood's manuscript and so could have been considered outside the terms of the original sale. In any case, they formed so small a part of the total work that a sympathetic editor would surely have left to Wood the right to publish them in the way he wanted. But Dr Fell subjected them to a strict personal scrutiny, and censored so many of them that Aubrey and his London friends suggested to Wood that he might himself publish a separate volume of those pages which had been rejected by the Dean. For these various reasons Wood obviously considered that his much beloved brainchild was strangled at birth, and to this attributed its failure to bring him the instant fame and recognition which was what he really wanted. The result was to make him become even more a recluse than he was already and to induce in him an increasing state of embitterment.

Over these years, which might be considered those of Aubrey's rehabilitation, his friendship with Wood played so central a part in his life – their correspondence being so often the only means through which one learns what Aubrey thought, felt and did over this period – that one tends to neglect the considerable part of his life outside it. He continued to pay intermittent visits to Broadchalke, still accomplished with a pretence of secrecy, although one would have thought this was in reality no longer necessary. In the spring of 1674 he went down to see his brother and mother. His mother had now settled in Bridgwater, and it was probably through her that Aubrey made the acquaintance of Andrew Paschall, the erudite vicar of Chedzoy, a parish, as the name suggests, in deep Somerset, some two miles to the west of Bridgwater. This acquaintance led to a correspondence which started in 1672 as a trickle but which became a flood when Aubrey, acting one would think under the commands of the Royal Society, enrolled him as one of his frequent correspondents. From then on there was a regular flow of letters between them, of which more than eighty survive in the Bodleian, difficult at first to read because of Paschall's old-fashioned calligraphic style and mainly dealing with mathematical matters, but concerned also with points and problems of scientific and antiquarian interest. On the odd occasion Aubrey brought these up, with a proper attribution, at meetings of the Royal Society. It must have been a considerable satisfaction to the intellectually minded vicar, stuck in the mud of Somerset, to know that he was in touch with, and on occasion had the ear of, so eminent a society. As often with Aubrey, acquaintance developed into friendship, and Aubrey would sometimes stay with Paschall, no doubt as a means also of seeing his mother. Paschall also sometimes came to London, where Aubrey introduced him to many of his eminent friends.

In the autumn of 1674 Aubrey was again at Broadchalke, and from there went on what was to prove to be his last visit to the friend for whom he always seems to have felt a particular affection and respect, Francis Potter. 'The last time I saw this honoured friend of mine was Octob. 1674. I had not seen him in 3 yeares before, and his lippitude [soreness of the eyes] then was come even to blindnesse, which did much grieve one to behold; he had let his beard be uncutt which was wont to be but little. I asked him why he did not get some kinsman ["cousin" inserted above] or kinswoman of his to live with him and looke to him now in his great age. He answered me that he had tryed that way and found it not so well, for they did begrudge what he spent; that 'twas too much and went from them: whereas his servants (strangers) were kind to him and tooke care of him.'[30] Francis Potter was not, in fact, to die until 1679, but Aubrey never went to see him again, probably finding it too sad a sight to see the ruin of this inventive and intellectually able man, who, if he had been born that much later, and so caught the tide of the new learning, as had Aubrey, might well have found the opportunities and recognition he deserved.

A sociable life
1673–6

Now that it was comfortably housed in Gresham College the Royal Society was the centre of Aubrey's social, as well as of his working, life. He was no longer a fringe frequenter of Whitehall as he had been in both Parliamentary and early Restoration days, nor was he any longer a member of an artistic circle such as that which used to meet regularly at the home of Samuel Cooper, although he continued to be on terms of friendship with individual artists, such as Cooper, Hollar and Faithorne, whom he both admired and liked. Yet since it had been given the seal of royal approval, the Royal Society had greatly developed as a social as well as a scientific centre. It had, in fact, formed a club within the club which the Society in reality was, meeting regularly on a Thursday after the weekly lecture. Members, however, often met there on other evenings as well. 'Our R. Soc. Club', Aubrey told Wood, included 'several Parl. men and courtiers, persons of great intelligence who commonly beare the news first to us'. On one occasion when, as Aubrey put it, his head was 'fuller of good wine than prudence' he had passed on an item of news obtained in this way, which was clearly confidential, before he should have done. Flushed not only with wine but with the excitement of whatever it was he had just learnt, he had 'immediately at the stationers shop by the Taverne' written a letter to Tom Mariet in which he gave an 'account which though I believe to be true as soon as I had sent the letter to the post-house I was troubled by an impulse of spirit that I had not donne well though it was to my old acquaintance and intimate friend from boyhood'. From Mariet Aubrey's news had quickly been picked up by the grapevine, reaching even Wood, whose letter referring to it troubled Aubrey 'more than any letter that ever I read, in my lifetime'.[1] However, being Aubrey, no doubt the indiscretion, whatever it was, would have been quickly forgiven and forgotten.

The members of the club meeting at Gresham College did not however necessarily adjourn to 'the Taverne'. They were more likely, in fact, to go to one of the several coffee-houses in the neighbourhood. The remarkably speedy spread of these since the early '50s when 'the first one in England' had been established in Oxford, had effected something of a social revolution, as Aubrey was later to describe in a letter to Wood of 30 September 1680. 'Heretofore, before coffee-houses, men could not be so well-acquainted with one another.'[2] Again in the covering letter he sent with the first instalment of his 'Lives' he referred to 'the extreme advantage of coffee-houses in the great Citie; before when men knew not how to be acquainted other than with their own Relations or Societies'.[3] Being the basically convivial person that he was it was perhaps one of Aubrey's greatest pieces of luck that his life in London should have coincided with the growth of the habit of coffee-housing.

From 1672 on one can see from a new viewpoint how large a part coffee-houses and coffee-housing played in Aubrey's social life. This is through the diaries of Robert Hooke, not only one of the most distinguished and ultimately one of the most famous members of the Royal Society, but as it's Curator the one most central to its existence. Hooke and Aubrey were thrown together in 1674, when Aubrey took on, first, the cataloguing of the Society's possessions and then its scientific correspondence, and so was working for much of the time at the college. But well before then they were clearly on close terms of friendship, as one can see from the number of times from its start that Aubrey figures in the diary. Not only was Aubrey a frequent companion, among several, of Hooke's when they prolonged their evenings after meetings in Gresham College by visits to the near-by coffee-houses and taverns, but Hooke frequently lent Aubrey the small sums of money he needed for his day-to-day needs. This was before Aubrey was receiving 'something of an honorarium' from the Society, and one would think between the visits to Broadchalke when it was likely he collected the small part of the farm's income that he kept for himself. There is a pathetic sequence of entries in the late autumn of 1673, which shows how short Aubrey was of money at this time. 'Oct. 14th. Lent Aubrey 20s. He promised to repay it.' 'Nov. 20th. Drank bottle of wine with Mr. Aubrey and Mr. Shortgrave. Bought of Mr. Aubrey Euclids works and 15 other books. Acquitted the former 20s. lent.' But then only five days later on 25 November, 'Lent Mr. Aubrey 20s. more.'[4]

Aubrey had an immense respect not only for Hooke's inventive intelligence but for his boundless energy which enabled him to be active on numerous projects at the same time, and always to be brimming over with new ideas. When Wood, who disliked Hooke only slightly less than Hooke disliked him, left him out of the list of eminent Oxonians which he attached to his *Historia*, Aubrey was strong in his rebuke of Wood's omission: 'Mr.

Hooke told me (who had looked over your booke) that you have left out as many eminent men as you have putt in. You have not mentioned him, which I desired. England has hardly produced a greater Witt'[5] (by which Aubrey seems to mean not so much 'wit' as we would understand it but rather what we would term 'intellect'). Six weeks later, on 4 November 1674, Aubrey is again reprimanding Wood: 'I shall advert you I am exceeding sorry you left out Mr. R. Hooke so eminent both at home and abroad.'[6] Not for itself – for Aubrey was never to become emotionally involved with Hooke, as clearly he was throughout with Wood – but for its results, his friendship with Hooke was to prove his most important relationship of the next fourteen years, a period which covered the happiest and most productive years of his later life. This was simply because during this time, in one way or another, he made the college his home. One does not know whether the arrangement was made primarily at the suggestion of Hooke, or of Aubrey's many friends among the members of the Royal Society, who were still concerned to provide him with the framework of a reasonable life. Most probably there was an element of both. Clearly it would not have been a workable arrangement at all had not the two men got on well together, but equally clearly as the Society had control over the college they had to give their permission and approval. It may even have been they who suggested the arrangement in the first place.

It was an arrangement that made all the difference to Aubrey's life – even if, while one can be virtually certain, from the fact that during this time all his correspondence was sent to 'Mr. Hooke's lodgings in Gresham College', that the college was his main place of work, one can not be sure that he lived, or lodged, there permanently. The alternative, which was that he lived in lodgings near by would have made little difference to the main fact that the college was now the centre of his London life and so his home. The evidence in Hooke's diary, which provides over this period by far the best record of Aubrey's London life, seems to point both ways. On the one hand there are entries which seem to show beyond doubt that they were lodging together – 'Home with Aubrey' – 'Smoked with Aubrey' – and, most convincing of all, 'Aubrey ill with cold. Spake to Horne to mend chamber.' On the other hand there are several entries in which Hooke writes 'went to Aubrey's', which he clearly would not have done if at that time they were living together. Also, Aubrey at the end of the autobiographical fragment which he added to the 'Lives', probably in late 1680 or early 1681, twice refers to lodgings in Bishopsgate – 'Rest at Mistress Morris near Gres. Coll', and again in the margin – 'Mistress Morr. in Hammond [?] Alley, Bishops Gate, farthest howse'.[7] The reality seems likely to have been that Aubrey stayed with Hooke when it was convenient, and when it was not he lodged nearby. Either way he had the use of the college and its capacious surroundings. These must have been a great improvement on the cramped conditions of the hospitable Henry Coley's house, or the necessarily limited liberty of the time when he lived between the Blackamore's Head and Wild's 'knick-knackery'. Aubrey would have enjoyed the surrounding sense of space which the college allowed and when he was not working, sauntering in the quadrangle, on its lawn, under its lime trees, in its arcade if it was wet. Altogether the college provided all the conditions suitable to a scholarly gentleman's life without any of the responsibilities which were normally its corollary. Being at the centre of the Society's life, the constant coming and going of the members provided also all the scholarly and social interest that Aubrey could possibly wish for. It really was an ideal arrangement, and was to prove such over a long period of years.

One gets a good idea of Hooke's character as it was in these earlier happier years from the one letter from Hooke to Aubrey that survives. Hooke's letter, dated 24 August 1674, written to Aubrey when he was on a visit to Broadchalke, shows his practicality, also his essential fair-mindedness. He was concerned with the hiring of a new assistant to replace 'Harry' who at the end of his apprenticeship was being 'preferred . . . to Mr. Mountain and I doubt not he will get his 150 pounds or 200p per annum'. Aubrey had heard of a possible replacement, the younger brother of an astrologer friend, Charles Snell, who lived at Fordingbridge, only a few miles distant from Broadchalke. Hooke was prepared to offer his assistant 'Meate, Drink but not much more . . . My reasons are because although he doe me service yet I shall assist him much more. I would not have him for less than 7 years'[8] – a hard but a fair offer, for at the end of seven years with Hooke his apprentice would have had the skills to set himself up for life. Although he came to see Hooke, Charles Snell's brother did not get the job because he stammered too badly, an affliction towards which Aubrey must have been sympathetic. In the end, however, there proved to be no job to get, for Harry decided sensibly that he would rather stay on as Hooke's no doubt now properly paid assistant – which he did, becoming in the end the official laboratory assistant for the Royal Society. This in itself was a considerable tribute to Hooke, showing that although exacting, he was a good master.

Aubrey's portrait of Hooke's personal appearance in his 'Life' is surprisingly unflattering. 'He is but of middling stature, something crooked, pale-faced, and his face but little belowe, but his head is lardge; his eie full and popping, and not quick, a gray eie. He has a delicate head of Haire, browne, and of an excellent moist curle.' In character Aubrey commended him as being 'as he ever was, very temperate, and moderate in dyet . . . [he] is a person of great vertue'. For Hooke's ability Aubrey's praise was unstinted. 'He is of a prodigious inventive head. He is the greatest Mechanik this day in the World.' Aubrey ended with some general comments: 'He is a Batchelour and I believe will never marie. His elder brother left one faire dau,' to whom Hooke was to develop, in its fullest sense, a passionate devotion. Aubrey finally sums up: 'In fine which crowns all, he is a person of great sincerity and goodness.'[9]

Hooke's diary was mainly a factual record of what he had done in the day, but inevitably some personal comment crept in, such as when 'Sir Jo. More' a distinguished mathematician, of whom Aubrey was to write a 'Life', became 'horribly fuddled'; or on the evening when Hooke, with Wyld, Aubrey and two other Royal Society friends 'discoursed about Universal Character, about preadamits [those who believed in the existence of man before Adam] and of creation. About insects. I told Wyld and Aubrey about flying. Wild cold. Drank port.' On 22 January 1676 a group met at Wren's house, where besides Wren himself 'were present Mr. Henshaw, Dr. Holder, Mr. Aubery and I. Eat vinegar, sugar, sturgeon'. A week later the same group met at the same place and 'discoursed about petrification of Bodies, about plaisters, about framing glasse, Form of arch, light gold statues, staining marble . . . about printing stuffe and guilding stuffe . . . about ghosts and spirits. By coach home. Eat sturgeon vinegar and sugar. Agreed not.' Hooke was clearly something of a hypochondriac, but evenings such as this would have tested the stomachs as well as the stamina of most people. In between these two meetings, on 19 January, Hooke had been 'taken ill with a violent fit of the collick after eating hart's tongue and cabbage, and drinking sack, chocolatt and tobacco'. On 25 March of the same year Hooke was 'at Garraways . . . Drank small beer made me sick. With Wyld . . . Aubrey. Sherry 10 times worse. At Cardinalls Cap. At home slept by fire till 2.'

Hardly surprisingly, considering the details of his diet that he records in his diary, Hooke seems to have had dyspeptic moods when he disliked whoever he was with, and viewed the world in general with displeasure and suspicion. Such a mood seems to have occurred in the middle of May 1676. On the 18th he noted, 'Wild and Aubrey till 11. Sottish company'. Two days later he writes: 'To Sir Chr. Wren . . . with Holder and Aubrey. Discourse nothing worth.' In the autumn of the same year he seems to have had a recurrence of this misanthrophic mood, under the influence of which he 'resolved to leave Royal Society'. At the main annual meeting of that year, on St Andrew's Day, there was 'much fowl play'.

How numerous the coffee-houses now were one can see from casting a net over the diary's entries of a few months – from which one ends up with a haul that shows Garraways as much the most popular, but mentions also visits to Childe's, Joe's, Fenwick's, Robert's, Charles', Martin's and Nell's. One can also see how frequently Hooke, Aubrey and their friends went there if one takes a sequence of entries such as those which followed the main annual meeting, always on St Andrew's Day:

> November 30th 1675 Annual meeting. Base doings, a packed Council 50 or more present. I was with Mr. Henshaw, Sir. J. Long, Mr. Hoskins, Mr. Hill, Mr. Aubrey. At Crown till 9 at night. Eat oysters, agreed well. At Garaways 2 dishes of chocolate and smoked 3 pipes. Agreed well.
>
> Dec. 9th Gar[aways] Mr. Hill, Wild, Aubrey etc. Smoked 4 pipes which brought away the flegm.
>
> Dec. 10th To Garaways. Sir Christopher Wren strange. Agreed upon new clubb to meet at Joe's. Mr. Hill, Mr. Lodowick, Mr. Aubrey and I to join to us Sir Jo. More, Mr. Wild, Mr. Hoskins – to begin to-morrow night at 7.
>
> Dec. 11th Mr. Hoskins here, to Joe's Coffe house where began New Clubb, Mr. Hill, Hoskins, Lodowick and I, at last Mr. Aubrey. Discoursed about Newton's new hypothesis.
>
> [On December 13th, Aubrey did not go to Garaways with Hooke and the rest of them, which was possibly as well, for they ate 'geese feet'.]
>
> Dec. 15 Mr. Aubrey with us till 11½ at night. Discoursed to him my Designe about new mechanical principal about flying.
>
> Dec. 16. At the Crown with Sir Wm. Petty, Aubrey.[10]

And so it went on. Inevitably at times one regrets Hooke's brevity. What were the base doings at the annual meeting? Why was Sir Christopher Wren strange and Wild cold? But on the whole, his diary gives a clear and convincing picture of an exceptionally convivial and conversational society, intellectually alert to all problems and possibilities, ever ready to talk about virtually anything.

If, perforce, Aubrey now passed the greater part of his time in London, he still had a life outside it. Besides the visits to Broadchalke, there were trips to Oxford to see Wood and 'the merry gang'. He also continued to stay on the country estates of his friends and relations, often for considerable lengths of time. For example, he told Wood in June 1675 of 'an imminent visit to Draycot Cerne [the home of the Longs]. I shall stay . . . till October.' This must have been for Aubrey a stay full of bitter-sweet memories of what had been, and of sad thoughts of what might have been. Yet the Wiltshire countryside would, no doubt, have shown its summer beauty to him as a landless visitor just as willingly as it had to him when he was a local landowner. Also, he had known Draycot and the Longs for so many years that it must have seemed almost like returning home – and, of course, a home without the responsibility, and so the worry and anxiety which overclouded much of his time at Easton Piers. One would hope and think that this and later stays at Draycot were particularly happy ones. Lady Long, as well as her husband, was clearly fond of Aubrey, and her husband's letters to Aubrey in London would often be accompanied by gifts of warm clothing or food, which obviously came from her. The Longs' youngest daughter Jane, at this time aged eighteen, was to be the subject of one of Aubrey's 'nativities' – in which he noted that she was born at an obviously inconvenient moment, 'about 2 p.m. and they went late to dinner because of her'. Maybe she, too, had a soft spot for Aubrey.

Periodically Aubrey also went to see Paschall at Chedzoy in Somerset, visits during the course of which he no doubt also saw his mother. On one late visit, in August 1685, the year before the death of his mother – so this would probably have been the last time he saw her – he happened to be there at the time of the Monmouth Rebellion. Monmouth's troops on their way to Sedgemoor burst into Paschall's house in the middle of the night, as Aubrey told Wood in a letter of 3 August – 'I went from London tuesday in Whitsonweeke into Somerset to an ingeniose friend of mine, and I came just that night as Monmouth began his rebellion. It was not without danger that I came hither. Monmouth's soldiers came into my friend Mr. Paschall's house and tooke away horses and armes, and came into my chamber as I was abed; but *Deo gratias* that Clowd is overblown.'[11]

There were still regular visits to Hothfield. One such occasion was in the autumn of 1676 when Aubrey wrote to Wood with obvious pleasure at being still a wanted and valued guest: 'My Lord of Thanet is inviting me into Kent and I can hardly refuse him.'[12] The preceding year, shortly after Aubrey had settled into Gresham College, he had received a curious couple of letters from Thanet written on successive days 3 and 4 May – the first of which was written in a patronizing manner very different from that he habitually used to Aubrey. 'With this you will receive a Protection according to your desire . . . I send it you under the proviso that you are my solicitor to look after my affairs in London; and for your salary that is agreed on. My mother hath lent me Thanet house Garden, where I intend to fit up two or three chambers for my use when I come to London privately, one of which as my menial servant you may make use of, when fitted up.'[13] The explanation for this odd letter followed a day later. 'I am not so ignorant as not to knowe that these sides of mine of the third instant [are not] fitting to be write unto a Gentleman of your Birth. The reason why I make myself such a proud, ill-bred Fellowe in it is the better to disguise the business you lately enjoyned me to do for you . . . I assure you this is the first Protection I ever gave, although I have in this nature been solicited by many. Were there anything of moment that I could serve you in, you might freely command him who is in great reallity your most affectionate and humble servant – Thanet.'[14]

Aubrey had obviously been more alarmed by his arrest than his cheerful letter to Wood after it leads one to think. This was clearly a safeguard against it happening again, theoretically at least. For anyone in a nobleman's employ was supposedly immune from arrest for debt, the assumption being that the nobleman would settle the debts himself, and that such an arrest would be a slight to his own person. Once again, Thanet's consideration, kindness and fondness for Aubrey shows through both letters.

Although Aubrey had turned down various suggestions that he should emigrate to America or the West Indies and had refused even Vaughan's offer to go on his staff to Jamaica, yet over these years he seems on occasion to have played the part of a go-between for those of his friends who were interested and rich enough to invest in America. Thus a letter from Thanet in April 1675 was in answer to one from Aubrey, clearly written on Wild's behalf, asking for advice about buying land there. 'I perceive that Mr. Wild has a mind to buy some land in New York, which place you suppose to be a fine country. You are the first that ever I heard term that part a delicious country. The winters are very long and tedious. They live on salt-meates and Fish, and have such vast snowes that they are forced to digg their wayes out of their houses, or they will be stiffled . . . If he will buy land in America let it be in the Bermudas where health abounds and safety is had.'[15]

The previous autumn Thanet, who had already bought land in the Bermudas, had sent Aubrey a request that was obviously aimed at Aubrey himself: 'I want some ingeniose person that would goe over to the Bermudas to bound my land, give me an accompt of the Soyle, and many other particulars. And when he has done so he may returne if he pleases on 1st opportunity.'[16] Aubrey, having refused Vaughan's much more tempting offer only a few months earlier, was unlikely to be interested, and clearly was not – for subsequently one finds him helping Thanet to find a steward for his Bermudan estate, who presumably would have done the surveying as well. Aubrey produced a candidate, whom Thanet was to interview in May 1676, who well may have been Charles Snell's stammering brother, who had earlier unsuccessfully applied to be Hooke's apprentice. For in one of three surviving letters from Snell – all of them starting 'Dear Gossip' – Snell asks if Thanet was still looking for a steward, and if so to consider his brother.

In later years Aubrey seems to have been something more than a go-between – in fact a salesman – for the gift of 1000 acres in Tobago that Capt. Poyntz gave him in 1688, which he records in *Faber Fortunae*, was 'for services that I did him to the Earle of Pembroke and the Earle of Abingdon'. A few years earlier Aubrey seems to have touted Tobago to Sir William Petty, but seemingly unsuccessfully. For in a letter of August 1685 Petty thanks Aubrey for 'proferring me in your thoughts to the purchase of Tobago . . . but the designe is as foreign and incongruous to my circumstances as anything can bee, for I am about 60 years old, am under some extraordinary thoughts concerning our affairs in Ireland, nor am I willing to be a Leader of Malcontents; nevertheless if there were but two or three such Partners as I did like and could trust I might venture £500 upon such a Designe.'[7]

It was unlikely that William Penn's gift to Aubrey of 600 acres in the newly bought and named Pennsylvania, which he suggested Aubrey 'should plant with French Protestants', and which Aubrey recorded in *Faber Fortunae*, was in consideration of similar services. It was much more probably an attempt to enlist Aubrey's aid in finding settlers and supporters. Penn had been elected, to Aubrey's pleasure unanimously, a Fellow of the Royal Society in 1681, the year before he set sail for America. But they had long known each other, even though Penn was eighteen years younger than Aubrey, because their family homes were close to each other in Wiltshire. Penn's was at Minety, some seven miles east of Malmesbury, and so some sixteen miles from Easton Piers. According to Aubrey, Penn's father, 'Sir William Penn the famous Seaman', whose fame and achievement as a Commonwealth admiral was second only to Blake's – he had led a West Indian expedition which captured Jamaica and subsequently served with distinction in the Restoration navy, both as a commander and as an administrator – 'was descended in a direct line from William Penne of Mynty who lieth buried in the Chancel floor here.'

In his 'Life' Aubrey tells that Penn first sensed he had a religious vocation at the age of eleven when at school at Chigwell in Essex: 'being in a chamber alone he was so suddenly surprised of an inward Comfort, and (as he thought) an external glory in the room . . . that from then on he had . . . the certainty that there was a God, and that the soul of man was capable of enjoying divine communication.' However, Penn could not find an anchor for his faith until while in Ireland, where he had been sent to avoid the plague, he heard of 'one Tho. Lowe, a tradesman of Cork [and] was so thoroughly convinced of the simplicity and selfe-denial of the people called Qu. that from thence he heartily supported that Judgement and Beliefe. Since which he has passed a life of great variety of circumstances – several imprisonments, one in Ireland, one in the Tower, 3 in Newgate.'

'Notwithstanding many odd adventures of his life he hath several times found favour from his Majesty.' Far the greatest favour of all was, of course, the munificent grant of Pennsylvania. Aubrey himself believed that this was by way of being the cancellation of a debt of '10,000 [pounds] owing by His

Majestie to his father (which with the interest of it came to not less than
20,000)'. But the real reason seems to have been that Charles II, wishing to
reward and honour Sir William Penn in the customary way for his services by
raising him to the peerage, was prevented from so doing by his son's
Quakerism, which would have made such an award virtually valueless. So he
gave the son Pennsylvania instead. As a result the younger William Penn
became the possessor of what must surely be one of the most extensive title-
deeds in history. It was measured in degrees of latitude and longitude. The
'Patent for Transference is from the beginning of the 40th degree to 43
degrees in Latitude and five degrees of Longtitude from Chisapeake Bay.'
On 4 March 1681 the grant was signed and sealed to 'the province which his
Majestie was pleased to call Pennsylvania, to which he is going this next
September 1681.' So Aubrey must have written his 'Life' in the spring or
summer of that year. However Penn did not actually sail until late August of
the following year – 'August 1682 26 Monday. This day about 4 o'clock p.m.
W. Penn Esq. went towards Deale to launch for Pennsylvania. God send him
a prosperous and safe voyage – Fri. Aug. 30 about noone he tooke shippe at
Deale.'

Aubrey liked both Penn's wife, and his father. Of his wife he wrote that
'she was greatly beloved' for her personal qualities 'and for one more . . . her
great skill in physic and surgery. She was a great fortune to her husband,
being worth to clear about £10,000. Her fortune and great good humour gave
her the opportunity of many suitors . . . she resisted their motions, till
providence brought a man of equal condition and faith to himself. Whose
marriage has been crowned with continuous affection.' Of Penn's father, the
Admiral, Aubrey wrote, '[he] was a man of excellent naturall abilities not
equalled in his time for the knowledge of naval affairs . . . Bred his son
religiously; and as the times grew loose would have had his sonne follow the
fashion and was extremely bitter at his retirement – but it lasted not
always . . . what is most remarkable – he that opposed his son's way because
of the crosse that was in it to the world's habitude, did himselfe embrace this
faith.'[18]

The year after Penn sailed for America Aubrey received a remarkable
letter written at 'Philadelphia, 13th of the month called June, 1683', not only
to him personally as an old and 'Esteemed Friend', but chiefly and clearly
aimed at the whole body of the Royal Society: 'I value myself much upon the
good opinion of those ingeniose gentlemen I know of the Royal Society.' In
his letter Penn gives a glowing report of the progress and prosperity of his
immense venture: 'all goes well, blessed be God . . . provisions we shall have
to spare – considerably – in a year or two unless very great quantities of
People crowd upon us. The Air, heat and cold resembles the heart of France.

The soyles, the springs many and delightfull. Fruits, roots, corne . . . as good as I have commonly eaten in Europe. I may say most of them better. Strawberries ripe in the woods in April, and in the last month, Peas, beans, Cherrys and mulberries. Many black walnut, chestnutt, Cyprus and white cedar and mulberry are here. The sorts of fish in these parts are excellent and numerous. Sturgeon leap day and night . . . We can hear them a bowshot from the Rivers in our beds. We have roasted and pickled them, and they eat like veal one way and sturgeon the other way. Minerals . . . in great store. I shall send [some] for Tryall. Vines are here in abundance . . . I have begun a vineyard, by a French man of Languedoc, and another of Poitou. Several people from other Colonies are retiring hither, as Virginia, Maryland, New England, Road Island, New York etc . . . I make it my business to establish a Virtuous Economy, and therefore sitt twice in council every week, with good success.' Aubrey – one would think mainly in his capacity as the Society's correspondent – had clearly been keeping in touch with Penn, for the letter ends 'I am debtor to thy Kindness for two letters – pray miss not to yield that content and liberality to – Thy very True Friend, Wm Penn.' It was signed with a great flourish and written throughout in a bold hand. At the end, Penn added a postscript – 'Particularly pray give my Respects to Sir Wm. Petty, my friend Hook, Wood* Lodwick and Dr. Bernard . . . Vale'[19] Most of the Fellows were of an age when their adventuring days were over, and were in any case set in their ways and their success, but there must have been some – particularly, one would think the enterprising and entrepreneurial Petty – who must have been tempted in their thoughts, and wished they were younger.

*   *   *

In August 1676 Aubrey's 'severall good friends who are great men', who at the beginning of 1674 had tried to persuade him into a parsonage, made another and, as it was to prove, final attempt. In a letter to Wood of 29 August he wrote, 'I am stormed by my friends afresh, viz. Baron Bertie [Abingdon], Sir W. Petty, J. Hoskyns, Bishop of Sarum [Seth Ward], to turn Ecclesiastique, but the K. of France grows stronger and stronger and what if the Roman religion should come in again? Why then (say they) can not you turne too? You . . . know well that I am no Puritan nor an enemy to the old Gentleman on the other side of the Alpes. Truly if I had a good parsonage of 2 to £300 per anno . . . it could be a shrewd temptation . . . Pray consider once more.'[20] Clearly this time Aubrey had come much closer to the cassock. How close seems to show in the agitation which backs a letter to Wood of a

---

*Wood was not a Fellow of the Royal Society, but Penn had probably known him through Aubrey.

fortnight later: 'If you die your papers may be examined. Therefore I would entreate you to burne (or blote out) a passage in a letter of mine, about 1674 or 5, wherein I expressed my friendship for the Ch. of Rome.' Aubrey pinpoints the letter by adding "twas when I was invited to take a benefice."[21] The passage he was referring to must surely have been that in the letter of 23 February 1674, in which he wrote that he was 'no enemie to them unless Irish Biggotts'. Aubrey's friends had shown themselves remarkably tolerant of his own religious tolerance, yet maybe now when it seems he may have been on the point of accepting their offer of finding him a pleasant and well-endowed parsonage, he feared that his Catholic inclinations – in reality only towards the monastic orders – might count against him. And maybe they did. For nothing came in the end of this, as of the earlier, offer. But a more likely reason for its failure seems to show at the end of his letter of August 1676 in which after praying Wood 'to consider once more' he tells him 'the next week I shall goe into Essex with my good friend Mr. Wyld . . . and perhaps may goe with him to Worcestershire.' If Aubrey had got his parsonage, and had found 'an honest curate' to run it for him – and one would have thought he would have had little difficulty in so doing – his ecclesiastical duties would have been minimal. Yet to some small extent they were bound to have curtailed his social activities. Also, Aubrey was generally very honest about himself to himself. Would he have felt happy as an ordained priest carousing with Wyld into the small hours? One would think not.

Throughout his life the study of the stars had always been of great interest to Aubrey and he set considerable store by their predictions. Yet it is curious to find so fatalistic a faith in someone who at the same time was an ardent and lifelong follower of the Baconian principle of independent enquiry. But if his belief that 'we are all governed by the planets', as he had written to Wood, absolved him too easily of all personal blame for the chain of disaster which had led to his bankruptcy, the sale of Easton Piers, and his absconding, yet over the difficult and depressing period of his delitescence it undoubtedly gave him some comfort and consolation. It also gave him a hobby – the collection of nativities or birth-charts, mainly of his friends, which he often refers to in his letters to Wood over this period. Wood himself seems to have been extremely dilatory in sending the details of his birth that Aubrey required. Exhortation follows exhortation. When eventually Wood gave in and sent Aubrey the date of his birth, he still seems to have been surprisingly vague and uninterested even about so basic a piece of information. In a letter of 23 March 1672, he told Aubrey, 'My nativity I can not retrieve, but by talking to an ancient servant of my father's I find I was borne on the 17th Dec.'[22]

Aubrey eventually produced – in a vellum-covered notebook to which he gave the title *Collectio Geniturarum* and the date 1677 – a collection of over sixty nativities each of which had a carefully drawn birth-chart, presumably done by Aubrey, probably with Coley's assistance. These gave usually only the bare facts of the date and place of birth, and where appropriate, death. But occasionally Aubrey's irrepressible taste for 'minuteness' broke in – about Robert Burton ''tis whispered that not obstante all his Astrologie, and his booke of melancholie that he ended his days by hanging himself'; 'Mistress Anne Radford', the widow of Aubrey's Trinity friend, 'has a solar face, thrives well, and has a good sound judgement; Mistress Grace [Hooke's niece] hath a hairy mole on her left pappe.' (How did Aubrey know?) Aubrey included most of his eminent friends – such as Dryden, Evelyn, Hobbes, Hooke, Pembroke, Pell, Penn, Petty, Wyld, Waller and Wren; but also Titus Oates, Ogilby, five Penruddocks, Thomas Pigot, John Stokes (the then owner of the manor at Kington St Michael), Charles Snell (his astrologer friend at Fordingbridge) and Jane Smyth, Wyld's mistress ('borne on the fifteenth of April between four and five in the morning – it thundered and lightened and the house was on fire then'.)[23] Altogether an oddly assorted collection. With its bare brevity work of this sort was probably as little suited to Aubrey's associative and essentially expansionist talent – one thing inevitably leading to another – as one could possibly find. Yet it was a useful pastime throughout a period when for Aubrey time may have been slow in passing. Collecting his 'nativities' may also have served another purpose. By turning his attention to the interesting figures of his time, even if for the moment he was only concerned with them as astrological material, may have helped to direct him down the road which led to his 'Lives'.

In his letters to Aubrey Thanet often referred to matters of business he wanted to discuss with him – these probably as much to do with the Bermudan estate as Hothfield. One such must have been delivered by personal messenger to Aubrey on 10 April 1679, the day on which it was written, for it contained an invitation for the following day, which must have been a Sunday – 'with such devout persons as you are tomorrow I conceive will be an idle day. Therefore I should be glad of your Company to-morrow morning at my lodgings, as early as you can. I have a little Businesse with you and then afterwards wee will eat a dish of meat together, at which I shall give you a bottle of most excellent Portugall wine.'[24] One hopes they enjoyed themselves, and it sounds as if they would have. For this was to be one of their last meetings, if not the last, Thanet dying suddenly later in the year. At his death, Aubrey must have mourned the loss of not only a good and generous friend, but of one who had played a particularly important part in his rescue in the early years of uncertainty and apprehension which followed his absconding, and who until his death continued to provide his life with an element of sheltering stability. Aubrey should have thanked his stars for such a friend at such a time.

A last florescence
1677–85

Aubrey had not been idle during the years since he had lost his money and Easton Piers. But with the exception of his *A Perambulation of Surrey*, in which he had achieved a great deal in a very short time, his method of working was always leisurely. As he wryly admitted himself, it was a method which 'had I not lived long . . . would have afforded but a slender harvest',[1] but until he was happily settled in, or around, the capacious quarters of Gresham College, and had time to look around, consider his position and purpose in life, his work had always been for other people. Mainly, of course, for Wood. As year followed year, and the greater part of them continued to be devoted to finding out information for Wood and sending it to him in scholarly rather than sociable letters – it is generally only in the last few lines that Aubrey writes about, and for, himself – one begins to resent on his behalf that he should do so much work, for such scant reward even by way of thanks. Wood's response was usually only a demand for further information, and the odd 'token' which brought Aubrey great delight but little financial relief or reward.

However, once Aubrey was settled in or around Gresham College there were signs of change. The causes of this were partly coincidental. After the publication of his *Historia*, Wood became much less demanding of Aubrey's time and trouble. In consequence, Aubrey's letters to him became less frequent and less impersonally informative. Aubrey, of course, now had to deal with the correspondence he conducted on behalf of the Society, but these letters involved little research, since he was now seeking rather than sending information. So, by force of circumstance, he now had more time to consider his own interests and affairs. Yet the changed and improved conditions of his life must also have played their part in restoring the self-confidence that was a prerequisite to producing worthwhile work of his own.

The first promising signs showed in a revival of interest in the 'Life' of Thomas Hobbes, which he had long been thinking of writing, and for which he had for some time been making notes. He had long ago voiced this intention to Hobbes himself as well as to Wood. Hobbes had in fact responded by sending him the draught of a short autobiography he had written in Latin, which did not however cover the last twenty-five years of his immensely long life. Round, and to, this Aubrey had made notes and additions, so that a considerable part of the groundwork was already done. But there was a restraint which held him back from proceeding for the moment much further, one which was bound to resolve itself in the course of time, and one which, in any case, he warmly welcomed while it lasted. This was simply that Hobbes lived much longer than he, or anyone else, expected. Looking at the later part of Hobbes's life one might, in fact, be excused for thinking that he was out to disprove his most famous dictum, and that life was not necessarily 'nasty, brutish and short'. In his instance it seems to have been 'pleasant, civilized and long'. He was immensely helped, as he had been throughout most of his life, by being able to live in the stately comfort of Chatsworth when he lived in the country, and in 'his lord's' town house – which Aubrey variously describes as being Little Salisbury House in the Strand, and then Newport House in Leicester Fields – when he was in London. But Hobbes had also taken good care of himself, restricting his diet, taking regular walks and even singing frequently from the book of 'prickt song', which Aubrey describes him as keeping permanently on his table, in order to exercise his lungs. In the mid seventies, which corresponded with his mid eighties, Hobbes was in London for some time, where Aubrey saw much of him, on one occasion taking Hooke to meet him. In a letter to Wood of 9 April 1674, Aubrey described Hobbes as still having 'his parts to admiration'. Hobbes eventually died at Chatsworth in 1679, when he was ninety – a great age for that, or any other, time.

Some time before Hobbes's death, Aubrey had sent his notes on his 'Life', with, presumably, Hobbes's autobiographical manuscript, to Wood at Oxford. His notes were already clearly of a considerable size, for Wood after reading them, told Aubrey that he should stop talking about adding notes to Hobbes's autobiography and refer to his work properly as his own life of Hobbes. However, there was a further snag which Aubrey had not earlier foreseen. This was simply that his 'merry' evenings with Wyld were taking their toll. In a letter to Wood, written on 9 April 1679, he wrote, 'I doe often chide myself as I lye abed to consider how much time Mr. E. W. and J. A. doe loose, and growe lethargiq.'[2] Again, in June, 'The trueth of it is that I and Mr. E. W. grow a little lethargique.'[3] Clearly, late nights did not help the progress of his 'Life' – as he acknowledged in a letter of 30 December: 'I am so much taken up by my Patron (E.W.) (besides my Lethargiquenesse) that I can not be so intent as I would on this Designe.'[4]

The solution, as Aubrey saw it, was to find an assistant. This, luckily, seems not to have been difficult. For on 17 January 1680, he wrote to Wood that he had acquired the services of 'a very learned young friend of mine'.[5] This was Dr Blackburn, who had recently taken his medical degree in Cambridge, but who, according to Aubrey, was at this time more interested in doing work of general scholarship than in practising medicine. In a letter to Wood of 10 February he again lauds Blackburn's scholarly qualities – 'I pitched upon an admirable young man' – at this point a hole in his letter breaks the thread of Aubrey's praise, but one picks it up again to find him describing Blackburn as 'one of the best scholars in London of his age'.[6] A week later he is allaying Wood's doubts and possibly soothing a niggle of jealousy: 'Dr. Blackburn is much your friend and will doe you all imaginable right. In all England you could not have landed upon such another.'[7] Aubrey wanted Blackburn primarily to translate his additional material into the Latin of Hobbes's autobiography, but also to give him the support and practical guidance that up to now Wood had supplied. This had taken the form of innumerable queries, with which Wood had soon lost patience: 'You should never ask these questions but do them out of hand forthwith – you have time enough.'

Having hived off on to Blackburn the task of shaping, translating and seeing through the press, the combined 'Life' of Hobbes, Aubrey, strangely, sat down to write yet another, this time in English, this time very short in length, which contained 'nothing that is in the Latin one'. 'I have writt 3 copies (improved) of Mr. Hobbes life,' Aubrey wrote in the letter in which he sang Blackburn's praises, 'I did not think I would have been so copious. It will be at least 8 sheetes.'[8] Although it has retained its separate identity, one can see from the copy, now a slim, bound volume which lies in its box in the Bodleian, labelled 'MS Aubrey 9', that it was the forerunner of the 'Lives'; and at the same time the spark which set off the amazing burst of creativity in which they were written.

Aubrey himself tells Wood – and us – how it all happened in two letters of which the first was written only a week after that in which he sang Blackburn's praises and told of his final personal version of Hobbes's 'Life'. 'Feb. 17th 1679 . . . On Sunday night [Aubrey writes 'Sunday' as a circle with a dot in the middle] it came into my minde to scribble a sheet of paper which I shall enlarge (much) viz. the life of the worthy and ingeniose knight Sir. W. Petty from the cradle, Sir Chr. Wren the like, as also Mr. Rob. Hooke.'[9] Four days later he enlarges on this momentous moment: 'It came into my mind Sunday last taking a pipe of tobacco in my chamber (my hand now being in)' – as a result of the practise which the eight sheets of Hobbes 'Life' had provided – 'to write my honor'd friend Sir W. Petty's life, which will be a fine thing, which, he shall p[er]use himselfe, and then it shall be left with your papers for Posterity hereafter to read.'[10] After this the flow was fast and furious. At the end of March Aubrey was telling Wood 'I have to my Booke of Lives made a Kalendar of 55 persons and have donne 20 of them. 3 or 4 leaves in a fol. Pray doe you your own selfe. I am glad you putt me on it. This morning being up by 10 [it was obviously one of Aubrey's early rising days] I writt two, one was Sir John Suckling of whom I wrote a leafe and a half in fol.' As he said he would, Aubrey had shown Petty his 'Life': 'Sir William Petty perused my copy and would have all stand' (Aubrey puts 'as A.W.' in brackets above).

However, Aubrey was not the only one at this time to be working fast and well. So too was Dr Blackburn. He had quickly completed his translation of Hobbes's 'Life' – too quickly it would seem for Aubrey's liking. In the same March letter in which he told Wood of his own astonishingly quick production of his 'Lives', he also wrote critically of Blackburn's progress 'I suffer the grasse to be cutt under my feet, for Dr. Blackburn will have all the Glory. 'Tis writt in a High style.' This led Aubrey to defend his own contrasting style of writing: 'Now I say the offices of a Panegyrist and a Historian are much different. A life is a short Historie, and there minuteness of a famous persons life is grateful.' With this countless of his readers will agree, for it is above all else 'the minuteness', the detail, which makes his characters live. In the margin of the same letter Aubrey told Wood that among the twenty Lives 'writt' were those 'of Sir Wr. Raleigh – 4 leaves not yet toucht . . . as much of my old friend Dr. W. Harvey, never yet toucht . . . Dr. Kettle' – all three of them notable 'Lives'. Two months later he told Wood 'My Memories of Lives (66)' had become 'a book of 2 quires close written and after I had begun it I had such an impulse on my spirit that I could not be at quiet till I had donne it.' He was still measuring himself against Blackburn – 'The Dr. says I am too minute, but a hundred years hence that minuteness will be grateful.'[12] Above 'minuteness' he wrote 'Sir Wm. Petty ordered me to be so.' Throughout the summer the 'Booke of Lives' steadily grew. At the end of September Aubrey was apologizing to Wood because he had not yet sent him the manuscript, which he had been promising to him since the spring. 'I thought long ere this to have . . . sent . . . my Booke of Lives but I have found more matter come upon me, so that I have yet about 16 Lives more to write; they will be in all about six score.'[13] It seems not, for the moment, to have grown above this, although for several years Aubrey was to continue to add the odd character to his collection as they came to mind and to hand. In February of the following year Aubrey promised Wood, 'I will send you about 120 Remarques of Lives.' This time he seems to have kept his promise.

This was almost exactly a year since it had come into Aubrey's mind while 'taking a pipe of tobacco in my chamber to write my honor'd friend Sir Wm. Petty's life'. It had truly been a miraculous year. For in it Aubrey had written the bulk of what was to become known as *Brief Lives*, the work for which he is now mainly famous, although some of his admirers would contend that his Wiltshire works are worth just as much. In reality the two should not be considered as rivals. For they are complementary. Between them Aubrey produced a landscape with figures – the landscape of the two parts of Wiltshire which he knew and loved; the figures, those of his friends and acquaintances, to which were added famous or notorious characters of the past about whom he had learnt through chatter in the coffee-houses, or from information that had come to him through the grape-vine which centred on the Royal Society. Behind his 'Lives' lay the same intense desire to report, and so rescue, whatever seemed worthwhile in the world around him that had backed much of his Wiltshire work – but this time he was concerned with the figures rather than the landscape. ''Tis pity', he regretted to Wood in the June dated letter which accompanied the manuscript and so did not reach Wood until the following year, 'that such Minutes had not been taken 100 years since or more, for want whereof many worthy mens Names and Notions are swallowed up in oblivion, as much as these also would have been had it not been through your Instigation.' Behind this, yet again, lay the simple desire which underlies much creative activity, which he had expressed in an early letter to Wood, 'I would fain, methinkes, do some good in the world before I dye.' It would surely be with Aubrey's consent to vary this slightly so that it reads 'to do some good work in the world' – which now he most certainly had. From the start Aubrey had no false modesty about the worth of his 'Lives'. 'They are fine things', he wrote to Wood in his letter of 22 May. In the September letter he declared 'I have found more matter come upon me, so that I have 16 Lives more to write . . . I believe never in England were delivered so faithfully and with so good authority.' In the covering letter that eventually went with the long delayed manuscript he wrote 'perhaps it is one of the usefullest pieces I have scribbled.'

Aubrey obviously felt he owed a considerable debt to Wood for suggesting the idea of writing the 'Lives'. 'I am glad you putt me on it,' he wrote in his March letter. In the June letter, he acknowledged his debt more fully – 'I have according to your desire, putt in writing these Minutes of LIVES, tumultuarily, as they occurred to my thoughts, or as occasionally I had information of them . . . 'Tis a Taske that I never thought to have undertaken till you imposed it on me saying that I was fitt for it by reason of my general acquaintance, having now not only lived above halfe a Centurie of yeares in the world but I have also been much tumbled up and down in it which hath made me much well knowne.'[14] It was certainly one of the greatest services that Wood did for Aubrey, yet as always it was one that was to his advantage also, for the 'Lives' provided much information that was invaluable in his own work. One can see how much he depended on it in a note of over a decade later, when Aubrey was seeking to gather together his manuscripts in order to place them for safe keeping in the Ashmolean. '11 Nov. 1691. Mr. Aubrey. I beseech you as you have been civil in giving this book to me at Oxon in Sept. '81. So I hope when you have done with it you'l return every part of it again to your servant. Ant. Wood.'[15] However, although it is clear that Wood had a hand in steering Aubrey towards the writing of his 'Lives' the whole process has so much the appearance of a self generated burst of creativity – of which the force had been gradually building up over years of frustration and harassment, finally released by the confidence which his work on Hobbes's 'Life' had given him – that one feels that even without Wood's help the 'Lives' would have emerged in the course of that miraculous year.

The cause of the delay in sending the manuscript to Wood was not only that 'more matter' was constantly coming upon Aubrey, but that he had 'deposited my Minutes of Lives in Dr. Pell's hands in Oct. last.' The main reason for this was Aubrey's affection and compassion for an old friend, a distinguished mathematician and divine who, in spite of his having two livings in Essex worth £400 a year, was living in a state of depressed destitution in an 'obscure Lodging in Jermyn St. – three stories high'. Aubrey was indignant that 'by this time (1680) this great learned man, famous both at home and abroad [had not] obtained some considerable Dignity in the Church . . . [no]lesse than a Deanery'. No doubt Aubrey hoped that reading his 'Lives' would cheer Pell up. But another reason was that Pell had been one of his informants. In most of his 'Lives' Aubrey interestingly gives the source of his information if it is not of his own finding or remembrance. Now Aubrey hoped that Pell 'would have made additions or amendments but (poor disconsolate man) I received it of him without any'.[16] This was not strictly true. Pell himself was the subject of one of the 'Lives' that Aubrey submitted to him. One can see on the manuscript of this that he has made several 'additions and amendments' and can be certain it is Pell's hand because Aubrey notes at one point 'This is his writing.' It is a small, neat hand such as befits a mathematician. For some reason, the ink that Pell used has turned golden with time, and his additions hang on the page like small gold chains. From them we learn that Pell had '4 sonnes and 4 Daughters, born in this order SD, DS, DS, DS', and that his parishes were notoriously unhealthy. 'At Febbing seven curates dyed within the first ten yeares.' Pell also lost his 'wife, servants and grandchildren'. One can understand that even 'an obscure Lodging in Jermyn St. next to the signe of the Ship [where] his Tenants and his Relations confin'd him of his Profits and kept him so indigent that he wanted necessary's, even Paper and Inke'[17] might be preferable to living in such a parish.

What one finds particularly astonishing in the creative process which produced the 'Lives' – remembering all the delays, hesitations and prevarication which surrounded Aubrey's earlier work – is the speed and ease with which he wrote it. 'I doe it playingly,' he had written in his March letter to Wood, and in his September letter he confirmed the pleasure and facility with which he wrote the 'Lives' – 'I doe these things with wonderful ease.' However, Aubrey himself gives the probable reason for this surprising change of tempo and attitude. He was writing of his contemporaries, but not for them. His audience was Posterity and a fairly distant one at that. So there was no need to worry about publication, or what people would think and say and do after it. In fact, being Aubrey, far the greater number of the 'Lives' were admiring and appreciative, and the subjects of them could only have been pleased and flattered. It was only the odd scandalous story, which his gossipy side could not resist, which might have caused trouble. But as it was, he wrote without check or constraint of any sort – and in consequence the flow was fast and the bowl full.

From the start Aubrey made his intention and his aim clear. In the first letter about the first of all the 'Lives', that of Petty, he had told Wood, 'it shall be left with your papers for Posterity to read;' and in that of 22 May when the 'Lives' had swollen to 'a book of 2 quires close written' he added 'few fitt to be published in my lifetime or yours'. In the letter which accompanied the first batch to Wood, he put it even more clearly, if crudely: 'I here lay downe to you the Trueth, the naked and the plain trueth and as near as I can . . . nothing but the trueth! which is here exposed so bare that the very pudenda are not hid . . . these arcana are not fitt to lett flie abroad, till about 30 yeares hence; for the author and Persons [Aubrey adds in a bracket above "like medlars"] ought to be rotten first.' In the same letter Aubrey quoted 'the saying of General Lambert "That the beste men are but men at the best"' – which clearly summed up his attitude not only to the 'Lives' but to life.

One can generally, but not always, judge the value that Aubrey himself put on his work, by the state of the manuscripts. The greater part of the 'Lives' are carefully transcribed. It is only the last, late added, 'Lives', which are obviously neither revised nor transcribed, that possibly show by their illegibility the results of a particularly late night with Wyld. To most of those in the main volume, Aubrey has added the coat of arms of the subject in the top left-hand corner of the first page, sometimes drawn in the brown ink he generally uses, sometimes painted. Occasionally, when it is a particularly important subject such as Petty, a nativity chart is added. On most pages there are the signs peculiar to Aubrey showing the place of an insertion – the carefully drawn hand pointing the way or the curious three-leaved clover-like plant only used when there are two or more insertions on one page. Personal touches such as these make anyone lucky enough to be given a glimpse of them in Duke Humfrey's Library feel very close to Aubrey.

1680 was not only the *annus mirabilis* during which the greater part of the 'Lives' were written, it was also remarkable for the publication of the Latin version of Hobbes's 'Life', under the title *Thomae Hobbes Angli Malmesburiensis Philosophi Vita*. Its appearance probably owed more to Blackburn's quick translation and competent arrangements than to Aubrey's additions and early instigation. In his letter of 22 May, Aubrey told Wood that 'this afternoon I shall see the proofs of the first sheets of Mr. Hobbes.' The printing was evidently intended to be financed by subscription, for Aubrey goes on, 'If you can get 14 to subscribe you shall have one Copie.' In the end however, there seem to have been few subscribers and so fewer copies. In September, Aubrey wrote to say that 'Mr. T. Hobbes life will be printed, and out, the next week. I will send you half a dozen copies.' Aubrey was obviously nervous of its reception. 'God deliver us from the fury and pride of some of our English Eps. [bishops].' But when it did come out, nobody took much notice – in fact a little of 'the fury and pride of some of our English Eps.' might have been welcome publicity. So Aubrey sent Wood only one copy: '[I] would have sent you one or two more as I did intend but I had but halfe a dozen in all, wh. was all that I had for my paynes; and the Dr. tells me that he had no more – but I doubt – our agreement was that what W. Crooke gave him he should have halfe . . . Be it how it will.'[18] As well as being doubtful about Blackburn's honesty, Aubrey was also angry with him because 'he is careless of my papers and keeps them not cleane.' He was also critical of some errors in the text, but pleased with the translation: 'he has donne it into very good Latin.' However, they seem to have remained friends, for the following year Blackburn was helping Aubrey to write out an advertisement for the spa at Seend, which was inserted in 'H. Coley's Almanack . . . but to no avail'. In 1695, the last year but two of Aubrey's life, when his sight was beginning to fail, he wrote in a sadly blurred letter to Wood – the last of that immensely long, immensely important sequence – 'I can not now read because of the Mist which comes to my Eies ever since I left Oxford – Dr. Blackb. advises me to drink the waters but I do not much mind.'[19] So evidently they remained in touch, and friends, for the rest of Aubrey's life.

Perhaps because 1680 was such a memorable year for Aubrey sometime in the course of it he jotted down in the autobiographical section of his 'Lives' the names of his particular friends – the 'Amici'. With one exception the names are those one would expect to find on such a list, Ettrick, Lydall,

Potter, Hoskyns, Wyld, Hooke, Hobbes, Wood, Petty, Long, Seymour, Seth Ward, Holder. The one exception is Sir John Stawell whom Aubrey notes as being of the Middle Temple. It seems likely that they studied there together, for they were of much the same age, Stawell being one year older than Aubrey, and that their friendship was formed at that time. There is otherwise, however, little surviving evidence of it, other than a note from Stawell which Aubrey kept. Stawell's home was at Bovey Tracey in south Devon, to which the first stage of his journey was to Salisbury, which was also Aubrey's destination when he went by coach to Broadchalke. The note is suggesting that they should travel together: 'There are three places in the Salisbury coach on Monday next taken up; no more; so that you may goe with me and make me truly happy in your company. I pray give earnest for a place immediately or goe in my boyes roome, and let him ride your horse (if you have horses sent). I will pay your coach hire. John Stawell.' In a postscript Stawell adds: 'Let me beg your favour in granting this earnest request. I will not admit a deniall. Let no slovenly, paltry, pittiful excuse be mentioned. We shall be truly merry on the progress.'[20] To someone as sociable as Aubrey one would think that such an invitation would be irresistible. Stawell, who died in 1669 at the early age of forty-four was long dead, like Lydall and Seymour, when Aubrey made his list. One senses a particular warmth of feeling to all three behind their inclusion after so long an interval.

Holding as he did so strong a belief in the power of the planets and after so exceptional a year as 1680 had proved to be, Aubrey must surely have anticipated that they were unlikely to be propitious in the one that followed. And so it proved to be. In September he wrote to Wood, 'I have lost several friends lately, amongst others my brother Tom dyed a fortnight since.'[21] One does not know who the other friends were. It is, in fact, difficult to think of any of Aubrey's close friends who died in that year. But as Aubrey did not forget friends quickly or easily, it may be that he was thinking back a couple of years to 1679, which had seen the death not only of Hobbes and Thanet, but also of Robert Wiseman – 'Robinet' – whose luck apparently ran out at the same time as Aubrey's, at the time of his absconding, for he never seems to have been happily settled afterwards. The death of Aubrey's brother Tom was so sudden that Charles Snell, Aubrey's astrologer friend who lived locally at Fordingbridge, to whom Aubrey had written to ask if he could find out details of his brother's death, replied that apparently he was dead before anyone knew he was ill. It was not only a cause of great grief to Aubrey but a practical disaster. For it meant that the responsibility for the running of the farm at Broadchalke reverted to Aubrey.

On the face of it this could be seen as a last chance for Aubrey to re-establish himself as a country-gentleman, a role which in every way except for his financial incompetence, he seemed well suited to play. Yet in reality what hope had anyone with no money behind him? For farming then as now needed a cushion of capital on which to fall back during the inevitable bad times – and even the seemingly competent Tom, who had kept the farm afloat for some fifteen years, and managed to provide Aubrey with a small but essential income, was found, after his death, to have been 'bound in bond for £60' to a Mr Hatchman, whom one would think was a local merchant or agent, or even the successor of 'Geo. Lawes, my Bayley'. Also, Aubrey, for all his interest in most aspects of country life, had had little experience of the day-to-day running of a farm. 'Geo. Lawes' had always done it for him. However, clearly the neighbourhood wanted the Aubreys to remain at Broadchalke. The Penruddocks organized a job for brother William in forestry, and on 19 December following Tom's death, Aubrey in London 'found a note in my chamber from my neighbour at Chalke, Sir. Jo. Saintlowe' (of Knighton Manor, which lies in a fold of the downs a mile east of Broadchalke), telling Aubrey that 'Dr. Lamphire was dangerously ill and would have me address myselfe to my friend Mr. Secretary Jenkins to procure it for me.' Dr Lamphire, as well as being one of Aubrey's 'merry gang' at Oxford, was Principal of Hart Hall. Such a position might have provided the income that would have enabled Aubrey to retain and run Manor Farm. He was obviously excited at the prospect, but doubted his suitability for such a job – 'I am an ignote fellow and but of little learning.' However, in the end the possibility never arose. Dr Lamphire recovered and lived for a further seven years. Had the possibility arisen, and had Aubrey been offered the job, one doubts whether, in fact, he could have brought himself to leave London, for there he and Wyld were, clearly, increasingly happy getting increasingly 'lethargique' together. 'If I should have it [the Oxford appointment] I should be like a weaned child to leave Mr. Wyld, who are inseparable and dote together till 12 or 1, at night.'[22]

Over the years of the late 1670s and early 1680s, Aubrey had acquired and obviously enjoyed a new friendship at Oxford. This was with Thomas Pigot, a young don at Wadham. One can see from his letters to Aubrey which survive in the Bodleian that Pigot was both able and ambitious. Aubrey thought highly of him, referring to him in one of his letters to Wood as one 'of whom we expect great things'. He had also considered him, before he found Blackburn, as a possible translator of the Hobbes 'Life'. The tone of Pigot's letters is often oleaginous, yet how else did an ambitious young man find advancement other than by seeking the acquaintance and friendship of those who could give it to him, such as the members of the Royal Society? Aubrey, as he always would, responded generously, and one can see from those to whom Pigot sends respects at the end of his letters that he introduced him widely around the very distinguished circles in which he habitually moved. One letter, dated 21 May 1678, which ends with a list of such respects is intriguing in itself. 'I have never met with any persons more deserving and obligeing than Mr. Aubrey and his Lady. You must pardon me if I could not treat them according to theyr merits for that had been impossible . . . their company was so pleasing and advantageous that I could not part with them, while they stayed at Oxford, not till I had seen them in the Stage-coach at Abington where I left them with a great deal of regret.'[23] Who was Aubrey's 'Lady'? We have no idea, but whoever she was, one is glad to hear of her. Pigot ended his letter by sending his respects to Hooke, Hoskyns, Lodowick, Haak – all Fellows of the Royal Society– as well as to Aubrey's Somerset correspondent, the Vicar of Chedzoy, Paschall, with whom Aubrey had put him in touch, but of whose work Pigot in his letters to Aubrey was somewhat disparaging, perhaps scenting a rival. He also sent his respects to Mr Wiseman. This, of course, was Robinet, the connection between them being that on Robinet's visits to London, presumably on business for Bathurst, he had often carried letters between them. Now he had come to find work in London, only to return to die in Oxford the following year. It had been Pigot who told Aubrey of his death, in a letter of 29 April 1679: 'Poor Mr. Wiseman dy'd here some time ago and I did carry him to the grave. You may imagine how much I am afflicted as I am sensible you will be troubled to hear it.'[24]

Pigot himself was to die in 1686, suddenly and unexpectedly, like Aubrey's brother Tom. His last letter to Aubrey – undated – had told of a pleasing promotion, although it was not a step in the direction Pigot most wanted to go: 'I have taken double orders and am instituted into a little living hardby, though not yet inducted. It is a pretty convenience with a fellowship, but I wish my lot may fall in London or somewhere near it that I might always enjoy your company and the worthy Society.'[25] Between this letter and his death Pigot was, in fact, to move into the area where he most wanted to be – in the centre of social London – becoming personal chaplain to the Earl of Ossory. It was in the Earl's London house in St James's Square that he died suddenly of 'a Feaver about one o'clock of the afternoon'. He was buried in St James's Church. Aubrey mourned the death 'of my worthy friend'. It was, indeed, a sad waste for with ambition as well as ability Pigot might have gone far.

Virtually the only personal possessions of any value left to Aubrey after his absconding were his books. However, had he been affluent one feels they would still have been those he most cherished. In recent years, through Wood and the younger George Ent, then living in Oxford, he had given some to the Bodleian, some to his old college, Trinity. In London, he had also given some to the Royal Society and in moments of particular poverty sold a few to Hooke. But now he seems to have been trying to sell all of those that he still

had with him in London as one sees from a letter from Isaac Newton, dated
22 December 1683: 'I acquainted our college with the contents of your letter
but the charge of building disables us from buying books at the present. Then
I went to the Vice-Chancellor, and he desires to know whereabouts the price
will be for the whole, and afterwards to have a catalogue. He knows not yet
whether the University will purchase them, their chest being at present very
low, but intends to propound it to the Heads of Colleges the next
opportunity.'[26] Newton signed his letter 'Your affectionate friend' – as he
had indeed shown himself to be.

Earlier in 1683, Aubrey had lost another friend, this time an old one: 'we
were borne the same weeke, and within 4 miles, and educated together.' This
was George Johnson, 'a deare, usefull and faithfull friend'. With his death
Aubrey considered he had lost 'an opportunity that I shall never have the like
again', for Johnson, already a judge, 'had the reversion of Master of the
Rolles; who generously gave me the Graunt to be one of his Secretaries,
which place is worth £500 per anno'. 'I should,' goes on Aubrey, obviously
carried away by the wonderful dream of finding at last his pot of gold, 'have
disposed the profit ad Majorem Dei gloriam, and have been useful and
grateful and benefactive to all my ingeniose friends – in which ranks AW has
one of the highest places.'[27]

Over these years, with the new found confidence which the writing of his
'Lives' and the publication of his 'Life' of Hobbes had given him, Aubrey
seems to have worked hard and well on two projects, his *Idea of Education*, on
whose title page he put the date 1683/4, and on his *Natural History of
Wiltshire*, the sorting and shaping of whose material, most of which dated
back, as he was to point out in his Preface, some fifteen years, was in itself a
creative process. On its title page he put the date 1685.

The Idea of Education is a curious, uncharacteristic Aubrey work, of which
possibly the most curious aspect is why he ever wrote it at all. But it had
clearly been in his mind, and on his table, for a long time, as is shown by his
early note in *Faber Fortunae*: 'The institution of my Idea for the Education of
young Gentlemen of quality, sc. from 9 – 18 yeares of age, in Derbyshire, or
Cheshire, London etc'.[28] Aubrey had undoubtedly spent a lot of thought on
his *Idea*, and as one would expect of such a brainchild, it showed clear signs of
its parentage. The system Aubrey advocated was humane. There was to be
none of the whipping which had been common at his own school, Blandford;
no early rising, from which he seems to have suffered almost as much; the
teachers (or 'informators') were to be 'sweet and even-tempered' for 'a boy
will never learn well of a teacher that hath an Antipathie to him.'[29] It was also
extremely snobbish: 'A cobblers son may have a good witt, and may
perchance be a good man; but he would not be proper for a friend to a person

of honour.'[30] It is interestingly innovative: if mathematics was to be the centre of the curriculum, 'Mechaniques' had to be recognized as the core of mathematics, for 'of all the studies there is not one so usefull to Mankind as this is – all the rest of the Mathematics are but in order for this.'[31] Some of his suggestions are surprisingly contrary to common practice then or now: 'too much reading of the Poets spoiles a good Prose-stile; for which reason I would have them to meddle as little with the Poets as is possible.'[32]

Aubrey saw his 'Institution' set up in 'a faire house with a little Parquet high-walled of about a mile or about', run by a Provost 'who should be a Gentleman . . . well-educated . . . and travelled' and 'above all else . . . neither the Provost or any of the Informators should marrie for if they should their daughters would debauch on the young Gent, not to say worse, to become their wives . . .' The three 'informators' were not to be English 'but chosen from Switzerland and Scotland'. There was also to be a 'Mathematical Teacher, a Rhetorician, a Logician, 10 or 12 Swiss or Dutch or Scottish Boyes. c. 15 yrs. that could speak Latin – to play with and instruct Gents – a Pen-man – a Dancing-master, a Cooke & scullions to speake Latin, a Butler, a Governess – to oversee Nurses, women and take care of Gents; the Butler or Porter to be a Barber, to shave their heads, etc; to keep them from lice'.[33] From all this one can see it was a totally impractical, totally impossible 'Idea' – but all the same it remains an informative, interesting, often amusing, Aubrey curiosity.

By contrast, the *Natural History* is characteristic Aubrey at its best. Aubrey, as he tells us in his Preface, had tried to get an antiquarian friend, Dr Robert Plot, who had already produced a *Natural History of Oxfordshire*, to edit it. However, Plot was too busy with his own work, and sent Aubrey's papers back to him, telling him that he must do it himself. So 'considering that if I should not doe this myselfe my papers might either perish or be sold at Auction – I have tumultuarily stitched up what I have many years since collected'.[34] Aubrey went on to excuse himself for possible errors and omissions on account of the length of time that had elapsed since the taking and the editing of the notes – 'It is fifteen years since I left the country and I have at the distance inserted such additions as I can call to mind.' But in fact there was no need for explanation or apology. The notes were much less 'tumultuarily' stitched up than one would have expected, Aubrey once again showing himself surprisingly methodical, arranging his book into two parts and dividing each part into several chapters on general subjects such as 'Rivers, Mineralls and Fossills, Fishes, Diseases and Cures'. There was probably a personal purpose behind the dedication to the Earl of Pembroke, behind the lengthy description of Wilton, and particularly behind the chapter 'Of Learned Men who had Pensions granted to them by the Earls of

Pembroke', but in general it is Aubrey at his most observant, dealing with a subject that particularly suited his 'minuteness', looking back at a well-remembered landscape and etching in a few local figures for good measure.

It must have been a shock coming back to the present day reality. At Broadchalke his affairs were clearly going from bad to worse, due not only to financial difficulties, but to increasingly bitter disagreement with his brother, William. A letter of 2 January 1686 shows the strain and stress he was under: 'I returned hither about St. Andrews tyde from Chalke where my domestique troubles were so great that I was hardly able to sustayne them – whether I shall be able to shake off the griefe, I know not . . . My brother and I are at so great a difference (too long now to relate) that I believe we shall ne'er be close again.'[35] But had they ever been? However, once again work provided some solace – until he was struck by a further blow – as he told Wood in a letter of 11 May: 'In Jan last I sett to work on my Nat. Hist. of Wilts, which I had just donne April 22 – rough-hewn and finished the last chapter, when at the evening I heard the sad news of the decease of my dear and ever honoured mother, who died at Chalke, but my brother has buried her with my father in North Wilts [Kington St Michael] – my heade has been a fountain of teares . . . I am now in a great deale of trouble – and Chalke must be sold. I hope to have some reservation to myselfe.' So, once again, the hard and often cruel facts of economic life had caught up with Aubrey. This time the difficulty of his situation was intensified by an increasingly bitter fraternal feud. Aubrey continues his letter to Wood by saying that he would 'shortly goe to Chalke, to see how matters goe there, and as soon as I can pick up a little money intend to see you in Oxon'. He ends 'God bless you and comfort me that I may live to finish and perfect my papers.'[36] Yet again, thought of work ahead came to his aid in a moment of crisis.

Final misfortunes, final graces
1686–97

Aubrey was sixty in 1686, and so on the threshold of old age. Apart from the recent difficulties at Chalke, the previous decade had, on the whole, been a peaceful, pleasant and productive one, in which there must have been much that he had enjoyed – the spacious surroundings of Gresham College, the stimulus of constantly mixing with the most intellectually eminent men of his age, the 'merry' evenings with Wyld, the 'coffee-housing' with Hooke and other friends, the periodic visits to Oxford, and to the estates of his friends in the country. Apart from the restrictions imposed by his 'gentle competence', which never seems to have been quite enough, Aubrey's life over this period had been as full and fertile – during it he had written his 'Lives' and shaped his *Natural History*, probably his two best works – as he could have reasonably hoped it would be. On the whole he seems to have been happy. There must, at that time, have seemed to be every reason to think and hope that the conditions and circumstances of his life would stay much the same for the rest of it.

But three unfortunate and unforeseeable twists of fate were to make the last eleven years of his life much less peaceful and pleasant than those of the decade which preceded them. These were the intensification of the dispute with his brother over the disposal of the lease at Chalke, to a point of bitterness that he could never have imagined at the time of his mother's death; the loss of his lodgings in, or around, Gresham College; and a bitter quarrel with Wood, which destroyed the friendship that had been the mainstay of Aubrey's emotional life since his absconding, and which one would have thought was indestructible.

Of the three, the most serious was probably the least obviously dramatic – the loss of his home in Gresham College. This was partly the result of a catastrophic change in Hooke's character, caused by the death, in 1687, of his niece, Grace, who had been living with him since 1672 when she was eleven. Grace was the only child of Hooke's only brother John, a grocer at

Newport where, according to Hooke, he had become mayor. In spite of this he seems not to have been at all successful, for Hooke was constantly sending him money. His financial worries were probably the reason why he sent Grace to live with his brother, and they were certainly the main reason why he hanged himself in 1678. Hooke became devoted to Grace, who in the due course of time became his mistress. She was also his constant companion, for Hooke, who had given her the best education he could, often took her about with him, both on business and pleasure, although the two, for him, were very much the same. As Grace was, not unnaturally, also interested in younger men, there were constant scenes when Hooke, coming home, found her sometimes in the company of, occasionally in bed with, one or other of them. Hooke should not logically have resented this, for on his side he seems to have had a succession of affairs with his serving girls. But undoubtedly he did, showing himself to be both possessive and jealous. Altogether, it seems to have become an extraordinary tangle of emotions to find in the background of this seemingly staid and single-minded scholar. The effect on Hooke of Grace's death was disastrous. According to a close friend, Edmund Waller, it totally changed his character.

With Hooke wrapped in the shroud of his sorrow, the college must have been a much less pleasant place in which either to work or to live. Yet, again one can not be sure whether Aubrey actually lived there or elsewhere for most of this time. A much earlier letter to Wood suggests that he rarely now lodged with Hooke. Aubrey was having trouble getting hold of letters sent to him at Hooke's lodgings – but 'I have now taken care with the deliveries of the Post letters to secure them for me – for Mr. Hook is not . . . within almost all day long . . . he lies abed all the morning, sitting up at study the night, and the afternoons he goes about businesse, so that the Post-men were weary at being disappointed.'[1] Yet the entry that Hooke records in his Diary about Aubrey being 'ill with cold. Spake to Horne to mend chamber' was dated '6. December 1688', and so a year after the death of Grace.

More personally serious for Aubrey than Hooke's grief, and consequent gloom, was the loss of his near-by lodgings with 'Mistress Morris' or whoever, for which one does not know the reason, but which one would think was simply because his landlady had died, retired or moved elsewhere. In consequence, he, too, had to move elsewhere, and so sometimes found himself living in conditions totally unsuitable for a man of his scholarly tastes and needs. This showed in a letter which he wrote to Wood on 5 September 1689: 'One would be apt to think (God bless me) that there was an evil genius did haunt me – I came to my pleasant lodgings at the end of Jan. last – a weeke after a schoolmaster takes the chamber above me; coming in at 12 or 1 and awakes me out of my sleep, and rises very early . . . The week after came a man and his wife and child breeding teeth, that cries day and night . . . But notwithstanding this I put on a resolution to begin to transcribe on the first of March. I had about a week's work left . . . when the chitt in the next chamber fell sick of the small-pox, and then the mother. So I was faine to lie at the Inne – because Mistress Smyth is afraid never having had them and fatt.' Obviously, under less infective conditions Aubrey could still fall back on Wyld's house in Bloomsbury when he was in need of a room. He goes on, 'I carried my MS out with me. I had the good luck to get a lodging in an empty house where I have layn 5 daies, and am on this day warnt out for new tenants to come in.' Aubrey decided to take refuge in Oxford. 'I intend by the middle of March to come to Oxford and bring my MSS with me and there finish them, which I cd. doe in a fortnight. In the meantime, pray consider where I should lye – whether at Mr. White's' – this was the chemist in Holywell, the street that runs behind New College connecting the Broad to the High Street, with whom Aubrey now seems to have habitually stayed when he was in Oxford – 'and board there, or els some other private place. I left with my laundresse a shirt, cap and cravat . . . (but then the P. of Orange came in). I hope she has not lost it for I would not bring shirts to stuff up my breeches and swelter in the coach.'[2]

Back in London, Aubrey's mail followed him to various addresses, most frequently to 'The Tobacco Roll and Sugar Loaf near Great Russell St'. This was near to Mistress Baylie's in Dirty Lane, Bloomsbury, where he lodged, and conveniently close to Wyld's house. He had a brief stay in another unspecified lodging which he found unsatisfactory. He also stayed for a while 'at Mr. Clarke's, over against the Kings Head in Wardour Street'; with 'Mr. T. Bridgeman in great Lincoln's Inn Fields', and with Dr Thomas Gale, the high master of St Paul's School. Thomas Gale was an old friend, a Fellow of the Royal Society, and a fellow antiquarian. The door of his house was to be increasingly opened to Aubrey, for whom during the final years of his life it was to become his main place of residence when in London. But these stays, and the moves they entailed, must have added up to an unsettled, and unsettling, way of life for an ageing man.

However, as on most occasions, Aubrey accepted his misfortunes with good grace. In particular, Hooke's grief-stricken withdrawal into himself never seems to have affected his feelings of respect and friendship for him. On 15 September 1689, one finds him joining in support of Hooke who was claiming that he, rather than Isaac Newton, discovered the theory of gravity. This was in a letter to Wood, suggesting that he should state as much in his forthcoming book. It turned out to be a joint letter in which Hooke's corrections and additions occupied about twice as much space as Aubrey's basic text. Aubrey writes – Hooke's additions in brackets – 'Mr. Rob. Hooke did in Ao. 1670 write a discourse called *An Attempt to Prove the Motion of the Earth* which he then read to the Royall Society . . . About 9 or 10 years ago Mr. Hooke writt to Mr. Isaac Newton of Trin. College, Cambridge to make a Demonstration of (this theory not) telling him (at first) the proportion of the gravity to the distance (nor what was) the curved line that was thereby made: Mr. Newton in his Answer to his letter (did expresse) that he had not (known) of it.' Hooke completed the letter with some forty to fifty lines explaining his theories, underlining five lines, central to the letter and central to his claim – 'these degrees and proportions of the power of attraction in the celestial bodys were communicated to Mr. Newton by Mr. R. Hooke in the year 1678 by Letters, as will plainly appear both by the copy of the said Letters and the Letters of Mr. Newton in answer to them, which are both in the custody of the said R. H.; both which also were Read before the Royall Society at their publique meeting as appears by the Journale book of the said Society.'[3] Eighteen months later, on 22 January 1691, one finds Aubrey urging Wood 'whatever you doe, pray take a special care to doe Mr. Hooke right against Mr. Newton: it is the greatest discovery that yet was made and Mr. Newton runnes away with the glory of it.'[4] Three months later he tells Wood, 'Mr. Hook has been very ill; we were afraid we would lose him; he was glad to be assured by me that you would doe him right against Mr. Newton, it comforted his spirits.'[5]

*   *   *

If Aubrey's forced move from Gresham College affected the conditions and character of his life more than any other of the various misfortunes which came upon him during the period, his dispute with his brother over the disposal of the lease at Broadchalke must have been the most hurtful. One so much regrets the distress which the dispute caused Aubrey that it is difficult to be fair to William, but a sequence of his letters in the Bodleian to Aubrey shows something of his side of the case, and that at the least Aubrey was remiss in not telling him what he intended to do. Only one of these letters is fully dated – 'St. James even. (July 24th), 1688'.

The other letters, one would think from their contents run from the previous May until June 1689. This covers the period of the 'Glorious Revolution'. The change of political climate that this involved may well have been at the root of William's problems, and so those of Aubrey. For William held an appointment as Keeper of a block of woodland under the overall control of the Lord Warden of the area who was 'Coll[onel] Penruddock', one of the family that had long been close neighbours and friends of the Aubreys. One would think that Penruddock was probably a supporter of James II and that it was for this reason he was dismissed. He was replaced by Sir Charles Raleigh. William, too, had been in the Militia: 'I took the Tost [presumably the oath of loyalty to James] one of the last Militia officers in Wilts, since Segamore Battle, when K. James was at highest, therefore unable to alter when he was declining.'[6] As soon as Raleigh took over, William, too, was dismissed. His next letter tells Aubrey that 'the Lady Raleigh has warned me out of the Lodge'. He asks Aubrey to try and persuade Raleigh 'that he must not displace me . . . , that I am no Papist, a man beloved of the country, and one that does not make a Prey on the forest, as some other Keep. doe, and must doe that have no other dependance'.[7] From this one would think that this was the period when Aubrey allowed William to run the farm, and that he was working the two jobs together. But soon he was to have neither, Aubrey seemingly having taken the running of the farm back into his own hands preparatory to the sale of the lease. William's letters, at first supplicatory, respectful, even affectionate, became increasingly recriminatory and bitter. In the end they became mildly threatening. William seems to have thought that he was in some way included in the lease – and may have been. Possibly their mother's interest had been passed on to him. 'I fear the end will be both changeable and troublesome, to discover each other's titles.' And again, in a later letter: 'You can not blame me if I side with that title I am like to lose least by.' He also knew how to hit where it hurt. Unluckily for Aubrey, the trunk of papers and books from his Easton Piers days, which for many years he had left in the safe keeping of the Longs at Draycot, had recently been sent across first to Mrs Penruddock, thence to Manor Farm: 'If I heard not from you I had delivered your studies, papers and books that have been so often demanded but if I can, I will keep the key until I hear from you.' Meanwhile the farm itself seems to have been left in a state of total neglect. 'Your hops are not poled, and your wheat . . . almost half eat up for want of removing.' William himself seems to have been in a pitiable plight – owing money at Kington St Michael to 'Thos. Stokes . . . for my board with him', for which he was expecting to be arrested, and at Chalke – 'I have not any money to buy food.' However, he still seems to have had his sheep, for 'Mr. Kitt. [Kitson] your agent threatened to sieze all my sheep and begin law with me.'[8] It was, clearly, a thoroughly unhappy and difficult situation for everybody.

Luckily, Aubrey seems to have found a patient and kindly purchaser. This was a Mr Kent, who, one would surmise from an earlier reference to some information that Aubrey obtained from 'one of Mr. Kent's plasterers' was a London builder. Possibly he had made his fortune in the spate of new building which followed the Great Fire. Aubrey himself gives two widely differing dates for the handover of the farm. In his *Collectio Geniturarum* he notes 'Possession of Chalke-ffarme given by Mr. Rich. Kitson', who was evidently Aubrey's solicitor as well as agent, 'to Mr. Jo. Martin', probably

Kent's solicitor, 'December the 9th. 4h P.M. 1687'. But in a letter of 24 April 1690 to Wood, Aubrey wrote 'After Michaelmas I parted as to Chalke Farm to Mr. Kent (to my great grief).'

During the intervening years it would seem that complicated and costly – but Kent would, of course, have been paying – legal consultations took place to determine the title of the lease which Aubrey was selling, and as to whether William had any right to part of the proceeds. The terms on which Aubrey was selling it seem to have been that Kent would clear Aubrey's farm debts and allow him a small annuity for the rest of his life. Even before the first handover, Aubrey describes himself as 'being perplexed and plagued with troubles from my brother and with running up and down with lawyers and Proctors'. After the second and effective date of possession on 5 July 1690, when Aubrey was lying 'dormant for feare of an arrest which will come to a matter of £90 which my brother could have settled for £12', he told Wood that William's 'rough humour hath putt all my business out of order and it hath made me doe him great prejudice and I have had to do with odd people.' He went on, 'If I am caught by the Bayliffs (my brother having been so unkind) I will end my days with that good woman Mrs. Baylie.' So, by then, Aubrey must have been reasonably content with his lodgings in Dirty Lane, close to 'The Tobacco Roll and Sugar Loaf'. After the second handover 'Mr. Kent and all his family went to Chalke to settle matters, and I thought to have sent some good old bookes to Oxon, but my brother in whose custody they were would not be spoken to, and absented himself. At Christmas I thought to have gone thither with Mr. K. but did not, and then he and my brother met and I am afraid between my brother and Mr. Kent's sonne all my best things are imbezilled. God help the helpless.'[9] It was a cry from the heart.

In January 1691, Aubrey wrote to Wood 'the later end of the Terme I expect my brother to come like a Fury and fall upon me and Mr. Kent.' In fact, in March both Aubrey and Kent were served with summonses on behalf of, and possibly by, William. But nothing more seems to have come of it, and by then Aubrey seems to have sufficiently recovered his spirits to write humorously 'I have got a new suite that I never expect to weare out.'[10] The arrest that he feared for the debt of '£80 and interest' finally came in October; but once again the long-suffering and ever-paying Kent came to the rescue. Aubrey wrote to Wood on 27 October: 'I thank God that I have yet my liberty. Mr. Kent compounded the debt that I was arrested for. My brother has been very unkind to me, and (God forgive me) I have undone him and myselfe . . . the trueth is I was never made to manage an estate, and was predestinated to be cosined and cheated.'[11] Although strictly speaking it would seem that Kent was only keeping to the terms of his contract in paying off Aubrey's ever-appearing debts one can but feel that including the cost of the legal proceedings to establish Aubrey's title the full cost of purchase must have come to much more than he anticipated and that Aubrey was lucky to be dealing with so honourable and kindly a man. In view of this it is sad to read in a letter to Wood after the sale that 'the farm does not prosper'. But this was in 1691, the first year of Kent's ownership. The farm may have needed a considerable length of time to recover from the Aubreys' management – or lack of it.*

*   *   *

What one might term the creative period of Aubrey's work, which seems to have reached its peak with the writing of the 'Lives', ended with the editing and shaping of his *Natural History*, in itself as creative a process as the original conception and note-taking. But there were still two vital tasks left for Aubrey to perform before he could be sure that he had done all that was in his power to preserve his work for posterity. First he had to make his manuscripts readable; then to find a place for their safe-keeping.

In the letter to Wood of 14 April 1690, in which he told him that he had handed over 'Chalke Farm to Mr. Kent', he added in brackets 'to my greate griefe, which I putt off as well as I can and I can not doe it better than by putting my papers in some method before I dye; for I have a great deale of worke on the loome.' In the same letter he had already told Wood, 'By the end of last October I had made an end of *Monumenta Britannica*, 3 volumes, and 1 vol. of Miscellanies.' In the previous year, he had revised and transcribed his 'Lives' which 'were so confused and so interlined that had I not donne it in my lifetime they would have figured nothing'.[12] A year later, as he told Wood in a letter dated 3 August 1691, 'On St. James Day (July 25th) I ended the 2nd part of my *Natural History of Wilts.*' By most standards, the discipline which Aubrey imposed on himself in order to transcribe the manuscripts seems not all that arduous. However, taking into consideration, as Aubrey did, that he was getting older – 'my candle blows low' – and that 'heart-breaking cares will shorten my life', perhaps the 'at least an howre . . . I transcribe one day with another' was reasonable. Also, late nights often led to late mornings – Aubrey, in any case, was rarely up before ten – and he was also, of course, still carrying on the correspondence of the Royal Society.

An unforeseen result of Aubrey's transcribing was that when his manuscripts became readable, they could be, and were, circulated among the members of the Royal Society. In consequence, he gained considerably in

*William Aubrey's last unkindness – but it was an unkindness to us rather than to Aubrey, who by then had been dead for six years – was, in 1703, to borrow from the Ashmolean 'Liber B', the second part of the second part of the *North Wiltshire Collections*, and then not to return it. It was not found among his effects when he died in 1707. So, no doubt, he had sold it, as he had sold so many of Aubrey's books.

respect and repute. He was, obviously, greatly pleased when the Royal Society ordered that a copy of his *Natural History* should be made at their expense and stored in their records, and likewise that when they learnt of his intention to send his manuscripts to Oxford for safekeeping, they asked that copies might first be made. 'I did not expect to be so highly honoured,' he wrote to Wood.

One new friend – he had long been an acquaintance – that this brought him was John Evelyn. In a letter of 27 January 1691, Aubrey told Wood, 'Mr. J. Evelyn I intend to see to-morrow: my old acquaintance and vertuous ingeniose friend.' Aubrey sent Evelyn the fair copy of his *Natural History*. One can still see, in the Bodleian, the occasional addition that Evelyn made, written in an elegant, considered hand that contrasts with Aubrey's scrawling, scurrying writing – but which yet has much more life in it than Evelyn's. He also, on 10 May 1692, sent Evelyn the manuscript of his *Idea*, after it had gone the rounds of the 'great and noble lords', who might have been likely to implement it – but without success. Aubrey wrote a somewhat gloomy accompanying note. 'In case I should happen to die before I call for this Idea; I desire you, then, to leave it with Mr. Hooke at Gresham college, to be put into my chest marked Idea: which is full of Bookes for this Designe. Sir, I pray God blesse you and yours.'[13]

Such new friends as Evelyn, even if they were old acquaintances, were particularly welcome at this time, for Aubrey had come to the age when he was starting to lose friends, among them some of those he most valued, in the only way that he was ever likely to – by their deaths. Petty died in 1687. Aubrey added a final note to the 'Life' which he had sat down to write in 'my chamber [after] taking a pipe of tobacco' some six years earlier, and which was to prove the first of many. 'Sr. W. Petty died at his house in Peccadilly Street (almost opposite St. James' Church) on fryday 16th day of December 1687, of a Gangrene in his foote, occasioned by the swelling of the Gowt, and is buried with his father and mother in the church at Rumsey in Hampshire.'[14] Aubrey adds neither lament nor praise – but one senses a feeling of completion, not only that a full and fruitful life had run full circle, Petty returning to his birthplace to lie beside his parents, but that Aubrey had finished his record of a remarkable man which was now there for posterity to read. Almost exactly two years earlier Aubrey's mathematician friend Dr John Pell had died in the poverty in which he had lived his last years – 'he had not 6d in his purse when he dyed.' According to Aubrey he 'dyed of a broken heart', but there are other more probable reasons of death at the age of seventy-four. Sir William Dugdale, one of his two antiquarian friends – the other being Ashmole – whom Aubrey saw regularly throughout many years of his London life, had died in the year that separated the deaths of Pell and

Petty. His Trinity friend Tom Mariet, whom he had lodged in his rooms at Fleet Street above 'the stationers at the signe of the Rainbow near Temple Bar' when he was sounding Monck on behalf of the exiled king to be, died in April 1691. 'My old acq. and deare friende . . . deceased in town about 10 days since. His 3rd wife broke his heart.' Seth Ward, who was one of 'the great men' who tried on several occasions to persuade Aubrey into a parish, and who without doubt would have found one for Aubrey in his diocese of Salisbury had he accepted – 'so prudent, learned and good a man that he honours his Preferment as much as his Preferment does him' – died in 1689. Aubrey considered that Ward had been killed by 'the black malice of the Deane of Sarum [who] printed sarcasticall pamphlets against him . . . For about a month before he died he lived on the stock and died a skeleton'.[15] But it sounds much more like cancer.

Aubrey went through the papers of both Pell and Seth Ward in order to save anything valuable 'from the Pies', as he wrote on some copies of mathematical letters of Pell's that he sent to Thomas Haak, an old friend and acquaintance of both of them. It may be that in Seth Ward's Knightsbridge house Aubrey was looking, in particular, for 'A Survey of Salisbury Cathedral', commissioned by Ward of Wren in 1667. He did not find it then, but most surprisingly, a copy of it came to Wood in the following year. In a letter of February 1690 Aubrey wrote to Wood, 'I shall put my left hand the next weeke to my 2nd part of my Nat. Hist. of Wilts: in the chapter on Architecture I would insert Dr. Wrenne's animadversions on Salisbury Church: therefore I desire you not to faile to bring it with you when you come hither, that I may transcribe it and will acknowledge it was from you that I had it; when I thought it was irretrievably lost.'[16] Wood was slow in either sending or bringing it and Aubrey's subsequent letters are full of exhortation, pleas, demands for its dispatch. But in the end it must have come to Aubrey, for a copy, possibly in his hand, lies among his 'Loose Papers' in the Bodleian.

It was well worth waiting for. In it Wren gives not only a detailed description of the cathedral and what needs to be done to repair and preserve it, but insight into his own ideas on architecture. 'The first architect's judgement I most justly commend . . . Gothick fabriques of later dates though more elaborate yet want the naturall Beauty which arises from the proportions of the first dimensions. For here the breadth to the height of the Naves, and both to the shape of the Iles, beare a good proportion; the Pillars and the intercolumnations (or spaces between pillar and pillar) are well suited to the height of the arches, the mouldings are decently mixt with large planes without affectation of filling every corner with Ornaments, which . . . glutt the eye. The windows are not made too great; nor yet the light obstructed with many mullions and transomes of Tracery works, which was the ill fashion of the next following age – Our Artist knew better, that nothing I could add beautie to light; he trusted in a stately and rich plainness that the marble shafts gave to his work.'[17]

Aubrey's quarrel with Wood only came in the last years of both their lives, and probably much of its ferocity came from that fact. Both were quarrelling not only with each other, but with the frustrations and failures in their lives. Long before then it seems, the fabric of their friendship was wearing thin. The fault for this, one would think, lay mainly on Wood's side. Aubrey was by nature essentially loyal, and indulgent of his friends' faults. It was common for even a casual acquaintance to become a friend for life, whatever he did. The range of his friendships was, too, widespread and ever growing. Wood, by contrast, had few friends and on those he had he was much more demanding. It was also undoubtedly important to him to be the dominant partner in the relationship. Over the many years when Aubrey was virtually working for him there can have been no doubt that this was so. But Aubrey's writing of his 'Lives' shifted the balance. In so doing Aubrey had not only proved his independence, but produced a work of far greater worth than any Wood was ever likely to achieve. Wood must have sensed and resented this. One would think, too, that at a time when because of his souring temper, and unsocial habits, Wood's life was contracting even within its already narrow limits he was envious of the full social life that Aubrey still led in spite of the fact that he had no money, nor any longer the backing of country possessions.

The most important strand in their friendship had always been their belief in the worth of their work. This they continued to share. Until now Wood's garrets had seemed the natural destination for Aubrey's work. He had, during a bout of illness, in the course of the writing of the 'Lives', written a will in which he had named Wood as what one might call his literary executor. But now Aubrey's long-standing friendship with Elias Ashmole had opened a much safer, more reliable and obviously longer-lasting depository for his work. This was in the Ashmolean Museum, founded and funded by Ashmole, and now well established in Oxford with a competent, caring and friendly curator in Edward Lhwyd. Wood's reluctance to hand over Aubrey's MSS made him now a hindrance rather than a help. Aubrey always remained fond of Wood, even in the depths of their quarrel, but he cared much more for his work. When the two conflicted there was no doubt where his priority lay. This showed clearly in a letter he wrote on 28 December 1688 after a visit to Ashmole. It can not have endeared him to Wood. It was only some five weeks since the Prince of Orange had landed in Torbay, and only a few days since James II had boarded the barge at Whitehall which would have taken him to Gravesend, whence he was to travel to Rochester, and so to France and exile. A wave of anti-Catholic feeling was sweeping the country, occasionally expressing itself in mob violence. 'Last Teusday I went to see Mr. Ashmole (whom I found ill). He lately received a letter from Dr. Plot [who had earlier refused to edit Aubrey's *Natural History* and was perhaps now trying to make amends] about the things I sent to Oxford, and sayes that he desired you to send to the Museum, but you denied him . . . Mr. Ashmole is most outrageously angry and charged me to write to you, as soon as I could, and to order you to put the Box in the Museum: for he looks upon you as a P.[apist] and forsooth so does the whole university . . . he sayes he expects to hear of you being plundered, and papers burnt, as at the Spanish ambassadors . . . and he further bids me tell you that if you shall further refuse to deliver the things sent down by me to Oxford that he will never looke upon you as a friend and will never give a farthing more to the University of Oxford.'

Wood must have been thoroughly alarmed by the time he had read this far, and must have been angered further when Aubrey continued to show a total lack of concern for the safety of Wood himself, which contrasted starkly with his concern for his manuscripts: 'I do desire you to send my box forthwith for feare that all my MSS should be rifled by the Mob.' He must also have been irritated when Aubrey inserted a totally inappropriate instruction to his laundress: 'When you see Mr. Chr. White – let him ask Liz my laundresse to keepe my shirt, for I was to be returned in a fortnight but the Times prevented me.'[18]

Aubrey had long been in correspondence with John Ray, a pioneering naturalist, whose long and dedicated labours eventually earned him the title of the father of English natural history. One would think that most of Aubrey's letters were on behalf of the Royal Society, for although interested in all aspects of country life, his particular concerns had always been antiquarian, agricultural and historical rather than botanical. However most of Ray's letters, of which thirteen survive, are in answer to botanical queries that Aubrey had raised. The first surviving letter, dated 18 August 1675, dealt with a personal matter. Aubrey asked whether he would consider being the travelling tutor to the son of Paschall's patron at Chedzoy in Somerset, Sir Francis Rolle. Ray refused on the grounds that 'travelling beyond sea is not consistent with my present relation and state of life.' This refusal had, in Aubrey's eyes, a horrific consequence which he notes on the bottom of Ray's letter: 'Failing to find someone suitable to take his son on his Grand Tour, Rolle was advised to send his sonne to an able divine that taught school at Newington – his sonne was sent thither, where within a 12 month his schoolmaster married him to his Niece; ten years older; and he was his father's only sonne.'[19]

Two years later Aubrey was again sounding Ray, this time to find out if he would consider standing for the Secretaryship of the Royal Society, but again Ray refused. At this time Aubrey was considering putting himself forward as a candidate. A year later an enquiry from Aubrey, seemingly about the purchase of some of Ray's botanical books, brought a reply which tells us much about Ray himself: 'True it is that Divinity is my profession' – Ray had been a Fellow of Trinity College, Cambridge from 1649 to 1662 – 'yet not lately by me undertaken . . . The study of plants I never lookt upon as my business – but my diversion only. Yet since I am not qualified to serve god and my generation in my proper function, I have been bold to bestow a good proportion of my time on it; nor have I yet given it quite over so that I have no thought of parting with any of my books on that subject.'[20]

Clearly what had started as a pen friendship had by then developed into a personal one. In the autumn of 1691 Aubrey sent Ray, by the 'Braintree Carrier, who lives at the Pewter Pot in Leaden hall Street, and goeth out of towne on Friday', the transcribed copy of his *Natural History* for corrections and comment. Ray was pleased and praising. 'You do so mingle so many utilia dicta that the book can not but take with all sorts of Readers.' But he was critical also on small points. 'Some words I have noted that do not sound well . . . I observed some particulars to be repeated . . . A great number of lacunae there are which you must endeavour to fill up.'[21] On the return journey the manuscript went astray. Ray, when he heard of it, wrote that he was 'much surprised and startled . . . Such an Accident as this never yet befell me . . . the loss of it would be inestimable'. However the manuscript must eventually have turned up for there is no further mention of its loss. Aubrey was, in fact, taking a considerable risk in sending his manuscripts about the country. When he sent his *Natural History* to Paschall at Chedzoy in Somerset, it arrived with its wooden box badly broken. A warm letter from Ray in the following year shows that Aubrey had been down to see him and his family at their Essex home in Black Notley. 'My wife and young girls . . . are indeed much pleased with the Glasse Microscope.' Ray was subsequently to be sent, to read and criticize several other manuscripts of Aubrey's – although noticeably not the 'Lives'. Their correspondence and friendship was to continue into the last years of Aubrey's life. The last dated letter from Ray was written on 7 May 1695, and was in answer to one from Aubrey evidently trying to raise subscriptions for, one would think, his *Miscellanies*. 'I life in a corner of the World barren of wits . . . but I will take a copy, and Mr. Dale another, and he will endeavour to get you other subscribers.'[22]

Aubrey's relationship with Ray was always a peripheral one but important none the less. It shows how well Aubrey spun the web of his friendships, and how widely he spread the listening posts which served both the Royal Society and himself. In the last years of his life he was to have another in Scotland, with Dr Garden of Aberdeen University, who was interested mainly in archaeological remains. In his West Country there was of course Paschall, and in Wales, when he was not looking after the Ashmolean in Oxford, Edmund Lhwyd. Aubrey, also, had an antiquarian friend who lived near Ripon, to whom he paid a visit in 1686. This was a great event for Aubrey, and the source of several entries in *Monumenta Britannica*. He brought back a plant he had picked on the Yorkshire moors, which he dried and sent to Ray for identification. Ray named it as *Grapholia vulgaris similis* and sent it back to him. It still lies between the pages of *Monumenta Britannica*. It is strangely moving when one turns over a page and comes to the actual plant that Aubrey picked on the Yorkshire moors three centuries ago. It makes the past seem much nearer at hand – which, of course, was the point of much of Aubrey's work.

Two much younger friends that Aubrey's work brought him at this time were Thomas Tanner, and Edward Lhwyd. Thomas Tanner was extremely young, still an undergraduate in his teens, when he first met Aubrey. He was to take his MA in 1696, the year before Aubrey's death, and in the same year to become a Fellow of All Souls. By then he was still only twenty-two. Even in these earlier years of his late teens when he first knew Aubrey he was obviously already well on the road to the distinguished antiquarian career that awaited him, and even more surprisingly seems to have been already well known to both London and Oxford publishers, with whom he tried to place Aubrey's work, particularly his *Natural History* and 'Templa Druidum', the first part of *Monumenta Britannica*. The price of these efforts on Aubrey's behalf was, of course, that he would be allowed to read, and to make use of for his own work, Aubrey's manuscripts. A sequence of letters in 1693 shows this proceeding apace. 'March 6th . . . I had your Remains of Gentilism and the Hist. of Wilts and deposited them as you bid me in Mr. Lloyds private custody' – 'May 10th . . . I desire you to let me hear from you as soon as you can about your Wiltshire Antiquities. If you can spare them I will order the Waggoner to call for them in a short time.' – 'Oct. 20th. As for your Templa Druidum I got it of Mr. Gibson a week since, for I could not be quiet till I had seen it and have since read it with a great deal of satisfaction.'[23]

Tanner, at this time, was also helping Wood to put his papers in order. The quarrel between Aubrey and Wood had not yet broken into the open, but it was clearly impending. Tanner, interested in and involved with the work of both men – he was to be one of Wood's literary executors – seems at this moment to have been running with both hare and hounds. For in the letter of 10 May in which he asks for Aubrey's 'Wiltshire Antiquities', presumably his *North Wiltshire Collections*, he adds, 'I shall scorn to be like Ant. Wood, viz. make use of your papers and acquaintance and at last not afford you a good word.'

Both Aubrey's interests and his inclinations seem to have pointed him much more strongly to Lhwyd than to Tanner. As Keeper of the Ashmolean, by then the designated depository for Aubrey's work, Lhwyd held a position of importance vital to Aubrey. In the course of their dealings he seems always to have been helpful, efficient and appreciative of both Aubrey and his work. In spite of the difference in age – Lhwyd was considerably older than Tanner, but would still only have been thirty-three in 1692 – they seem to have established a bond of personal friendship which strengthened during the few years that Aubrey still had to live. Ashmole died in 1692, leaving most of his money to the Museum, to the disgust, so Aubrey tells us, of his wife, who shortly after his death – again, according to Aubrey – married a stone-cutter of Lambeth, where Ashmole had had a house. It may have been Ashmole's death which prompted Aubrey to make a list of the manuscripts which were already in the keeping of the Museum and the care of Lhwyd. This included 'Antiquities of Wiltshire' (his *North Wiltshire Collections*); *Monumenta Britannica* in 3 parts; 'Memoire of Naturall Remarques in Wilts' (his *Natural History*); 'Perambulation of halfe the County of Surrey'; *Miscellanea*; *Lives*, 3 parts; Mr. Th. Hobbes' life in English: *Idea of Education*; *A Collection of Genitures*; *Easton Piers delineated*; *Faber Fortunae.*' So all his main works are here. But there were also more recent works, which show that if he no longer contemplated, or possibly was capable of, work of the calibre of his *Natural History*, his *Monumenta Britannica*, his *North Wiltshire Collections* or his 'Lives', that he was still an inveterate collector of original and unusual facts. His collections of these were often the first of their kind. Such was the *Remaines of Gentilisme*, a collection of folk-lore. So, too, was *Villare Anglicanum*, a list of English place-names with occasional notes. He had also written 'An apparatus of the Lives of English Mathematicians', now bound in with the 'Lives'; 'A Collection of divine Dreames from persons of my acquaintance worthy of beliefe' – this was probably the section entitled 'Dreams' in his '*Miscellanies*': and 'A Collection of approved Receipts'. There were also three manuscripts still to come – *Adversaria Physica*, *An Introduction to Architecture* and *Some Strictures of Hermetick Philosophy*. There was also his collection of *Letters, writt to me from about 100 ingeniose persons*, of great interest and value to anyone seeking information about Aubrey. Altogether there were twenty-two items noted. It was an impressive list, an impressive achievement.[24]

The long-brewing quarrel between Aubrey and Wood finally broke out at the end of 1692. As one would expect, Wood's attack was far the most violent and venomous, but it came out of a deep reserve of bitterness; Aubrey was simply angry, but surprisingly so for a generally mild and gentle man. The quarrel took place against the background of Wood's expulsion by the Oxford authorities from the University for two years, and their imposition of a fine of £40, for having alleged in his *Athenae et Fasti*, of which the first volume had been published in 1691, the second in the summer of 1692, that Clarendon, when Chancellor, took bribes when considering the appointment of judges.

This allegation was based on a letter from Aubrey, written as long ago as January 1671, in which when writing about a relation, Judge David Jenkins, who had suffered a long period of harsh imprisonment under the Commonwealth, Aubrey regretted that after the Restoration 'he was not made one of the Judges of Westminster Hall, and he might have been (he told me) if he wd. have given money to the Chancellor; but he scorned it.' But if Aubrey provided the information, the responsibility for the printing was, surely, entirely Wood's. Aubrey was constantly reiterating that all he wrote about his contemporaries, or famous figures of the immediate past, was only for posthumous publication – 'the author and the persons (like medlars) ought to be rotten first.' If Wood disregarded this, then surely the fault was entirely his?

On Aubrey's side, his anger was caused by the discovery, when Wood reluctantly returned Part Two of the 'Lives', that some forty pages had been cut out. This caused Aubrey's furious note, headed 'Ingratitude' in his manuscript, in which he wrote: 'This part . . . Mr. Wood haz gelded from pag. I to pag. 44 and other pags. too are wanting, wherein are contained trueths; but such as I entrusted nobody with the sight of, but himselfe, whom I thought I might have entrusted with my Life. There are severall papers that may cutt my throate.' Aubrey added a postscript of personal protest: 'It was sticht up when I sent it him.' He dated it 'Novemb. 29, 1692.'[25] There was an element of fright in Aubrey's anger. This was fuelled by the unkind remark of the Earl of Abingdon, whose now dead wife had been a distant relation of Aubrey's, and on whose estate in Wiltshire Aubrey frequently stayed, that the present Clarendon intended to sue him, not only for his remarks about his father's corruption, but also for a virulent anonymous attack on the court called 'Advice to a Painter'. With this, of course, Aubrey had had nothing at all to do. As it proved, Abingdon's remark that Clarendon intended to sue Aubrey on these two counts was totally false. When tackled again, Abingdon admitted he had said as much only 'to putt me in a fright'. One wonders that Aubrey ever went again to stay at Lavington, Abingdon's estate, but he did frequently.

The core of the quarrel between Aubrey and Wood shows in the exchange of two letters, the first from Aubrey, written on 2 September 1694. Wood, in exile from the university, still seems to have lived in Oxford, whence Aubrey had recently returned: 'I have been ill ever since I came back from Oxford . . . of a serfeit of Peaches. I was fain to send to Kit White for a good, lusty Vomit . . . but abstinence hath pretty well settled me again. Your unkindness and choleric humer was a great addition to my ilness. You know I always loved you . . . I tooke paines enough to serve you. I was told by severall at Oxford that you can never afford me a good worde.' Aubrey then repeats much of the accusation he wrote in his note on the manuscript under the heading 'Ingratitude' – 'You have cutt out a matter of 40 pages, out of one of my volumes, as all the Index. (was ever anybody so unkind). I remember you told me there were some things in it that would cut my throat. I thought you so deare a friend that I might have entrusted my life in your hands, and now your unkindness does about break my heart.'[26]

This letter provoked the broadside that Wood had, clearly, been longing to deliver: 'When I was in your company last at Oxon, you told me I had cutt your book and so in your most wicked and silly letter of the 2nd. Sept . . . Now I must let you know that before you disturb my mind by word of mouth and by letters, especially by that rascally letter that had been soaked in a bucket of ale, you should have examined this matter and brought the book with you, to show me where the Leaves were cut out . . . but this you have not done, but go on with stuff and tattle to abuse without end . . . Another thing . . . when a suite was commenced against us [?] by the Earl of Clarendon, your poore spirit was so much affrighted that after twenty yeares acquaintance you took away your books in your Kodpiece.'[27] Clearly, Wood minded the loss of Aubrey's manuscripts and books much more than the loss of Aubrey's friendship. Much of his letter, of course, was bluster, but it was also the letter of a man at the end of his tether. As it was to prove, it was also that of a man close to the end of his life.

Towards the end of the following year, 1695, at the beginning of which Wood's exile was officially ended, he developed an internal obstruction which made it difficult, in the end impossible, to pass water. Mentioning this to an academic acquaintance, Robert South, with whom he was walking, he received the heartless reply that if he could not make water, he would have to make earth. This so annoyed Wood that, in a last flare-up of spirit, he returned to his house, and altered the notes on South's life to his disfavour. He faced his impending death with courage, arranging his papers, seeing to their safekeeping in the hands of the university, even reconciling himself with his sister-in-law. He died on 28 November. Aubrey mourned his death in a letter of 19 March, 1696, to Thomas Tanner. He wrote, 'I am extremely sorrowful for the death of my deare Freinde and old correspondent Mr. Anthony Wood: who (though his spleen used to make him chagrin and to chide me) yet we could not be asunder, and he would always see me at my Lodging, with his dark Lanthorne, which should be a Relick.'[27]

*   *   *

As one can see from the list of works that Aubrey had already placed in the Ashmolean by 1692, he had virtually completed the two final tasks that he had set himself – the transcription and deposition of his work in a place of

safe-keeping – in his effort to secure its immortality. But in the course of
the following fifteen months he was to receive three frightening reminders
of his own mortality. On 20 March 1693, he was mugged. 'I lighted upon
Thieves that robbed and wounded me sorely. I kept my chamber for a
weeke and have since been on a course of Physick.' Aubrey had fifteen
wounds on his head. He had barely recovered from this when he had
another attack – this time of gout. He wrote to Wood in October, 'After my
recovery of wounds by the Thieves I fell extremely ill of the Gowte for two
months . . . it had almost carried me off.' On 4 January 1694 he had a mild
apoplectic fit – from which he quickly recovered – but, at the very least, he
must have seen it as a warning of things to come.

However, in the same year, he must have been cheered by the probability
of publication – not, as one would have wished, for his *Natural History*, but
of his *Miscellanies*. In this, as Aubrey acknowledged, he was greatly helped
by another old acquaintance, who again, prompted, one would think, by the
reading of Aubrey's now readable manuscripts and the realization of their
worth, had become a friend. 'I am exceedingly obliged', Aubrey wrote in a
letter to Wood, on 4 April, 'to my old Acquaintance, Mr. John Dreydon for
his friendly advice and recommendation.' Dryden, in fact, wanted his own
bookseller to print it 'but he will print only Plays and Romances. So I am
obliged to do it by subscription.' However, clearly, all his friends were now
rallying round, for 'it doe begin pretty luckily'.[29] His *Miscellanies*, the only
work of his to be published in his lifetime, was published in 1696. Clearly
not one of his important works, there is yet a lot that is unmistakably
Aubrey, that will please and interest his admirers, such as the story about
'Mrs Cl. of S. in the county of S. had a beloved Daughter, who had been a
long time ill, and received no benefit from her Physicians. She dream'd that
a friend of hers deceased, told her that if she gave her daughter a Drench of
Yewgh compounded that she would recover. She gave her the drench and it
killed her. Whereupon she grew almost distracted. Her ChamberMaid to
complement her and mitigate her Griefe, said surely that could not kill her;
she would adventure to take the same herselfe. She did and died also. This
was about the year 1670 or 1671. I knew the Family.' Or again, under the
heading 'Glances of Love . . . It is strange that as one walkes the streets
sometimes one shall meet with an Aspect (of Male or Female) that pleases
one's soule; and whose Natural Sweetness of Nature we could boldy rely
on.' It was in the chapter on 'Apparitions' that Aubrey told about the now
famous phantom, quoted by Sir Walter Scott in *The Antiquary*, that, when
questioned, 'disappeared with a curious perfume and most melodious
twang'. It is pleasing that Aubrey lived to see at least one of his works in
print.

Over these last years, the emphasis of Aubrey's social life inevitably shifted from 'merry' evenings with Wyld and 'coffee-housing' with his Royal Society friends, to long country visits to relations and friends. He often stayed with the Earl of Abingdon at Lavington, but one would doubt whether Aubrey enjoyed these visits as much as those to his other friends. Abingdon always seems to have been complaining about something or other – for example that Aubrey was indirectly responsible for the number of people coming to the spa at Seend (which, at last, seems to have found the fame for which Aubrey had long been working) who might disturb the game on his near-by estate. More often, and more pleasantly, Aubrey stayed with Sir John Aubrey either at Boarstall or at Llantrithyd. From Llantrithyd Aubrey wrote on 29 October 1695, to Lhwyd, 'I am extremely caressed here by my noble Chief Sir JA where I am treated with all the varieties that the sea and land afford . . . In the afternoon we shove the Tankard and Bottle one to another in the bond of peace'[30] – which can not have been at all good for his gout.

Although Wood himself was to live until November 1695, their friendship was clearly dead after their quarrel. Aubrey made a few faint-hearted efforts to revive it, but with little response from Wood, and so with little success. In its place, for the scholarly companionship interest and encouragement that he always needed, Aubrey turned more and more to Lhwyd, particularly in these last years. From a letter written to Lhwyd on 18 July 1695, one is sorry to see that Aubrey's eyesight was now failing. This was the greatest of all ills for him since it cut him off from so much that he valued. 'Since I came from Oxon I have a mist in my eies; some vapours I suppose rising from the spleen upon my so soon leaving your good company at Oxd. which did very much vex me . . . I can hardly read a letter, but I write by guess.' To this letter Aubrey added a postscript dated 15 August: 'My eies are little mended . . . I have delivered this morning a Box of Books for you and Gloucester Hall. I hope it may come safe but the box is very feeble.' So too was Aubrey's handwriting. 'God knows whether I shall ever come to my beloved Oxford again.'[31] However, nine days later he was clearly intending to, writing to Lhwyd on 24 August, 'I shall come to Oxford about a week hence.' He had sent down 'by Mr. Rush the Bargeman Two Trunkes . . . one a sealeskin, the other blackleather, a great chest with Idea and my name writt on it, and two great Boxes . . . My eies do mend but very slowly. My candle grows low.' So, too, did that of 'my deare friend Mr. Edm. Wyld [who] grows very very weake and I feare can not long continue.' Aubrey now signs himself as he often did to Wood – 'Tuissimus. JA.'[32]

Several of Aubrey's letters to Lhwyd now carry echoes of his earlier letters to Wood when they were in the full flush of their friendship. In his letter of the end of October 1695, after his description of Sir John Aubrey's lavish hospitality, Aubrey adds, 'but I declare I am near so well pleased as with a college commons . . . in your good company.'[33] He ended a letter, still from Llantrithyd, the following February. 'I must never forget your many Civilities and friendships to me. I think the time long till I see you here.'[34] One would think, from the run of these two letters and of a third one in March, all written to Lhwyd from Llantrithyd, that Aubrey spent the whole of that winter there. He was extremely fortunate in having so kind and generous a relation and friend, yet one feels that if it had not been Sir John it would have been another. Looking back, one sees a long succession of friends from Thanet to Sir John who gave Aubrey hospitality during his penurious years. But no hospitality is ever totally one-sided, even when the main intention is charitable. Aubrey must always have been a genuinely welcome guest, giving much back in the way of good and interesting company for the much that he received.

Sir John had obviously at some time also extended his hospitality to Lhwyd, but Aubrey's March letter showed that for the moment he was to be disappointed in his hope of Lhwyd's coming to Llantrithyd. 'I did expect you this month, with a great desire of enjoying your good company, but you acquaint us you shall not come hither till August . . . Sir J. A. bids me tell he would not have you come hither till September for June, July and August he shall spend at Boarstall; he usually returns from Boarstall hither about the 10th or 12th of Sept., by that time I shall return hither.'[35] By now having deposited the manuscripts in the Ashmolean – although one suspects from his later mention of the various deliveries of the sealskin and black leather trunks, and the boxes, that there was a certain amount of putting in, taking out and putting back in again – Aubrey was collecting impersonal objects of interest for the Museum. In his March letter he goes on to tell Lhwyd, 'I have now gott of Mr. Wyld's Gentlewoman [presumably Jane Smyth] the Armorie Dictionary for you and also Mr. Potter's dividing compass which he invented and made with his own hand.' Aubrey generally ends his letters by asking to be remembered to his various friends in Oxford, of which there still seem to have been plenty, even though the days of 'the merry gang' were now long past. In this letter he sends his 'humble service . . . and respects to Dr. Woodroff and his good Lady, to my cosen J. Aubrey, Esq [presumably Sir John Aubrey's son] and Mr. Hopkins; and to my friends of Jesus College, and Mr. Lloyd of Madg. Coll.'. In a postscript Aubrey sent his 'humble service to Dr. Bathurst.'[36]

It must have given considerable pleasure to Aubrey that he was now on good terms again with Bathurst, for their friendship went such a long way back. But there had been a period when they seem to have drifted apart. Bathurst had married late in life a wealthy widow whose money, together

with that from his stipend as Dean of Wells, he put to good use by improving
and adding to the buildings of Trinity. One senses from the odd remark of
Aubrey's that Mrs Bathurst did not approve of him. Even as late as 1689,
when after Seth Ward's death Aubrey wrote to Bathurst suggesting he might
compose Ward's epitaph, he received a snappy refusal, saying that Bathurst
considered himself to be of an age when he should be thinking of his own
epitaph, not of someone else's. But there could be no doubt of the friendship
and the desire to help which showed in a letter of 25 August 1693 'I am glad
to find that you have resumed the thoughts of publishing your *Monumenta
Britannica* and that Dr. Gale's annotation will further improve it . . . I am not
like to be in Oxford till October. When I am there I shall be writing to
promote your affairs in what way I am able.'[37]

In London, the friends who seem closest, who were kindest, and in every
way cared the most for Aubrey over the last years, were, undoubtedly, the
Holders – and not only in London. In 1693 Aubrey had recuperated from the
combination of the hurt he had received in the mugging and from the severe
attack of gout by taking 'the fresh aire and good entertainment at my cosen
Freemans, married to Sir John Aubrey's sister', whence 'Dr. Holder', who,
as well as in London, lived in the near-by vicarage, 'carried me to Cambridge
and brought me acquainted with the Heads of Houses, who kindly
entertained me.'[38] This was the sort of recuperation that Aubrey most
needed – good talk, good company, against a background of affection. The
Holders had the great advantage for Aubrey that they still lived for most of the
time in London, so he could turn to them there in times of trouble, as he
evidently did in the midsummer of 1695, when he was troubled with his
eyesight. He received in return a note from Holder headed 'Amicissime – I
am much troubled for the defect in your Ey. It is most likely it came at the
cold . . . I know of nothing but Time, and keeping warm, and sparing of it to
recommend you. If you wish of a safe and harmless medicine, the Break
Spectacle Water, you may have it of Mr. Hemmings . . . who lives at the
Pestle and Mortar in St. Martin's Lane.'[39] Aubrey had long had both respect
and affection for Holder and his wife Susanna, Wren's sister – as they for him
– and had written a joint 'Life' in which he said of the Doctor 'if one would
goe about to describe a perfect good man [I] would draw the Doctors
character'; and of Susanna '[she] is not less to be admired in her sex and
station than her brother Sir Christopher and (which is rare to be found in a
woman) her excellences doe not inflate her.'[40]

In the summer of 1696 Aubrey was again at Llantrithyd, but seems not to
have spent the following winter there, for on 29 December he wrote from
London to Lhwyd to wish him 'a happy New Yeare and all success in your
noble undertaking. I have sent you by Mr. Bennet of the half Moon in Paul's

ch. yard a copy of Mr. Love's Scripture Rules'. Since it was mid-winter one is glad to see from 'Mr. Bennets' address that Aubrey was undoubtedly again staying in the house of Dr Gale, the high master of St Paul's School.

Aubrey had kept in touch with, and still on occasion went to see, Lady Long, now the widow of Sir James who had died in 1692. It was supposedly to see her that Aubrey set out from London at the beginning of June 1697. He stopped for the night at Oxford, most probably at the house in Holywell of Kit White, his chemist friend, and died in the course of it, one would think of an apoplectic fit similar to the one he had suffered in 1694. The register recorded his burial: '1697. John Aubery. A stranger. Was Buryed June 7th.' One knows that it was only a technical term for someone who did not live in the parish, but even so – Aubrey, a stranger in Oxford! No one, even among those who lived there all their lives, could have loved Oxford more, nor have been more faithful in his love from the day he came there as an undergraduate in May 1642, until the night of his death, fifty-five years later. Trinity College made some amends by claiming him as its own, and burying him in the space reserved for Trinity men in the church of St Mary Magdalen, which still stands on a now traffic-bound island at the end of the Cornmarket and so little more than a hundred yards from Trinity College itself. But it was only his twentieth-century friends who put up a plaque to his memory. In the south-east corner of Kington St Michael church, Aubrey shares another as one of Kington's 'Two most famous sons' with John Britton, the nineteenth-century antiquary who did much to rescue Aubrey's work and revive his reputation. One wishes, however, that Aubrey had a memorial to himself, and that it was on the other side of the church where his parents and his Lyte ancestors are buried. His real memorial, however, is, of course, the collection of his manuscripts in the Bodleian. But as one takes one of the volumes in which these are now bound out of its case, and turns the pages, one realizes that it is not only a memorial, it is a still living work.

Epilogue

Some of the questions raised at the time of Aubrey's bankruptcy by the drastic change in the conditions and style of his life, answered themselves in the course of the second part of it. Losing his money and his home, Aubrey inevitably lost much of his independence, and was thereafter largely dependent on his friends, who, happily, never failed him. Yet he was never totally dependent on any one friend in particular. His long and important friendship with Wood was basically a working relationship which, on his side, Aubrey supplemented with a great deal of affection which Wood rarely reciprocated – except in the early years of their relationship when Wood was still somewhat in awe of Aubrey as a Fellow of the Royal Society and a friend of the famous. But Wood apart, Aubrey had plenty of eminent, wealthy, and well-inclined friends to whom to turn in time of need. As it happened, he hardly had to turn. They presented themselves. Witness Thanet. He was at most an acquaintance until he became Aubrey's ever-welcoming host at Hothfield. But if Thanet had not appeared, some other member of Aubrey's wide circle of friends surely would have done. When Aubrey's visits to Hothfield ended with Thanet's sudden death some eight years after he first invited Aubrey to stay, there were still visits to the Henleys at Bramshill, to the Longs at Draycot, to the Holders and the Freemans in Hertfordshire, to Sir John Aubrey at Boarstall and Llantrithyd, and to the Earl of Abingdon at Lavington. Edmund Wyld frequently took Aubrey to his manor in Essex, and occasionally to his other estates in Bedfordshire and Shropshire. When in London, the wealthy, eccentric, sociable and scientifically-minded Wyld was an ideal crony and patron but in his absence Aubrey would undoubtedly – because he was a likeable, intelligent and entertaining companion – have found others to be merry with, as he had at Oxford. There was also the perpetual coming and going at Gresham College of the members of the Royal Society who provided company, stimulus and food for thought as well as the 'gentle competence'. In other words, Aubrey while being almost totally dependent on his friends in general for all that made his very changed life worthwhile, yet because of their number, he had within their charmed circle, considerable freedom of choice and action – and so some measure of independence.

There can be no doubt, however, that Aubrey's enforced exile from

Wiltshire did cut him off from what had been until then his main source of
material and of inspiration. Apart from his brief saunter through Surrey, in
the course of his *Perambulation* – and how different the course of his later life
and the character of his later work might have been had this led, as he hoped,
to subsequent surveys throughout Britain – his main topographical and
antiquarian work, the work through which he expressed his deep-rooted
desire to preserve what he could of both past and present, was to complete, in
so far as he could, his *North Wiltshire Collections*; thereafter to sort out, tidy
up and transcribe his *Natural History* and his *Monumenta Britannica*. All of this
was important but hardly original work. Yet with one door now barred,
another unexpectedly opened. Led to it amid the circumscribed and
humdrum surroundings of his work for Wood, and along the often prickly
path of his preparations for his *Life of Hobbes*, it opened into a storehouse of
riches, which unknown to him had been accumulating over the years in the
course of his social life. It led, of course, to the wondrous moment when, after
his pipe of tobacco, he settled down to write the first of his 'Lives'.

It is a temptation, but a mistake, to balance the weight of the Wiltshire work
in the early part of his life, against that of his 'Lives' in the later. The two do
not equate or compete, but taken together they immensely extend the size of
the canvas and the scope of his achievement. There is also little point in trying
to distinguish whether Aubrey, in his refusal to face facts on his way to
financial ruin, was being admirably consistent to his true self, in a
Shakespearian sense, or simply stupid. Aubrey was being Aubrey, he could
be no other, but in so being, when it came to practical and financial matters,
his lack of interest and competence often had disastrous results. Had
circumstances been kinder to Aubrey and he hd managed to retain Easton
Piers, Broadchalke and enough of his money to lead the life to which he was
used, one wonders what shape his later work would have taken. There can be
little doubt that he would not only have completed his *North Wiltshire
Collections*, but set about covering south Wiltshire as well. He had already
announced it as his wish and intention to do so, and was admirably placed
with his two homes, one in the north and one in the south, to do so. Also, with
practice he would probably have worked quicker and better – his *Perambulation* had shown how well he could work at a set task in a limited period of time
if he had to. A complete and completed survey of the whole of Wiltshire
would have been a work of quite a different stature from the fragment whose
mainly hidden charms lie in the Bodleian.

Given more congenial conditions Aubrey would certainly have added
something to his *Natural History*. Although, when he had tidied and
'tumultuarily' stitched up his notes, they made a remarkably complete and
seemingly freshly-painted picture. Had he had some money to put towards

the printing Aubrey would almost certainly have been able to have had it published in his lifetime. This would have been pleasant for us as well as for him, since like most of Aubrey's manuscripts they tend to lose more than they gain by editing. Roy, my son, put the reason for this nicely when commenting on the *Idea of Education*, of which he transcribed the greater part, as well as that of the 'Lives', for my home consumption during his post-graduate year at Oxford – 'In a scholarly work written to a clearly defined end, it is the afterthoughts, parentheses and fragments that are necessarily pruned. The loss in many cases is not great, yet these "irrelevancies" often create an impression of spontaneity, and provide the enjoyment of variety. If one pruned Aubrey's fragments and irrelevancies there would be nothing but a stump left, but there is little temptation to do so in any case. I find the scraps and sidelines very entertaining, the tumultuarier the better, and I feel that one is closer to the living Aubrey in this aspect of himself. The tendency has been to excuse or minimize his lack of organization in order to enhance his standing as a scholar. Aubrey would have been grateful for this, he had tried to do the same, yet did not succeed in changing his nature. So why should posterity?' One has only to compare the only published versions of the *Natural History* caringly edited by John Britton, with whom Aubrey shares his memorial in Kington St Michael church, first printed in 1847, with the original manuscript, to see what Roy means.

Aubrey would also, no doubt, have extended the range of his *Monumenta Britannica* by journeying further afield had he been able to afford to do so; for example, to see the stones and circles of north Wales and so compare them with Stonehenge. But as he recounted in *Templa Druidum* he 'never had the opportunity'. Yet apart from his immortal account of the hunting trip which led to the rediscovery of Avebury, and the undying interest of his finds at Stonehenge, *Monumenta Britannica* was essentially a foundation on which future archaeologists and antiquarians could build. And so it has proved, pointing the way notably for Dr Stukeley in the eighteenth and Sir Richard Hoare in the nineteenth centuries. But in the nature of things the value of a guide-book of this sort is bound to be diminished by the subsequent sweep of ever-spreading research. So, today, his *Monumenta* is little more than an archaeological and historical curiosity and a personal reminder of Aubrey. Would Aubrey have written his 'Lives' if the more leisurely conditions of the early part of his life had continued? One must doubt it. He might easily have written the odd pen portrait of friends and acquaintances he particularly admired and liked, such as Petty, Harvey, Wren, Hooke. But the manner of his writing of the 'Lives' has so much the air of an outburst of pent-up frustration, increasing during the ten years when he was doing virtually no work of his own, and very little that was worthy of him, that one cannot believe that he would have built up the head of steam which suddenly found so miraculously creative an outlet. So, in all probability, in his work there would have been more landscape but fewer figures.

*   *   *

Posterity was much slower in recognizing the worth of Aubrey's work than even he anticipated. He would have been pleased that his *Miscellanies* went eventually into four editions – but that was over a span of more than a century and a half. After its first publication in 1696, it was reprinted in 1722, 1784 and 1857. Curiously, for with so much on offer it seems strange that a relatively short although attractive work should be chosen, it was his *Perambulation of the County of Surrey* that was the first to be printed after his death. It was edited, with a biographical memoir, by Dr Richard Rawlinson, an ardent antiquarian throughout his life – which overlapped with that of Aubrey by six years – whose valuable lifelong collection of manuscripts is now, like those of Wood and Aubrey, in the Bodleian. His version of the *Perambulation* was published in 1718/19. But in it Aubrey's text was much amended, and the main sources of information about his life not then available.

From his main works – his *North Wiltshire Collections*, *Natural History of Wiltshire*, *Monumenta Britannica* and, of course his 'Lives' there was total silence for well over a century after Aubrey's death. The real breakthrough came in the middle of the nineteenth century, when two local men, one by birth, one by adoption, made notable contributions to the knowledge of both Aubrey and his work. John Britton, who was born in Kington St Michael, the son of a copyholder, who was also maltster, baker, shopkeeper and smallholder, and who, not surprisingly considering his diverse activities, went bankrupt, showed a dedication equal to Aubrey's in becoming one of the leading antiquaries of his day. He wrote a brief biography of Aubrey, which inevitably was somewhat light on the personal details of his life, but had the great merit of including the greater part of Aubrey's autobiographical notes, and also his list of astrological 'Accidents'. He also edited the *Natural History*. It was a great advance to have the greater part of the manuscript in print, but Britton was very selective in his editing. Perhaps one's outlook changes with the centuries but the passages he leaves out often now seem among the most interesting, because of the detail of a now so distant age.

Canon Jackson was an admirable editor of *North Wiltshire Collections*, appreciative of Aubrey's achievement and of Aubrey himself, adding the weight of his learning to the local knowledge which he had acquired as Rector of Leigh Delamere. His church would have been that in which Aubrey was taught by Robert Latimer. Jackson was intent to let Aubrey speak for himself, and did not wish to show 'the Father of Wiltshire History in any other costume but his own'. However, the extent of Jackson's notes and knowledge – on which one can hardly fault him – which on average occupy three quarters of each page, tends to dwarf Aubrey's text. Would it have been kinder to Aubrey if Jackson had printed his 'Notes' separately at the end of the book – or even as a companion volume?

Two 'Selections' from Aubrey's 'Lives' appeared on either side of the turn of the eighteenth into the nineteenth century, but it was not until the end of that century that a reasonably full and competent edition was produced by Andrew Clark, who had earlier turned Wood's diaries and other papers into his *Life and Times*. Then there was a long lull, until in succeeding years, shortly after the end of the Second World War, two books were published which more than any others have succeeded in bringing Aubrey and his work to the notice of the general public. Anthony Powell's *John Aubrey and his Friends* was published in 1948; Oliver Lawson Dick's *Aubrey's Brief Lives* in 1949. Powell's *Aubrey* was the informative biography that had long been needed and all subsequent students of Aubrey owe it and him a considerable debt. In Lawson Dick's presentation of the 'Lives' there was a great deal of clever scholarship, particularly in his biographical introduction, but there was also an element of showmanship, which was just what was wanted to give back to the 'Lives' their essential spontaneity and sparkle. Perhaps it was this that caught Patrick Garland's eye, and led to his adaptation of *Brief Lives* for the stage. This clever distillation of the essence of the 'Lives', and the brilliant characterization of Aubrey by Roy Dotrice, have between them probably widened Aubrey's public more than any published work. Anthony Powell also published, in 1949, a selection of *Brief Lives*. It is a more personal and so less comprehensive selection than Lawson Dick's but captures much of the quintessential Aubrey. Its more personal quality together with its smaller format – as published by the Cresset Press – makes it a delightful bedside book. More recently, Michael Hunter's *John Aubrey and the Realm of Learning*, published in 1975, although primarily the work of a scholar for scholars, and concentrating mainly on Aubrey's intellectual interests, is throughout thought provoking and refreshing reading. With all this post-war production there is an encouraging and increasing ground swell of interest in Aubrey so that it is now rare to read about any aspect of his period and not find a reference to him, and quotations from his work.

So, at very long last, Aubrey seems to have found a posterity that values his work at its true worth, a posterity that is properly 'gratefull . . . for his minuteness'. For it is this above all else that distinguishes his work. His eye and taste for detail, whether human or historical, archaeological, antiquarian or topographical, enable him to raise before our minds eye a vivid picture of whatever he is describing. Within the framework of events in which he played little part, in an age of exciting original thought to which he added little, he yet made a highly important contribution of his own. He not only recorded the background detail of the countryside in which he lived, and of those areas he visited in the course of his researches – many of the buildings wherein have, as he feared they would, since disappeared – but brilliantly brought to life the characters who inhabited his world, both in town and country. In so doing he shows us not only how much has been lost but how much remains; and while showing us clearly the distinctive difference of his age from ours, shows us also its recognizable similarity. It is a remarkable achievement, and brings his past much closer to our present. In consequence, as we return from Easton Piers, after meeting Aubrey, to Junction 17 of the M4 – and so from past to present – it seems a much shorter distance.

Sources

By far the greatest part of the material for this book comes from Aubrey's manuscripts in the Bodleian. Those that I have used are:

MS. AUBREY 1 AND 2 *The Natural History of Wiltshire*

MS. AUBREY 3 *The North Wiltshire Collections* but Liber A only, Liber B having been borrowed and never returned by his brother William, after Aubrey's death

MS. AUBREY 4 *A Perambulation of Surrey* The only one of Aubrey's MS of which only a photographic copy, and not the original, was available

MS. AUBREY 5 *Villare Anglicanum*, followed by a list of those works which Aubrey had already handed over to the Ashmolean, dated 1692

MS. AUBREY 6, 7 & 8 His 'Lives'

MS. AUBREY 9 *Life of Hobbes*

MS. AUBREY 10 *The Idea of Education*

MS. AUBREY 12 & 13 Letters to Aubrey

MS. AUBREY 17 *Designatio de Easton Piers*

MS. AUBREY 21 Loose Papers, including *The Country Revel*, Aubrey's Will and Wren's Survey of Salisbury Cathedral

MS. AUBREY 23 *Collectio Geniturarum*

MS. AUBREY 26 *Faber Fortunae*

MS. Top. Gen.c 24 & 25 *Monumenta Britannica*

Aubrey's letters to Wood are contained in:

MS. WOOD F39

MS. BALLARD 14 which also contains a copy of Aubrey's 'Accidents' of which the original now seems lost

I have also used:

MS. ASHMOLE 1814 Edward Lhwyd's correspondence A–D

MS. ASHMOLE 1829 *Reliquae Lhwydianae* Vol X

MSS. TANNER 25 and 456a Letters

MSS. RAWLINSON J p. 6

MS. WOOD 51

For Aubrey's *Miscellanies*, his only work to be printed in his lifetime, I have used the 1721 edition

The books about Aubrey that I have found particularly useful are:
JOHN BRITTON *Memoir of John Aubrey*. 1845
ANTHONY POWELL *John Aubrey and his Friends*. 1948
OLIVER LAWSON DICK The Introduction to *Aubrey's Brief Lives*. 1949
MICHAEL HUNTER *John Aubrey and the Realm of Learning*. 1975

About Wiltshire:
Aubrey himself is by far my best informant, but otherwise:
J. E. JACKSON Notes to his edition of *Wiltshire Collections* 1862
J. E. JACKSON *Kington St Michael*
The Victoria History of Wiltshire. Vol. 4 (1959) and Vol. 13 (1987)
N. PEVSNER *Wiltshire*. 1963
Kilvert's Diary. Vol. 2. Edited by William Plomer. 1960 edition

About Oxford:
ANTHONY WOOD *Life and Times*. Edited by Andrew Clark. 3 vols 1891–1900
C. E. MALLET *History of the University of Oxford*. Vol. 2. 1924.
H. BLAKISTON *Trinity College*. 1898
H. H. SMITH *New College and its Buildings*. 1952
MARGARET TOYNBEE & P. YOUNG *Strangers in Oxford*. 1973
ANN FANSHAWE *Memoirs of Lady Fanshawe*. 1905
F. J. VARLEY *The Siege of Oxford*. 1935

About the Royal Society:
THOMAS SPRAT *History of the Royal Society*. 1664
THOMAS BIRCH *History of the Royal Society*. 4 vols. 1756–7
Diary of Robert Hooke Edited by Henry Robinson & Robert Adams. 1935
Notes and Records of the Royal Society:
VOLUME 15 Douglas McKie. *Origin and Foundation of the Royal Society*
VOLUME 23 P. M. Rattansi. *Intellectual Origins of the Royal Society*
VOLUME 23 Christopher Hill. *Intellectual Origins of the Royal Society*
VOLUME 27 R. G. Frank. *John Aubrey, John Lydall, etc., at Commonwealth Oxford*

General:
DAVID OGG *England in the Reign of Charles II*. 2 vols
DAVID OGG *England in the Reign of James II and William III*.
I Vol. These cover the second part of Aubrey's life for which they provide excellent background. They are written with an attention to 'minuteness' that would have delighted Aubrey

H. R. TREVOR-ROPER *Religion, the Reformation and Social Change.* 1967 The essay 'Three Foreigners' was invaluable in providing the background to Aubrey's friendship with Hartlib

EDMUND FITZMAURICE *Life of Sir William Petty.* 1895

H. F. HUTCHISON *Sir Christopher Wren.* 1976

MARGARET ESPINASSE *Robert Hooke.* 1956

JOHN EVELYN *Diaries.* Edited by D. S. de Beer. 1955

HELEN DARBISHIRE *The Early Lives of Milton.* 1932

RICHARD OLLARD *Clarendon.* 1987

N. G. BRETT-JAMES *The Growth of Stuart London.* 1935

JOHN HEARSAY *London and the Great Fire.* 1965

ANTONIA FRASER *Cromwell. Our Chief of Men.* 1973

ANTONIA FRASER *King Charles II.* 1979

C. V. WEDGWOOD *The King's Peace.* 1953

C. V. WEDGWOOD *The King's War.* 1958

JOHN KENYON *The Civil Wars of England.* 1988

References

A curved bracket inside a quotation indicates an insertion by Aubrey. A square bracket means my insertion.

In the case of several consecutive quotations from the same source, I have put the number at the end of the last one. In the case of a particularly long gap between quotations from the same source I have repeated the number.

Letters from and to Aubrey during January, February and March sometimes pose a dating problem. This seems to have been a transition period when both the old calendar, when the year ran to the end of March, and the new one such as we use today, were both used. Most of the letters written by Aubrey and his correspondents during these months are dated with both years – thus 'January 15 67/68' – but in the cases where they are not, one can only go by the sense or the sequence of the letters into which they fit, to know in which of the two years they were written.

Chapter One

1. J. E. Jackson, *Kington St Michael*, pp. 37–8
2. MS.Aubrey 3 f.56
3. MS.Aubrey 3 f.59
4. MS.Aubrey 3 f.66
5. MS.Aubrey 6 f.76
6. J. E. Jackson, *Kington St Michael*, p. 43
7. *Kilvert's Diary*, Vol. 2, pp. 20–21
8. MS.Aubrey 3 f.59
9. MS.Aubrey 3 f.67
10. MS.Aubrey 3 f.66
11. MS.Aubrey 17 f. 3
12. MS.Aubrey 3 f.59
13. Aubrey's *Natural History of Wiltshire*, edited by John Britton, 1847.
14. MS.Aubrey 3 f.66

Chapter Two

1. MS.Aubrey 8 f.105
2. MS.Aubrey 7 f. 3
3. MS.Aubrey 6 f. 20

4. MS.Ballard 14 f.139
5. MS.Aubrey 7 f. 3
6. MS.Aubrey 3 f. 65
7. MS.Aubrey 6 f. 76
8. MS.Aubrey 7 f. 3
9. MS.Top. Gen. c. 24 (*Monumenta Britannica*) Vol. 1, f. 23
10. MS.Aubrey 12 f.238
11. MS.Aubrey 7 f. 3
12. MS.Aubrey 2 f. 18
13. MS.Aubrey 9 f. 33
14. MS.Aubrey 9 f. 36
15. MS.Aubrey 7 f. 3
16. MS.Aubrey 2 f. 18
17. MS.Aubrey 7 f. 3
18. MS.Aubrey 10 f. 8
19. MS.Aubrey 7 f. 3
20. MS.Aubrey 2 f. 36
21. MS.Aubrey 10 f. 8
22. MS.Aubrey 10 f. 83
23. MS.Aubrey 10 f.166
24. MS.Aubrey 10 f.166
25. MS.Aubrey 10 f. 89
26. MS.Aubrey 7 f. 3

Chapter Three

1. MS.Aubrey 7 f. 3
2. MS.Aubrey 7 f. 3
3. MS.Aubrey 6 f.57
4. *Aubrey on Education*. Edited by J. E. Stephens. p. 120
5. MS.Aubrey 10 f.97
6. MS.Aubrey 7 f.57–9
7. A. Wood, *Life and Times*. Edited by Andrew Clark. Vol. 1, p. 53
8. MS.Aubrey 6 f.58
9. A. Wood, *Life and Times*. Edited by Andrew Clark. Vol. 1, p. 68
10. MS.Top.Gen. c.24 (*Monumenta Britannica*) f.266
11. A. Wood, *Life and Times*. Edited by Andrew Clark. Vol. 1, p. 69
12. A. Wood, *Life and Times*. Edited by Andrew Clark. Vol. 1, p. 99
13. Ann Fanshawe, *Memoirs*. 1905 Edition, p. 56
14. M. Toynbee and P. Young, *Strangers at Oxford*
15. *Miscellanies*, p. 37
16. MS.Aubrey 6 f.59
17. MS.Ballard 14 f.99
18. MS.Aubrey 21 f.75
19. MS.Aubrey 7 f. 3

Chapter Four

1. MS.Aubrey 2 f. 45
2. MS.Aubrey 2 f.163
3. MS.Aubrey 1 f. 21–2
4. MS.Aubrey 2 f.111–2
5. MS.Aubrey 1 f.163
6. *Victoria History of Wiltshire*, Vol. 4, p. 56
7. MS.Aubrey 1 f. 46
8. MS.Aubrey 2 f. 86
9. MS.Aubrey 2 f. 46
10. MS.Aubrey 2 f. 78
11. MS.Aubrey 1 f. 81
12. MS.Aubrey 1 f. 60
13. MS.Top.Gen. c.24 (*Monumenta Britannica*) f.181
14. MS.Aubrey 1 f.126
15. MS.Aubrey 7 f. 3
16. MS.Aubrey 1 f.162
17. MS.Aubrey 8 f. 10
18. MS.Aubrey 23 f. 86

19. MS.Top.Gen.c.24 (*Monumenta Britannica*) f.232
20. *Miscellanies* p.41
21. MS.Aubrey 3 f. 10
22. MS.Aubrey 1 f. 5
23. MS.Aubrey 3 f. 11
24. MS.Aubrey 1 f. 6

Chapter Five

1. MS.Aubrey 12 f. 35
2. MS.Aubrey 7 f. 3
3. *Wilts. Archaeological Magazine*. Vol. 26, p.347
4. MS.Aubrey 7 f. 3
5. A. Wood, *Life and Times*. Edited by Andrew Clark. Vol. 1, p.129
6. MS.Aubrey 6 f. 57
7. MS.Aubrey 8 f. 60
8. MS.Aubrey 12 f.296
9. MS.Aubrey 12 f.292
10. MS.Wood F.39 f.368
11. MS.Aubrey 7 f.105
12. MS.Aubrey 7 f. 93
13. MS.Aubrey 7 f. 93
14. MS.Aubrey 3 f. 11
15. MS.Aubrey 6 f.121
16. MS.Tanner 456a f.19
17. MS.Aubrey 10 f.119
18. MS.Aubrey 7 f. 3
19. C. E. Mallet, *History of the University of Oxford*. Vol. 2, p.376
20. H. Blakiston, *Trinity College*. p.141
21. MS.Aubrey 12 f.306
22. H. Blakiston, *Trinity College*. p.130–2
23. MS.Aubrey 10 f.134
24. MS.Aubrey 12 f.292
25. MS.Aubrey 12 f.298
26. MS.Aubrey 1 f. 5 (Margin)

Chapter Six

The quotations from Aubrey's account of his discovery of Avebury are all taken from his Introduction to his 'Templa Druidum' – MS.Top.Gen. c.24 (*Monumenta Britannica*) f.23–6. Otherwise –

1. MS.Aubrey 8 f.21

2. MS.Top.Gen.c.24 (*Monu-
    menta Britannica*) f.35–7
3. MS.Top.Gen.c.24 (*Monumenta Bri-
    tannica*) f.44

Chapter Seven

1. *Miscellanies.* p. 10
2. MS.Aubrey 7 f.   3
3. MS.Aubrey 10 f. 28
4. MS.Aubrey 6 f. 43
5. MS.Aubrey 6 f. 46
6. J. E. Jackson, Notes to Aubrey's
    Wiltshire Collections. p.87
7. MS.Aubrey 6 f. 39
8. MS.Aubrey 23 f. 82
9. MS.Aubrey 6 f.60–2
10. MS.Aubrey 6 f. 63
11. MS.Aubrey 7 f.   3
12. MS.Aubrey 3 f.106
13. MS.Aubrey 26 f. 25
14. MS.Aubrey 12 f.298
15. MS.Aubrey 12 f.310
16. MS.Aubrey 12 f.302
17. MS.Aubrey 6 f. 13
18. Notes and Records of the Royal
    Society: Vol. 23. P. M. Rattansi
    *The Intellectual Origins of the Royal
    Society*
19. MS.Aubrey 7 f.   3
20. *Miscellanies* p.91
21. MS.Aubrey 2 f. 41
22. MS.Aubrey 2 f.33–4
23. MS.Aubrey 1 f.136
24. MS.Aubrey 6 f. 63
25. MS.Aubrey 12 f.312
26. MS.Aubrey 21 f. 75
27. MS.Aubrey 7 f.   3
28. MS.Aubrey 7 f.   3

Chapter Eight

1. MS.Aubrey 7 f.   3
2. MS.Aubrey 2 f.115
3. MS.Aubrey 2 f.123
4. MS.Aubrey 2 f. 98
5. MS.Aubrey 2 f. 84
6. MS.Aubrey 13 f.164
7. MS.Aubrey 1 f.164
8. MS.Aubrey 8 f. 94
9. MS.Aubrey 6 f.17–19

10. MS.Aubrey 13 f.277
11. MS.Aubrey 6 f.64–6
12. H. R. Trevor-Roper, *Religion, the
    Reformation and Social Change.*
    'Three Foreigners'
13. MS.Aubrey 12 f.155
14. MS.Aubrey 6 f.67–74
15. MS.Aubrey 6 f. 17
16. MS.Aubrey 13 f. 23
17. MS.Aubrey 13 f. 24
18. MS.Top.Gen. c.24 (*Monumenta Bri-
    tannica*) f.198
19. MS.Top.Gen.c.24 (*Monumenta Bri-
    tannica*) f.91
20. MS.Top.Gen.c.24 (*Monumenta Bri-
    tannica*) f.183
21. MS.Top.Gen.c.25 (*Monumenta Bri-
    tannica*) f.20
22. MS.Top.Gen.c.25 (*Monumenta Bri-
    tannica*) f.20

Chapter Nine

1. A. Wood, *Athenae et Fasti.*
2. Thomas Sprat, *History of the Royal
    Society.*
3. Notes and Records of the Royal
    Society, Vol. 23. P. M. Rattansi
4. MS.Aubrey 6 f. 92
5. MS.Aubrey 8 f. 21
6. Notes and Records of the Royal
    Society, Vol. 23 P. M. Rattansi
7. Helen Darbishire, *The Early Lives of
    Milton*
8. MS.Aubrey 2 f. 83
9. MS.Aubrey 8 f.   9
10. MS.Aubrey 6 f. 98
11. MS.Aubrey 6 f. 99
12. MS.Aubrey 12 f.153
13. MS.Aubrey 6 f. 17
14. MS.Aubrey 3 f. 10
15. J. E. Jackson, Introduction to the
    Wiltshire Collections, p. vii
16. MS.Aubrey 3 f. 98
17. MS.Aubrey 3 f. 99
18. MS.Aubrey 3 f. 91
19. MS.Aubrey 3 f. 95
20. MS.Aubrey 3 f.106
21. MS.Aubrey 3 f.107
22. MS.Aubrey 3 f.106
23. MS.Aubrey 3 f. 97

24. MS.Aubrey 3 f. 97
25. MS.Aubrey 3 f. 97
26. MS.Aubrey 3 f. 95

Chapter Ten

1. MS.Aubrey 9 f. 41
2. MS.Aubrey 9 f. 38
3. MS.Aubrey 9 f. 41
4. MS.Aubrey 9 f. 52
5. MS.Aubrey 12 f. 85
6. MS.Aubrey 13 f.102
7. J. Britton, *Memoir of John Aubrey.*
   p. 37
8. MS.Ballard 14 f.158
9. MS.Aubrey 6 f. 81
10. MS.Aubrey 8 f. 93
11. MS.Aubrey 13 f.230
12. MS.Aubrey 13 f.233
13. MS.Aubrey 13 f.231
14. MS.Aubrey 13 f.235
15. MS.Aubrey 12 f.194
16. MS.Aubrey 13 f.254
17. MS.Wood F.39 f.160
18. T. Birch, *History of the Royal Society*,
    Vol. 1
19. MS.Aubrey 12 f.164
20. MS.Aubrey 21 f. 56
21. MS.Aubrey 12 f.102
22. MS.Wood F.39 f.149
23. Anthony Wood, *Life and Times.*
    Vol. 2 p.117
24. MS.Ballard 14 f.158 'Accidents'

Chapter Eleven

1. MS.Aubrey 1 f. 34
2. MS.Wood F.39 f.199
3. MS.Wood F.39 f.121
4. MS.Ballard 14 f.158 'Accidents'
5. MS.Ballard 14 f.158 'Accidents'
6. MS.Top.Gen.c.25 (*Mon. Brit.*) f.37
7. T. Birch, *History of the Royal Society.*
   Vol. 2
8. MS.Top.Gen.c.24 (*Mon. Brit.*) f.241
9. MS.Aubrey 9 f. 43–5
10. MS.Aubrey 12 f.174
11. MS.Aubrey 6 f. 26
12. MS.Aubrey 3 f. 39
13. MS.Aubrey 1 f. 81
14. MS.Top.Gen.c.24 (*Mon. Brit.*) f.241

15. T. Birch, *History of the Royal Society.*
    Vol. 2
16. MS.Aubrey.Top.Gen.c.25 (*Mon. Brit.*) f.112
17. MS.Aubrey 26 (*Faber Fortunae*) f's 5, 8, 7, 27, 12
18. MS.Aubrey 26 (*Faber Fortunae*) f.15
19. MS.Aubrey 26 (*Faber Fortunae*) f.2
20. MS.Aubrey.Top.Gen.c.25 (*Mon. Brit.*) f.134
21. MS.Aubrey 26 f. 20
22. T. Birch, *History of the Royal Society.*
    Vol. 2
23. MS.Aubrey 26 f's 10, 19, 34, 8, 7, 18

Chapter Twelve

1. MS.Aubrey 3 (Preface) f. 10, 11
2. MS.Aubrey 7 f. 3
3. MS.Wood F.39 f.202
4. MS.Aubrey 13 f.263
5. MS.Wood F.39 f.129
6. MS.Aubrey 7 f. 3

Chapter Thirteen

1. MS.Aubrey 7 f. 3
2. MS.Wood F.39 f.129
3. MS.Wood F.39 f.141
4. MS.Wood F.39 f.141
5. MS.Wood F.39 f.369
6. MS.Aubrey 7 f. 3
7. MS.Wood F.39 f.148
8. MS.Wood F.39 f.141
9. MS.Aubrey 13 f.263
10. MS.Wood F.39 f.147
11. MS.Wood F.39 f.147
12. MS.Wood F.39 f.141
13. MS.Aubrey 21 f. 9–21
14. MS.Aubrey 13 f.263
15. MS.Wood F.39 f.131
16. MS.Wood F.39 f.135
17. MS.Wood F.39 f.138
18. MS.Wood F.39 f.138
19. MS.Wood F.39 f.169
20. MS.Aubrey 23 f.106
21. MS.Aubrey 23 f.107
22. MS.Aubrey 1 f.115
23. MS.Wood F.39 f.387
24. MS.Aubrey 6 f.100
25. MS.Wood F.39 f.160

26. MS.Wood F.39 f.163
27. MS.Wood F.39 f.166
28. MS.Wood F.39 f.169
29. MS.Wood F.39 f.173
30. MS.Wood F.39 f.178
31. MS.Aubrey 6 f. 25

Chapter Fourteen

1. MS.Wood F.39 f.190
2. MS.Top.Gen.c.25 (*Mon. Brit. Chronologica Graphica* 1) f.189
3. MS.Wood F.39 f.188
4. MS.Wood F.39 f.426
5. MS.Wood F.39 f.188
6. MS.Wood F.39 f.199
7. MS.Wood F.39 f.203
8. MS.Wood F.39 f.204
9. MS.Wood F.39 f.214
10. MS.Wood F.39 f.214
11. MS.Ballard 'Accidents' 4 f.158
12. MS.Aubrey 8 f. 53
13. MS.Wood F.39 f.221
14. MS.Wood F.39 f.223
15. MS.Wood F.39 f.231
16. MS.Aubrey 4
17. MS.Ballard 14 f.96
18. MS.Wood F.39 f.234
19. MS.Wood F.39 f.241
20. MS.Wood F.39 f.255
21. MS.Wood F.39 f.261
22. MS.Wood F.39 f.252 and 253
23. T. Birch, *History of the Royal Society*, Vol. 2
24. MS.Wood F.39 f.261
25. MS.Wood F.39 f.411
26. MS.Wood F.39 f.141
27. MS.Ballard 14 f.98
28. MS.Ballard 14 f.99
29. MS.Wood F.39 f.271
30. MS.Aubrey 6 f. 63

Chapter Fifteen

1. MS.Wood F.39 f.328
2. MS.Wood F.39 f.347
3. MS.Aubrey 6 f. 12
4. Hooke's *Diary*, Edited by Robinson and Adams. 1935
5. MS.Ballard 14 f.111
6. MS.Ballard 14 f.113

7. MS.Aubrey 7 f. 3
8. MS.Aubrey 12 f.186
9. MS.Aubrey 6 f. 32
10. Hooke's *Diary*, Edited by Robinson and Adams. 1935
11. MS.Wood F.39 f.377
12. MS.Wood F.39 f.301
13. MS.Aubrey 13 f.217
14. MS.Aubrey 13 f.218
15. MS.Aubrey 13 f.213
16. MS.Aubrey 13 f.211
17. MS.Aubrey 13 f.102
18. MS.Aubrey 8 f. 34
19. MS.Aubrey 13 f. 98
20. MS.Ballard 14 f.119
21. MS.Wood F.39 f.301
22. MS.Aubrey 23 f. 87
23. MS.Aubrey 22 f's 29–47
24. MS.Aubrey 13 f.227

Chapter Sixteen

1. MS.Aubrey 7 f. 3
2. MS.Wood F.39 f.316
3. MS.Wood F.39 f.324
4. MS.Wood F.39 f.334
5. MS.Wood F.39 f.337
6. MS.Ballard 14 f.124
7. MS.Ballard 14 f.126
8. MS.Ballard 14 f.124
9. MS.Ballard 14 f.126
10. MS.Ballard 14 f.127
11. MS.Ballard 14 f.130
12. MS.Wood F.39 f.340
13. MS.Wood F.39 f.347
14. MS.Aubrey 6 f. 12
15. MS.Aubrey 13 f.270
16. MS.Aubrey 6 f. 51
17. MS.Aubrey 6 f. 52–4
18. MS.Wood F.39 f.350
19. MS.Wood F.39 f.451
20. MS.Aubrey 13 f.191
21. MS.Wood F.39 f.357
22. MS.Ballard 14 f.134
23. MS.Aubrey 13 f.115
24. MS.Aubrey 13 f.120
25. MS.Aubrey 13 f.133
26. MS.Aubrey 12 f.347
27. MS.Wood F.39 f.137
28. MS.Aubrey 26 f. 18
29. MS.Aubrey 10 f. 11

30. MS.Aubrey 10 f. 10
31. MS.Aubrey 10 f. 38
32. MS.Aubrey 10 f. 24
33. MS.Aubrey 10 f. 11
34. MS.Aubrey 1 f. 7
35. MS.Wood F.39 f.377
36. MS.Ballard 14 f.139

Chapter Seventeen

1. MS.Wood F.39 f.401
2. MS.Wood F.39 f.395
3. MS.Aubrey 6 f. 30
4. MS.Wood F.39 f.412
5. MS.Wood F.39 f.424
6. MS.Aubrey 12 f.176
7. MS.Aubrey 12 f.178
8. MS.Aubrey 12 f.184
9. MS.Wood F.39 f.406
10. MS.Ballard 14 f.146
11. MS.Wood F.39 f.435
12. MS.Wood F.39 f.386
13. MS.Aubrey 10 f. 1
14. MS.Aubrey 6 f. 15
15. MS.Aubrey 7 f. 86

16. MS.Wood F.39 f.417
17. MS.Aubrey 21 f. 69
18. MS.Aubrey 12 f. 1
19. MS.Aubrey 13 f.168
20. MS.Aubrey 13 f.170
21. MS.Aubrey 13 f.174
22. MS.Aubrey 13 f.179
23. MS.Aubrey 13 f.198
24. MS.Aubrey 5 f.123
25. MS.Aubrey 7 f. 2
26. MS.Ballard 14 f.155
27. MS.Tanner 456a f.48
28. MS.Aubrey 24 f.198
29. MS.Wood F.51 f.5
30. MS.Ashmole 1829. Vol. 10, f. 31
31. MS.Ashmole 1829. Vol. 10, f. 26
32. MS.Ashmole 1829. Vol. 10, f. 28
33. MS.Ashmole 1829. Vol. 10, f. 31
34. MS.Ashmole 1829. Vol. 10, f. 35
35. MS.Ashmole 1829. Vol. 10, f. 13
36. MS.Ashmole 1829. Vol. 10, f. 13
37. MS.Aubrey 12 f. 23
38. MS.Wood F.51 f.6
39. MS.Aubrey 12 f.169
40. MS.Aubrey 6 f. 88

Index

DA 93 .A8 T95 1991
Tylden-Wright, David, 1923-
John Aubrey

NOV 1 7 1992

DEMCO

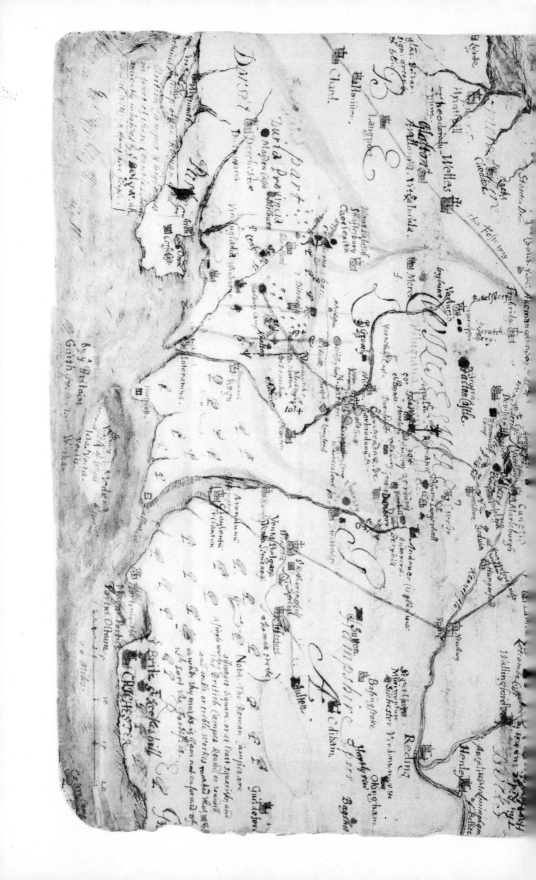